Dutch Americans and War:
United States and Abroad

Dutch Americans and War:
United States and Abroad

Edited by Robert P. Swierenga, Nella Kennedy, Lisa Zylstra

Copyright 2014 Van Raalte Press
All rights reserved

Van Raalte Press is a division of Hope College Publishing

Editorial Address: A. C. Van Raalte Institute
                     Theil Research Center
                     9 East Tenth Street
                     Holland, MI 49423

Mailing Address: PO Box 9000
                     Holland, MI 49422-9000

                     vanraalte@hope.edu
                     www.hope.edu/vri

Printed in the United States of America
ISBN 978-0-980 1111-9-4

Copy Editor: JoHannah Smith
Cover Design: Nella Kennedy and Russell Gasero
Page Layout: Russell Gasero

Papers from the Nineteenth Biennial Conference of the Association for the Advancement of Dutch American Studies, Central College, Pella, Iowa, 6 – 8 June 2013.

Cover, *top row, l-r:* Dirk B. K. Van Raalte, Civil War (JAH), John Luyben, Spanish-American War (*Souvenir History of Pella, Iowa,* Pella: Booster Press, 1922); *bottom row, l-r:* Dirk Bruins, WWI (JAH), Ernest Gerritsma, WWII (Don Sinnema), Dave Fetters, Vietnam War (JAH)

Phillip E. Webber

An ever-curious scholar, insightful mentor, and thoughtful friend

Contents

Foreword and Acknowledgments   xiii
   Introduction   xv

Part I   Civil War

1. Henry P. Scholte and Abraham Lincoln: Compatriots in the Civil War
   Ronald D. Rietveld   3
2. Two Holland, Michigan, Boys in the Union Army
   Marten C. P. Rustenburg   31
3. Wooden Shoes to Brogans: Klaas Zuidema and the Civil War
   Michael Swanson   43
4. WilliamVandever: Presbyterian, Congressman, General
   Douglas Firth Anderson   53
5. A Dutch Colony in Tennessee as a Casualty of the Civil War
   Janet Sjaarda Sheeres   67

Part II   Spanish-American War and First World War

6. For Humanity's Sake: Abraham Kuyper, the Spanish-American War of 1898
   George Harinck   89
7. Loyalties in Conflict: Theodore F. Koch Confronts the First World War
   Robert Schoone-Jongen   107
8. Dutch Americans in World War One: In the Fog of International Law
   Huug van den Dool   117
9. Abraham Johannes Muste: American Pacifist Extraordinaire
   Gerlof Homan   129

Part III Second World War

10. Home Front: Holland, Michigan, in the World Wars
    Robert P. Swierenga ... 137
11. Packing Underwear, Cod Liver Oil, and Stockings: Holland, Michigan, Responds to War-Ravaged Netherlands, 1940s
    Nella Kennedy ... 159
12. By Trial and Error: The Experience of a Dutch Escape Line in the Second World War
    Bruce Bolinger ... 177
13. One Soldier's Experience of War in the Pacific: Sgt. Ernest Gerritsma's Diaries and Letters in the Second World War
    Donald Sinnema ... 201
14. Dutch Propaganda Films in America: Documentaries from the Netherlands Information Bureau in the 1940s
    Henk Aay ... 221

Part IV Vietnam War

15. Dutch American Attitudes and the Vietnam War
    David Zwart ... 253
16. The Moral Fog of War: A Christian Vietnam Veteran's Perspective
    Sylvan Gerritsma ... 271

Part V Dominies, Language, and the Arts

17. Hendrik Pieter Scholte Roils the Christian Seceded Church in the Netherlands, 1834-1846
    Eugene Heideman ... 287
18. Significance of Hendrik Pieter Scholte's Vision of Church and State
    Emo Bos ... 309
19. From Amsterdam and Antwerp to Otley and Harrison: The Rise, Fall, and Restoration of the Maverick Rev. Arie Gerrit Zigeler
    Earl Wm. Kennedy ... 323
20. On the Shift to Standard Dutch: Pella, Iowa, Compared to Holland, Michigan
    Jaap van Marle ... 351
21. Gerhard Hendrik Nollen: Portrait of the Artist
    Susan Price Miller ... 363

Index ... 379

Illustrations

Rev. Henry P. Scholte, 1862	4
Franklin Street, Pella	4
Scholte House, overlooking Central Park, 1870s	6
Beardless President Abraham Lincoln, 3 June 1862	7
Secretary of State William Seward	8
Scholte's desk in his upstairs study	14
Lincoln's inauguration, 4 March 1861	18
Governor Samuel Kirkwood	21
Scholte's church, built 1855	28
Johannes Van Lente in uniform	32
John Douma with Civil War volunteers at homecoming	33
Tebbs Bend hospital in Atkinson Griffin House	36
Guarding the vault	40
Johannes Van Lente by the fountain he designed in Centennial Park	41
Headstone at the gravesite of Nicholas Zuidema	44
Rebel prisoners at Camp Morton	46
Nicholas Zuidema with two of his children	51
Hon. William Vandever	55
Gen. William Vandever, Col. William H. Coyl, and Col. Francis J. Herron	58
Lakota Chief "Sitting Bull"	61
Early portrait of Anna Maria Margaretha (Mienette) Storm-van der Chijs	68
Later portrait of Maria Margaretha (Mienette) Storm-van der Chijs	76
Newton A. Patterson	79
Plaque on 1 Breestraat for AMM Storm v.d. Chijs	86
Abraham Kuyper	96
Banquet, Holland, Michigan, 1898	99
Varia Americana, 1899	100
Cartoon, Baltimore's Merchants Club	102
Pella train station, 1898	104
Edward Matthews	119
Nicolas Williams	119
Abraham Muste lecturing at Pendle Hill	131
Muste arrested at the Army Induction Center, New York	133
Peace March in New York City	134
Red Cross wagon in parade	140
Army howitzer attracts curious onlookers in Holland	141
Family and friends send the "boys" off on the train at Holland depot	143
Second World War ration book with gas coupons	147
Holland High School students collect scrap metal	148
Women march in Liberty Loan parade in 1918	150

Hart & Cooley's Holland Division of Fafnir Bearing won the coveted "E Award" for exemplary production	152
Chris-Craft's 8,000th Navy Landing Craft	153
Willard G. Leenhouts	155
Army Specialized Training Program, Lubbers Hall, Hope College	156
Newspaper ads demonstrate textile shortage during the war	162
Church Herald advertisement	166
Queen Wilhelmina Fund poster	168
Willard C. Wichers	169
Women of Prospect Park Christian Reformed Church	171
Thank-you letter from a school in Werkendam	174
Karst Smit in Jagers uniform	179
Assisting the Keesing family	185
Van der Heijden family	187
Dick Los and Jan van Dongen	192
Karst Smit and *marechaussees*	193
Three escape routes	195
Elise Chabot and Charlotte Ambach	197
Pvt. Ernest Gerritsma	205
USAT *Willard A. Holbrook*	208
Map of the 147th Field Artillery in Australia, New Guinea, and the Philippines	210
LSTs Landing on Noemfoor Island	213
Gerritsma with his blitz buggy and buddies	216
Ernest and Marie Gerritsma's wedding photo	219
Estimated 1940s NIB film attendance by service region	223
NIB-Holland: first page of film-showing report for September 1945	228
NIB-Holland: estimated yearly attendance of films, 1940s	229
NIB-Holland: estimated attendance by film during the 1940s	230
NIB-Holland: estimated film attendance by place, 1940s	233
NIB-Holland: film attendance by type of borrower	235
Foreign-policy-directed and culture-directed films shown during the 1940s	236
Making new land with dike mats. Film: *New Earth*	240
Ferrying cars across a canal with a destroyed bridge. Film: *Friesland*	244
NIB-Holland letterhead during the 1940s	245
Maps of the United States and the Dutch East Indies superimposed. Film: *People of the Indies*	246
Oil storage tanks and refineries on Curacao. Film: *Netherlands America: Holland in the Western Hemisphere*	247
Model integrated Javanese village. Film: *Netherlands East Indies*	249
One of many soldiers in Vietnam	257
Photo from *Church Herald* article questioning Vietnam War effort	259
Advertisement in the *Banner*	261
Guides distributed by the Young Calvinist Federation	262
A chaplain in Vietnam	263
"Project Thank-You Vietnam"	264
In defense of military action	266

Gerritsma in front of "hootsch"	274
Helmeted Gerritsma at "hootsch"	275
De Reformatie, 1845	288
Hendrik de Cock	292
Hendrik P. Scholte	292
Anne Maurits C. van Hall	292
Anthony Brummelkamp	292
Letter from Scholte to J. A. Wormser	298
Wouter Verschuur, *Ten Days Campaign*	310
Summons to pay fine for meeting illegally	313
King Willem II	315
Scholte's library in the Scholte House	318
Rev. Arie Gerrit Zigeler	324
De Kleine Komedie, formerly Scottish Missionary Church	329
Zigeler's evangelization building, Rehoboth	330
Share issued 15 December 1869 for Rehoboth	331
Interior of the *Plantagekerk*	335
SS *Rotterdam I*	340
First Reformed Church, Harrison, South Dakota	346
Central Park Café, Pella, Iowa	353
Conversing on Franklin Street, Pella, Iowa	358
Pastoral Scene	364
Portrait of Mrs. Hendrik Eysink	368
Self-portrait with Marble Pillar	369
Self-portrait	372
The Farm	374
Landscape with Pine Trees	377

Foreword and Acknowledgments

Lisa Zylstra

The Association for the Advancement of Dutch American Studies met for its nineteenth biennial meeting at Central College in Pella, Iowa, in June 2013. The AADAS board chose the theme "The Dutch American Involvement in War: US and Abroad," at the 2011 conference in Wisconsin. Since the 2013 conference would occur during the sesquicentennial commemoration of the Civil War, Marten Rustenburg suggested the board consider the theme of Dutch Americans in times of war. Knowing that Pella sent one-twelfth of its population and Central College sent all but four eligible men to serve the Union, it seemed an appropriate topic and venue for such an examination of the impact of war on the Dutch in America.

AADAS president, George Harinck, organized the conference papers into sessions starting with early Pella history and moving into a chronological look at the experiences of Dutch American individuals and communities during the Civil War through the conflict in Vietnam. Other papers examined the impact of a Dutch American pacifist and a variety of other topics of interest.

In addition to the lectures on the Dutch American war experience, the local conference organizers sought to bring Pella's history to life for conference participants. The pre-conference tour day included visiting the Hendrik Scholte family home, touring the Pella Historical Village and Vermeer Mill (the largest working windmill in North America), as well as taking a guided bus tour of Pella. That evening, participants and members of the community enjoyed the locally written and produced play, *The Dominie's Wife*, a fictionalized account of Hendrik Scholte's wife, Mareah, coming to terms with life in America.

During breaks between conference sessions, participants could look at several different displays including the history projects of local fifth graders focusing on the founding of Pella, a display and discussion about Central College during the Civil War, and a video of local Dutch immigrants talking about their experiences in the Netherlands during World War II. At the AADAS banquet, the Dutchesses, a group of area high school girls performed Dutch songs and klompen dances for the audience. The evening was capped off as Dr. Ronald Rietveld pieced together the political involvement of Pella's founder (Rev. Hendrik Scholte) during the election of Abraham Lincoln, as well as his friendship with Secretary of State William Seward.

As a result of the success of the 2013 AADAS conference, the Archives and Documentation Center of the Reformed Churches (Liberated) and the Roosevelt Study Center in the Netherlands in conjunction with the Pella Historical Society have begun the process of planning a conference in 2018 to examine the life and work of Hendrik Pieter Scholte (1805-1868), commemorating the 150th anniversary of his death.

As the conference host, I would like to express deep gratitude to all who helped make the conference a success. Thank you to the AADAS board, especially George Harinck, Dick Harms, and Mary Risseeuw for all of your help and advice. Thank you to Yvette Hoitink for help with the website and developing online registration. Thanks also to my local conference planning committee and support staff: my husband, Brian Zylstra, my parents, Ralph and Elaine Jaarsma, and our good friends and co-conspirators, Henry and Milly Vande Kieft and Ronald and Ruth Rietveld. Thank you also to Central College (Lowell Olivier-Shaw and Lori Witt) and the Pella Historical Society for sponsoring the conference and for all of the logistical help.

Introduction

Robert P. Swierenga

Since the mid-nineteenth century, the successful prosecution of American wars involved the entire population. Wars had become total, including immigrant groups like the Dutch, who were caught up in conflicts before they had mastered the language of the land or before they had even become citizens. Wars actually hastened assimilation as immigrants stood shoulder to shoulder with Americans of all nationalities in fighting the nation's wars and defending the home front by their labor and sacrifice.

This volume recounts Dutch American responses from the Civil War to the Vietnam War, both as citizens and soldiers. That the immigrants of 1847 in Pella, Iowa, and Holland, Michigan—the midwestern mother colonies—would have such strong commitments to the Union in 1861 is nothing less than amazing. But the Dutch were also torn. Was abolishing slavery more important than preserving the Union? Neither Pella nor Holland voted for Abraham Lincoln, the Great Emancipator. Rather, they preferred Stephen Douglas, the "Little Giant," in 1860 and in 1864 Peace Democrat, General George McClelland. The anti-immigrant American—or Know Nothing—Party, which many immigrants considered a branch of the Whig Party, made them wary of the new Republican Party, which also had roots in the Whig Party. The Democratic proclivities of the Pella and Holland citizens were all the more remarkable, since their respective immigrant leaders, Henry P. Scholte and Albertus C. Van Raalte, had joined the new Republican Party in 1859. These strong men were expected to carry their untutored countrymen at the polls, but they both failed miserably.

McClelland's platform called for ending the bloodshed by conceding peace to the Confederacy and allowing the breakup of the Union. Similarly, in the First World War, some Dutch immigrants were so angered by the brutal British conquest of their Afrikaner cousins in the Boer War (1899-1902) that they sided with Kaiser Wilhelm and the Germans when war broke out in 1914. Some were hounded by hyper patriots for criticizing President Woodrow Wilson's seemingly pro-British diplomacy or for objecting on church-state grounds to American flags in the sanctuary during worship services. Those in Peoria, Iowa, a village in the greater Pella colony, suffered the burning of their church and Christian school at the hands of nativists who resented their thriving farms and community.

Scholte was the premier national politician among the nineteenth-century Dutch immigrants, as Ronald Rietveld proves in the opening chapter, which originated as the keynote address of the conference that gave birth to this book. Scholte, as a member of the Iowa Republican Party delegation, cast his vote for Abraham Lincoln for president and Hannibal Hamlin as vice president at the Republican National Convention in Chicago. Subsequently, Scholte, as editor of the *Pella Gazette* and as translator into Dutch of Republican campaign literature during a stay of several weeks in Washington in the spring of 1860, campaigned energetically for the Lincoln-Hamlin ticket with his pen. While there, Scholte conferred several times with New York Senator William Seward, a leader of the Lincoln campaign team. On his return to Pella, Scholte stopped in Springfield, Illinois, and met with Lincoln at his law office; he returned to Washington for Lincoln's inaugural. The campaign activities led to Scholte's friendship with Lincoln and Seward, which continued through the war and the 1864 campaign.

Rietveld uncovers for the first time the extensive Scholte correspondence with Lincoln and Seward that forms the backbone of his chapter. Scholte offered Lincoln advice in the campaign on snaring the "immigrant vote," and during the war, he encouraged the beleaguered president and urged him to press the war vigorously. He also joined the long list of office-seekers by asking the president for the appointment as minister to the Netherlands. Lincoln demurred, although no Lincoln letters to Scholte are extant. Scholte's correspondence with Seward was more extensive, and fortunately, most of those letters survive. This chapter shows that the voluminous research and writings on the Lincoln administration still leave room for scholarly lacunae, such as his ties with the Dutch American immigrant leader Henry Scholte of Pella.

Scholte's friend and colleague, Rev. Albertus C. Van Raalte, leader of the West Michigan Holland colony, similarly worked with a will for Lincoln and the Union cause, but he never went on the campaign trail. Van Raalte used his church pulpit and his "bully pulpit" as editor of *De Hollander* to support the Lincoln-Hamlin ticket, and when war came, he urged Dutchmen to volunteer. In the first year, 125 men from Holland Township volunteered, including two of Van Raalte's sons and eight Hope College students. Son Dirk came home minus his right arm, which had been amputated after taking a bullet in the conflict. Ultimately, 424 Hollanders from Ottawa County enlisted and twenty (5 percent) made the ultimate sacrifice. Still, Dutch American soldiers were under-represented by thirteen points, compared to their proportion of the county population.

Some thirty Holland "boys" kept diaries and letters, as did many soldiers in the nation's wars. Martin Rustenburg features the stories of two, Johannes Van Lente and Jan Douma, which offer first-hand accounts of life in the camps and on the battlefield. Both were members of the 25th Michigan Infantry. Van Lente enlisted early in 1862 and saw service in southern Kentucky against Confederate General John Hunt Morgan and his "fearsome cavalry," which culminated in Morgan's defeat in the Battle of Tebbs Bend. The 25th was then joined to Gen. William T. Sherman's army in time for the infamous "March to the Sea" and the burning of Atlanta.

Jan Douma enlisted late, in March 1865, and did not see military action, but he had an interesting career nonetheless. His first assignment was routine, to guard Confederate prisoners at Camp Butler in Springfield, Illinois. His second assignment was far from routine. Following Lincoln's assassination, he and part of the 24th Michigan Infantry Regiment, including his friend and fellow "Holland boy," Mathew Notier, were assigned to guard the funeral train bearing Lincoln's remains to Springfield for burial. After the ceremony, the two stood guard at Lincoln's tomb. This was quite a responsibility for the eighteen-year-old Douma, who later recalled that at the time he was more concerned with his stomach than the president's bier. When Douma died in 1939, he bore the distinction of being the last surviving Civil War veteran in Holland, Michigan.

Klaas Zuidema was another Civil War soldier with a unique story, although Michael Swanson had to stitch it together from public and military records, since Zuidema did not leave a diary or letters—at least none have been found. He enlisted in March 1862 at Indianapolis, Indiana, less than a year after emigrating from the province of Groningen in the northern Netherlands. He was assigned to the 60th Indiana Infantry and, like Douma, was first tasked with guarding Confederate prisoners at Camp Morgan in Indianapolis. Then his unit joined the Michigan 25th in pursuing Morgan's raiders in southern Kentucky.

While on horseback in pursuit of the enemy, Zuidema suffered a hernia and was sent back to Indianapolis, where he lay in the hospital for three months, without reparative surgery. Late in 1862 he rejoined his regiment and completed his three-year enlistment in the western campaign to capture Vicksburg and secure control of the vital Mississippi River. But he was hobbled by his hernia for the duration and frequently was excused from guard duty because of it. Late in his term he contracted a respiratory illness and that brought him an assignment to the Pioneer Corps, a unit of soldiers unable to fight but useful for menial engineering tasks, such as improving roads and bridges and building fortifications. Zuidema lived out his post-war years as a rolling stone among fellow Groningers in Lafayette, Indiana; Kalamazoo and Muskegon, Michigan; and finally in Fulton, Illinois, where he is buried. Zuidema is one of the thousands of unheralded soldiers who fought to restore the Union.

Another Civil War soldier of Old Dutch ancestry was Democratic Congressman William Vandever of Iowa, a Dubuque lawyer who enlisted as a colonel in the Ninth Iowa Infantry in July 1861. Douglas Firth Anderson recounts Vandever's near death experiences in the Battle of Pea Ridge, Arkansas, and his rapid rise in the ranks to general. Congressman Vandever, a Presbyterian by faith and who identified himself as "religiously Dutch," was well connected, which saved the day when the "political general" refused to resign his seat in Congress. This refusal presumably violated the Constitution, which forbade a member from holding another federal "office" at the same time. The refusal also displeased some soldiers under his command with Republican proclivities, who left unflattering assessments of his generalship. Unfortunately, Vandever left no letters or diaries to shed light on his military career, which took him to Vicksburg, Mississippi; Brownsville, Texas; and finally Marietta, Georgia, to guard Gen. Sherman's flank as he closed in on Atlanta. After the war, Vandever became a US Indian Inspector who was critical of the commissioner of Indian Affairs for the military handling of the Lakota Sioux and Chief Sitting Bull, whom Vandever met and befriended. Vandever lost his political post in 1878, after the Republican Ulysses Grant administration came to power.

Janet Sjaarda Sheeres describes another aspect of the Civil War: how the war led to the demise of the Dutch colony at Kingston in Roane County, Tennessee. This colony was unique in that it was founded by a woman, Anna Maria Margaretha (Mienette) Storm-van de Chijs, in 1857. This is the only Dutch colony known to be led by a woman. Storm-van de Clijs was a wealthy philanthropist and social reformer who had tenuous ties to the Dutch Reformed Church in America. She had the misfortune to locate in what became in 1861 a Confederate state, and Union forces in 1863 torched her buildings. By then, she had returned to the Netherlands. The ultimate blow to the Tennessee colony was the lack of a Dutch Reformed church and clergyman, which spelled the end of such ventures almost everywhere Dutch Reformed immigrants settled. Mienette Storm-van de Clijs lived to the ripe old age of eighty-one and died in Delft in 1895, rich in honor for having lived a "useful" life.

The Spanish-American War of 1898 is an oft forgotten conflict because of its brevity and minimal casualties. The exploits of Teddy Roosevelt's Rough Riders, however, catapulted him into the vice presidency. The longest lasting impact was the United States conquest of Cuba and the Philippine Islands from Spain. Both island nations were promised eventual independence after a period of American tutelage in democratic governance. United States expansion into the Philippines was especially controversial, both at home and abroad. Netherlands neo-Calvinist theologian and politician, Abraham Kuyper, who after delivering the prestigious Stone Lectures at Princeton University in October 1898, went on a national speaking tour in Dutch American communities, during which he defended the rights of smaller nations against world powers and specifically opposed US policy toward the Philippines. George Harinck, director of the Protestant Documentation Centre at the Free University of Amsterdam, a school founded by Kuyper and where his papers are housed, describes Kuyper's American tour and cogently explains his differentiation of the legal and moral facets of international law as it related to President William McKinley's expansionist foreign policy.

The First World War, which brought an end to the Great Migration of the nineteenth century, forced Dutch Americans to surrender their precious "Dutchness" for American ways and acculturate more rapidly than they were wont to do. Part two contains four chapters that reveal various aspects of "loyalties in conflict." Robert Schoone-Jongen, who is writing a book on the fabled real estate promoter Theodore F. Koch, a Dutchman with German family roots, notes how Koch's idealistic view of human progress that rendered war obsolete, clashed with the realities of a world war in which armies employed poison gas, tanks, and other "inhumane" weapons. Koch's land dealings involved German investors, so his properties fell under the Trading with the Enemy Act of 1917 and were seized by federal officials. Koch spent the war years desperately trying to redeem his properties from the US Custodian's Office, while his son and namesake, Theodore William Koch, enlisted and fought in the US Army. The family was truly torn by conflicting loyalties.

The "fog of international war" also snared many Dutch immigrants in military conscription campaigns, even when as non-citizens they were exempt from the draft. Huug van den Dool explores this little known aspect of American draft policy based on a sampling of forty-three biographies that he uncovered by Internet searching and chance conversations with genealogists. He concludes that Dutch American males of draft age were enrolled under one of five classes: naturalized citizens, American-born *de facto* citizens, declarants who had filed First Papers, non-declarants who had not filed and had no intent to do so, and Dutch nationals who volunteered. Non-declarants comprise the problematic category. Neither marriage nor changing family names proved sufficient. Not knowing English, nor understanding their legal rights, and lacking legal counsel, caused some to be drafted extra-legally. Van den Dool describes how some non-declarants as full citizens of the Netherlands nevertheless succumbed to pressure by recruiting agents and joined the US military. They were told that unless they enlisted they could never become American citizens.

The Second World War was truly a "total war" in scope and intensity. It affected everyone, whether civilian or military. Part three contains six chapters that illustrate various aspects of that impact. Gerlof Homan describes the life and activities of the Abraham Johannes Muste, a Dutch Reformed Iowan and Hope College alumnus, who was a pacifist extraordinaire during the Second World War, the Cold War, and the Vietnam War. Muste remained an unreconstructed pacifist despite the Holocaust and military expansion by Soviet Russia, North Vietnam, and Red China. He preached civil disobedience, tax resistance, and non-violent demonstrations and joined a peace delegation to North Vietnam.

In total wars the home front was as necessary for victory as were the front lines. Robert Swierenga describes how the residents of

Holland, Michigan, supported the two world wars with their labor, money, and sacrifice as consumers. Dutch Americans participated wholeheartedly in both conflicts, although in the first war nativist crusades caused needless hurt when the Dutch were mistaken in the public mind as Germans. As patriotic Americans, the Dutch obeyed rationing and conservation edicts and price controls, planted "Victory Gardens," bought war bonds, and worked overtime in defense plants to make war materiel for the military. In the first war only one-quarter of civilian production was diverted to war needs, but in the second conflict the entire economy was commandeered for war production. Swierenga tells how Hope College went to war each time, and he shows that the wars speeded the pace of Americanization in immigrant communities like Holland.

Winning the war was the first priority, but Dutch Americans were also concerned for the plight of their countrymen in the Netherlands suffering under the heel of Nazi occupation for more than five years, especially during the Hunger Winter of 1944-45. As Canadian and US forces liberated the Netherlands in the spring of 1945, the extent of the suffering became known, and the Dutch "cousins" sprang into action by packing underwear, cod liver oil, and stockings, as Nella Kennedy tells in detail for the first time. Kennedy first tells of deprivation during the war from looting and confiscation by German troops of food, fuel, and materials, including radios and even bicycles. After liberation, Reformed Church women took the lead in gathering used clothing, shoes, toiletries, kitchen utensils, and even toys. Women knit wool sweaters by the dozens. Church basements became packing, storage, and shipment centers. In Holland the relief effort was guided by Willard Wichers, the local Netherlands consul general. Kennedy follows the goods to the Old Country and describes the distribution networks there. She closes the chapter with expressions of gratitude that completed the circle of compassion.

During the war the Dutch citizens took the war into their own hands as fifth columnists, called *onderduikers* (literally "under divers"), who engaged in sabotage, hiding men from forced German labor, sheltering Jews, and smuggling downed allied pilots to England. Bruce Bolinger provides the first study of the inner workings of Dutch "escape routes," based on a case study of the Smit-Van der Heijden Line, named after its leaders, Karst Smit and Eugene van der Heijden. These heroes and their associates placed their lives on the line, and thirteen gave their all in the effort, although Karst and Van der Heijden had to go into hiding when their line collapsed in November 1943. Readers will be captivated by this thrilling story of cunning and intrigue in the service of freedom.

Besides the European theater, the war in the Pacific involved millions of servicemen and women. One of them was Ernest Gerritsma of Sioux County, Iowa, who kept a diary, despite an absolute ban on such writings, and managed by the most cunning schemes to smuggle the six surreptitious volumes home. Donald Sinnema tells the story of the diaries and the military experiences in Australia and Dutch New Guinea of the soldier-author who later became his father-in-law. War stories abound, but diaries from the front lines are very rare, given the strict military policy forbidding them. Gerritsma's diaries show his sharp eye for the absurd and the tragi-comic in army life. An added plus is that his strong Dutch Reformed character shines brightly in his writings.

Another aspect of the war was the program begun by the Dutch government to win hearts and minds in America by the creation of "propaganda" films for distribution and screening in the United States by the Netherlands Information Bureau (NIS). This was the first time the Dutch government waged an intensive public diplomacy campaign of this kind. Fortunately, Netherlands consul Willard Wichers, head of the Holland, Michigan, NIS branch, saved a large collection of these films. Geographer Henk Aay is the first scholar to analyze these films produced in the 1940s, which were screened widely in the United States from the 1940s into the 1970s. As part of his book-length study in progress, Dr. Aay used computers to analyze yearly film borrowing reports, more than eleven thousand in number, which show distribution by film and attendance per showing by Dutch American and non-Dutch viewers. Aay here reports the first results of that analysis. The films tout the themes of Netherlands war resistance and the royal family in exile in Canada, land reclamation and water policy, historic cultural traditions, and the "benevolent" government policies in the Dutch colonies in southeast Asia and South America.

The Vietnam War presented Dutch Americans with another challenge, to weigh the morality of American involvement in a civil war in Asia. Most backed the war effort, but increasing numbers, especially among the young, joined the anti-war movement. David Zwart studied the religious press in the Reformed and Christian Reformed denominations to ascertain the many voices that were heard. As casualties mounted, he found an increasing skepticism among both clergy and laity about the war strategies and even whether to be involved at all. He concludes that the war forced Dutch Americans to rethink the

American part of their identity, with the result that many clung more firmly to their Dutchness.

Many Dutch descendants saw the war up close and personal as part of the US military. Sylvan Gerritsma, a son of the Ernest Gerritsma whose smuggled diaries formed the basis of chapter thirteen, was one such soldier who afterwards penned his thoughts about combat as one acting in a "moral fog." A committed Dutch Calvinist, Gerritsma reflects on the meaning of his combat training and the battlefield requirement to kill or be killed, from the perspective of his Christian faith. While he does not offer a prescriptive conclusion, it is clear that he understands how being trained in the military to kill may change one from the inside, and that it takes great wisdom to remain humane and even sane. This thoughtful treatise on the morality of war from a combat veteran is worth careful study.

Because the AADAS 2013 conference took place in Pella, four chapters in part four relate not to war but to the life and work of Dutch American clerics and artists and the language transition demanded of Dutch immigrants. In chapter seventeen, Eugene Heideman, a retired professor, cleric, missionary, and functionary in the Reformed Church in America, argues persuasively that Scholte was the true father of the Secession of 1834, since he instigated the secession of Hendrik de Cock, who has often been ascribed that place. Yet Scholte was drummed out of the church in 1840 for disregarding synodical actions. The Secession of 1834 began as a protest against theological declension in the national church. Government persecution sparked the emigration to America in the 1840s of thousands of Seceders, which led to the founding of the Holland and Pella colonies. Eugene Heideman has a book in press on Scholte as the leading churchman of the Secession, based on his religious periodical, *De Reformatie*, and the annual church synods of the nascent denomination.

Emo Bos, a retired Netherlands jurist, in chapter eighteen examines Scholte's decision in 1839 to seek legitimacy for his Utrecht congregation from King Willem II, based on a careful analysis of Scholte's views of civil authorities and their relationship to the institutional church. Both in the Netherlands and Iowa, Scholte gave Caesar his due, but he never gave Caesar what belonged to God. Bos shows that Scholte, paradoxically, had a negative view of the state, believing that its principles derived from Satan rather than from God. Scholte perceived correctly, Bos concludes, that it is impossible to have lasting peace between church and state; they are fundamentally at odds.

The struggling Seceder congregations in America had a more practical problem than civil laws and policies. They needed ministers, and in their desperation, they welcomed men in their pulpits with checkered pasts. Some had never been ordained; others were divorced or living in adultery, and yet others had abandoned wives and children or left financial scandals behind. Earl Wm. Kennedy explores one such preacher. In chapter nineteen, he details the notorious career of the maverick pastor Arie Gerrit Zigeler, both in the Low Countries and across North America. Zigeler had the remarkable ability to rise, fall, and pick himself up again, not once, but several times. After founding a tabernacle in Antwerp, he left it in bankruptcy and began an independent ministry in Amsterdam. In 1872 he deserted his wife and family, leaving her destitute, and shipped to America with a woman half his age, appearing in Chicago. He wandered in the "American wilderness" for thirteen years, including Pella, until finally gaining ordination in the historic Reformed Church in America and closing out his career in honor. The moral of the tale, Kennedy concludes, is that "humbled, chastened, and repentant sinners can still be fruitful ministers."

Jaap van Marle, a Netherlands linguist and long-time student of language change among Dutch Americans, in chapter twenty reports on field work he carried out in Pella and Holland, Michigan, in which he compares the use of the Dutch language among numerous respondents. He reports that Pella folks experienced a unique development: they maintained Standard Dutch, that is "proper" Dutch, rather than the dialects they had spoken before emigrating, whereas in West Michigan, Dutch speakers conversed in their local dialects, and not in standard Dutch.

In the final chapter, art historian Susan Price Miller provides the first portrait of the noteworthy but forgotten Pella artist, the Dutch-born and trained Gerard Nollen (1830-1901). Nollen was a painter, photographer, and artist, first in Pella and later in Keokuk, who was known in the nineteenth century for his portraits of leading Pella citizens, local scenes such as the central square, the Scholte house, the *Pella Gazette* office, pastoral landscapes, and several self-portraits. Miller examines Nollen's techniques, genres, and major works. Although "one of the most unknown great artists in America," no art gallery has yet mounted an exhibition of his paintings. Perhaps Miller's writings will bring a revival of interest in his work.

PART I

Civil War

CHAPTER 1

Henry P. Scholte and Abraham Lincoln: Compatriots in the Civil War

Ronald D. Rietveld

Henry Peter Scholte founded his Holland *kolonie* in the new state of Iowa in 1847 with the intent of making its history and heritage his own. His desire for renewal rather than continuity led him into politics, law, business, banking, and a refined American lifestyle, much to the bewilderment of his immigrant followers. Scholte played a serious and active political role in the Civil War era and made important contributions to his county, state, and country. Within a decade, it was said that he displayed "a political knowledge of the country of his adoption that is possessed by very few, even of our gray-headed patriots and politicians."[1]

The looming question in the body politic was whether slavery should be allowed to spread into the territories acquired in the Mexican-American War. The binary option was "for or against slavery." Pella and

[1] Hans Krabbendam, *Freedom on the Horizon: Dutch Immigration to America, 1840-1940* (Grand Rapids, MI: Eerdmans, 2009), 67; Robert P. Swierenga, "The Ethnic Voter and the First Lincoln Election," *Civil War History* 11 (March 1965): 27-43; reprinted in *Ethnic Voters and the Election of Lincoln*, ed. Frederick Luebke (Lincoln: University of Nebraska Press, 1971), 229-50; John H. Yzenbaard, "H. P. Scholte and the 1856 Presidential Campaign in Michigan," *Annals of Iowa* 3, no. 42 (Summer 1973): 37.

Fig. 1.1. Rare portrait of Rev. Henry P. Scholte, 1862 (*Scholte House Archives*)

Fig. 1.2. Very early photo of Franklin Street, Pella (*Pella Historical Society Archives*)

Marion County in general voted for the Democratic Party, but by 1860 that had begun to change, as many joined the Republican Party. Scholte made the switch in 1859 and laid out the reasons in his mouthpiece, the *Pella Gazette*. The Democratic Party, however, remained dominant in Pella.[2]

Scholte had been a Democrat up until 1859, when the territorial issue of slavery caused him to change political parties. "Once more I feel at home in my political connection, [which harmonizes with] my honest and well-digested convictions, conclusive to the peace and happiness of our beloved country." *Our beloved country*; the Hollander had become a loyal American! His object as a Republican newspaper editor was "the conversion of political sinners and heretics; the conviction of the misinformed and misguided and the strengthening of the faithful lovers of liberty, independence, and Union."[3]

The Iowa Republican State Convention met in Des Moines in January 1860, and the delegates selected Scholte as a delegate at large to the Republican National Convention which met in Chicago's famous "Wigwam" in May. Scholte wrote: "I have always been an opponent of Slavery without approving the Abolitionists, which I consider as a visionary political sect, well able to destroy but not to build up, and connect with other wild theories such as woman's rights, spiritualism, and free love tending to sap the foundations of our national system and to make a mud pool of libertinage and lawlessness of our country."[4]

Wigwam convention

Shortly after Scholte was chosen as delegate, he corresponded with New York Senator William H. Seward and sent copies of his little book, *American Slavery*. Seward appeared to be Scholte's choice for the Republican Party's presidential nominee. By early April 1860, Scholte was convinced that "Seward will be our candidate and next President, if the Republicans do not spoil themselves by dissension." "On my own hook," Scholte noted, he circulated a recent Seward speech in Congress as "a most excellent production . . . [and] a greater victory over his assailants than he would have achieved if he had made the most effective

---

[2] Kommer Van Stigt, *History of Pella, Iowa and Vicinity*, 1897, trans. by Elizabeth Kempkes (Pella, IA: Scholte House Foundation, 1995), 115.
[3] Mills, "Iowans Helped Nominated Lincoln," 4; *Burlington Weekly Hawk-Eye*, 30 July 1859.
[4] 18 Jan. 1860, *Scholte Journal* 2, 1856-62, private collection; Lubbertus Oostendorp, *H. P. Scholte: Leader of the Secession of 1834 and Founder of Pella* (Franeker: T. Wever, 1964), 185.

Fig. 1.3. Scholte House, overlooking Central Park, 1870s
(*Scholte House Archives*)

self defence [*sic*]." Scholte informed Seward that his speech "has made a great many Democrats in Iowa totally silent and that the hearts of his friends are gladdened." Scholte promised to translate the speech into the "Holland Language." Democratic Senator Stephen Arnold Douglas of Illinois, known as the "Little Giant," however, declared that Seward's speech was "the most powerfull [*sic*] exposure of his unfitness for such an exalted position as President of the United States."

After the Chicago convention, Senator James Grimes of the Iowa congressional committee asked Scholte to consider spending a month at Washington to oversee printing campaign literature in the "Holland" language. Scholte agreed and added: "In that case I would be grateful to be one of the committee to bring the nomination to Mr. Seward." Clearly, Scholte still backed Seward's nomination as the party's nominee.[5]

The Republican National Convention opened on 16 May 1860, with thirty-four Iowa delegates and eight votes. Scholte was one of them, chosen to represent Dutch and German immigrants in Iowa. "I was one of the vice-presidents of the Chicago Convention," he later

[5] *Scholte Journal*, 17, 21, 27 Jan. 1860; Henry P. Scholte to William H. Seward, Cincinnati, OH, William H. Seward Papers, University of Rochester Library, NY, 11, 12 May 1860 (hereafter Seward Papers).

Fig. 1.4. A beardless President Abraham Lincoln, 3 June 1862 (*collection of author*)

noted proudly, along with William M. Stone of Knoxville (later Iowa's Civil War governor). A quarter of the delegates and alternates were lawyers, and only five were farmers. Nineteen later served in the Union army, and at least two died at the front. At age fifty-five, Scholte was one of the oldest Iowa delegates at Chicago's Tremont House, where a large number of Republican delegates had gathered.[6]

Before a roaring crowd of eleven thousand, balloting began on 18 May 1860 for the Republican nominee for president. William Penn Clarke of Iowa City rose to give Iowa's vote on the first ballot. The Iowa delegates scattered their strength among six candidates, with Lincoln and Seward each snaring two. Scholte was still a Seward man, but he came under the influence of Lincoln men at the Tremont House and ended up casting his vote for Lincoln. He wrote later: "At the time my preference was for Seward, but afterwards I became perfectly satisfied with the election of Lincoln."[7]

No other northern state distributed its strength as widely as Iowa. Seward led on the first ballot with 173½ votes but fell short of the 233 necessary for nomination. Lincoln was a strong second with 102½. On the second ballot, Iowa gave Lincoln 5 and Seward 2. Seward moved up to 184½, but Lincoln made a mighty leap to 181 and carried the

---

[6] George Mills, "How Iowans Helped Nominate Lincoln at Wild Convention," *Des Moines Register*, 14 Feb. 1960, 4-5; Ronald C. White Jr., *A. Lincoln: A Biography* (New York: Random House, 2009), 321-29.

[7] *Scholte Journal*, 18 May 1860; Mills, "Iowans Helped Nominate Lincoln," 4-5; Scholte undated manuscript, Scholte House Archives.

Fig. 1.5. Secretary of State William Seward (*collection of author*)

nomination on the third ballot with 231½ votes. The Iowa delegation held firm at Lincoln 5 and Seward 2. With Lincoln the victor, Iowa made their vote unanimous. There must have been some pitched battles among the Iowa delegates at Chicago's Tremont House. But Scholte made only a brief note in his journal on 18 May 1860: "Nomination of A. Lincoln for President and H. Hamlin Vice President."[8]

Scholte backs Lincoln in the presidential campaign

Abraham Lincoln received his formal notification of nomination in his own parlor on 19 May 1860, when the Republican committee arrived in Springfield. Instead of joining the Springfield delegation or attending the Iowa Republican State Convention on 23 May in Iowa City, Scholte left by train for Cincinnati en route to Washington.[9]

On the train Scholte penned a letter to Seward and expressed regret for Seward's defeat at the Chicago convention. "I can assure you dear sir that the only reason, wherefore your name was not triumphantly carried through the Convention, was the fear infused in several delegates that the Republican Party was yet not strong enough to elect you." Scholte assured the senator that "your true friends" had battled manfully until the last, but the die was cast, and "we have to wait four years more." There were "many tears in manly eyes when the result was announced," he added to assuage Seward's loss. Scholte then added

---

[8] Mills, "Iowans Helped Nominate Lincoln," 4; White, *Lincoln*, 321-29; *Scholte Journal*, 18 May 1860.

[9] Earl Schenck Miers, *Lincoln Day by Day: A Chronology, 1809-1865*, vol. 2, 1849-60, ed. William E. Baringer (Washington: Lincoln Sesquicentennial Commission, 1960), 281; White, *Lincoln*, 332; *Scholte Journal*, 19 May 1860.

the line: "I can yet be hardly reconciled with the idea that an advancing army with a broken front of the enemy before them [i. e., the split of the Democratic Party into northern and southern candidates], should pronounce it impossible to win the battle under its acknowledged leader [Seward] and select a second rate general [Lincoln]." But there was little choice, "We have however to submit, and I for my part will do what I can to secure the election of Lincoln, in the conviction that if he becomes President of the United States, he will request you to be and to remain the leader of the van as Secretary of State and then everybody will acknowledge that you are in fact the soul of the administration, and the next Convention cannot but acknowledge by acclamation as the first and last choice of the Republican party."

In Washington Scholte likely stayed at the Willard Hotel near the White House while he translated into Dutch, Republican campaign material and speeches of both Lincoln and Seward for the Republican Congressional Committee, for which he received a stipend of $45.[10]

While still at the capital, Scholte received Seward's reply to his Cincinnati letter, in which he had expressed the wish to return to Pella by way of New York and visit him in his Auburn home. Evidently, Seward apprised him that he would be in Washington, so Scholte visited him there on 1 June 1860. A week later Scholte dined at Seward's home across from the White House at Lafayette Park. There is no record of what transpired, but the men certainly discussed campaign strategies.[11]

While he was away from home, Scholte and his wife Maria wrote each other faithfully. On 9 June, Maria pleaded with him to return home. This ended Scholte's visits with Seward in Washington. Yet, Scholte wrote, "I entertain still the hope to see you next time President, and I can hardly reconcile myself with the idea that it cannot be this time." Then he added: "There is, however, a Providence, and we must obey."[12]

Scholte returned home by way of Springfield, where on 13 June 1860, he visited with Lincoln in his "barrowed" office in the Illinois State House. During the visit, Thomas Hicks completed his portrait of Lincoln, the first ever painted, that very afternoon. The artist commented on his subject: "His eyes had an inexpressible sadness . . . with a far-away look, as if they were searching for something they had seen long, long

---

[10] *Scholte Journal*, 23 May; 9 June 1860; Scholte to Seward, 19 May, 10 June 1860, Seward Papers.
[11] Scholte to Seward, 10 June 1860, Seward Papers; *Scholte Journal*, 26 May, 1, 7 June 1860.
[12] *Scholte Journal*, 26 May, 7, 9 June 1860; Scholte to Seward, Seward Papers.

years ago." At the time, a close friend of Lincoln's said: "It is an exact, life-like likeness, and a beautiful work of art. It is deeply imbued with the intellectual and spiritual, and I doubt whether anyone ever succeeds in getting a better picture of the man." This is the Lincoln Scholte saw, and he was duly impressed. "Not a man of us who saw Mr. Lincoln but was impressed by his ability and character." Lincoln personally invited Scholte to attend his inauguration if elected president.[13]

The *dominee* finally arrived home at Pella on 16 June 1860. His travel adventure to Chicago and Washington took nearly forty days.[14] Scholte wrote Seward about his visit with Lincoln at Springfield. Although he "always" felt "a little disappointed" not having Seward as "our candidate," Scholte said, "I was more reconciled since I have had the opportunity of being a few hours alone with Lincoln. . . . He feels the burden of his position, and he does not expect an easy chair if he should be elected." Scholte concluded with the hope that Lincoln would surround himself with "trustworthy advisers and administer our Government so credible for the Republican cause that we can place you the next time." "For my part," he assured Seward, "I . . . will do what I can to secure the election of Lincoln." Although Scholte had indeed taken Seward's measure, Lincoln was yet to prove himself."[15]

1860 presidential campaign

Scholte campaigned energetically in the 1860 contest, believing that Iowa would give a large majority for the Republican tickets. "I have occupied my spare time since my return for several papers in our State," he boasted to Seward. Through September and October, Republican orators like Scholte fired away from Iowa stumps before large crowds. Lincoln's life story had wide appeal to Iowa's common people. The emphasis was on Lincoln's humble start, his honesty, his conservatism, his western heritage, and his favoring homesteads and railroads, as well, he was a friend of immigrants, such as the Germans and Dutch.[16]

---

[13] *Scholte Journal*, 13 June 1860; Charles Hamilton and Lloyd Ostendorf, *Lincoln in Photographs: An Album of Every Known Pose* (Morningside: Dayton, OH, 1985), 114; Schenck Miers, *Lincoln Day by Day*, 283; White, *Lincoln*, 351-52; "A Visit to Lincoln," *Burlington Weekly Hawk-Eye*, 2 June 1860.

[14] *Scholte Journal*, 10 May to 16 June 1860; White, *Lincoln*, 351-56; "A Visit to Lincoln," *Burlington Weekly Hawk-Eye*, 2 June 1860.

[15] Scholte to Seward, 16 Aug. 1860, Seward Papers; Scholte, "Douglas and Breckinridge," 19 Sept. 1860, *Burlington Daily Hawk-Eye*; Scholte, "Enslaving of Freemen in our National Territory," 27 Oct. 1860, *Burlington Daily Hawk-Eye*.

[16] Scholte to Seward, 16 Aug. 1860, Seward Papers; Edward Younger, *John A. Kasson: Politics and Diplomacy from Lincoln to McKinley* (Iowa City: State Historical Society of Iowa, 1955), 108.

The 1860 campaign was one of the most vigorous and exciting in Marion County. In July Scholte sent campaign "communications" to the Dubuque *Times,* Chicago's *Press and Tribune,* and the *Sheboygan Nieuwsbode,* a Wisconsin paper. Editor Jacob Quintus harshly criticized Scholte's political activism. "See how now in a country where we have more freedom of religion, he deserts his pulpit to become an attorney, publish a paper, [and] gad about speaking in behalf of a party which extends slavery." Quintus had earlier criticized Scholte when he campaigned as a Democrat in Michigan in 1856.[17]

Scholte attended mass meetings for Lincoln in Knoxville, the Marion County seat, and at Oskaloosa, the county seat of the neighboring county of Mahaska. Scholte declared: "We will elect Lincoln and Hamlin and maintain inviolate the treasure of Liberty, Independence and Union delivered to *us by our fathers* [italics mine]."[18]

The campaign rhetoric and pageantry gave little evidence that the nation was engaged in one of the most fateful presidential elections in its history. Borrowing the log cabin, hard cider razzle dazzle that the Whigs had used to elect the Harrison-Tyler ticket in 1840, the Republican Wide-Awake Clubs held torchlight parades, barbecue picnics, and rail-splitting contests for "Honest Abe." There were thousands of young men who marched in gigantic rallies, "wearing colorful, glazed capes and smart military caps, well-disciplined and drilled," as they "marched in solid columns to the blare of brass bands and cadenced cheering." There were also impressive floats, sometimes from as far away as fifty miles.

The Republicans held a rally in Pella on 11 October 1860 that was considered "a rousing success." Never again would Pella witness such political demonstrations! There was a "fine" turnout of over five thousand, but unfortunately, in "unpleasant weather." At first, the large throng poured out to the north end of town to Grundman's Grove, where a speaker's stand had been built for the celebration. But because of the cold, piercing wind, they "repaired" to the street (Washington Street) in front of Scholte's home. Driving through the streets, a wagon hauled a heavy log. Besides the driver, there were two other men on the wagon, each carrying an ax and other tools necessary for rail splitting. As the procession proceeded, men were busy splitting rails amid the deafening "hurrahs for Lincoln." A dray man, who owned a large dog, taught the dog to wag his tail and bark when anyone hollered three

---

[17] *Scholte Journal,* 7 July 1860; Scholte, "How We Know What Slavery is," *Burlington Weekly Hawk-Eye,* 8 Sept. 1860; *Sheboygan* (WI) *Nieuwsbode,* 7 Oct. 1856.
[18] Yzenbaard, "Scholte," 38.

cheers for Douglas, and he growled and snarled and acted as if he would eat the person up if he cheered for Lincoln.[19]

Democrats also held their rallies, which seemed to increase as the election approached. During the torchlight procession across from Scholte's home on the night of the eleventh, a rock came hurtling out of the crowd and hit a marcher on the head in that Republican rally. A fight broke out, and both J. Murray Cox and Wyatt Earp, Pella Wide-Awakes, were injured by "cowardly rowdies" throwing rocks. Thus, Democratic and Republican groups sometimes clashed violently. The morning after the rally in Pella, it was reported that one of the Democrats in that "rumpus" was walking the streets with a revolver in one hand and a club in the other creating a disturbance. Pella's mayor issued a warrant, and the city marshal arrested six Democrats.[20]

In order to snag the Dutch vote in Marion County, Scholte made three major addresses in the "Holland Language": two in October and one on 2 November, just four days before the election.[21] During this time he also directed a political rally in "Garden Square" on 11 October and a smaller meeting at his personal residence. When the Democrats proposed to have a public rally in Pella, it was believed that Scholte, whose "prejudices against the democratic party were so strong," would not allow them to use Garden Square across from his home. Nicolas P. Earp, Wyatt's father and a leading Pella Democrat, encouraged the Democratic officials to ask Scholte for his permission anyway. Indeed, he granted the privilege, on the condition that no horses be allowed on the ground. He declared later: "I have always permitted the use of my grounds for the enjoyment of the public, with the consideration to do no damage, and I do so still."[22]

Lincoln's election and secession

Election Day was 6 November 1860! Scholte simply noted: "Election of A. Lincoln." Then he gave the Lake Prairie Township tally

[19] Younger, *Kasson*, 108; Van Stigt, *History of Pella*, 115; John Van Sittert, "Recalls the Campaign of Lincoln and Douglas," *The Good Ol' Days of Pella's Past* (Pella, IA: Pella Historical Society, 2004).

[20] *Pella Chronicle*, 7 May 1964; George Mills, "Fights, Fiery Speeches, Roaring Cannons Enlivened Wild Campaign of 1860 in Iowa," *Des Moines Register*, 21 Feb. 1860; "How a Dubuque Democrat's Stand on a Slavery Issue Wrecked 1860 Convention and Led to Lincoln's Victory," *Des Moines Register*, 23 Oct. 1860; Wyatt Earp came to Pella in 1850 with his family and left for the West in 1864; "The Pella Rally—Wide Awakes Arouse Support for North," Pella *Chronicle*, 7 May, 1964.

[21] *Scholte Journal*, 10, 23 Oct., 2 Nov. 1860.

[22] William Fisher, et al., Appellee vs. M. H. E. Beard, Appellant, Supreme Court of Iowa, December Term, 1874, 78, 79, 88.

of 199 votes for the Republicans and 398 votes for the Democrats. Scholte's best efforts had not delivered the Dutch vote; they remained loyal Democrats. In the state, however, Lincoln's victory was assured; he carried sixty of eighty-five counties. Douglas carried twenty-five counties. Lincoln also carried the Electoral College vote and was elected the next president of the United States.

When Pellians learned the election results, Republicans prepared for a "great blowout" victory party with a huge bonfire, augmented by firecrackers. After the noise and celebrations died out, Scholte prepared to leave for Lincoln's inauguration on 4 March 1861 in the nation's capital.[23]

In the winter of 1860-61, Iowa's senators and representatives in Congress took no part in a last-ditch effort to find a compromise that might again save the Union and prevent civil war. Henry Clay of Kentucky—Lincoln's favorite Whig, as well as Scholte's—was dead. Within days of Lincoln's election, southern states began preparations for seceding from the Union. Scholte considered this totally unnecessary. "The Republican Party has openly declared that the State rights of the South shall be respected, and that any unlawful invasion of any State must be punished," he wrote on 4 December. "A President elected upon that platform, would betray the party which elected him, if he should infringe upon the Constitutional rights of the South, and nobody has any fear in that respect for Abraham Lincoln. . . . There is at present, no real cause of danger . . . and if we only keep cool, self-possessed, but at the same time firm and prepared, the present crisis will soon be over, and business resume its natural course." Then he quoted the Democrat president "Old Hickory," Andrew Jackson: "The Union, it must be preserved."[24]

At this same time, in the midst of growing tension in the nation, Scholte sat down at his desk in his second floor office and wrote to both President-elect Lincoln and Secretary of State-elect Seward. Sadly, there is no surviving Lincoln response.[25] "The contest is over," Scholte rejoiced to Seward, "and we are the victors. . . . Now comes the trial if we can maintain the ground taken." He believed that the challenge was "to hold our ground under the administration of our next President

---

[23] *Scholte Journal*, 6 Nov. 1860; "And Old Time Political Campaign," *Pella Chronicle*, 22 June, 1916.

[24] Joseph Frazier Wall, *Iowa: A Bicentennial History* (New York: W. W. Norton & Company, Inc., 1978), 107; Scholte, "The Present Crisis," *Burlington Daily Hawk-Eye*, 5, 10 Dec. 1860, *Scholte Journal*.

[25] Scholte to Seward, 5 Dec. 1860, Seward Papers.

Fig. 1.6. Scholte's desk in his upstairs study
(*collection of author*)

and Providence spares your life, then we have a change [chance?] next time to bring your name forward." Meanwhile, he told Seward that he would like to see him at London or Paris [as an American minister] "where we need an efficient Representative, and I should not object to be in some minor Country." Things in Europe were also critical and would not remain without influence on the United States. "I hold it for certain that in a few years we will see a remodeling of the Political map of the old world," he averred. Scholte expressed an eagerness to be in Washington, but he had several court cases to attend to in Knoxville.[26]

South Carolina declared independence as a Republic on 20 December 1860, and other southern states followed quickly. Scholte declared this was an effort to make slavery national and liberty or freedom sectional. If the Republican Party abandoned its political confession of faith and surrendered to the Secessionists, "we might as well cease voting at Presidential elections, and let the slave holders designate in future who shall fill the Presidential chair and occupy the Federal offices, and declare all the Free States open to Slavery. Submission to southern secessionists would demoralize the entire nation and stamp us with infamy before the world." Lincoln was no abolitionist, and southern leaders knew that, but they would rather

[26] Ibid.

deceive southerners and force them into rebellion. The Republican Party would not abdicate. "We can love those who hate us," Scholte wrote. "We can repay curses with blessings, we can pray for those who injure us, but we cannot give up what a kind Providence has given to our Fathers, and transmitted to us—National Liberty Independence and Union." Again, an adopted Holland son claimed the inheritance of "our [American] fathers."[27]

Since the actual declaration of Secession by South Carolinians, along with the probability that other States would soon take the same step, the question for Scholte remained "can Secession be successful?" Writing from his study on 31 December 1860, he editorialized, "Our decided opinion is that it cannot.... If the North is only quiet, but firm, forbearing without cowardice, secession will kill itself.... No person has been able to bring forward a single fact to show that Mr. Lincoln holds any doctrine inimical to the South." But he admitted that there was "no doubt that we are as a Nation in the midst of a Revolution."[28]

The matter of corruption in the incoming administration was on Lincoln's mind. "We need a total reform in the administration of the government," Scholte told Lincoln, "in particular so far as honesty is concerned." Lincoln himself must be "honest but the same ought to be the known character of your Secretaries." Scholte, essentially, was sending a warning to the president-elect. "I have spoken to nobody about it, but having taken an active part in your nomination and election, I should like to see your administration successful at home and abroad." Clearly, Scholte was proud of his efforts on Lincoln's behalf. Although the "present state of things looks gloomy," he added, "I have no doubt but a firm and honest administration will not only be able to preserve the Union but also restore confidence and good will." Scholte signed off "with the best wishes of prosperity for your administration and the Blessings of Providence for you and your family." He was Lincoln's "true friend.[29]

Senator Seward's speech in the US Senate pleased Scholte, and it even silenced Iowa Democrats. He wrote Seward, "I hope to come to Washington to witness the inauguration of Mr. Lincoln and the

---

[27] H. P. Scholte, Pella, "Must the Republican Party Abdicate," *Burlington Daily Hawk-Eye*, 27 Dec. 1860.

[28] H. P. Scholte, "Can Secession Be Successful?," ibid., 5 Jan. 1861; Scholte, "Our Present Condition," ibid., 26 Jan. 1861.

[29] *Scholte Journal*, 5 Dec., 1860, 11, 24, 25; Scholte to Lincoln, 8 Jan. 1861, Lincoln Papers, Library of Congress, Manuscript Division (Washington, DC: American Memory Project, [2000-2002]).

installation of his Cabinet." Knowing that Seward was much occupied, Scholte still solicited his opinion on a wholly unrelated matter. "I am very desirous to know your opinion in reference to my idea of a new Jewish Republic in Palestine.... We would certainly not object because such a Republic would resemble ours for a good deal."[30]

Lincoln's inauguration

At least one hundred Iowans joined the vast Republican throng that descended on Washington for Lincoln's inauguration. "Some came to give confidence and support to the new administration in [the midst of] the nation's greatest crisis. Some sought political rewards, and others hoped to cash in on the Republican victory by fat government contracts," posited one authority of that day. A small Iowa group temporarily took a "half-house, with double parlors and five rooms upstairs" just back of the National Hotel, where they could meet and have their meals. It was said that "everybody from Iowa" visited them. That included H. P. Scholte.[31]

Scholte traveled to Washington by way of Philadelphia and found that Lincoln had passed through the city the night before. Lincoln traveled secretly to the capital because of threats on his life.[32] Scholte learned of this in Philadelphia. "I see from the papers here that Mr. Lincoln has reached secretly Washington and that there was remors [sic] of an attack upon him." It angered Scholte that southern leaders might attack the president-elect. "It would be more than Satanic when the Southern leaders are in contact with assassins. My blood boils sometimes, and nevertheless I feel the necessity of keeping cool."

Scholte wrote Seward that "Lincoln will discover at Washington that direct contact with the affairs of Government is a little different from receptions along the road.... I hope that he will prove a genuine Statesman and otherwise have the good sense to hear [sic] to the counsels of those who know how to steer during the storm." Although the "present circumstances" could not be "handled without gloves," Scholte had no doubt that the South would finally repent. But he "should not wonder if the desperate leaders would hasten a conflict so as to draw the border States to their side." This was also Lincoln's

[30] Scholte to Seward, 1 Feb. 1861, Seward Papers.
[31] Leland L. Sage, *A History of Iowa* (Ames: The Iowa State University Press, 1974), 150-52; Grenville M. Dodge to Annie Dodge, 4, 17, Mar. 1861, Grenville M. Dodge Papers, State of Iowa Archives, Des Moines; Dodge manuscript biography, Dodge Papers; Younger, *Kasson*, 3.
[32] White, *Lincoln*, 378-82.

great fear. "I always feel glad that you will be the leading spirit of the cabinet," he wrote Seward. "Time is what we need at present" because "the organization of the militia in several States is far from complete, and our naval armaments must certainly be increased in case of war." Scholte concluded with a declaration: "I am firmly convinced that our principles must finally triumph, they are right and have the acknowledgment of the civilized world."[33]

In Washington Scholte took a room at the Willard Hotel, where he had lodged the year before. The first evening, on 25 February 1861, he attended a reception for "Lincoln & Lady," who received visitors for two hours in the Willard Hotel parlors. Two days later, Scholte joined the Iowa delegation for another visit with the president-elect, again at Willard's, the same day that Illinois Senator Douglas made an impassioned plea for conciliation of the South.[34]

In the midst of inaugural excitement, Scholte deliberately put himself forward, because the Iowa congressional delegation and the governor had recommended him as the American minister to the Netherlands. The Iowans understood that anti-immigrant Know-Nothings had frightened Dutch immigrants in Iowa, Michigan, and Wisconsin, and thereby discouraged prospective immigrants from the Netherlands. Scholte's appointment would allay their fear. But to Scholte's disappointment, Lincoln appointed James Shepherd Pike of Maine as the minister to the Netherlands, where he served from 1861 to 1866. Pike had been the Washington correspondent of Horace Greeley's *New-York Tribune* and Seward's "most resourceful maligner."[35]

Inauguration Day dawned on a cloudy, raw morning on 4 March 1861. About thirty thousand people gathered to hear his first inaugural address. No inaugural address had ever been delivered in such turbulent times. For some days, there had been rumors of threats to Lincoln himself and repeated attempts to prevent his inauguration. Scholte listened as Lincoln's high-pitched voice and his Kentucky accent could clearly be heard by the throng. After speaking nearly thirty minutes, Lincoln appealed to "the mystic chords of memory" to "swell the chorus of the Union, when again touched, as surely they will be, by the better

---

[33] Scholte to Seward, 23 Feb. 1861, Seward Papers.
[34] *Scholte Journal*, 25, 27 Feb. 1860; C. Percy Powell, *Lincoln Day by Day: A Chronology, 1809-1865*, vol. 3, 1861-65, 22-23.
[35] Hans Krabbendam, "No Return for Henry P. Scholte," *AADAS News: Association for the Advancement of Dutch American Studies* 5 (Fall 2004), 2, 4; Jay Monaghan, *Diplomat in Carpet Slippers: Abraham Lincoln Deals with Foreign Affairs* (New York: The Bobbs-Merrill Company, 1945), 68.

Fig. 1.7. Lincoln's inauguration, 4 March 1861 (*collection of author*)

angels of our nature." And then he placed his hand on the Bible, raised his right hand, and repeated the presidential oath of office.[36]

The cheering began, and Senator Douglas, his old rival in love, law, and politics, stepped forward, one of the first to congratulate the new president. Back in Pella, when the stagecoach arrived the next day with the news of a quiet inauguration, the citizens staged another "blowout" that same evening, replete with a bonfire, firecrackers, and several speeches. The entire crowd closed with the singing of "America."[37]

On 11 March 1861, before leaving the nation's capital, Scholte sat down and wrote letters of gratitude to Lincoln, Seward, and Iowa's senators, James Grimes and James Harlan, expressing his appreciation for their courtesy and gracious reception. The next day, he left by train for home via St. Louis. The weary traveler arrived home on 17 March, after almost a month away, much to his wife Maria's relief.[38]

Scholte fights the Civil War

Less than a month after Scholte's return home, the nation was shaken by the Confederate attack on the federal fort in Charleston

---

[36] White, *Lincoln*, 388-94;
[37] White, *Lincoln*, 388-94; "An Old Time Political Campaign," *Pella Chronicle*, 22 June 1916.
[38] *Scholte Journal*, 11-16 Mar. 1861.

Harbor, South Carolina. Federal forces under Major Robert Anderson soon surrendered. And war came!

During the war years, Scholte continued to carry on correspondence with the much beleaguered president. None of Lincoln's letters to him have survived in Pella, but copies of five Scholte letters to Lincoln are extant, four of which he kept for his own reference.[39] On 8 August 1861, Scholte sent a letter of warning to the president: "During my stay in Washington, I soon discovered that your administration was surrounded by greedy office seekers, and the means to obtain success was not much different from former Democratic Administrations, and I must say I turned in disgust from our National Capitol." Scholte himself was no longer an office-seeker. He counseled Lincoln: "Dear Sir. Your present position is one of the most difficult and critical in the world, but if you put your trust in God, He will give you wisdom and strength to hold the helm of our Ship of State with a strong hand."[40]

In a letter written from Pella, probably sometime in 1861, Scholte warned the president: "I consider it a great calamity for our Country if the present Democratic Party should gain the ascendancy." Scholte believed that Lincoln was "an antislavery man like myself, but unwilling to destroy Society by trying impracticable theories, like the Radical abolitionists." He warned Lincoln: "I am convinced that, if the war is not prosecuted with the utmost vigor, the South will be recognized by European Powers and our Nationality at an end." This, of course, was also a great concern for the president.[41]

During that dark summer of 1862, with the Union forces in retreat, Scholte continued his correspondence with Lincoln's Secretary of State Seward about legal matters. But the Dutch leader had no idea that Lincoln was wrestling with the possible use of his military powers as commander-in-chief to emancipate slaves in the area of rebel resistance. One of Lincoln's friends observed that the president "looks weary, care-worn, and troubled." On 14 July, along with Secretaries Seward and Gideon Welles, the president rode to the funeral of Secretary of War Stanton's infant child. On the way, Lincoln disclosed his intention to emancipate slaves, if the war did not end soon.

Three days later, Scholte wrote the president again. This missive was less political and much warmer in tone. "In the acknowledgment

---

[39] One Scholte letter to Lincoln, dated Jan. 1861, concerning the possible appointment of Simon Cameron of Pennsylvania, is in the Lincoln Papers, Library of Congress. Four letters are in the Scholte Collection at Central College, Pella, IA.
[40] Scholte to Lincoln, 8 Aug. 1861, Scholte Collection.
[41] Ibid., 7 Dec. 1861.

of the heavy burden resting at present upon your shoulders, I wish to address you a few words of Sympathy." He forwarded to Lincoln resolutions that he had introduced and unanimously adopted in "our Township and subsequent in our Republican County Convention. . . . You will clearly see my stand in the present critical condition of our beloved Country." The letter revealed a tender heart, "Dear Sir! In the solitude of my study room I often reflect upon the dangers surrounding you, but I can also assure that my unobserved prayer often rises for you to the throne of Grace, for wisdom, discernment, fortitude and perseverance in the present critical struggle for our National existence."[42]

Scholte closed with a sermonette: "Dear Sir! Human wisdom cannot save our nation, and you are not unaware that calculations of human wisdom in our difficulties have already oftentimes failed. There is, however, a Supreme Wisdom and Power who will not disappoint any man who puts in reality his trust in Him, who can save with few as well as with many." He concluded with a prayer for Lincoln's spiritual strength. "Dear Sir! It is my earnest wish and prayer that you may be strengthened against all pressure of every ultraism, and that you may retain your yet unsullied name [character], and carry t[h]rough your very dangerous and troublesome administration the very honorable name of honest old-Abe—You can rest assured that you have at least in me one praying friend in Iowa." Probably in response to this letter, Scholte received a return letter from President Lincoln on 30 July 1862, but this letter appears to be lost.[43]

Scholte's "whole heart" was in the war. Had he not been fifty-six years old, he would have been among the first volunteers, just as he had done as a "remarkable young man" in his native Holland during the Belgian War for Independence. He declared: [I have] "always preserved my sword, used in the defense of my native country against rebellion." Scholte sought to serve his adopted country in the time of another "rebellion" in every possible way. He believed more men were needed in the field, and he used his influence to "stir up as many as possible." He requested "authority to enlist men and send them up." The Iowa Adjutant General could dispose of his services, he said, and he would "directly provide for an office [to recruit]." All he needed were instructions and the different corps for which enlistments could be made."[44]

[42] Ibid., 17 July, 1862, Scholte Collection.
[43] Ibid.
[44] Scholte to Nathaniel B. Baker, 27 Sept. 1861, Adjutant General of Iowa, General Correspondence, 1861, State of Iowa Archives, Des Moines (hereafter Adjutant

Fig. 1.8. Governor Samuel Kirkwood (*collection of author*)

Scholte guards the home front

While awaiting a commission, Scholte actively recruited young men for service from Pella and the surrounding area. He opened a recruiting office in the log cabin in Garden Square [Central Park], and maintained constant contact with Governor Samuel Kirkwood and Iowa's senators. Already in December 1861 Governor Kirkwood and Secretary of State E. Sells had recommended Scholte's military appointment to Secretary of War Simon Cameron in Washington, DC, "without designating any particular place." Scholte forwarded their recommendation to Cameron. In December he was studying Army regulations. He continued to swear in volunteers to the Iowa regiments and handled passes for enlisted boys.[45] Scholte received his recruiting commission on 10 February 1862 and Adjutant General Nathaniel B. Baker thanked him for his "patriotic motive" to serve "his adopted country."[46]

General Correspondence); Maurice G. Hansen, *The Reformed Church of the Netherlands* (New York: Board of Publication of the Reformed Church in America, 1884), 299, 301.

[45] *Scholte Journal*, 14, 16 Dec. 1861.

[46] Ibid., 10 Feb., 21 Mar. 1862; Baker to Scholte, 10 Feb., 1 Mar. 1862, Adjutant General Correspondence.

By June 1862, Scholte had sought to serve as a spiritual advisor and chaplain to the soldiers in the Iowa 3rd Regiment Volunteer Infantry, where his son-in-law, surgeon Benjamin Franklin Keables, was serving. From Corinth, Mississippi, on 3 June, Dr. Keables wrote his wife Sarah, Scholte's eldest daughter, stating that he did not think they would be able to have a chaplain in the 3rd Iowa Regiment until they were more permanently settled. But he hoped to get better acquainted with the men and "then he would try and get an invitation extended to him if the Regiment was not disbanded." At any rate, Keables was sure that Scholte "would very much dislike the way we have to live and march here." Besides, he told Sarah, there "was a financial burden. It would cost at least $100 to $200 for a respectable outfit." But in a matter of days, by 18 June, Keables wrote that "there appears no opportunity at present for a chaplain in this Regiment as they all think it is useless." Scholte must have been disappointed again.[47]

At the same time, Scholte remained active in both county and state Republican politics. He attended the Iowa State Republican Convention in July 1862, and in September he received a commission to take the votes of the 33rd Iowa Regiment at Oskaloosa's Camp Tuttle. A soldier of the 33rd recorded in his journal of 14 October that it was "Election Day," and "H. P. Scholte of Pella having been previously appointed commissioner to take the vote of the 33rd appeared in camp soon after breakfast." At nine o'clock in the morning the regiment was assembled and elected Judges of Election by acclamation; Scholte recorded their votes.[48]

Scholte next worked to form a Pella Home Guard. He asked Governor Kirkwood to introduce in the Iowa Legislature a "law to provide for the arming of home guards composed of men over 45 and those under that age if they are not drafted for the US" Scholte believed that the times were such "that the State ought to have a force ready to repel invasion and to suppress rebellion within its borders." If approved, he would procure arms and "directly organize one or two companies" from among local Hollanders who were not naturalized citizens and thus not subject to the draft. "I belief [sic] that everyone who has made this State his home, and has all the privileges, must also share in the burdens, particular Hollanders, who by law of their native land have lost their citizenship" as soon as they emigrated. "If you can get arms,

---

[47] Benjamin Franklin Keables to his wife Sarah Scholte Keables, 3, 18 June 1862, Benjamin Franklin Keables, Civil War Letters, Scholte House Archives, Pella, Iowa.
[48] Scholte Journal, 23 July, 14, 17, Sept., 14 Oct. 1862; John S. Morgan's Journal, John S. Morgan Papers, State of Iowa Archives, Des Moines.

do not forget to give us a supply at least for one company." Governor Kirkwood was having a difficult time of it. He was conducting three wars: one with the Missouri Secessionists and Iowa Copperheads on the southern border, one with Native Americans in northwest Iowa, and the third with supplying the state's quota of troops for the Northern Government.[49]

By March 1863, Congress after much debate, enacted a new conscription act that might include the foreign-born. That fear prompted some Hollanders in 1864 to return to their homeland or go to the far west. Scholte warned Adjutant General Baker that "there is here amongst the Hollanders a great stir to leave the State on account of the impending draft." Then he added: "It seems that they have so much Copper in the head that there is no possibility of getting any reasonable argument in their brains."

The "Copperhead Movement," an antiwar faction of the Democratic Party, created much animosity, fury, and repression in Iowa during the war years. It became difficult to define disloyal and even traitorous behavior. In deep concern Scholte made a promise to the governor: "I shall do all in my power to sustain our Government and to defeat the plans of the traitors and their secret allies here, and I shall therefore . . . not shrink from joining a legal Militia Company, if we can be provided with means stronger than words." As late as August 1864, Scholte wrote Adjutant General Baker: "You know as well as I do that we have in our neighborhood a good many who are tainted with Copperheadism, and I think it of the greatest importance to have here an armed band of organized loyal citizens." Scholte was sure that there were no arms in his vicinity belonging to the state and there was need for an armed company in the region. This would be the role of the Pella Guards.[50]

As early as July 1862, Scholte offered city lots "as a small token of our regard for our brave volunteers" to every man from Pella and Lake Prairie Township who enlisted and formed a Union army company from

---

[49] Henry P. Scholte to S. J. Kirkwood, Aug. 28, 1862, S. J. Kirkwood Papers, State of Iowa Archives, Des Moines; Henry Warren Lathrop, *The Life and Times of Samuel J. Kirkwood, Iowa's War Governor* (Iowa City, IA, 1893), 167-69.

[50] Andy Reddick, *Squelching the Secessh: Iowa's Role in the Civil War* (Baltimore: Publish America, 2007), 37-38; Van Stigt, *History of Pella*, 177; Scholte to Baker, 13 Jan., 9 Aug. 1864, Adjutant General of Iowa; Scholte to Kirkwood, 5 Nov. 1862, Adjutant General Correspondence; Hubert H. Wubben, *Civil War Iowa and the Copperhead Movement* (Ames: Iowa State University Press, 1980), 39-40, 65; Benjamin Franklin Keables to Sarah Scholte Keables, 10 Feb. 1862, Keables Civil War Letters, Scholte House Archives.

the South Congressional District of Iowa before 1 September 1862. The company would take up "arms in the Service of the United States, for the suppression of a most unholy rebellion, and for the reestablishment of the Constitutional Authority in every part of the union." Scholte gave sixty-one lots to men of Company G of the 33rd Iowa Infantry Volunteer Regiment, upon their return to Pella.[51]

Meanwhile, the Union army under Gen. George B. McClellan made an ignominious retreat from the Virginia peninsula after the shameful battle at Second Manassas or Bull Run. McClellan had also failed to pursue General Robert E. Lee of the Army of Northern Virginia after the battle of Sharpsburg, Maryland or Antietam Creek. Senators grumbled over Lincoln's failure to fire McClellan, abetted by inside leaks coming from Lincoln's Cabinet secretaries Salmon P. Chase, Edwin M. Stanton, and Caleb B. Smith, who all blamed Scholte's friend Seward for the troubles. The primary source of the anti-Seward movement was Treasury Secretary Chase. The critics demanded Seward's head, although Lincoln knew he was innocent of intrigue. Moreover, the move against Seward was an unconstitutional interference in the senatorial role of advising and consenting to the executive branch. Lincoln believed this to be a constitutional crisis.[52]

Scholte was badly shaken. It seemed that the Lincoln Administration was in trouble, and he expected to hear about a "change of Secretaries." "I must confess," he wrote a friend, that "I have always been a friend of Seward, [yet] my confidence in him is greatly impaired as Statesman and Diplomatist." He believed President Lincoln to be perfectly honest, but began "to doubt his ability for governing in such a State of things as we see since the rebellion." Part of Lincoln's problem was that he tried to act as the servant of the people by following public opinion, instead of leading and shaping it. If he acted more and talked less, "I think we would have been farther in subduing rebellion." Lincoln could not please his critics. The *Washington Chronicle* concluded late in the war: "Some have chided him for being too fast; others for being too slow; but all must see that he has kept pace with the country, neither rising with its exultation, nor sinking with its depression, but steadily, calmly, constantly, directly moving on in the path of progress and liberty."

[51] *Dubuque Times*, 18 Sept. 1863; Van Stigt, *History of Pella*, 116; Recorded Deed for A. J. Sperry, 18 Nov. 1862, John Nollen, Mayor of Pella; Henry P. and M. H. E. Scholte [Civil War] Lot Proposal, 28 July 1862, Central College Archives.

[52] David Von Drehle, *Rise to Greatness: Abraham Lincoln and America's Most Perilous Year* (New York: Henry Holt and Company, 2012), 350-51.

Scholte resorted to the biblical tactic of issuing jeremiads. "O that the Nation could see and acknowledge that God is displeased with our National conduct, and that therefore we are in trouble," he wrote. The Bible says that "the fear of God is the beginning of Wisdom . . . but our present politicians seem to consider themselves smart enough without that."[53]

During that same winter of 1862-63, General Ulysses S. Grant wrestled with the problem of how to crack the Vicksburg, Mississippi, defenses. Vicksburg is situated on a high bluff above the eastern bank of the Mississippi River and protected from the north by hills and swamps. Vicksburg was under siege for forty-eight days, and Grant failed to take the city by assault twice. The battle settled into a siege. Iowans were there from Pella and Marion County. Vicksburg fell on 4 July 1863, and the Mississippi River flowed "unvexed to the sea" for the Federals. Pella celebrated.[54]

In October 1863 Scholte was again appointed commissioner to take the vote of the men in the 33rd Iowa Volunteer Infantry, then camped at Little Rock, Arkansas. The election was held at the colonel's tent. Recent Union military victories had vindicated Republican policies, and the 33rd Iowa cast 295 votes for Iowa's next governor, William M. Stone, former colonel of the 22nd Iowa Infantry and wounded at Vicksburg. His Democratic opponent, General James M. Tuttle, received only forty-five votes. Scholte's return trip up the Mississippi River was threatened by Rebels firing on the boats. But Scholte arrived safely home.[55]

The "Peace Democrats" in the 1864 election demanded an armistice to negotiate a settlement with the South and stop the slaughter. These "Copperheads" angered many fighting men, especially when they returned home on furlough. Both "Peace Democrats" and "Copperheads" belonged to the Democratic Party in Iowa, and many could also be found in Pella and the surrounding area. As early as February 1863, Scholte wrote his son-in-law Dr. Keables that there were "certain persons—*naming them*—who were openly expressing the wish that there would be a revolt in the North against the Government." In fact, Dr. Keables wrote home to his wife, Scholte's daughter, that despite

---

[53] Henry P. Scholte to H. D. Hazen, 23 Dec. 1862, Nollen Papers, Pella Historical Archives, Pella, Iowa; *Washington Daily Chronicle*, 12, 14 Jan. 1864; Kenneth J. Winkle, *Lincoln's Citadel* (New York: W. W. Norton & Company, 2013), 407.
[54] White, *Lincoln*, 550-51; 570-71; 579.
[55] Sage, *A History of Iowa*, 164; Benjamin Franklin Keables to Sarah Scholte Keables, 27 Aug.; 5, 12 Sept. 1863, 10 Nov. 1864, Keables Civil War Letters, Scholte House Archives; Poll Records of 31-40 Regiments, Iowa Infantry, 1863, 7, State of Iowa Archives, Des Moines.

her fear of trouble at home in Pella, it would be "of short duration. The majesty of the law will be maintained, and the traitors in your midst will be arrested, and the quicker it is done, the better." Both Scholte and Keables, one a former Democrat now Republican, the other still a Democrat, were angry with Henry Hospers, editor of the Pella *Weekblad* (established in 1860), and Scholte's future son-in-law John Nollen, Pella's mayor since 1860, for holding that the war was a failure and that peace should be immediately negotiated.[56]

Presidential election of 1864

The presidential campaign of 1864 was a difficult one for Republicans and War Democrats who supported the Union. Lincoln carried Iowa easily with 88,966 votes to Democrat General McClellan's 49,586. McClellan won at least twelve Iowa counties and came close in several others. There were nearly fifty thousand votes cast for Lincoln, the majority from Iowa soldiers fighting in the war. Lincoln had a nine-to-one margin in absentee ballots. Iowa also went for Lincoln in 1860. Lincoln's Electoral College majority was 212 votes to McClellan's 21. In Marion County, the vote for president stood: "Lincoln, 1,459; McClellan, 1,453, a victory of six votes for the President." Part of McClellan's strength came from the fact that thousands of Iowa pioneers came from southern states.[57]

On 10 April 1865, news reached Pella by telegraph that General Lee had surrendered his Army of Northern Virginia to General Grant at Appomattox Court House in Virginia.

Celebrations began in Pella! As always, the center of activity was in and around Garden Square, in front of Scholte's home. The Square was surrounded on all sides with a high Osage Orange hedge. There were no entrances or exits except at the four corners of the Square. A high platform was built on the east side on which was gathered a large consignment of fireworks. The event was widely publicized and drew an immense crowd as night came on. The celebration was to begin with fireworks. But at the very start, sparks from a shooting skyrocket set the entire supply of fireworks aflame, and a wild and dangerous situation occurred. The explosives flew in all directions into the entire crowd, wounding and burning many, some seriously. Pandemonium broke out and people rushed for the hedges. Some were injured in getting

---

[56] Benjamin Franklin Keables to Sarah Scholte Keables, 10 Feb., 30 Mar., 2 May 1863, Keables Civil War Letters, Scholte House Archives.
[57] *History of Marion County, Iowa* (1881), 421.

through or over them, and others trampled underfoot. The well-planned celebration was a dire disaster, but fortunately there was no loss of life. This was a tragic way for Pella to celebrate the end of four years of war![58]

Scholte mourns Lincoln's assassination

Five days after Lee's surrender to Grant, another tragedy struck. The telegraph brought word to the Pella railroad station that President Lincoln had been shot and had died. The undertaker's assistant went door to door with the announcement. Townspeople were stunned; they walked about speaking softly and even whispering. Flags appeared, draped in black crepe or black cloth. On 21 April 1865, editor Hospers' *Weekblad*, a Democratic sheet, published the community response:

> President Lincoln Assassinated—With deep emotion we write these words—his bitterest opponents in state affairs, approved of his methods of restoring peace, and the entire North depending on him. Formidable indeed, reader is this blow! Dreadful the crimes of the one who perpetrated the same! All seemed to point to an early return of peace. Lincoln's magnanimity towards the rebels was making many friends for himself in the North and now?—He is suddenly taken from the scene by the hands of an assassinator. We repeat—'Great is the shock!' and to be despised is he who does not feel deeply touched by the nation's great loss!
>
> True it is that we did not see eye to eye with Lincoln's administration, but it was not the man, the President, but the policy that we opposed. The last fifteen days of Lincoln's administration were approved by all. His mild attitude towards the rebels gave strong hope of an early settlement. But this policy has now been stemmed by assassination. The perpetrators of this terrible murder must be severely punished; even a haven of refuge in some foreign land must not, as the price of a foreign war, be given the degenerate. We trust that a wise Providence, whose actions we have not the right to question, will order all to result in what is best for our land.[59]

The day after Lincoln's death was Easter Sunday. Dominee Scholte, the friend of the president, draped his pulpit at Scholte Church on West First Street with the American flag during that morning's

---

[58] Pella *Chronicle*, 2 June, 1932 (article by W. H. H. Barker).
[59] Van Sittert, "Campaign of Lincoln and Douglas," *Good Ol' Days of Pella's Past*; *Pella Weekblad*, 21 Apr. 1865; Van Stigt, *History of Pella*, 122.

Fig. 1.9. Scholte's church, built 1855, razed 1916 (*Pella Historical Society Archives*)

worship service. One lady, whose husband was a staunch Democrat, but who wished to hear Scholte deliver his sermon, covered her face with a shawl so that she could not see the pulpit but could hear his sermon.[60]

Pella's public buildings were draped in black mourning crepe for thirty days. On the day of Lincoln's death, 15 April 1865, Governor William M. Stone of Iowa was in Washington and issued a proclamation setting aside 24 April as the day on which all of Iowa should jointly humble themselves before Almighty God. The *Weekblad* recounted the Pella observance: "All business houses and public places were closed. The various religious-minded gathered in their respective places of worship." Scholte also held a memorial service in his church.[61]

Back in September 1861, Scholte had written that his "whole heart" was "in the present war." After four years of a horrific carnage, with the tragic loss of twenty Pella boys, the death of the nation's wartime president, and his unfulfilled dream of a foreign post,[62] Henry

---

[60] A. Vander Meide, "When Lincoln was Assassinated Dominie Scholte Draped His Pulpit with the American Flag," *Good Ol' Days of Pella's Past*.

[61] Van Stigt, *History of Pella*, 122.

[62] Out of the 250 Pella volunteers, Pella casualties included 40 wounded, as well as the 20 who were killed or fatally wounded. There were 63 Dutch volunteers

P. Scholte could take satisfaction in his efforts to be of service to Pella, Marion County, and the nation. This Dutch immigrant leader fulfilled his deep desire to be of use to his "adopted country" in time of civil war, although he had been unable to move much of the Pella Dutch vote into the Republican fold. Indeed, Scholte was no stranger in a strange land, although he still had a warm heart for the spiritual life of his home country—he was proud to be an adopted son.

---

enlisted in infantry and cavalry regiments. The Pella numbers do not include the 250 volunteers from Central University, and the 26 who volunteered for service but never returned. See *Souvenir History of Pella, Iowa, 18-22* (Pella: Booster Press, 1922), 134-35; *History of Pella, Iowa, 1847-1987* (Pella: Pella Historical Society), 163.

CHAPTER 2

Two Holland, Michigan, Boys in the Union Army

Marten C. P. Rustenburg

Henry Beets in 1908 compiled a list of the 386 men from West Michigan who served in the Civil War. All of them wrote letters home, but only a handful of the missives, written in an amalgam of Dutch and English, found their way into historical archives.[1] This chapter tells the story in their own words of two men from the Holland colony—Johannes Van Lente and Jan Douma.

Van Lente was the sixth of eight children in the Van Lente family that emigrated in 1847 from the city of Zwolle, in the province of Overijssel, to join Van Raalte's colony in the woods of West Michigan. Frederick, the father, was a carpenter and cooper. The family immigrated in response to a severe economic downturn, made worse by the potato crop failure of 1845 and 1846, which affected tradesmen and farmers alike. With borrowed money, the family of ten made the journey July 1847.[2]

---

[1] Henry Beets, *Abraham Lincoln, zijn tijd en leven* (Grand Rapids: Hulst & Sevensma, 1909), 217; Jeanne Jacobson, Elton J. Bruins, and Larry M. Wagenaar, *Albertus C. Van Raalte: Dutch Leader and American Patriot* (Holland: Hope College, 1996), 66.

[2] Janice Van Lente, ed., *The Civil War Letters of Johannes Van Lente* (Holland: Yankee Girl Publication, 1992), 1.

Fig. 2.1. Johannes Van Lente in uniform (*Joint Archives of Holland*)

Johannes Van Lente

Once settled, they cleared land and started farming. Two of the boys, Johannes and Hein, worked the land, while Frederick found work in his trade. From family stories that have survived, it is known that Frederick made roofing shingles for many of the log cabins. Later the family donated their cooperage skills to construct the pillars for Pillar Church.[3] The Van Lente family was musically talented. Johannes asked his consistory for permission to start a church choir. When that was denied, he began a "singing school."[4] The school survived for several generations and performed at many public events.

Jan Douma was born in January 1847 in the village of Ee in the province of Friesland. His father, Romke, was also a carpenter.[5] Ten years later the Douma family of eight, plus Mrs. Johanna Douma's brother, Wiebe Mokma, a widower with four children, left their homeland. Mokma died during the voyage, so the Doumas took in the orphaned children and raised them.[6] The families travelled directly to Michigan to join Van Raalte's colony.

When the Civil War broke out, the Holland colony was immediately affected. Rev. Van Raalte was very aware of the issues that led to the

---

[3] From personal interviews with Janice Van Lente and Van Lente, *Civil War Letters*, 3.
[4] D. M. Tripold, *Sing to the Lord a New Song*, 49.
[5] Personal letter to Barb Lampen, granddaughter of Jan Douma, from the Rijksarchief in Friesland.
[6] Randall P. Vande Water, *Holland Happenings, Heroes & Hot Shots*, vol. 2 (Holland, MI: self published, 1995), 124.

Fig. 2.2. John Douma with Civil War volunteers at homecoming; *l-r, seated*: Cornelius J. Lokker, Berend H. Eppink, Matthew Notier; *standing*: Germ W. Mokma, Gerrit J. Nyland, John Douma (*Joint Archives of Holland*)

war and decidedly took up the cause of the North. He strongly urged the young men of the colony to enlist, and two of his own sons signed up. Johannes Van Lente and some of his friends enlisted in August of 1862. His enlistment papers state that Johannes, age twenty-seven, was a farmer. He was 5 feet 5 ½ inches tall, somewhat short even for those times when the average solder was between five foot five and five foot nine.[7] Johannes and some of his friends were assigned to the Twenty-Fifth Michigan Infantry, Company I.

Johannes wrote many letters home, and the family preserved them; they even survived the Holland Fire of 1871. This chapter is enriched by these letters, which provide an intimate window into the life and times of a Civil War soldier. Van Lente's great-granddaughter, Janice Van Lente, inherited the letters and had them translated. The first letter, dated 7 September 1862, was sent from Kalamazoo, where Johannes and his compatriots were mustered into service and spent the month. The letter painted a positive picture; the camp opened daily with a Psalm and a song. It likely was Johannes' first encounter with the "world out there," and he sensed immediately that there would be

---

[7] Jacobson, Bruins, and Wagenaar, *Van Raalte*, 53; Van Lente, *Van Lente Letters*, 4.

challenges to his religious convictions. He wrote about being exposed to "all sorts of temptations," although he does not identify them.[8]

The letters reveal strong and deep family ties. One included a photograph of Johannes in uniform, which has also survived. The letters also show his strong sense of patriotism. He wore his uniform with pride, and he was a true son of Uncle Sam. This national loyalty later became somewhat of a divisive element in the colony. Johannes was quick to impugn the motives of men who did not support the Union cause. Every letter also told of his health and well being, in an attempt to reassure his worried parents and siblings.

In early October 1862, his unit left Kalamazoo by train for Indianapolis. It was Johannes' first train ride, and he reported the experience in detail, including descriptions of the various towns en route. In Niles local citizens treated the troops kindly and brought them coffee by the bucketsful. From Indianapolis the unit travelled on to Louisville, Kentucky. Johannes' first letter from below the Mason-Dixon Line revealed his negative feelings toward the South. He also had his first encounter with the realities of war when he saw a prison-of-war camp in Indianapolis. His impressions were that these "rebels" were nothing more than a poorly equipped bunch of rag-tag men. He also encountered a large number of Northerners there who had been prisoners of war but were released after swearing never again to pick up arms against the South. The war hit home very personally when he heard of the death of his friend and former tent mate, Arie Rot. Disease claimed Rot, as it did a majority of the casualties in the war. The news hit Van Lente hard, and he shared his despondency in passionate and spiritual terms. He began chiding tent mates to set their spiritual house in order and frowned on any lighthearted frivolity.[9]

Johannes wrote little about the fighting, with two significant exceptions. We learn more about the campaigns of the Twenty-Fifth Michigan from the letters of Benjamin Travis of Company E than from anyone else. Johannes' first detailed account of an engagement was in a letter of 23 January 1863 from Bowling Green, Kentucky. He noted that the brigade built breastworks in anticipation of an attack by John Hunt Morgan's cavalry, a fearsome group. In a letter dated February 1863, Van Lente reported that 2nd Lieutenant Jacob O. Doesburg returned to Holland because "he couldn't take it any longer." Johannes caustically said that Doesburg suffered from "Morgan fever," meaning he was a

---

[8] Van Lente, *Van Lente Letters*, 9.
[9] Ibid., 13, 18.

coward. Officially, however, Doesburg was discharged on account of disability.[10]

The Michigan Twenty-Fifth Infantry and Morgan's raiders engaged in several skirmishes in the area of Munfordville, Kentucky, but none were of great consequence. The Union troops took a few prisoners, who Johannes described as rude and belligerent. His unit then marched to Louisville, across a scenic landscape dotted with large farms and slaves working in the fields.

Van Lente's letter of 4 February 1862 revealed a sense of discouragement with the progress of the war. "As I notice here and there, it is not going too well with the war. Oh, the Lord save our Country, because as far as we can see, our Country is done for."[11] Over time, his feelings vacillated according to particular information the troops received, which may not always accurate. In any case, Johannes always evaluated the war from the perspective of his faith and religious convictions.

The other engagement that Johannes described in detail had some significance in the outcome of the war. Unfortunately, the news of this battle and its significance was eclipsed by the battle of Gettysburg. This battle, called the Battle of Tebb's Bend, or the Battle of Green River, took place near Campbellsville, Kentucky, on the Green River. In a very bloody fight, the Michigan Twenty-Fifth under the command of Colonel Moore was greatly outnumbered. The troops knew that Colonel Moore was disliked by his superiors who had sent him on this assignment in hopes of the unit suffering an overwhelming defeat. The troops, in fact, loved this leader as a father figure and obeyed him eagerly. Johannes even compared him to Van Raalte.

The tactics that Moore worked out consisted of cutting down trees to make a sort of blockade, behind which the Union troops took cover. Hiding behind the tree trunks, they were able to pick off the rebels so effectively that every charge was repelled. The boys in blue had also efficiently picked off the cannoneers, so that the rebels had to pull the cannons back from the battle. At dusk a truce was declared so that the dead could be buried. Travis wrote: "Within an hour after the battle, I went out to look at the rebel dead, and found most of them shot through the breast and head. . . . The location of the wounds showed the accuracy of our aim. . . . Captain De Boe had been detailed to bury the rebel dead, which was done by placing them all in one trench, with

---

[10] Ibid., 30.
[11] Ibid., 27.

Fig. 2.3. Tebbs Bend hospital in Atkinson Griffin House, erected ca. 1840 (*courtesy Janice Van Lente*)

nothing to distinguish one from another. Our own dead were properly buried with military honors and with as good grace as the sorrows of the occasion would permit."[12] Captain De Boe was in charge of Company I, to which Johannes was attached.

Johannes in his letter described some of the gory details of the battle, but added the comment: "Too much to mention."[13] Near the battlefield was a log cabin that served as a field hospital, receiving wounded from both the North and South. On 4 July 1988, the Holland-Zeeland Civil War Roundtable went to the battle site and erected a monument to commemorate the battle. The Holland American Legion color guard participated in the ceremonies, along with Janice Van Lente, who was startled to find blood stains on the wood floors that were still visible. It was an emotional experience for her and her children to think about the fact that her great-grandfather was involved in bringing the wounded there.

The effect of this battle was that John Hunt Morgan's units were so decimated that they were never a major threat for the rest of the war, although Morgan carried out a lot of nerve-wracking raids until he was captured in Ohio. The Battle of Tebb's Bend turned the tide of the war in the Ohio Valley. The flag of truce that Morgan sent was shredded into pieces as mementos. Johannes sent his scrap to his family

---

[12] Van Lente, *Van Lente Letters*, 54.
[13] Ibid., 56.

enclosing it in a letter dated 24 July 1983. This letter also notes the capture of Vicksburg and Port Hudson and the apprehension of John Morgan, whom Van Lente labeled a torturer. A letter found among the Van Raalte papers adds an interesting footnote to this battle in which the soldiers expressed their appreciation for correspondence from their pastors in the Holland colony. In an act of gratitude for sparing them in the Battle of Green River, the men sent a thank offering to Van Raalte to be used for Kingdom causes. It was signed by thirty-one soldiers, including Van Lente.[14]

As mentioned before, family and friends were of primary concern. Despite bad weather, inadequate and dilapidated tents, and the lack of creature comforts, Johannes did not complain to his family back home. In spite of sleeping in unheated tents in the snow, Van Lente's primary complaint was about delays in receiving mail. "It isn't so easy for me when I don't receive any letters from you. So I can imagine how you people feel when a letter arrives from one of the other boys and not from me. Dear Father and Mother, it is really not my fault. . . . I can't understand that you don't receive any greetings from me or that you don't hear from me. Dears, I hope that if you don't receive my other letters, that you will receive this one for sure."[15]

As noted above, music was important in the Van Lente family and Johannes occasionally exchanged sheet music and included in his letters a song he had composed. His father was also very capable of writing a song and may have written compositions for the choir. It appears that his brother Hein was giving singing lessons, but it did not go well. Johannes wrote in May of 1863 of his consternation upon learning of the "downfall of your song school." He encouraged him to start again with a new choir.[16]

The Michigan Twenty-Fifth was part of General William T. Sherman's "March to the Sea." On 14 May 1864, while advancing on Atlanta, there was some serious fighting around Resaca, Georgia, and Johannes was deep in the middle of it. His good friend, Cornelis van Dam, died in that fight. Janice wrote: "During the confusion of battle . . . Johannes also lost his knapsack and all of his belongings. After lying in the water for several hours, he became ill with pneumonia and was (hospitalized). . . . During his recuperation at the hospital in Marietta, Johannes served as a cook."[17] None of Van Lente's letters from this six-

[14] Ibid., 59, 66.
[15] Ibid., 28.
[16] Ibid., 48.
[17] Van Lente, *Van Lente Letters*, 81.

month period have survived, but he did begin saving his father's letters, which fill in some details.

No mention is made in the letters from home or from Johannes about the re-election of Abraham Lincoln in November 1864. Pessimism seemed to rule about the war and on the home front. "I noticed already in the first letter your downheartedness about the condition of the country," Johannes wrote. "It is true our country is now in a lamentable condition, but I really believe that you are worrying too much about this business when you talk about the war. . . . I wrote you this before, that I think it is going to come to a destruction of the South, and then they will have to give up . . . It will have to come to the point where they will have to surrender unconditionally. . . . Let's be thankful for the things that are happening today. Also thank the Lord especially for such a general as Sherman. Dear ones, we may see him as a second Washington."[18]

The letters become more upbeat in April 1865. Although the fall of Richmond is not mentioned, Johannes' father expressed gratitude "for so many blessings shown, especially now these last times," which have "visibly revealed the hand of the Lord by blessing our weapons and the downfall of the Rebellion."[19]

The assassination of President Lincoln cast father Frederick into despair for the future. "Now I write something that you probably already know, that horrible blow which struck our Country about the murder of our President. What a blow that was for us and that this great Statesman [William Seward] almost had his throat cut. How shattered we were. You cannot imagine how our Colony was immersed in mourning, especially since we received such happy news a few days before, that Petersburg and Richmond had been captured and that General Lee had laid down his weapons."[20]

Johannes's next letter, dated 22 April 1865, notes simply that "everything is quiet, there is armistice." Johannes explained the devastation that Sherman's army had inflicted on civilians as a just punishment. "I say, 'away with this disgrace slavery.' As long as we keep this in America we can't expect everlasting peace. And that's why we are working on it and that's why I think it best to finish it right."[21] Johannes was mustered out at Salisbury, North Carolina, on June 24 and traveled to Grand Rapids, where his family met him on the last leg of his journey home.

[18] Ibid., 119.
[19] Ibid., 127.
[20] Van Lente, *Van Lente Letters*, 129.
[21] Ibid., 131, 133.

Jan Douma and six friends were mustered in during the last months of the war, on 29 March 1865, in Kalamazoo. According to the enlistment papers, he signed up for one year. He was somewhat taller than Johannes, measuring at five foot eight. The Douma family arrived in Holland in 1857 and settled in Fillmore Township of Allegan County. In his enlistment papers, Jan's occupation is farmer.[22] His companions who signed up with him were Cornelius J. Lokker, Berend H. Eppink, Matthew Notier, Germ W. Mokma, and Gerrit J. Nyland. Douma and Notier were assigned to the 24th Michigan Infantry regiment, which unit earned the nickname, "Iron Brigade." For a time, the regiment got a reprieve from the fighting and was assigned to garrison duty at Camp Butler in Springfield, Illinois.[23]

One of the many scams perpetrated during the Civil War was for men to sign up to get the government bounty and then desert from training camp only to sign up again under a different name to collect another bounty. To stop this practice, recruits were sent to an enclosed camp, called a "Rendezvous," which was guarded by veteran units. The 24th Regiment was engaged in that duty along with guarding a prison camp. It was not pleasant duty, because the wet and muddy Camp Butler was notorious for filth and disease.

It was in this setting that Douma and Notier were brought to Springfield that spring of 1865. The new recruits were not always received kindly. In his book on the Twenty-Fourth, Donald Smith wrote: "The new recruits were, in most cases, barely tolerated, many of the men believing that they had joined because the outlook for further combat by the organization was dim."[24] Douma and Notier were guarding prisoners when the news came of Lincoln's assassination. Many years later, in an interview published in the *Holland Sentinel*, Douma recalled vividly the day when word of the fatal shooting was brought to their camp as he and Notier were guarding rebel prisoners. "The bulletin was flashed over the telegraph and passed from mouth to mouth in a few moments. There was a hush over the camp broken only by the shout of a rebel prisoner that he was glad Lincoln was dead. A northern soldier struck him to the ground with a blow to the mouth."[25]

When the regiment was notified that it was assigned to the funeral ceremonies, "the men were drilled with special care for the treasured duty . . . until they appeared at their best. New uniforms were issued;

---

[22] *Holland City News*, 2 Feb. 1939; enlistment papers of Jan Douma, National Archives.
[23] Vande Water, *Holland Happenings*, 2: 122.
[24] Donald Smith, *The Twenty-Fourth Michigan, Of the Iron Brigade* (Harrisburg, PA), 248.
[25] *Holland Sentinel*, 12 Feb. 1930.

Fig. 2.4. Guarding the vault: Jan Douma (*left*) and Matthew Notier (*right*), with their muskets at arms (*Abraham Lincoln Presidential Library and Museum*)

muskets, brass, and shoes polished until they shone, and the whole topped off with a new issue of black hats, feathers, and white gloves."[26] On May 4th the regiment left Camp Butler for the funeral ceremonies. The 24th Michigan stood at the head of the military escort along with units from Iowa, Wisconsin, and of course, Illinois.

It was not likely that the entire Twenty-Fourth took part of the funeral entourage, but Douma and Notier were assigned to guard the vault that was to hold Lincoln's body until the grave proper was completed. It was guarded until the body was placed in the vault and secured. Their assignment was memorialized when a photographer took their picture while they were on duty. It was published in the book, *Twenty Days*, a pictorial book about the Lincoln funeral.[27]

The next day the units returned to their normal routines. Preparations were being made to begin the process of mustering out the soldiers. We are left to wonder what Douma and Notier felt during these events. Here were a couple of teenage farm boys being exposed to an historical event of monumental proportions. We get a glimpse of

[26] Smith, *Iron Brigade*, 252.
[27] D. M. Kunhardt and P. B. Kunhardt, *Twenty Days* (New York: Castle Books, 1965), 249.

Fig. 2.5. Johannes Van Lente (*on right*) as a middle-aged man by the fountain he designed in Centennial Park (*Joint Archives of Holland*)

this from another interview recorded in a news article on the occasion of remembering Lincoln on his birthday: "Mr. Douma, then a young man of eighteen was on guard the entire day as the cortege was moved down the street. He recalls how the casket was borne in army fashion on a flag draped gun caisson. . . . Mr. Douma is frank in saying that he was more concerned that day in not being able to stop for a meal than in the significance of the day."[28]

Epilogue

After the war, both Van Lente and Douma returned to their farms, married, and raised large families. Both anglicized their names to John. Both suffered greatly in the Holland Fire of 1871. Providentially, Van Lente's letters survived. In later years, Johannes became a carpenter and then as gardener for the city of Holland. He designed the fountain in Centennial Park. Johannes also carried on the singing school his father had started. He died in 1911 and is buried by the statue of the Civil War Soldier in Pilgrim Home Cemetery. After giving up farming, Douma worked as custodian at the First State Bank. At the time of his death in 1939, he had the distinction of being the last surviving Civil War veteran in Holland, Michigan.[29]

---

[28] *Holland Sentinel*, 12 Feb. 1930.
[29] Van Lente, *Van Lente Letters*, 141, 144; *Holland Sentinel*, 1 Nov. 1986, 31 Jan. 1939.

CHAPTER 3

Wooden Shoes to Brogans: Klaas Zuidema and the Civil War

Michael Swanson

The municipal cemetery in Fulton, Whiteside County, Illinois, is situated atop a picturesque limestone bluff overlooking the Mississippi River. Among the assorted gravestones, many of which attest to the Dutch heritage of the community, are those in a small section for veterans of nineteenth-century wars. One of the men buried here, Nicholas Zuidema, served as a private in the Civil War with a regiment out of Indiana as shown on his headstone.[1]

Zuidema emigrated from the Netherlands in that fateful year of 1861, arriving in New York on the sixteenth of August.[2] Born in the province of Groningen to a family of limited means, he likely had little understanding prior to leaving his homeland seven weeks earlier of the significance of the bombardment at Fort Sumter on 12 April

---

[1] Although he was generally known by the given name of Nicholas in American records, his given name at birth in the Netherlands was Klaas.

[2] Claas Zuideman [sic], Bark Helvetia Passenger Manifest, 16 Aug. 1861; *Passenger Lists of Vessels Arriving at New York, New York, 1820-1897* (National Archives Microfilm Publication M237, roll 214); Records of the US Customs Service, Record Group 36; National Archives, Washington, DC.

Fig. 3.1. Headstone at the gravesite of Nicholas Zuidema, Fulton Cemetery, Fulton, Illinois (*courtesy of Crystal Smith, Fulton, Illinois*)

1861. Nor did he probably conceive, upon his arrival, that he would be a participant in the protracted war that ensued. What more could be learned about the life of this Dutch immigrant and, in particular, his experiences in the deadly and prolonged conflict that polarized our country? Moreover, what circumstances caused him to eventually settle in Fulton after serving in the Indiana regiment?

Klaas Zuidema and the 60th Indiana Infantry

From 190,000 to 210,000 men served in Indiana military units during the Civil War, and of these, from 24,000 to 27,000 (about 13 percent) lost their lives. The numbers are imprecise given poor record keeping. The greater number of participants, including those serving in the Navy, is etched into the south face of the Indiana Soldiers and Sailors Monument in downtown Indianapolis, which was completed in 1901. The total number of 210,000 represents nearly 75 percent of the eligible men living in Indiana at the time.[3] Roughly two-thirds of the deaths during the Civil War are attributable to disease and other non-combat causes, while only one-third resulted from actual warfare. As a state, Indiana ranks fifth overall in the number of troops furnished for the war.

---

[3] "Soldiers and Sailors Monument" (Indiana War Memorials Foundation, 2013), http://www.indianawarmemorials.org/index.html (accessed 12 Sept. 2013). The smaller estimate is in "Union—Troops Furnished and Deaths" (The Civil War Home Page, 2009), http://www.civil-war.net/pages/troops_furnished_losses.html (accessed 29 May 2013).

It is not known if Zuidema wrote any letters during the Civil War (none have been located), but official military records make it possible to piece together basic facts of his service. In addition, a pension file in his name has been preserved at the National Archives. Documents in this file provide a glimpse into his prior military experiences. On 1 March 1862, Zuidema enlisted in Indianapolis for a three-year term and was assigned to Company G of the 60th Indiana Infantry.[4] On the enrollment form, Zuidema is described as being 5 feet 7½ inches tall, with light hair, blue eyes, and a fair complexion. His occupation is recorded as farmer, and he claimed Amsterdam, Holland, as his nativity. It is not known why Amsterdam was recorded on this form. Zuidema was one of four men to be enrolled into Company G on that date, and they were the last four privates to join the Company.[5]

The 60th Regiment was created at Evansville in November 1861, and enrollment was completed after the unit was ordered to Indianapolis in February 1862.[6] Ten days after his enrollment, Zuidema was mustered in and promptly stationed at Camp Morton on the outskirts of Indianapolis. Established as the state fairgrounds a few years earlier, the property was converted into a soldiers' training facility in 1861, when the prospect of war was imminent.[7]

The grounds were renamed Camp Morton in honor of Governor Oliver Perry Morton and were taken over by the federal government early in 1862 for the purpose of housing Confederate prisoners. The first prisoners to be detained at Camp Morton were from the capture of Fort Donelson in Tennessee. Over the span of a few days in February 1862, thirty-seven hundred prisoners arrived. When it was known these prisoners were coming, Governor Morton requested several partially-filled regiments to serve as prison guards. Among these regiments was the 60th—ten companies strong under the command of Colonel Richard Owen. The companies of the 60th were distributed around the boundaries of the camp, along with remnants of other regiments. Company G occupied a position midway, along the west side of the camp border.[8]

[4] Nicolaus Seidema; *Card Index to Indiana Civil War Records* (Family History Library Microfilm 1570894) Indiana State Library, Indianapolis.
[5] Enlisted Men of Company "G." Sixtieth Regiment Infantry." *Report of the Adjutant General of the State of Indiana* VI (1866): 12.
[6] Ann Turner, *Guide to Indiana Civil War Manuscripts* (Indianapolis, IN: Indiana Civil War Centennial Commission, 1965), 194-95.
[7] Hattie Lou Winslow and Joseph R. H. Moore, "Camp Morton 1861-1865. Indianapolis Prison Camp," *Indiana Historical Society Publications* 13, no. 3 (1940): 238-50.
[8] Winslow, "Camp Morton," 277.

Fig. 3.2. Rebel prisoners at Camp Morton, Indianapolis, Indiana, ca. 1862-65 (*unattributed, Prints & Photographs Division, Library of Congress, LC-DIG-ppmsca-33994*)

At this time, there were no military rules or guidelines regarding the treatment of prisoners of war. Other prison camps were not much more than cesspools, where death and disease were common occurrences. For the prisoners at Camp Morton, the capable leadership of Colonel Owen proved fortuitous. Owen's manner of oversight of the prisoners was termed paternalistic. He was a strict disciplinarian, who demanded that his orders be followed to the finest detail. This was balanced by his sympathetic views of the plight of the prisoners and his provision of adequate facilities for them. Owen created a set of rules that allowed the prisoners essentially to govern themselves, an idea unheard of at the time. They were allowed to engage in wholesome and educational activities, but if any rules were broken, Owen was swift and decisive in handing out discipline. His respectful and even-handed approach in the treatment of Confederate prisoners would serve him and the 60th well some months later.[9]

The 60th remained as the principle regiment in charge of the prisoners until 20 June 1862, when it was dispatched for active service to Louisville, Kentucky.[10] Shortly thereafter, the regiment continued about thirty miles farther south to Lebanon Junction. There is little doubt that Zuidema was part of this campaign to reinforce Union positions and protect against counter attacks. Documents in his pension file indicate that either in September or early October of 1862, his regiment

[9] Winslow, "Camp Morton," 262-65.
[10] Turner, *Indiana Civil War Manuscripts*, 194.

encountered the cavalry of Confederate General John Hunt Morgan in southern Kentucky, somewhere between Bowling Green and Glasgow.[11]

Injury and illness

Zuidema, in pursuit of the enemy, was thrown from his horse and injured when attempting to jump a fence. He spent a few days in the regimental hospital in Bowling Green but returned to active duty three weeks later. It is somewhat perplexing that Zuidema, who served in an infantry regiment, was on horseback. The pension documents do not elaborate on this nor do they mention anything about his horsemanship. The injury turned out to be a rupture (hernia) in the left inguinal area that manifested itself about two months after his hospital stay. The nature of this injury would certainly have limited his ability to carry out his duties as a soldier.

General Morgan is one of the interesting personalities of the Civil War. His cavalry unit, informally known as Morgan's Raiders, raided Union-held territory on several occasions in order to disrupt transportation infrastructure by destroying bridges and rail lines. His men also plundered Union supplies and captured and paroled numerous troops. In the summer of 1863, Morgan and his raiders began their most ambitious campaign by making their way into Indiana and Ohio. Pursuing federal troops finally captured him near the Pennsylvania border, but he escaped prison several months later and returned to raiding until he was killed in action at Greeneville, Tennessee, in September 1864. Considered a loose cannon by his superiors, Morgan is now regarded as having been more of a nuisance than anything else to the Union. At the time his daring exploits were glorified in the Southern press, but the ultimate loss of his cavalry was a significant blow to the Confederate cause.

About the time Zuidema suffered his accident, seven companies of the 60th, along with various other troops at the Union garrison at Munfordville, Kentucky, were forced to surrender to Confederate General Simon Bolivar Buckner, part of General Braxton Bragg's army. Munfordville was a strategic point due to the nearby railroad bridge over the Green River, which was a critical supply route for advancing forces.[12]

---

[11] Nicholas Zuidema (Pvt., Cos. A & G, 60th Ind. Inf., Civil War) pension application no. 403,934, certificate no. 578,186, Department of Veterans Affairs, Record Group 15; National Archives, Washington, DC.

[12] H. Engerud, US Colonel (retired), "The Battle of Munfordville, September 14th-17th, 1862," *Indiana History Bulletin* 50, no. 11 (1973): 127.

Buckner was one of the generals who had previously surrendered at Fort Donelson and was imprisoned with his men at Camp Morton. Realizing that men of the 60th, including Owen himself, were part of the captured forces and recalling their previous treatment as prisoners by Owen, Buckner's unit quickly paroled the companies of the 60th.[13] They returned to Indianapolis to reassemble the regiment.

It remains unclear if Company G was among those captured at Munfordville. In any case, Zuidema would have also been transported back to Indianapolis to rejoin the 60th. In November 1862, the 60th made its way to Memphis and became part of the Army of the Mississippi.[14] In a physician's affidavit included in his pension application, Zuidema was treated for a rupture in early 1863 near Young's Point, Arkansas. The affidavit stated that Zuidema was excused from guard duty a number of times by a regimental surgeon as a result of his injury. The location of this Young's Point seems to be in error and more than likely was Young's Point, Louisiana, situated on the Mississippi River about nine miles upriver from Vicksburg, Mississippi. Young's Point, Louisiana, had fallen under Union control only a few weeks previously and was used as a staging point in preparation for the siege of Vicksburg in the summer of 1863. On 10 January 1863, the 60th was involved in the Battle of Arkansas Post in nearby Arkansas. This victory by the Union paved the way for the ultimate prize of Vicksburg and control of the entire Mississippi River.

There was only one other mention of Zuidema's Civil War experiences in his pension documents. He developed a severe case of bronchitis near the end of his term of service, in March 1865, which caused him to be susceptible to bad colds, particularly in damp weather. His compiled military service record, however, provides a few more details.[15] In March or April 1863, he received a five dollar reduction of pay for an undisclosed violation. He was then detached to a pioneer corps about September 1863 until April 1864.

The pioneer corps

The creation of a pioneer corps, attached to each regiment, was the idea of General William Rosecrans. Rather than designating random

---

[13] Winslow, "Camp Morton," 284.
[14] Turner, *Indiana Civil War Manuscripts*, 194.
[15] Compiled service record, Nicholas Seidema, Pvt., Cos. A & G, 60th Indiana Infantry; Carded Records Showing Military Service of Soldiers Who Fought in Volunteer Organizations During the American Civil War, compiled 1890-1912, documenting the period 1861-66, Record Group 94; National Archives, Washington, DC.

soldiers to do some of the menial engineering work, such as improving roads, disassembling enemy fortifications, and repairing bridges, two soldiers from each company were detached and organized into these groups, thus enabling advancing troops to move more efficiently.[16] Men in the pioneer corps did not see active duty, but were expected to work hard. It is possible that Zuidema possessed a certain skill that led to his assignment in a pioneer corps, or perhaps his chronic hernia problems prevented him from adequately performing as a regular soldier, and this was the next best option. Whatever the case, Zuidema spent a significant portion of his three-year enlistment in this capacity.

Upon returning to the 60th from his pioneer corps, Zuidema was temporarily transferred to the 67th Indiana Infantry in the spring of 1864, but he returned to his old company a couple of months later. On 13 December 1864, Company G was broken up, and Zuidema, along with the remaining men, were transferred to Company A, which began as an all-German company of the 60th. Klaas was mustered out on 22 March 1865 in Indianapolis after satisfactorily completing his three years of military service.

Although there was no specific mention in Zuidema's various military records, the 60th played an active role in the siege of Vicksburg in late May to early July, 1863.[17] It then participated in the siege at Jackson, Mississippi, and later fought primarily in Louisiana and Texas. The regiment returned to Indiana on furlough in mid-1864, but because it had not fulfilled its mandated term of service, it returned to fight in Louisiana until early 1865. Recruits that had joined the 60th after its original muster were transferred to the 26th Indiana.[18]

Life after the Civil War

After being mustered out, Zuidema returned to Lafayette, Tippecanoe County, Indiana, where he filed naturalization papers in May 1865. Lafayette was home to a small community of Groningers beginning in the mid-1830s, when Klaas Janszoon Beukma from the area of Zuurdijk decided to settle there.[19] At the time of the 1860

---

[16] Geoffrey L. Blankenmeyer, "The Pioneer Brigade," http://www.thecivilwargroup.com/pioneer.html (accessed 2 June 2013).
[17] Turner, *Indiana Civil War Manuscripts*, 194.
[18] Of the sixty-eight privates who served in Company G, 60th Indiana Infantry, 14 (21 percent) deserted, 10 (15 percent) died, 16 (24 percent) were discharged (two for disabilities), 24 (35 percent) mustered out 21 Mar. 1865, 1 (1 percent) was promoted, and 3 (4 percent) were transferred.
[19] Lucas, Henry S. *Netherlanders in America* (Ann Arbor, MI: University of Michigan Press, 1955), 34-38.

Federal Census, there were more than twenty-five thousand individuals enumerated in Tippecanoe County and, of these, 143 were born in the Netherlands. Shortly after the war, Zuidema moved to Michigan possibly to be near his older sister Grietje, her husband Hendrik Suikerbakker, and their two children when they emigrated in 1866. Shortly thereafter, the Suikerbakker family settled in Muskegon County. Despite multiple attempts, it has not been possible to locate Klaas Zuidema in the 1870 Federal Census.

In November 1872, at Vriesland in Ottawa County, Zuidema married Anna Bos, who was fifteen years his younger. She was the daughter of Simon and Geertje Bos, Dutch immigrants from the municipality of Zijpe, province of Noord Holland. According to the marriage record, Muskegon was listed as Zuidema's residence. Klaas and Anna had twelve children together. Clearly, his persistent hernia problems did not prevent him from carrying out certain activities! One child, Simon, drowned at the age of sixteen, while Anna died of dyspepsia in 1895 and was interred in Georgetown Cemetery in Ottawa County.

About 1899, Klaas and most of the children moved to Fulton, Illinois. His apparent reason for relocating there was to be near another sister, Trientje, who had come to Whiteside County in 1885 with her husband, Klaas Wiersema, and several children. With his advancing age and possible complications from his prior maladies, Zuidema likely needed assistance caring for his younger children. While cutting and splitting wood at his house in Fulton on 9 April 1901, Klaas suffered an acute heart attack and died.

Determining when and where Zuidema was born in the Netherlands proved to be no minor task. His initial settlement in Lafayette and subsequent residences in Muskegon and Fulton were strong indications he was a Groninger. His 1862 enlistment record and all later US records, however, state he was born in Amsterdam. To complicate things further, different dates of birth were recorded on other assorted documents. In the early stages of this research, there was also a problem locating relevant American records, until it was discovered that Zuidema's surname was often spelled Seidema or Seidma. There were no Zuidemas enumerated in the censuses of 1850 or 1860 for Tippecanoe County, though there was one Sidemaugh [sic] family of five there in 1870. The head of this family appears to be a Groninger named Dutmer Zuidema, who is not a close relative to Klaas Zuidema.

Fig. 3.3. Nicholas Zuidema with two of his children, ca. 1900 (*courtesy Mary Faber, Fulton, Illinois*)

The ship manifest for the bark *Helvetia* included a Hendrik Zuideman, who was later determined to be a brother to Klaas.[20] Hendrik later settled in West Michigan. The remaining eight Dutch passengers were also Groningers, including a Spolema [*sic*] and members of an Aardappel family who eventually settled in Whiteside County, Illinois. Birth information for Klaas Zuidema was discovered by first locating the marriage record in the Netherlands for his sister Trientje (the sister in Muskegon County was found more recently). This record revealed the names of her parents. With this information, it was possible to determine that Klaas was born 14 September 1839 in Den Andel, municipality of Baflo, province of Groningen, the son of day-laborer Pieter Rijpkes Zuidema and his wife Hendrikje Pieters Bult.[21] Like Klaas, his father Pieter had twelve children, but with two different wives (Hendrikje died in 1842). Ten children were born in Den Andel, while the two oldest were born in Vliedorp, municipality of Ulrum.

As a newly-arrived immigrant and likely with limited knowledge of the issues prompting the Civil War, what motivated Zuidema to enlist? To attempt an explanation, the experiences of German immigrants were explored. Germans formed the single largest immigrant group

---

[20] Helvetia Manifest, 16 Aug. 1861.
[21] Klaas Pieters Zuidema, Aktenummer 51, Geboorteregister Baflo, 1839; *Registers van de Burgerlijke Stand, 1811-1940* (Family History Library Microfilm 108939); Rijksarchief, Groningen, Netherlands.

serving in the Civil War and more has been researched and written about them than other immigrant groups in this regard. In addition, Germans comprised a large percentage of the men serving in the 60th Indiana. Extending these observations to Zuidema, he very well may have identified with the Republican ideals for liberty and equality promoted by President Lincoln, but any political or patriotic leanings he may have had would have been secondary reasons for enlistment. For a relatively new immigrant, more practical needs would have had a greater impact upon his decision.[22]

The need to support himself financially in this new country was almost certainly his primary factor for enlisting. The promise of a steady income of thirteen dollars per month with food, clothing, and other amenities seemed to outweigh the risk to life and limb. For Zuidema these practical considerations were substantiated when he applied for an invalid pension in June 1880. As a Civil War veteran, he had been receiving the standard pension of four dollars per month. His pension application sought to increase that amount due to his claimed disability resulting from his war injury. The various documents in this part of his pension file (an application was also made after his death for support of his minor children) are confusing and sometimes contradictory. Zuidema could not accurately recall dates and even claimed that he suffered a double hernia in 1862. In any case, he was successful in obtaining an increase to eight dollars per month in 1884 and then to twelve dollars per month in 1890. All the while, he continued to farm. Notwithstanding the perceived effect of his injury during this time, the fact that he pursued a claim of invalid status from the government supports the proposition that practical needs were his chief reasons for enlistment.

During this ongoing remembrance of the 150th anniversary of the Civil War, places like Camp Morton, Munfordville, Young's Point, and Arkansas Post do not normally come to mind. These and many other locations, however, were places where the two sides, North and South, encountered one another in battle and as conquered foes. The records documenting Klaas Zuidema's experiences during the Civil War provide only glimpses into his term of service. Many questions remain. He was an ordinary soldier, but his story, among thousands of others, constitutes the fabric of this defining era in American history.

---

[22] Walter D. Kamphoefner and Wolfgang Helbich, eds., *Germans in the Civil War: The Letters They Wrote Home*, trans. Susan Carter Vogel (Chapel Hill, NC: The University of North Carolina Press, 2006), 25-28.

CHAPTER 4

William Vandever: Presbyterian, Congressman, General

Douglas Firth Anderson

Few people today have ever heard of William Vandever (1817-1893). On the one hand, that is odd, since, among other things, he was a two-term Congressman from Iowa, a Civil War general, a US Indian Inspector, and, after he moved to California, again a two-term Congressman. Moreover, because he sponsored the House bill in 1890 that resulted in the creation of what are now Yosemite and Sequoia National Parks, there is an 11,947 foot mountain named for him in the Sierra Nevada.

On the other hand, Vandever wrote no memoir. Neither was he a spell-binding speaker. Indeed, despite the important positions he held, he had few noteworthy accomplishments to point to. Even his national park bill seemed to be at the behest of others, notably the Southern Pacific Railroad, rather than of his own initiative. He was not a leader who inspired followers, either in Congress or in the Union army. For all his federal positions, he was more ordinary than extraordinary. His comparative typicality as a white middle-class male of nineteenth-century America helps highlight Karl Marx's dictum that "circumstances make men just as much as men make circumstances."[1]

Why, then, should we consider him? For one thing, Vandever claimed Dutch ancestry. Near the end of his life, he explained in a letter that he was "of Holland, not of Sweedish [sic] descent." This distinction was important to him because Captain Myron Van Der Weer—"the common patriarch of all the Vandevers in America"—moved to Delaware, originally a Swedish colony, soon after arriving in New Netherland in 1635. On his mother's side, Vandever was, he declared, "a Jersey Ten Eyck of pure unmitigated Dutch descent."[2]

For another thing, as a loyal Republican House member from Iowa, Vandever played a role in the coming of the Civil War, and he dutifully helped fight for the Union and to end slavery. In the 1870s, as a US Indian Inspector, he came to oppose the military when the federal government forcefully subjugated various American Indian peoples during the so-called Grant's Peace Policy years.

Finally, Vandever sustained a Christian faith that at a minimum seemed to provide him with a moral grounding amid the contingencies of life. Indeed, it is Vandever's faith-based moral compass that links his military ties with his "Holland descent." Vandever was too far removed from his seventeenth-century Dutch ancestors to think of himself as ethnically Dutch. He did, however, seem to think of himself as religiously Dutch. When he recounted his "Holland descent," besides surnames, he also noted that the Vandevers had been "staunch reformers."[3] The adult Vandever was a staunch Presbyterian who developed a certain unease with the military.

Federal officeholder and the warfare of the 1860s and 1870s

Father William Vandever (1790-1869) was born in Delaware, while son William was born in 1817 in nearby Baltimore, Maryland. The family soon moved to Philadelphia, where young Vandever received sufficient schooling, so that when he moved to Rock Island, Illinois, in 1839, he could take up surveying and edit a newspaper. Married in 1847,

---

[1] Quoted by David Nasaw in "AHR Roundtable: Historians and Biography. Introduction," *American Historical Review* 114 (June 2009): 578.
[2] Photocopy of William Vandever to B. A. Stephens, 28 Dec. 1886, folder of documents by Vandever from other collections, unnumbered box, William Vandever Papers, Special Collections, Charles C. Myers Library, University of Dubuque (hereafter, Vandever Papers).
[3] "Having been staunch reformers, some of the early kin may have been treated to a hot steak or a cold chop under *Alva* when he ruled the Netherlands" (ibid.).

Fig. 4.1. Hon. William Vandever, between 1855 and 1865 (*Library of Congress Prints and Photographs Division*)

he moved to Dubuque, Iowa four years later, where he clerked with the US Surveyor General's Office. In 1853 he began to practice law.[4]

Politically, Vandever began as a Whig. When, however, the Republican Party was organized in Iowa, he readily joined it. As a Republican he won election to the US House in 1858. This was surprising, since his hometown Dubuque had been Democratic politically, and it had no significant Dutch American enclave. Instead, it was the center of the Roman Catholic Diocese of Dubuque, sustained through the nineteenth century with large numbers of Irish and German immigrants.[5] Vandever's election, though, was part of a statewide turn to the new Republicans. He was re-elected in 1860.

Vandever was not an abolitionist, but he was outspoken against slavery. In Congress, he attacked the extension of slavery through Stephen A. Douglas' "popular sovereignty" doctrine. What was at issue, he argued in 1860, was "the extension of slavery upon the one hand and its restriction on the other."[6] Yet he was not one who sought war. Instead, he participated in a last-ditch peace convention in Washington, DC, in early 1861.[7]

---

[4] Ibid.; *Dubuque Daily Times*, 25 July 1893; *Washington National Tribune*, 15 Dec. 1887; *Weekly Dubuque Tribune*, 1 June 1853.

[5] Timothy R. Mahoney, "The Rise and Fall of the Booster Ethos in Dubuque, 1850-1861," *Annals of Iowa* 61 (Fall 2002): 371-419; Jacob Van der Zee, *The Hollanders of Iowa* (Iowa City, IA: State Historical Society, 1912), 103; William E. Wilkie, *Dubuque on the Mississippi 1788-1988* (Dubuque, IA: Loras College Press, 1987); Robert Cook, "The Political Culture of Antebellum Iowa," in *Iowa History Reader*, ed. Marvin Bergman (Ames, IA: Iowa State University Press and State Historical Society of Iowa, 1996), 86-104.

[6] *Congressional Globe*, 36th Cong., 1st sess., App. (27 Apr. 1860), 270. Accessed through http://lcweb2.loc.gov/ammem/amlaw/lwcg.html.

[7] "Vandever, William (1817-1893)," *Biographical Directory of the United States Congress, 1774-Present*, http://bioguide.congress.gov/scripts/biodisplay.pl?index=V000031.

The war came, nonetheless, in April 1861. Vandever was in his mid-forties, and he had no military training. It happened that he was in Davenport when President Lincoln's initial call for troops came in by telegraph. Since the telegraph did not extend farther into Iowa at the time, the congressman personally took the telegram to Governor Samuel J. Kirkwood's home in Coralville.[8] Vandever did not, however, join the first rush of volunteers. Only after participating in the special session of Congress in July did he enlist as the colonel of the Ninth Iowa Infantry, US Volunteers.[9]

Vandever saw combat more than once as commander of a brigade at the Battle of Pea Ridge, Arkansas (7-8 March 1862). Reportedly, he had at least one horse shot from under him then, and again three years later, at the Battle of Bentonville, North Carolina (19 March 1865). Another time when his command was surrounded, the troops fought first on one front, then the other, capturing a Confederate battle flag on each front. For his role at Pea Ridge, he was promoted to brigadier general, and for "gallantry" at Bentonville, he was breveted to major general. He also commanded a division in the spring of 1863 that successfully blocked a Confederate raid into southeast Missouri.[10]

Other Iowa officers, however, were promoted more quickly and were given more responsibility. For example, his regiment's lieutenant colonel, Francis J. Herron, was wounded and captured at Pea Ridge; he was awarded the Medal of Honor and later was Vandever's superior

---

[8] H. W. Lathrop, *The Life and Times of Samuel J. Kirkwood, Iowa's War Governor* (Iowa City, IA: published by the author, 1893), 115. "Vandever took the train to Iowa City, to get to Kirkwood's farm in Coralville: 'Upon his arrival he found the Governor in boots and overalls caring for his flock on the Coralville farm.'" Dan Elbert Clark, *Samuel Jordan Kirkwood* (Iowa City, IA: State Historical Society of Iowa, 1917), 180.

[9] A bare summary of Vandever's military service is in his Civil War Pension Record, 1893, photocopy of National Archives and Record Administration (NARA) record, in William Vandever biographical file, Ventura County Historical Collection, Ventura County Museum of History and Art, Ventura, CA.

[10] Vandever's report on the Battle of Pea Ridge is in Adjutant General of Iowa, *Official Records, 1861-1866* (Des Moines: Adjutant General of Iowa, 1866), Official Army Records 1862 – pt. 1: 90-92, on O. J. Fargo, ed., *Civil War and Iowa: Greyhounds and Hawkeyes* (Creston, IA: Green Valley Area Education Agency and State Historical Society of Iowa, 2000), CD-ROM; William L. Shea and Earl J. Hess, *Pea Ridge: Civil War Campaign in the West* (Chapel Hill: University of North Carolina Press, 1992), 176. On Bentonville, see Record and Pension Office, US War Department, *The War of the Rebellion: A Compilation of the Official Records of the Union and Confederate Armies* (Washington, DC: Government Printing Office, 1883-99), series 1, vol. 47, pt. 1: 72, 486; for recognition of his gallantry, see ibid., pt. 3: 613, accessible at http://ebooks.library.cornell.edu/m/moawar/waro.html. On the Cape Girardeau campaign, see Adjutant General of Iowa, *Official Records*, Official Army Records 1863 – pt. 1: 57-60; Stephen B. Oates, "Marmaduke's Cape Girardeau Expedition, 1863," *Missouri Historical Review* 57 (1962): 237-47.

officer. Another example was Grenville M. Dodge of Council Bluffs. Dodge's brigade was next to Vandever's at Pea Ridge. Dodge was also wounded there, and he soon was building, or rebuilding, railroads; eventually, he commanded a corps under General William Tecumseh Sherman. Samuel R. Curtis, like Vandever a Republican congressman from Iowa, became the overall commander of the Union forces at Pea Ridge.[11]

Several things probably account for Vandever's relative obscurity as a Union general. He did not identify himself with Dutch Americans or any other particular group, ethnic or otherwise, so he had no supporting community. Clearly he was a "political general," who as a professional politician was named a military officer, despite having no military training. Samuel Curtis resigned from Congress to take a military appointment; Vandever did not. Indeed, Vandever's refusal to resign brought on a case against him in the House, since the US Constitution prohibits members of Congress from holding another federal office at the same time.[12]

Vandever's refusal to give up his seat in Congress did not endear him to Iowa's Republicans or the soldiers under his command.[13] In 1862, while leading a brigade outside Helena, Arkansas, Vandever apparently upset some with a local truce that appeared to be too generous to the Confederates. Alonzo Abernethy of the Ninth Iowa recorded in his diary: "Went to Helena & returned to find the camp in an uproar of excitement because some Rebel Officers had been making considerable purchases" at the army's contracted grocer. A few days afterward, brigade officers and Vandever had an "inharmonious" meeting "owing to differences of opinion." Abernethy noted that the officers nonetheless signed a paper "asserting their unabating [sic] confidence [in] Col. Vandever's integrity, patriotism, & bravery."[14]

---

[11] On Herron, Dodge, and Curtis at Pea Ridge, see Shea and Hess, *Pea Ridge*, passim; Terry Beckenbaugh, "Curtis, Samuel Ryan," and Don L. Hofsommer, "Dodge, Grenville Mellen," in *Biographical Dictionary of Iowa*, eds. David Hudson, Marvin Bergman, and Loren Horton (Iowa City: University of Iowa Press, 2008), 114-16, 132-34.

[12] For the House case regarding Vandever, see *Congressional Globe*, 37th Cong., 2nd sess. (8 May 1862), 2021-23, and 3rd sess. (20-21 Jan., 14 Feb. 1863), 403-7, 427-34, 742-43, 963-71.

[13] The House Republicans let the case against Vandever drag on until his term ended. Meanwhile, Republicans in Vandever's district nominated William B. Allison instead of Vandever for the 1862 election. Allison's victory launched his political career in Congress, but it left Vandever bitter. Douglas Firth Anderson, "Allison, William Boyd," in *Biographical Dictionary of Iowa*, 13-16.

[14] For the tensions over the truce, see Alonzo Abernethy, Diary, 13-17 Nov. 1862, transcription, State Historical Society of Iowa Library and Archives, Des Moines;

Fig. 4.2. Gen. William Vandever flanked by Col. William H. Coyl (*left*) and Col. Francis J. Herron (Johnson Brigham, *Iowa: Its History and Its Foremost Citizens*, 1918)

More than one soldier in the Thirty-Eighth Iowa Infantry did not remember Vandever very fondly. As their brigade commander during the summer of 1863, he pushed them in the sultry heat of the lower Mississippi Valley region in ways that gave no hint of sympathy with them. In 1864, Surgeon J. Moore, concerned with "getting proper food for the sick" during Gen. Sherman's Atlanta campaign, blamed Vandever, whom he pointedly characterized as "a hackneyed and effete politician." Gen. Oliver O. Howard early in 1865 sent Vandever from his command to Sherman's, along with a note that Vandever and another officer would do better to "retire" and make room for "our young officers." Finally, J. Thompson of the First Iowa Cavalry, who served for a time under Vandever, wrote an extensive and unflattering assessment of him:

> General Vandever ... lacks both the will and the energy, but more, the ability of a successful leader. The history of his military life is

---

for multiple mentions of Vandever based on varied sources for the Thirty-Eighth Iowa, see David Wildman, *Iowa's Martyr Regiment: The Story of the Thirty-Eighth Iowa Infantry* (Iowa City: Camp Pope, 2010), 99, 133, 136, 165.

a history of the man—tame and unromantic, exhibiting nothing striking or remarkable—never sinking below, nor yet rising above his chosen level.[15]

No letters or diary of Vandever's from the Civil War are extant, so we can only guess at his perspective on his war experiences. He was present at the capture of Arkansas Post and during the siege of Vicksburg.[16] He also participated briefly in Gen. Nathaniel P. Banks' Brownsville, Texas, campaign.[17] Much of Vandever's military service was on other than the front lines. Now and then he was in Washington attending Congress; for the first half of 1864, he was in Iowa recruiting and organizing new and veteran regiments.[18] For most of the rest of 1864, he was commander of the District of Marietta, Georgia, while Sherman closed in on Atlanta. Twice he was assigned to a court martial. The first was in the fall of 1863, when in New Orleans he presided over the trial of Col. Joseph S. Morgan, Ninetieth New York Infantry, for drunkenness and misconduct before the enemy. The officer's conviction was suspended by Gen. Banks.[19] The second time was from December 1864 to January 1865 in Louisville. Brig. Gen. Thomas W. Sweeny was tried on multiple charges, including striking his superior officer, none other than Iowan Grenville M. Dodge. Vandever ended up presiding over the court, which acquitted Sweeny.[20]

Vandever was mustered out of service in August 1865, a few days short of four years from his enlistment.[21] He tried to resume his law practice in Dubuque, but that did not provide steady income—perhaps due, in part, to fallout from his reluctance to leave Congress. Steady income did not come until his next federal post, that of US Indian Inspector in 1873.[22]

---

[15] For Surgeon J. Moore's comments on Vandever, see Adjutant General of Iowa, *Official Records*, Official Army Records 1864, pt. 2: 129; for Gen. Howard's comments, see *War of the Rebellion*, series I, vol. 47, pt. 2: 70; for the comments on Vandever by J. Thompson of the First Iowa Cavalry, see the section on Vandever, 3-4, in A. A. Stuart, *Iowa Colonels and Their Regiments* (Chicago, 1865), in Fargo, *Civil War and Iowa*, CD-ROM.

[16] Ezra J. Warner, *Generals in Blue: Lives of the Union Commanders* (Baton Rouge, LA, 1992), 523.

[17] *War of the Rebellion*, series 1, vol. 26, pt. 1: 412, 789, 897 and Pt. 2: 414.

[18] Adjutant General of Iowa, *Official Records*, Official Army Records 1864, Pt. 1: 51-52.

[19] *War of the Rebellion*, series 1, vol. 39, pt. 2: 526, pt. 3: 45-381; vol. 26, pt. 1: 205-6.

[20] Records of the Judge Advocate General, US Army, Court Martial of Thomas W. Sweeney, Case LL2995, NARA. Sweeny's surname is spelled with the additional "e" throughout the trial documents.

[21] Civil War Pension record, 1893.

[22] The following discussion of Vandever as Indian Inspector is based on Douglas Firth Anderson, "'More Conscience than Force': US Indian Inspector William

Inspectorships were newly created, mid-level posts in the Office of Indian Affairs. Under the Commissioner of Indian Affairs, inspectors had the power to investigate operations and to suspend and temporarily appoint personnel at assigned Indian agencies. Between 1873 and 1878, Vandever visited various Indian agencies. Although these years are known in the history of United States-Indian relations as the ear of Grant's Peace Policy, this was a time when the military enforced peace. It was also a time when the War Department and its supporters were making a strong bid to take Indian affairs from the Interior Department back to the War Department, where they had been originally. This was known as "the transfer issue."

Where did Inspector Vandever—of "Holland descent"—find himself regarding the military and warfare with American Indians? In his fourth year as inspector in 1876, he had gained confidence in offering his critique of federal Indian policies. At the time, the army was moving to force all Lakotas back to their assigned agencies, despite provisions otherwise in the 1868 Treaty of Fort Laramie. Particularly outraging Lakotas was the army's failure to keep gold-seeking Americans out of the Black Hills, an area designated as part of the Great Sioux Reservation by the Laramie treaty. In his report after visiting the Red Cloud and Spotted Tail Agencies, Vandever bluntly told the Commissioner of Indian Affairs: "We are now experiencing the bitter fruits of war with a barbarous race, who are only seeking to defend from invasion the country we had guaranteed to them by solemn treaty." He emphasized that "the military should be restrained from further aggressive movements at this time."[23]

As the spring turned into summer, events in the northern Plains escalated. On 17 June, Lakota warriors and their allies turned back an army column under Gen. George Crook at the Battle of the Rosebud. On 25 June, Lakotas and other warriors killed Lt. Col. George Armstrong Custer and over two hundred men of the Seventh US Cavalry at the Battle of the Little Bighorn. On 30 June, Vandever reported to the Commissioner about his meeting with Lakota leaders at the Red Cloud Agency, Nebraska. He reiterated his view that the regional turmoil was the fault of the federal government: "The present troubles have been occasioned by a palpable violation on the part of white men of the provisions of the treaty of 1868, and a failure of the government

---

Vandever, Grant's Peace Policy, and Protestant Whiteness," *Journal of the Gilded Age and Progressive Era* 9 (Apr. 2010): 167-96.

[23] William Vandever, *Report on Affairs at Red Cloud and Spotted Tail Agencies* (Washington, DC: Department of Interior, Office of Indian Affairs, 1876), 7.

Fig. 4.3. Lakota Chief "Sitting Bull" (1831-1890) in 1885

to protect from encroachment the territory guaranteed to the sole use of the Indians by solemn treaty stipulation." Apparently without knowledge yet of the battles of 17 and 25 June, he also reiterated that the militarization of federal policy only "stirred [the Lakota] up to active hostilities."[24] Vandever was clearly a reformer in American Indian policy.

Armed conflict in the West continued in 1877, but Vandever's agencies were in the Southwest, where the military presence was strong but hostilities simmered rather than boiled. He spent some three months involved with affairs at the San Carlos Agency, Arizona Territory. Various Apache groups had been concentrated there since 1874, when Agent John P. Clum arrived.[25] Appointed by the Reformed Church in America, Agent Clum had, like Vandever, Dutch roots and Presbyterian affiliations. When Vandever arrived at San Carlos in May, Clum had resigned. The Inspector stepped into the vacancy, Clum staying in touch from nearby Tucson.

[24] William Vandever, *Report Relating to Disposition of Indians at Red Cloud and Spotted Tail Agencies* (Washington, DC: Department of Interior, Office of Indian Affairs, 1876), 10-11.

[25] On Clum, see Douglas Firth Anderson, "Protestantism, Progress, and Prosperity: John P. Clum and 'Civilizing' the US Southwest, 1871-1886," *Western Historical Quarterly* 33 (Autumn 2002): 315-35.

Clum and Vandever strenuously objected to military interference in the inspection of agency supplies. This was part of the larger political battle over transferring the Office of Indian Affairs from the Interior Department to the War Department. "The greatest obstacle to the success of the Indian Service in Arizona," Vandever wrote the Commissioner, "is the constant interference of the military." That he had not forgotten his remarks of 1876 was made clear a few days later, when he warned: "If army councils are permitted to direct the administration of Indian affairs in this territory, the Sioux war will be supplemented here within six months." By June, he was telling the Commissioner that "the army debauches and demoralize [sic] the Indian." To former Commissioner George Manypenny, Vandever commented, "Outbreaks are generally commenced by our army and not by the Indians."[26]

In August, Vandever expressed outrage over the apparent failure of the army to include the Commissioner as a recipient of the army's reports on supplies. "A more discourteous and unfriendly act," Vandever wrote, "on the part of an officer of one department toward those connected with another department, can scarcely be conceived."[27] Unfortunately for Vandever, his letter was published as part of a pamphlet by former Agent Clum, who was continuing his feud with Gen. August V. Kautz. The pamphlet escalated political tensions in Washington, DC over the transfer issue, so much so as to bring a reprimand to Vandever from Secretary of the Interior Carl Schurz.[28] In early 1878, Secretary Schurz refused to reappoint Vandever to the post of Inspector.

Vandever's termination came in part because in 1878 the Hayes administration was replacing the Grant administration. His termination also was a way for the Interior Department to mollify the War Department. Yet Vandever's pointed comments about the army and about federal violations of treaty obligations had a moral bite. His disdain for regular military officers as a group—"shoulder strap gentlemen" he termed them in one of his letters—arguably has a heft that may have roots in his Civil War experience.[29] In short, an important reason Vandever lost his federal civilian post was for objecting too much to the militarization of federal Indian policy.

[26] Vandever to Commissioner of Indian Affairs, 20 May, 25 May, 1 June 1877; Vandever to George W. Manypenny, 24 June 1877, folders May, June 1877, box 7, Vandever Papers.
[27] Vandever to Commissioner of Indian Affairs, 6 Aug. 1877, folder Aug. 1877, box 7, Vandever Papers.
[28] Carl Schurz to Commissioner of Indian Affairs, 6 Sept. 1877, folder Sept. 1877, box 7, Vandever Papers.
[29] Vandever to Commissioner of Indian Affairs, 1 June 1877, folder June 1877, box 7, Vandever Papers.

Religiously Dutch

Vandever invoked not only the ethnicity but also the religiosity of his Dutch ancestors in his 1886 letter. They were, in his words, "staunch reformers." Two clusters of evidence taken together suggest that he self-consciously continued in the Reformed tradition he ascribed to his forebears.

As an adult, Vandever persistently affiliated with Presbyterians. A Presbyterian minister presided at his wedding in 1847.[30] In Dubuque in the 1850s, he was a member and an officer of the First Presbyterian Church, an Old School congregation. In general, Old School congregations were opposed to revivalism, inter-denominational crusades, faith-based political activism, and theological innovations.[31] In 1857 Vandever was also a trustee of Alexander College, an Old School Presbyterian preparatory school and college that folded during the economic contractions of the banking Panic of 1857.[32] After 1855, however, Second Presbyterian Church was organized in Dubuque. Second was a New School congregation, which body tended to support revivalism, inter-denominational crusades, and political activism. Many members left First Presbyterian to join Second Presbyterian, presumably also the Vandever family. In 1903, over a decade after the Vandever family had moved to California, the two congregations merged. While there is no direct evidence of Vandever's membership after the 1850s, his wife, Jane Vandever, was a deaconness of Second Presbyterian, and his daughter, Florence, attended Second Presbyterian's Sunday school.[33]

Moreover, from 1882 through 1885, Vandever was a member of the board of directors of the German Theological School of the Presbyterian Church of the Northwest.[34] The school had been founded in 1852 by Holland-born Adrian Van Vliet as a theological training school for German-speaking pastors. In 1870, when the Old and New School Presbyterians reunited nationally, the Dubuque seminary came under the control of the General Assembly of the denomination. By

---

[30] Civil War Pension Record, 1893.
[31] [Committee on History] *A History of One Hundred Years, 1850-1950: Westminster Presbyterian Church, Dubuque, Iowa* (Dubuque, IA, 1950?), 11, 14, Special Collections, Charles C. Myers Library, University of Dubuque (hereafter UD).
[32] Steven Baule, Alexander College, appendix A, p. 2, 10 Dec. 1986 typescript paper for Dubuque Area History, Dr. Auge, UD.
[33] *Westminster Presbyterian*, 35; Florence Vandever letter in Letters and Correspondence for B. M. Harger, Sunday School Superintendent, Westminster Sunday School, 1864-1914, Dubuque, Iowa, Scrapbook, UD.
[34] Board of Directors, German Theological Seminary of the Northwest, Minutes, 1880-1890 ledger: 47, 77, UD.

the 1880s, it was more actively broadening its identity beyond that of the German Presbyterians.[35] In 1884 Vandever moved to Ventura, California. While his church membership there is unclear, it is clear that his funeral service in 1893 was Presbyterian.[36]

At various times Vandever tied his thinking, perspective, and actions to his religious convictions. Before the Civil War, he delivered a major, though unremarkable, speech to the House of Representatives opposing the expansion of slavery into territories. The speech is laced with religious analogies. Lambasting Democratic claims that the Missouri Compromise needed repealing, Vandever made a biblical analogy:

> In the annals of the world there is, perhaps, but one parallel for the facility with which the Democratic party of to-day clothes its monstrous heresies in the garb of truth; and that is when Satan, with dissembling speech, incited mother Eve to treason against high Heaven, saying that she should not surely die as a penalty for her transgression.

He also scorned those who viewed slavery as "an institution sanctioned by God, a missionary institution, which is calculated to rescue from barbarism the millions of Africa, and to bring them under the christianizing influences of the peculiarly disinterested philanthropy of our southern brethren."[37]

Biblical and missionary allusions were not uncommon at the time, of course. More explicit evidence of perspectives and actions informed by personal religious sensibilities, however, comes during and after Vandever's US Indian Inspectorship. In 1875 he sided with the Methodist Agent at the Round Valley Reservation in California in opposing a petition by the Catholic Church for permission to erect a church and a priest's home on the reservation. "Dissensions and strife would necessarily result," he wrote, and to allow the Catholics in would undercut the Methodists' laudable work in "training and instructing the Indians in moral and religious duties." Besides, he said, the priest was an "enthusiast" and a "lunatic."[38]

---

[35] Alvin J. Straatmeyer, *Child of the Church: University of Dubuque 1852-2008*, ed. Joel L. Samuels (Cedar Rapids, IA: WDG Publishing, 2008), 1-20.

[36] John E. Baur, "William Vandever: Ventura's First Congressman," *Ventura County Historical Society Quarterly* 20 (Fall 1974): 23.

[37] *Congressional Globe*, 269-70.

[38] Vandever to Commissioner of Indian Affairs, 4 June 1875, in US Office of Indian Affairs, *Reports of the Field Jurisdictions, 1873-1900*, roll 3, microform M1070, California Superintendency, National Archives and Records Administration, Rocky Mountain Region, Denver.

Vandever was a man of his times. As a Protestant, he was not prepared to view Catholicism with much favor. Neither was he prepared to consider sympathetically Indian desires for cultural autonomy. Yet in 1876, when the Peace Policy was unraveling in the northern Plains, Vandever explicitly pointed out to the Commissioner of Indian Affairs that the troubles were caused by federal failure to abide by the Laramie Treaty. Amid his comments on the situation among the Lakota in June 1876, he recommended that supplies be sent to the agencies immediately, for morality's sake as well as for prudential reasons: "Unquestionably, it would be far cheaper to feed them than to fight them. To confine them to the reservation to starve, or to kill them if they attempt to leave, would be inhuman."[39]

The following January, in a letter to Presbyterian J. Elliot Condict, Vandever was even more explicit.[40] Despite the constraints of what I elsewhere term Vandever's "Protestant whiteness," his Reformed Protestantism was on display in his explaining to Condict his views on federal Indian policy.[41] "If our government is based on Christian principles," he wrote, "it should display more conscience than force in dealing with the Indians." Military intervention only exacerbated a deteriorating situation. "The events of the past season," Vandever observed, "ought to satisfy every impartial mind, that the Indian problem cannot be solved through the intervention of the Army." Instead, law and Christian civilization were what were needed:

> Law and civilization go together; Indians on or off their reservations, must be brought under the restraints of law. They need civil law, not military or martial law, to civilize them. . . . Unfortunately for the Indian and for the whites, the Government has never offered the Indian anything in lieu of his barbarous customs; any improvement that has been wrought among the Indians in this particular is owing to the labors of Christian missionaries and not to the influence of the government.

The "North American Indian," although "wild" and "savage" from Vandever's perspective, deserved humane treatment for religious reasons: "He is a man, he has a soul; Christ died for him."[42]

---

[39] Vandever, *Disposition of Indians at Red Cloud and Spotted Tail Agencies*, 9.
[40] For Condict, see J. Elliot Condict, "Our Indians and the Duty of the Presbyterian Church to Them," *Presbyterian Quarterly and Princeton Review* 5 (Jan. 1876): 76-93.
[41] Anderson, "'More Conscience than Force.'"
[42] Vandever to J. Elliot Condict, 4 Jan. 1877, folder 2, box 7, Vandever Papers.

William Vandever, I believe, is best understood as religiously Reformed or Calvinist. For him, his Dutch identity was scarcely ethnic but instead largely religious. He seems to have viewed himself as a participant in a heritage of "staunch reformers." For him, being a "reformer" seems to at least have meant being Presbyterian, living with integrity as an individual, acting with integrity as the citizen of a nation purporting to be civilized and Christian, and regarding others as those for whom Christ died. This was the English variant of Calvinism. Further, his faith informed his life, notably his opposition to the expansion of slavery and his critique of the militarization of federal Indian policy. Both of these developments left him in tension with public policies.

Vandever left historians with few insights as to his inner life. Nevertheless, a declaration he made in connection with his support of a prohibition law in Iowa can serve as concluding evidence of the broadly Reformed character of his outlook:

> The law promulgated from Sinai lost none of its force by the rejection of it. . . . The commands of that law, rewritten by the finger of God, though but imperfectly obeyed by the children of men, remain in force to this day without abatement of one jot or tittle, as the foundation of all civil authority and social order, as well as of religious obligation.[43]

Perhaps for a moment he even thought about adding that this meant even "shoulder strap gentlemen" were answerable to God.

---

[43] William Vandever, "Good Words from Gen. Wm. Vandever, one of Iowa's Best Men," broadside, 1882, Vandever Paper

CHAPTER 5

A Dutch Colony in Tennesse as a Casualty of the Civil War

Janet Sjaarda Sheeres

The American Civil War is well documented. Numerous books and articles recount the atrocities, the battles, and the loss of life. Even now, a century-and-a-half later, many of these battles are re-enacted regularly. According to the *New York Times*, "Far more books have been written about the Civil War than about any other event in American history."[1] Nevertheless, some of the lesser confrontations did not make the headlines, and over time these stories have faded from our collective memory. Such is the story of a small, ill-fated Dutch colony that was being established in Roane County, Tennessee, in 1858, three years before the Civil War began.

The few Dutch families that had settled in the southern states by 1860 were not part of any larger Dutch settlement.[2] The Dutch,

---

[1] http://www.nytimes.com/ref/opinion/civilwar-booklist.html, 13 Sept. 2013.
[2] According to the 1860 United States Federal Census, there were approximately 450 Dutch scattered over the 10 southern states of Alabama, Arkansas, Florida, Georgia, Louisiana, Mississippi, South Carolina, North Carolina, Tennessee, and Texas.

Fig. 5.1. Early portrait of Anna Maria Margaretha (Mienette) Storm-van der Chijs (*courtesy Adria, Kennisinstituut voor emancipatie en vrouwengeschiedenis, Amsterdam*)

averse to slavery, avoided the South.[3] While many of the Dutch that had arrived in the 1600s owned slaves, later nineteenth-century immigrants opposed slavery. Men like Albertus C. Van Raalte in Holland, Michigan, Hendrik Scholte in Pella, Iowa, and Pieter Zonne in Sheboygan County, Wisconsin, all had chosen northern states for their settlements. So who would choose Tennessee as a possible site for a Dutch colony? This chapter recounts the vision of a wealthy Dutch widow, Anna Maria Margaretha Storm-van der Chijs,[4] to create a colony in Tennessee to benefit young Dutch orphans and how the Civil War interfered with those efforts.

Family history

Anna Maria Margaretha, or Mienette, as she was called, was born in a stately house at no. 1 Breestraat in Delft, the Netherlands, on 26 August 1814, the youngest child and only daughter of Jacobus van der

[3] Jacob van Hinte, *Netherlanders in America: A Study of Emigration and Settlement in the Nineteenth and Twentieth Centuries in the United States of America*, ed. Robert P. Swierenga, trans. Adriaan de Wit (Grand Rapids, MI: Baker Book House, 1985), 426. For instance, Texas had been rejected partly because of its support of slavery, which many of the Dutch viewed as unchristian.

[4] Unlike American women who write their married name behind their maiden name, e.g., Hillary Rodham Clinton, Dutch women write their maiden name behind their married name and add a hyphen, hence Storm-van der Chijs – Storm being her married name and van der Chijs her maiden name. And because her last name is rather lengthy, I will use Mienette instead.

Chijs (1776-1833) and Anna Susanna Bagelaar (1778-1846).[5] Her wealthy merchant father imported tea from China and Japan and exported butter and cheese. The family belonged to the city's upper class, and many important people from the business and political sector visited the home, aptly called *De Wereld* (the world). Mienette, who, according to her brother Jacobus was rather spoiled, had connections with the Dutch Royal House, and counted Queen Sophia (1818-1877) among her friends. Her maternal grandfather, who was adjutant to King Willem II, brought her in contact with Queen Sophia, the first wife of King Willem III, resulting in a lifelong friendship between the two.[6]

Her formal education, which included private lessons in language, music, and the arts, was augmented by traveling with her father to many European capitals, and later, as a young woman, traveling on her own. In 1833 she traveled to South Africa, where her brother Jan Theodore lived. Here she received the news that her father had died. She immediately returned home to Delft to live with her mother. On 29 January 1845, she married *Dominee* Willem Storm (1808-1845) a Dutch Reformed church pastor.[7] Willem died two months after the wedding; the marriage did not produce any children. She had lived with Willem in Utrecht for the two months of their marriage but then returned home again to live with her mother who died a year later.

Back in Delft, Mienette busied herself with social work, and as a member of Dorcas, a ladies aid society, she assisted single women, needy widows, and large families by helping them with food, clothing, and heating fuel as well as finding work for the women so that they could support themselves. From the Dorcas minutes it appears that Mienette was often absent due to her travels abroad. But when home, she was very active in the society.[8]

In 1846 she founded the Leer en Werkschool voor behoeftige Meisjes (Educational and Vocational School for Impoverished Girls), a

---

[5] She had three older brothers: Pieter Otto (1802-1867), Jan Theodorus (1806-1841), and Jacobus (1813-1888).

[6] H. M. Bonebakker-Westermann, et al., eds., *Delftse Vrouwen van Vroeger door Delftse vrouwen van nu* (Delft, Delftse Vrouwen Raad, 1975), 68. Unfortunately, according to the Dutch Royal House Archives, Queen Sophia had all her correspondence destroyed before her death.

[7] A. J. Van der Aa, *Biographisch Woordenboek der Nederlanden*, 12 vols. (Haarlem, J. J. Van Brederode, 1874), 17: 1026. Willem Storm was born in Rotterdam in 1808. He studied at Leiden and served congregations in Heijenoord, Leiderdorp, Delft, and Utrecht. He died on 29 Mar. 1845. He must have been Mienette's pastor when he served in Delft.

[8] Huiberta P. Hogeweg-de Haart, *Anne Maria Margaretha Storm-van der Chijs* (Amsterdam: Internationaal Archief voor de Vrouwenbeweging, 1955), 2.

school in which young women from well-to-do families who had fallen on hard times could be trained in various household duties and then placed in suitable jobs.[9] She fostered a special love for orphans and would often entertain them in her home.

Exceptional for this era was that after her father's death, Mienette managed her own finances, much to the chagrin of her brother, Jacobus, who felt that females had no business engaging in financial matters. In 1843 she successfully negotiated a contract with the city of Delft to build a row of ten rental homes on the Cellebroerssteeg. And once, when visiting Madrid, she told King Emanuel II (1820-1878) that the railroads in Spain were in poor shape, not knowing that he owned the railroads. When she was apprised of this fact, she proposed to the King that she invest money in his railroads and that he hire engineers from Delft to repair them. He agreed, and this became another profitable enterprise for her.

World traveler

After her mother's death in 1846, Mienette was free to come and go without any family obligations. She moved out of the large home on the Breestraat into smaller quarters on the Verwersdijk. Her wealth allowed her to indulge herself in her passion for world travel. Her passport reveals that she visited almost all the European countries.[10] These trips brought her in contact with the leading citizens of these countries. She even managed to gain an audience with Pope Pius I in 1848, which was a rare occurrence for a Protestant.

In 1847, when Van Raalte was looking to the United States to plant a colony, she traveled to South Africa again, where she founded a colony at the Cape for seventy Dutch orphans. She financed the trip, including room and board, for these young colonists, and provided each with a small stipend. At age twenty-one, each could decide to stay in South Africa or return home. The colony became a huge success, and Mienette visited it often.

Mienette was not the only one working to alleviate poverty and the plight of orphans. The philanthropist, Rev. Otto G. Heldring

[9] Ibid., 3. The school was meant to help girls from better social backgrounds whose families had fallen on hard times. Girls from lower class backgrounds, it was assumed, could easily find work in factories and as domestics, which was not the case with the girls from the upper classes. The school became a success and celebrated its 25th anniversary in 1871.

[10] Including Germany, Austria, Italia, Spain, Portugal, France, Poland, Russia, Turkey, Denmark, Sweden, and Norway.

(1804-1876), a leader of the *Réveil* and active in improving conditions for the poor and orphans, founded the Commissie ter overzending van jonge lieden als dienstboden naar de Kaap de Goede Hoop (Committee to send young people as servants to the Cape of Good Hope).[11] This committee may have followed Mienette's example of choosing South Africa as a place to send Dutch teenagers because it was in great need of laborers for the Dutch settlers. Between 1854 and 1860, 378 Dutch teenagers were shipped to South Africa to work.[12] Mienette's three main interests were education, agriculture, and the arts. With the first she hoped to help women support themselves, and with the second, she hoped to educate farmers on how to be more productive.

The Netherlands experienced an economic depression in the 1840s that forced many citizens to seek public assistance. The loss of the potato crop in 1845 and 1846 caused mass hunger and food riots, and eventually led thousands to immigrate to America, beginning in 1846. Most settled in the midwestern states of Michigan, Wisconsin, Illinois, and Iowa.

Interest in America

Her interest in the United States had been kindled by reading the *Declaration of Sentiments* published in 1848 by a group of Quaker women that included Lucretia Mott. The women declared that the rights and responsibilities of females were equal to those of males. After corresponding with the group, Mienette packed her bags again and, accompanied by her friend and travel companion, Maria van den Bosch, traveled to the United States in 1856, where Mott welcomed the pair in her home.[13]

---

[11] For more on this movement, see Ivo Sicking, *In het belang van het kind: Nederlandse kinderemigratie naar Zuid Afrika in de jaren 1856-1860* (Utrecht: Vakgroep Geschiedenis der Universiteit Utrecht, 1995).

[12] Two groups of orphans ended up in Graaf-Reinett, South Africa, where Rev. Andrew Murray Sr. was pastor of the Dutch Reformed Church. Murray's two sons, Andrew Jr. and John Murray, studied theology at the academy in Utrecht from 1845 to 1848 and there became fluent in Dutch. This was at about the time when Storm-van der Chijs' husband was a pastor in Utrecht, and she would have acquainted herself with these two young men and with the situation in South Africa, having been there and having a brother there. For more on the Murrays in the Netherlands, see J. Du Plessis, *The Life of Andrew Murray in South Africa* (London: Marshall Brothers, Ltd., 1919).

[13] Maria van den Bosch was Mienette's travel companion for nearly forty years, until her death in 1884. Because her name is such a common Dutch name, and because Mienette's biographers do not give any more details about Maria, I have not been able to find her birth date or place.

A fervent abolitionist, Mott strongly opposed slavery and spoke out publicly to the point of promoting public boycotts of foods and goods produced by slave labor.[14] Mienette's original intent of traveling through the United States had been to write a book about her experiences. After meeting with Mott and other abolitionists, Mienette may have conceived the idea of establishing a colony in America for Dutch orphans to prove to slave owners that it was possible to make a profit without using slave labor. Owning slaves had long been practiced in the southern states while the northern states had tacitly accepted it. President Millard Fillmore expressed a common view when he stated, "It is an existing evil, for which we are not responsible. We must endure it, and give it such protection as is guaranteed by the Constitution."[15] That is, until the Fugitive Slave Act of 1850 landed the reality of slavery ominously on the doorsteps of the northern states, and more and more abolitionists began to agitate against the system.[16]

America was supposed to be a shining example of democracy to the "old nations" of Europe where attempts at democratization were often unsuccessful.[17] How could America be this example if it enslaved a large part of its population? Mienette also viewed America as a beacon of democracy and hope.[18] Consequently, she wanted to be part of the catalyst for change in the slavery situation as evidenced by her statement in the *Leeuwarder Courant* "The example of free laborers will have a positive effect on the Negro population and by the anticipated

---

[14] Mott was a member of the American Anti-Slavery Society (AASS) founded in 1833. By 1838 the society had 1,350 local chapters with approx. 250,000 members. From 1840 to 1870, it published a weekly newspaper, the *National Anti-Slavery Standard*. The South began a similar boycott, exhorting people to "use, eat, drink, wear, or buy nothing under the sun from north of the Mason/Dixon line." Tony Horwitz, *Midnight Rising: John Brown and the raid that sparked the Civil War* (New York: Holt, 2011), 262.

[15] Horwitz, *Midnight Rising*, 36.

[16] The Fugitive Slave Act required Northerners to aid in the capture of runaway slaves. Harriet Beecher Stowe's answer to this law was to publish *Uncle Tom's Cabin* in 1852. The book was immediately translated into many languages, including Dutch, and distributed in the Netherlands the same year. Mienette would have been familiar with the book. Slavery was again very much in the foreground in 1856 due to the passage of the Kansas-Nebraska State Act of 1854, opening up those states for settlement. The Act allowed each state to decide for itself if it wanted to be a slave-owning state or not, resulting in violent clashes between pro-slavery and anti-slavery settlers.

[17] The idea of America as an example of democracy was first introduced by Alexis de Tocqueville, who described the United States as "exceptional" in 1831 and 1840.

[18] Mienette compared America's freedoms, values, hospitality, and opportunities to Europe's in a series of articles in *De Hollander*, Feb., Mar., and Apr. 1858.

expansion of the colony Christian charity will gain the upper hand over the misery of slavery."[19]

With this in mind, she traveled extensively throughout the southern states searching for a possible place to found her colony. She settled on Roane County in East Tennessee, an area that, although in a slave-owning state, was not populated by slave-owning plantations.

The state of Tennessee joined the Union in in 1796. As an offshoot of North Carolina, it embraced the right to own slaves. Nevertheless Tennessee, an upper southern state, was not as heavily invested in slave labor as the states of the Deep South. Most slaves in Tennessee were house slaves as opposed to plantation workers. East Tennessee especially was pro-union, and Mienette apparently felt the area safe for her experiment.

Armed with letters of introduction from King Willem III (1792-1849), Mienette obtained ready access to powerful and influential people in the United States.[20] From New England she traveled to Washington, DC, to attend Congress and visit with President James Buchanan (1791-1868) in the White House.[21] She then traveled to New York to visit Worp Van Peyma, a well-to-do Frisian farmer, who had immigrated in 1849 and founded a Frisian colony at Lancaster in Erie County, New York. Van Peyma's farm included an impressive manor home surrounded by beautiful gardens.[22] Being a social reformer like Van Peyma, Mienette made his farm her American headquarters for the first year, while she took excursions to Tennessee and other parts of the country.

In a letter of September 1858, Van Peyma wrote to his friends in Friesland, "Last winter we had the pleasure of entertaining a certain widow, Mrs. Storm of the Netherlands. This lady is not afraid to travel. She has crisscrossed almost all of America and earlier almost all the countries of Europe. Currently she is traveling in Canada. *As a very competent and pleasant woman to host, I don't have to tell you that she has many stories to tell. She is very taken with America.*[23] Mienette returned the

---

[19] *Leeuwarder Courant,* 14 Oct. 1857.
[20] Bonebakker-Westermann, et al., *Delftse Vrouwen,* 75. King Willem III did insist that Mienette, for decorum's sake as a friend of the Dutch Royal House, travel first class. She preferred to travel third class but acquiesced to the King's demands.
[21] *De Hollander,* 9 Sept. 1857; 14 Apr. 1858. She was accompanied to Congress by Horatio Seymour (1810-1886), governor of New York from 1853 to 1854 and again from 1863 to 1854.
[22] Van Hinte, *Netherlanders in America,* 163.
[23] Worp Van Peyma to friends in Friesland, September 1858; Van Peyma Collection, Tresoar, Leeuwarden.

compliment by asserting that Van Peyma's suggestions for her colony were of immense help.

In August 1857 she published her plans for a colony in Tennessee in a lengthy, three-and-a-half column article in the *Sheboygan* [Wisconsin], *Nieuwsbode*, the first Dutch-language newspaper for Dutch immigrants.[24] Stating her goals and choice of location cogently, she noted that the lack of factories in Knoxville and Kingston drove up transportation costs to import goods. She was especially interested in building steam sawmills, brick factories, beer breweries, and leather tanneries.

Visit with Van Raalte

In late September 1857, she visited the Dutch colony of Holland, Michigan, staying at the home of its founder, Rev. Albertus C. Van Raalte.[25] No doubt this visit gave her the opportunity to discuss the pros and cons connected with colonization and also to benefit from Van Raalte's decade-long expertise. During her stay in Michigan she experienced the vicissitudes of the Michigan winter and reported to the *Leeuwarder Courant*, "It is only the 30th of September and people have used their stoves for fourteen days already. Here one has to be prepared to live for eight months in the cold." This fact convinced her that once she had her colony up and running, she would draw many Dutch settlers from the northern states, if only to escape the harsh winters.[26] While in Holland, she had hundreds of copies of her plan printed in brochure form by the printers who published *De Hollander*.[27] Copies of her plans were also mailed to her many contacts in the Netherlands.[28]

Dutch Reformed church connection

Although Van Raalte's own motives were driven more by a desire for freedom of religion and Christian day schools, he would have been

---

[24] *Sheboygan Nieuwsbode*, 25 Aug. 1857
[25] *De Hollander*, 9 Sept. 1857.
[26] *Leeuwarder Courant*, 15 Dec. 1857.
[27] *De Hollander*, 7 Oct. 1857. Jacob Quintus, publisher of the *Nieuwsbode*, accused Hermanus Doesburg, editor of *De Hollander*, of plagiarizing his (Quintus') paper in these brochures, which Doesburg countered by saying that Mrs. Storm was quite capable of forming her own words, and it was her words that were printed.
[28] Her agent in the Netherlands was Jan Pijnappel, located at the Rokin in Amsterdam. Pijnappel was a merchant who also dealt in butter and cheese and had a partner named van der Chijs. Pijnappel was born 28 Aug. 1791 and died 13 Nov. 1864 in Amsterdam, at 73 years of age. He was also a member of the "Maatschappij tot Nut van 't Algemeen."

impressed with Mienette's social conscience to assist her indigent compatriots.[29] He may also have suggested that she contact the Domestic Mission Board of the Dutch Reformed Church in America to establish a mission outpost in Tennessee, because that same month a lengthy article in *Dagblad van Zuidholland en 's Gravenhage* of 22 September 1857 suggested that there was a good probability that the mission board might become involved in this new colony. The church could help by contributing to the support of a missionary from the Netherlands for the proposed colony.

Mienette was a member of the Reformed Church in the Netherlands and as such would naturally have turned to the Reformed Church in America for assistance. Van Raalte had enjoyed considerable material and financial support from the Dutch Reformed Church in America when founding his colony, and when a year later in 1858 the crops in the Holland colony were complete failures, he again turned to the mission board for help.[30]

There is, however, no mention of a potential outreach in Tennessee in the minutes of the *Acts and Proceedings of the General Synod of the Reformed Protestant Dutch Church in North America* from 1858 through 1861. This may have been due to the fact that the Board of Domestic Missions was experiencing financial difficulties, to the point that "the Board have been under the necessity of denying all applications from new stations."[31] Reason for the decline in contributions was stated by the board as being the result of the economic depression the United

---

[29] Henry S. Lucas, *Netherlanders in America: Dutch Immigration to the United States and Canada, 1789-1950* (Ann Arbor: University of Michigan. Reprint, Grand Rapids: Eerdmans, 1989), 308. In 1868 when Van Raalte deliberated about a possible site for another Dutch colony, he toured the south and spent some time in Knoxville, Tennessee (Van Raalte to Oggel, *De Hope*, 21 Oct. 1868). Defending his choice of Virginia, as far as the weather was concerned, he cited Mienette's choice of location in the eastern part of Tennessee, stating that she had chosen the eastern part of the state because of the climate (E. J. Masselink, *Holland, Michigan, Residents in the Civil War* [Calvin College Archives Collection 360, box 1, folder 2]). In 1864 when his son was wounded in the Civil War, Van Raalte immediately traveled south by train but was allowed to go only as far as Knoxville. At that time he may have been able to find out what happened to Mienette's colony. Van Raalte knew that Mienette still owned the property, and perhaps he wanted to check out the possibility of purchasing it but decided against it.

[30] C. "Holland Colony Michigan," *Christian Intelligencer*, 9 Sept. 1858. "Crops here are a complete failure [due to drought], and there is a request to the Board of Domestic Missions for a monetary sum to prevent many in the Holland colony from starving."

[31] *The Acts and Proceedings of the General Synod of the Reformed Protestant Dutch Church in North America, convened in the city of Newark, N.J. June 1858* (New York: Board of Publication of the Reformed Protestant Dutch Church, 1858), 351.

Fig. 5.2. Later portrait of Anne Maria Margaretha (Mienette) Storm-van der Chijs (*courtesy "Oprechte Haarlemse Courant"*)

States had experienced following the financial panic of 1857.[32] This turn of events was also unfortunate because an on-site spiritual leader often helped draw other settlers to a colony.

Advertisements

Back in Lancaster, Mienette followed up her *Sheboygan Nieuwsbode* article with a similar one published in the 14 October 1857 issue of the Frisian newspaper, *Leeuwarder Courant*:

> **Lady seeks boys for her colony.** The Widow Storm, née van der Chijs, from Delft traveled through the United States with the idea of writing a book about her adventures. And not that only but these past six months the purpose [of her travels] has especially been directed to establishing a new Dutch colony in one of the American States. According to her, Tennessee is the most suitable.
>
> "For the past fourteen days I have stayed again at the Frisian family Van Peyma, who received me so kindly last year. I have just arrived from my third visit to Tennessee, accompanied by an experienced engineer whom I took along to get his opinion regarding my plans to develop land and start a colony. I do not regret this difficult and costly trip, because I am indebted to this

---

[32] Ibid., 353.

man for his ideas with respect to the building of a sawmill, as well as that of factories. In general he shared my opinion regarding the advantageous lay of the land and bemoaned the fact that the Hollanders had settled mostly in the Northern states, while the Southern states offer so much more prosperity since the growing season is longer and the harvest more abundant. It is my hope, therefore, that I will win over my friends, the Van Peymas, and other well-to-do Frisians and Groningers already here [in America] not only as participants in my project but that they, as well as many Hollanders in Wisconsin and Michigan will follow me to live and work there. Here [in the north] the winter season can take up to eight months, during which at least three months all mechanical work must stop, while in the south one can keep working. In addition the land here is expensive compared to what it produces, while in the south, land is on average three-quarters the price of that in the north, so that right away one saves on capital investments and interest. In the south there are not yet factories, even though consumer goods are in demand and have to be transported from the north which makes them very expensive. These high prices will stay in effect because the rich planters of Louisiana, Alabama, Florida, etc., do not regard price an object to their comfort and luxury. With energy, capital and knowledge, there are fortunes to be made in Tennessee.

If my plans to found a colony in the slave-state of Tennessee succeed, I will have the wonderful prospect that through Dutch capital and Dutch colonists, Tennessee could become a pearl in the crown of a free [from slavery] America. The example of free laborers will have a positive effect on the Negro population and by the anticipated expansion of the colony Christian charity will gain the upper hand over the misery of slavery. With the increase in population, the completion of the railroads, which will complete the railroad network in mid America, and provide direct access of the colony with the Mississippi, the original land purchase will increase ten times over. Tennessee exceeds many other states in riches of geology and minerals, is very suitable for growing grapes and the founding of a brick factory, as I wrote earlier.

I hope now to find the same enthusiasm in my fellow countrymen for this project. Besides the initial ten to twelve young lads to work on my already purchased 450 acres, I will soon need several hundred if I can find enough backers so that I can expand the acreage. I would hope that the directors of orphanages in the Netherlands will work with me and send me strong healthy lads. In no time they will earn back the advanced travel costs, and after only a few years will enjoy an independent living. In many parts of this area many heads of household earn from two to four dollars daily, and thereby can provide a carefree life for their families. The average laborer here enjoys meat three times a day, which gives him strength and energy to do his work. In comparison, how poor is the lot of the average laborer in the Netherlands, and how wonderful the opportunity for them to be able to better their futures."[33]

Mienette did not mention the name of the engineer whom she had engaged to travel with and advise her. She did, however, know well Tennessee's mineral riches. From 1840 to 1845, the engineer co-edited *the Agriculturist*, a journal Mienette would be familiar with, since she contributed to similar journals in the Netherlands.[34]

She realized that traveling throughout the northern and western states was difficult in wintertime, and so she chose to winter in Cuba, returning to Lancaster in the spring of 1858.[35] Mienette used this time to write a series of lengthy articles in *De Hollander* about the United States Congress and how it worked. With her characteristic drive to educate, she contrasted the make up of the Senate and House of Representatives, which was composed of elected citizens, to that of the Dutch parliament, which consisted of members of the nobility. She covered topics such as how much the members were paid per day, the various states and territories they represented, the religious make up of the members, the American eagle, and the current economic crisis.[36]

The agent

Just as Van Raalte had found in Judge John Kellogg of Allegan, Michigan, a trusted adviser regarding the choice of land for his colony, Mienette found a valuable resource in Newton A. Patterson, a young attorney in Kingston, Tennessee. As a member of the Roane County Agricultural Society, Patterson's knowledge of the possibilities for the improvement of land use, agriculture, weather conditions, and

---

[33] *Leeuwarder Courant*, 15 Dec. 1857, translated by author.
[34] Troost died in 1850, so the two would not have met. For more on Troost, see Henry Grady Rooker, "A Sketch of the Life and Work of Dr. Gerard Troost," *Tennessee Historical Magazine* 3 (1932-33), 3-19.
[35] *De Hollander*, 9 Sept. 1857; *Zierikzeesche Courant*, 14 Oct. 1857.
[36] *De Hollander*, 3, 10 Feb. 1858, 3 Mar., 1858, 14 Apr. 1858.

Fig. 5.3. Newton A. Patterson
(*courtesy Patterson family*)

transportation matched her needs and her interests. Speaking fluent English, Mienette could converse one on one with Patterson, and their views on almost everything meshed. Patterson was a devout Christian and a family man. He, like Mienette, used newspapers to expand his interests and did not hold back from publishing his anti-slavery views. At one time he was sole publisher of the *Gazetteer,* Roane County's first newspaper.[37] During his life Patterson published hundreds of articles in area newspapers having to do with agriculture in the Roane County.[38] He was the one, no doubt, who pointed out to her the advantages of purchasing the 450 acres along the Clinch River in Roane County. The river would give her access to markets until the railroads were laid to Kingston.

In the *Nieuwsbode* of 25 August 1857, Mienette outlined a detailed cost analysis of her plans to grow grapes for wine, which would fetch one dollar per bottle, and for which the market was excellent. She

[37] Willie Hardin Bivins, "Newton Alexander Patterson," *Tennessee Ancestors*, Aug. 1996. Patterson was born in 1827 in Meigs County, TN. He was admitted to the bar in 1853, establishing a law practice in Kingston in 1854. After the Civil War, he became a judge and taught law at East Tennessee Wesleyan University in Athens. Because Patterson was against slavery, his father-in-law, Ramsey, was at first against the marriage of his daughter to Patterson. When the two did marry, he gave Elizabeth a female slave and her two-year-old child as a wedding present, and there was not much Patterson could do about having a slave in his household. To make sure his progeny would know about his anti-slavery feelings, he added the phrase "To be manumitted when funds are raised" in the margin next to their names on the 1860 USFC. Because he was the census taker, he was able to add the line.

[38] Willie Hardin Bivins, *Memories of our Ancestor Newton Alexander Patterson* (Oklahoma City, s.p. 1999).

estimated that her twelve sawmills would be able to cut fifteen hundred board feet of lumber per hour, which could be shipped to Chattanooga to the lumber dealers and fetch thirty-three dollars per one thousand feet. Sheep would also provide profitable wool.

The colony

Mienette's name is recorded in the Roane County Tax lists of the 1st District (Kingston and outlying areas) for 1859, which indicates she purchased this acreage in 1858.[39] There are no records of deeds, so she did not have it recorded. In 1867 the land is listed as "Patterson, N.A., Agent for Mrs. Storm." In 1871 the property is listed as "Patterson, N.A. Agent."[40] Therefore, according to the tax lists, she still owned the property in 1871.

The 1st district was located east and north of Kingston, on the south side of the Clinch River, approximately four miles from town. In order to gain approval for her project from the authorities, Mienette went straight to the top and met with Isham G. Harris (1818-1897), Tennessee's governor from November 1857 to 1862. She was confident that he would sanction her plans and plead her cause in the state assembly. She realized that her proposal might be met with some opposition, since Tennessee was divided about the slavery issue, and Mienette, by bringing in colonists, was trying to prove that one could make a profit without using slave labor. What Governor Harris told Mienette is lost to history, but what is known is that he led Tennessee's secession from the Union and was instrumental in recruiting thousands of confederate soldiers.

Despite this lack of the governor's endorsement, Mienette nevertheless had two farm houses and buildings built and the interiors furnished, and she imported farm equipment from the Netherlands, as well as Frisian horses and cattle.[41] The idea was to employ ten young men (two smiths, four carpenters, one cooper, one wooden shoe maker, and two gardeners) and four girls with sewing skills. These orphans, all no older than sixteen years, would be provided free passage plus pocket money. In return, they would indenture themselves to the colony until the age of twenty-one, at which time they could become American citizens and

---

[39] 1859 Roane County Tax Records 1st District Compiled by Robert L. Bailey; STORM, Mrs. A.M.; 450 acres - value $1000; http://www.roanetnheritage.com/research/index.htm.
[40] Information from tax lists, Roane County Archives supplied by Robert L. Bailey, archivist.
[41] Hogeweg-de Haart, *Storm-van der Chijs*, 6.

be free to choose to work elsewhere for themselves. Her colony manager began the process of selecting orphans to be brought over.

It is speculation, but not without merit, that one of the carpenters she employed was a young Dutch immigrant by the name of Gerard Ebben from Gennep, Limburg. Ebben had immigrated in 1847 at the age of twenty-two and first settled in Morgan County, Tennessee, just north of Roane. By 1857 he is listed on the Roane County tax records and living just a few houses down from Patterson, Mienette's agent. It is reasonable to assume that Patterson would have known this Dutch neighbor and that he recommended him to Mienette, who then hired him as part of her building team. Ebben, able to speak both English and Dutch, could supervise the young Dutch carpenters she hoped to bring over. Or, Ebben may have read about Mienette's plans, contacted her and when hired, moved to Kingston.[42]

In the Netherlands, her compatriots applauded her efforts. Citing the success of the thousands of Dutch in Chicago and of the Germans in Walhalla in South Carolina, the article in the Dutch newspaper, *Handelsblad*, lauded her plans as "highly commendable."[43] Nevertheless, not everyone sanctioned the plan. The *Nieuwsbode* published negative reactions in late 1857 and early 1858. Concerns about the project were that Tennessee was a slave-owning state and that she would run into difficulty with other landowners. They also claimed that the climate was too warm for Hollanders and that the cost of land in Tennessee was prohibitive.[44]

Henry Lucas blamed the 1857 financial crisis for ruining her plans. This is unlikely because Mienette was well aware of the economic situation. She had a solid grasp of finances and economics and would occasionally enter that great male bastion, the Amsterdam Stock Exchange, to see how her stocks were doing. To prove her point, she published two lengthy articles in the *Sheboygan Nieuwsbode* in late 1857 about the influence of America's economic crisis in Europe and in the Netherlands in particular and how it would impact the founding of her proposed colony.[45]

In one of her communications to the Dutch newspapers, she recounted the economic crisis and its possible impact on her colony,

---

[42] United States Federal Census, 1850 and 1860; Roane County Tax Lists for 1857, 1859, 1862, and 1869, Roane County Wills Recorded in the Deed Books. That he was a trusted member of the community is evidenced by the fact that in 1864 Ebben was named as executor of an estate.
[43] *Handelsblad*, 19 Sept. 1857.
[44] Lucas, *Netherlanders*, 308.
[45] Ibid.; *Sheboygan Nieuwsbode*, 24 Nov., 29 Dec. 1857.

notably raising land prices. But she figured that the American economy was resilient enough to weather the crisis, which she expected to moderate in a matter of months. Additionally, she thought that the crisis might have a positive effect in that Americans would cut back on their extravagant lifestyle.[46]

It turned out that the crisis did not impact the southern states as negatively as it did the northern states. While Mienette could, to some degree, predict the economic outcome, she could not have foreseen that the United States would become embroiled in a protracted Civil War. It is more likely, therefore, that the Civil War, and not the economy, ended her dream. This is also the conclusion of her biographer, Hogeweg-de Haart.[47]

Civil War

In 1859, when Mienette was busy purchasing land and materials for her colony by which she hoped to prove that by peaceful means she could be successful without the use of slave labor, another person hoped to do away with slavery using force. John Brown (1800-1859) believed than nothing less than an armed insurrection would abolish slavery. With weapons provided by northern abolitionists, Brown led a small band of whites and a few blacks to raid the United States Armory at Harpers Ferry in October 1859. The armory housed at least one hundred thousand muskets and rifles with which Brown hoped to arm slaves who would then rise up against their masters. The raid was unsuccessful ending in the death and execution of seventeen of the twenty-four men involved. Nevertheless, it exposed the fear of Southern slave owners that a large-scale revolt by slaves was a reality.[48]

Large crowds greeted Brown's funeral train from Virginia to Vermont, and church bells tolled at each stop. Southerners, seeing and reading about this outpouring of sympathy for Brown, came to regard most Northerners as Brown sympathizers, and began to increase their military budgets, and crack down on "infiltrators."[49] Even though Mienette had already bought the property before Brown's raid, it was perceptive on her part that she, an abolitionist sympathizer, had chosen the location for her colony in an area not heavily dominated by slave owners.

---

[46] *Leeuwarder Courant*, 12 Dec. 1857.
[47] Hogeweg-de Haart, *Storm-van der Chijs*, 6.
[48] For more on John Brown's raid, see Horwitz's, *Midnight Rising*.
[49] Horwitz, *Midnight Rising*, 262. The British Consul in Charleston, South Carolina, wrote on 9 Dec. 1859 "The Northern Merchants and Travelers are leaving [the South] in great numbers."

The region that she had chosen in Roane County was solidly pro-Union before the Civil War.[50] The election of the anti-slavery candidate, Abraham Lincoln, as president of the United States must have reassured her that her plan would succeed. She was still in the United States when he was elected. Given her interest in and solid knowledge of the American political system, she must have been greatly discouraged that by the time Lincoln was inaugurated in March 1861, seven of the southern states had seceded from the Union. Still, Tennessee had not yet made that decision at the time. It took several votes, but in the end Tennessee, the last state to do so, also seceded. It joined the Confederate States in June of 1861.

Confederate States of America

With Tennessee now part of the Confederate States of America, Mienette's colony was located in a foreign country, a country that had chosen slavery as a legitimate right. She was, in effect, in hostile territory. The warnings in the 1857 articles in the *Sheboygan Nieuwsbode* might now perhaps be realized. Nevertheless, Roane County, situated in East Tennessee still seemed safe for the time being. East Tennessee had voted firmly against separation on 8 June 1861, while West Tennessee voted in favor, so that the deciding vote came from Middle Tennessee which earlier had voted against secession but by February had voted in favor, resulting in ratifying the popular vote.

Even after Tennessee's secession from the Union, the citizens of Roane County aligned themselves evenly between North and South. Militia companies raised in the county were also evenly divided. On April 6 and 7, 1862, a major battle between North and South took place at Shiloh, Tennessee.[51] The Confederates achieved an early success but lost the battle on the second day. The ensuing loss of life on both sides shocked the nation, and it became clear that the war would not be as short as predicted earlier. The *Middelburgsche Courant* of 23 August 1862 reported that "especially in Kentucky, Missouri, and Tennessee guerilla tactics and cruelties against Yankees increased." Although they had lost at Shiloh, the Confederates gained and retained control of East

---

[50] Roane County, like much of East Tennessee, was against seceding from the Union. Only 454 voted for separation from the Union, while 1,568 voted against. **Vote in Roane County in 1861 For Separation or No Separation**, compiled by Robert L. Bailey, Roane County Archives.

[51] Hiram Isham also took part in the battle at Shiloh, TN. Also fighting on the Confederate side was Henry M. Stanley, who would find fame as the person who found David Livingstone in Africa.

Tennessee and Roane County until September 1863 through a series of skirmishes.[52]

During one of these clashes, Mienette's buildings were burned down and her caretaker killed. Her property was likely destroyed in the spring of 1862, because Mienette, not one to give up, remained in the United States until the summer of 1862 in hopes of reviving her colony as soon as the war ended. With increasing hostilities and her property destroyed, she returned to Europe in the fall of 1862. The Civil War effectively stemmed any large-scale immigration for those years, and there are no records of any Dutch orphans ever traveling to the area.[53]

Her agent, Patterson, stayed in Kingston and remained neutral in the war. In a biography of Patterson, her great-grandfather, Willie Hardin Bivins states that the family believed that he may have been a Secret Service Agent working for the Union.[54]

On 24 November 1863, General Joe Wheeler's cavalry was attached to General Longstreet and made a determined attempt to take Kingston. After a brisk fight, the Confederates withdrew that day. There continued to be numerous skirmishes during that November, but Union forces regained the territory. When Mienette learned this fact, she returned to the United States in 1864 to personally assess the damage to her property. Always the entrepreneur, she took along thirty-two folding models of various windmills she wanted to introduce to the New World. These windmills were such a success that from their sale she almost recouped her Roane County losses.[55]

Agricultural specimen

During her years in the United States, she shipped over four hundred species of plants and seeds to the Netherlands and introduced several new varieties such as the Mexican potato, sweet corn, and Wisconsin wild rice.[56] This brought her recognition at the exhibition for

---

[52] Albert H. McGeehan, ed., *My County and Cross: The Civil War Letters of John Anthony Wilterdink Company I, 25th Michigan Infantry* (Dallas: Taylor Publishing Company, 1982), 55. It is interesting to note that Michigan's 25th Infantry, Company I, which consisted of men from Holland Michigan, were in Kingston, Tennessee, from 12 to 29 November 1863 engaged in skirmishes. Van Raalte traveled to Knoxville in 1868 and may have found out what happened to Mienette's colony at that time.

[53] The 1860 United States Federal Census lists 23 heads of households born in the Netherlands living in Tennessee, none in Roane or surrounding counties.

[54] Bivins, "Patterson," in *Tennessee Ancestors*, 84.

[55] Bonebakker-Westermann, et al., *Delftse Vrouwen*, 76.

[56] *Zierikzeesche Courant*, 10 Nov. 1860. This paper reported that in November of 1860, Mienette was in Green Bay, WI.

the *Maatschappij van Landbouw* (the agricultural society) held in Haarlem in 1863, and a year later she was granted an honorary membership in the *Maatschappij tot Bevordering van Tuinbouw in Zeeland* (the society for the advancement of horticulture in Zeeland). Additionally, in her travels throughout America, she studied the development of industry, trade, and agriculture, and published articles in journals such as the *Economist* and *Journal for Home Economics* in which she described the Cooper Institute, where girls were taught not only the traditional women's occupations but also accounting and telegraph operation.[57]

Later years

Storm continued to travel until well into the 1870s. In November 1869, she attended the opening of the Suez Canal. In 1871, when word reached Europe that Dr. David Livingstone was lost in Africa, Mienette set out immediately to find him. There, in the interior of Africa, staying in a small hotel, she unexpectedly found herself face to face with her own brother who had the same idea.[58]

Her travels were a source of inspiration for her activities in the Netherlands, where she continued to concentrate on education for girls and work opportunities for women. She founded the Industrial School for girls and spearheaded a campaign to allow women to become pharmacists. Besides those endeavors, she encouraged women to engage in dairying and flower and vegetable growing. For many years she held readings on these subjects all over the country. Her celebrity status was such that her travels made newspaper headlines.

In 1870 the *Goessche Courant* reported that she was seen in the south of Italy.[59] In 1877 the *Zierikzeesche Courant* reported that Mevrouw Storm van der Chijs "is getting ready to set sail for Australia to study the norms and customs especially in Sidney and Melbourne."[60]

Why did Mienette, with all the financial means she had at her disposal and her boundless energy for travel, not try again to found a colony in America after the Civil War? After 1865 she may have been barred from taking Dutch teenagers out of the country to work in the United States. The shipping of 378 Dutch teenagers to South Africa between 1854 and 1860 became problematic when news filtered back to the Netherlands that some of these children had been mistreated.

---

[57] Her book, *Het Cooper's Instituut te Nieuw-York* was published in The Hague by the Belinfante Brothers in 1863.
[58] Bonebakker-Westermann, et al., *Delftse Vrouwen*, 81.
[59] *Goessche Courant*, 26 Apr. 1870.
[60] *Zierikzeesche Courant*, 4 Aug. 1877.

Fig. 5.4. Plaque on 1 Bree straat: "Here Lived and Worked AMM Storm v.d. Chijs: world traveler, pioneer feminist" (*courtesy K. Spiero, Archief Delft, coll. Beeld en Geluid 31585*)

This caused such a public outcry that by 1865 the Dutch government stopped the sending of teenaged orphans to South Africa, and in all likelihood the same measure was applied to other countries, including the United States, where distance also would prohibit oversight.[61]

Mienette's life's motto was "*Nuttig wezen*"—be useful. With her considerable wealth she could have lived a life of ease and leisure. Instead she chose to be useful. As such she lives on in the biennial Storm-van der Chijs Scholarship awarded to female students at Wageningen Agricultural University in the Netherlands. She died in Delft on 1 January 1895 at age eighty-one, and with her died her dream of a colony for Dutch orphans in the United States. Nevertheless, she would have rejoiced that in her lifetime slavery had been abolished by the Emancipation Proclamation; this was, after all, one of her fervent goals.[62]

---

[61] Sicking, *In het belang van het kind*.
[62] To ensure the abolition of slavery in all of the United States, Lincoln pushed for passage of the Thirteenth Amendment. Congress passed it by the necessary two-thirds vote on 31 Jan. 1865; it was ratified by the states in December of the same year.

PART II

Spanish-American War and
First World War

CHAPTER 6

For Humanity's Sake: Abraham Kuyper and the Spanish-American War of 1898

George Harinck

Neo-Calvinism is historically known for its impact on Dutch religion, education, politics, and media. It was a national phenomenon, and the international influence has been restricted to religion, theology, philosophy, and higher education. Neo-Calvinists have tried to extend their influence internationally more broadly, especially in the decades after the First World War, when internationalism in Europe had its first high tide. But their efforts were restricted to support of the League of Nations and to international conferences in the 1930s of the *Internationale Calvinistenbond* (International Calvinist league) for academics (mainly theologians), and the international (including American) outreach of VU University in Amsterdam.[1]

Neo-Calvinists, however, considered their impact far wider than these organizations. From the start of the active political involvement,

---

[1] George Harinck, "'We may no longer restrict our horizon till one country': Neo-Calvinism and Internationalism in the Interbellum Era," in *European Encounters: Intellectual Exchange and the Rethinking of Europe (1914-1945)*, eds. Carlos Reijnen & Marleen Rensen (Amsterdam/New York: Rodopi, 2013). Translations from the Dutch are by the author, unless indicated otherwise.

neo-Calvinists had an international agenda, especially in its European context. Abraham Kuyper (1837-1920) took a special interest in the United States, given his preference for its political system, especially in relation to civic freedom and the public role of religion. When in America in 1898, he had an opportunity to apply his Calvinist ideas on international relations to the actual situation in this country, then waging war on Spain. What was Kuyper's view on the role of the United States in world politics, and how did he appreciate America's interventions in Cuba and the Philippines? And was there anything specifically Calvinist in it?

Background: the ideas of Groen and Kuyper on internal law

The political branch of the Dutch neo-Calvinist movement was rooted in the ideas of Guillaume Groen van Prinsterer (1801-1876) and the anti-revolutionary politics he developed in the Netherlands beginning in the 1830s. He was part of an international network of intellectuals like Edmund Burke, Friedrich Julius Stahl, and Francois Guizot, who developed a conservative alternative to the political views produced by the Enlightenment and the French Revolution. Groen maintained that this revolution was not a reaction to a suppressing regime, but the movement "had a life of its own, not restricted to the limits of retroaction. It was born from a doctrine; from a *theory of freedom* ... that displaced all that was not according to this so-called freedom."[2]

Over against this theory of freedom, developed in the eighteenth century, Groen propagated the principle of the Reformation: "Is it freedom? Certainly not. Like the Gospel, the Reformation preaches freedom—a freedom that is grounded in the higher principle of *subjection*. Freedom is the result of, and subjection to, the principle."[3] The Reformation wants freedom, not to limit the authorities of rulers and governments, not to get political prerogatives, but to serve and keep His commandments. The only way to oppose the principle of revolution effectively is by excluding its influence and affirming the anti-revolutionary principle. According to Groen, this is possible only by acknowledging that the foundation of laws is God's law and order, citing Louis Vicomte De Bonald: "Revolution has begun by the

[2] Guillaume Groen van Prinsterer, *Ongeloof en revolutie. Eene reeks van historische voorlezingen* (Leiden: S. and J. Luchtmans, 1847), 120; English edition and translation by Harry Van Dyke, *Unbelief and Revolution* (The Groen Van Prinsterer Fund, VU Amsterdam, 1973).
[3] Groen Van Prinsterer, *Ongeloof en revolutie*, 155.

declaration of the rights of man; it will not end but by the declaration of the rights of God."[4]

As to international politics, these views resulted in Groen's stress on the need for a legal foundation of international affairs, with reference to the Christian character of Europe and in opposition to the European impact of the French Revolution. This legal aspect was closely related to belief in a divine order in history. The practical result of this standpoint was a rather rigid view on international politics: change was often equated with revolution, and Groen showed a clear preference for European nation states that were Protestant. In his metahistorical approach he defended both a spiritual European unity and national diversity.[5]

Abraham Kuyper, Groen's successor in the 1870s as political leader of the neo-Calvinist movement in the Netherlands, politicized the more-or-less religious view on international politics of his predecessor. He developed a political program based on Christian principles and in 1879 founded the Anti-Revolutionary Party (ARP). In this program, foreign affairs was dealt with in an article on national defense:

> It seeks to promote a vigorous defense of our national independence by reinforcing the sense of justice, fostering knowledge of our history, affirming our popular liberties, practicing a skilled diplomacy, and by legislating an organization of the standing armed forces and the reserves on land and sea that, after improving life in the barracks and aboard ship and after abolishing the replacement system, relies for its strength above all on the morale of the soldier.[6]

The ARP posited the idea of the nation over against cosmopolitism. In former days, Kuyper argued, people had a sense of the diversity of nations and the differences between peoples. "Everywhere you witnessed that rich splendor of multiformity that speaks to you and that embodies an idea and that proves to you that your nation has a right to an independent existence."[7]

---

[4] Groen Van Prinsterer, *Ongeloof en revolutie*, 7, translation from French by Nella Kennedy. Louis Gabriel Ambroise Vicomte De Bonald (1754-1840) was a French anti-revolutionary thinker.
[5] J. P. Bijl, *Europese antirevolutionair. Het Europabeeld van Groen van Prinsterer in tekst en context* (Amsterdam: VU University Press, 2011).
[6] *Guidance for Christian Engagement in Government: A Translation of Abraham Kuyper's Our Program [Ons program]* (Amsterdam: J. H. Kruyt, 1880), translated by Harry Van Dyke (Grand Rapids: Christian's Library Press, 2013), 259.
[7] Ibid., 260.

From this sense of national origin and independence the conviction followed that "just as every nation is a moral organism, of which provinces and municipalities are the articulations, so also the nations of our continent in their turn together constitute one large organic whole, of which each people is a living member and each nation, large or small, is one of the constituent parts."[8] Kuyper claimed the Christian origin of this conviction and characterized it as the moral foundation for international relations.

In opposition to this view of international relations, Kuyper maintained that in the nineteenth century international law no longer guaranteed the right of existence to all nations. Its purpose was to sacrifice "the nations' right of independent existence to a certain imaginary right of Europe's peoples to form large agglomerates and to eliminate every barrier and every obstacle that still prevent the merger and blending of the life of nations. [Hence], international law, in this modern view, increasingly causes the smaller nations to disappear and to be robbed of the primordial *right to exist*."[9] To make his case, he pointed to the dangers of the politics of Napoleon, of the socialist's international ideal, and of the colonial policies of Great Britain, for example, toward the Boer Republics in South Africa. And the worst thing, according to Kuyper, was that smaller nations were not upset by this new internationalism, but welcomed it and rejected nationalism as old-fashioned patriotism.

In Kuyper's ideas on international affairs, he distinguished between a legal and a cultural view. In his legal view his maxim was the principle of law—as grounded in God's creation ordinances. International relations are not defined by power relations but by the creative plurality of peoples, and therefore these relations have a moral base that needs legal expression. Thanks to Christianity, relationships among European nations were based ultimately not on power and threat but on treaties and written law. Many texts of specific treaties in European history, therefore, started with a reference to the sovereignty of God.[10]

Given this moral character of international affairs, Kuyper was open to the emerging idea of an international *community*, a European-law community, and Europe as a Christian family of peoples.[11] When from

[8] Ibid.
[9] Ibid., 263.
[10] Ibid., 261.
[11] Roel Kuiper, *Zelfbeeld en wereldbeeld. Antirevolutionairen en het buitenland, 1848-1905* (Kampen: J. H. Kok, 1992), 112-14.

the 1870s interest grew in a general legal regulation of international affairs, Kuyper's Anti-Revolutionary Party stressed the meaning of international law as objective and binding law, and not as something conventional that could not be enforced.

This was the legal aspect of his view on international affairs. But there was also a cultural view, which saw Calvinism as the eminent worldview that since the sixteenth century defined the course of civilization. This worldview operated independently of the politics of nation states, but Dutch people played a vital role as bearers of Calvinism. The Dutch were a link in the life stream of civilizations, from the Greek and Roman civilizations through the Middle Ages, via Calvin's Geneva to France, the Netherlands, Scotland in Europe, and then in the seventeenth century crossing the Atlantic Ocean to North America. Kuyper's prediction that the United States would take a leading international role in the twentieth century was not based on an analysis of power relations but on its Calvinist character. In 1899 Kuyper wrote: "Calvinism is an independent general tendency which, from a mother principle of its own, has developed an independent form both for our *life* and for our *thought* among the nations of Western Europe and North America, and at present even in South Africa."[12]

This cultural view was as nationalistic as it was non-political. Kuyper's nationalism was not determined by social Darwinism. The essence of his nationalism was not language but Calvinistic faith, which would find its way within a nation organically. The result would be a change in politics through the *conscience* of politicians and diplomats, as well as legal or political enforcement. This cultural view was not shared by Kuyper's fellow Dutch politicians, and he mainly used this imagery when addressing his supporters. To them, the cultural aspect of the ARP's foreign policy stance was essential.

In theory this cultural view could have influenced the foreign policy and diplomacy of the Netherlands, but it never did. The three Christian coalition governments that were in office before the First World War (1888-91, 1901-5, 1908-13) did not deviate from the Dutch policy of neutrality and emphasis on international law. But Kuyper himself actively applied his cultural and legal views to international affairs. As prime minister from 1901 to 1905, he showed a vivid interest in foreign policy—to such a degree that he was nicknamed as minister of international travels. He stressed the moral responsibility

---

[12] Abraham Kuyper, *Calvinism. Six Stone-Lectures* (Amsterdam-Pretoria: Höveker and Wormser; Edinburgh: T. & T. Clark; London: Simpkin, Marshall, Hamilton, Kent & Co.; New York-Chicago-Toronto: Fleming H. Tevell, 1899), 9-10.

of the Netherlands to lead its colonies to more independence ("ethical policy")—he did not view colonies as a part of the Dutch nation—and he pushed for the Peace Palace to be located in The Hague. These views were in line with the general preference for international law in Dutch politics. There was not much debate in Dutch politics that the international role of the Netherlands was defined by moral position and neutrality, not by power. Kuyper only differed with his fellow-politicians on the foundation of this law.

It is clear that Groen's and Kuyper's views on international law and international relations were firmly based in the conviction that God's laws and ordinances were the grounding principles which had to be obeyed but with respect to the diversity of nations, whose existence was not accidental, but willed by God. In order to defend this state of affairs, cosmopolitan ideas had to be opposed, and the rights of nations, great or small, had to be vindicated. In practice, this outspoken Christian view on international relations did not differ much from the political position of other Dutch political parties. This view, given the smallness of the Dutch nation, was defended not by force but on moral grounds.

The application of Kuyper's cultural view to the United States

Kuyper did not apply his neo-Calvinist views on international affairs solely in the Dutch political arena. An example of this is his visit to the United States in 1898. In that year the Spanish-American War had broken out, and the United States had captured San Jago (Santiago de Cuba) first and then the entire island. Spain was defeated, and Cuba became an independent state under American guardianship. In the Netherlands not much attention was paid to this war on the other side of the Atlantic. Cuba was *terra incognita* to the Dutch. In the Dutch press hardly any attention had been paid to tensions between Spain and Cuba over the previous decades, and though the Dutch had experienced difficulties in their colonies as well, especially in Aceh in the Netherlands East Indies, similarities were only suggested, not explored.[13]

In the Caribbean the Netherlands possessed the Antilles and Surinam but had few contacts with Spanish and Roman Catholic colonies in that region. The country was known for its tobacco—the Havana cigar was introduced in the Netherlands at the end of the

---

[13] *De Gids* 60 (1896): 375, 429.

nineteenth century—and sugar cultures, but before 1900 hardly any Dutchmen had visited Cuba.[14]

When the Cunard Line steamer *Lucania*, with Kuyper aboard, sailed into New York harbor in August 1898, he was immediately confronted with this war. His first letter to his wife mentioned the war:

> What was very nice when arriving at the pier [on 27 August] was seeing the American warships from San Jago, a fleet of 15 ships. On Monday [29 August] I also saw the return of the 71st regiment from San Jago, 330 of the 1,080 men, all the others killed, wounded or ill. And even of those 330, there were a whole lot who had to ride in horse carts. Most interesting otherwise. At least 400,000 people, all wild with enthusiasm. The troops looked exhausted and weak. A chaplain led the way, and when they had arrived all heads were bared, and in the open air a prayer of gratitude [was said]. So very different than in our country. That is the after effect of Calvinism.[15]

Especially in this final remark about the "after effect," Kuyper's culturally-embedded view of international affairs was apparent. Calvinism upheld a nationalism that was grounded in the belief in God who had created nations, in the realization that the nations depended upon Him, and to whom the nations therefore were to be grateful in response. That was the background of what Kuyper saw in Manhattan. The enthusiasm of the New Yorkers was citizenship at its best.

In the Stone Lectures Kuyper delivered in October 1898 at Princeton Theological Seminary, the flagship institution of the Presbyterian Church in the United States, he was explicit about the relationship between Calvinism and the United States: "The fundamental idea of Calvin has been transplanted from Holland and England to America, thus driving our higher development ever more Westward, until on the shores of the Pacific it now reverently awaits whatsoever God has ordained."[16] Whatever the future would be, Kuyper

---

[14] The first travel accounts by Netherlanders were: P. Reineke, *Indrukken eener reis door Louisiana en Cuba in 1901* (Amsterdam: De Bussy, 1901) and Hendrik P. N. Muller, *Door het land van Columbus: Vereenigde Staten, Mexico, Cuba, Costa-Rica, Colombia, Venezuela, Trinidad, Curaçao, Suriname. Een reisverhaal* (Haarlem: Erven F. Bohn, 1905).

[15] A. Kuyper to J. H. Kuyper-Schaay, 1 Sept. 1898, in George Harinck, ed., *Kuyper in America: "This is where I was meant to be,"* transl. Dagmare Houniet (Sioux Center: Dordt College Press, 2012), 9-10.

[16] Kuyper, *Calvinism*, 36.

Fig. 6.1. Abraham Kuyper, honorary doctorate, Princeton University, 22 October, 1898 (*Historical Documentation Center for Dutch Protestantism*)

took it as a fact "that the broad stream of the development of our race runs from Babylon to San Francisco." This implied that in Europe as well as in the United States the conflict between Calvinism and the French Revolution—the antithesis detected by Groen, strictly defined—was the fundamental issue. Kuyper's struggle was America's struggle and vice versa.

On 22 October, the day following the last of his six Stone Lectures, Kuyper received an honorary law degree from Princeton University. In his word of thanks, he related his view of the effects of Calvinism on the American nation to the recent war against Spain:

> Even during your latest war my Calvinistic recollection stirred my warmest sympathy for your splendid achievement on sea and land. I felt as if you gave the final death blow to the very power my ancestors had run down. . . . The result remains, that we checked Spain's sway over Europe, and that you broke down its colonial empire.[17]

It was Calvinism and its political liberties that connected the Netherlands and the United States.

The Princeton speech "succeeded so well," he wrote to his wife, "that it ended in sustained applause. . . . The people were all beaming,"

---

[17] "Toespraak door A. Kuyper, 1898" (Dossier Amerika, Kuyper Archives, Historical Documentation Center for Dutch Protestantism, VU University Amsterdam.

a lady noted.[18] An Oxford professor who received an honorary degree on the same occasion was astonished by what Kuyper said "slowly and solemnly." The Oxford don wrote his wife in England that this was "the most remarkable speech I have heard for a long time.... One felt as if the seventeenth century had visibly risen upon us to give the last curse to Spain."[19] Later on during his visit to the United States, Kuyper repeated this comparison, condensing it into the *bon mot* that it took the Dutch eighty years to defeat Spain while the Americans needed only eighty days.[20]

British politicians at this time spoke in a different tone about the Spanish-American War. Prime Minister Lord Salisbury, addressing the Conservative Primrose League in the Albert Hall on 4 May 1898, offered a social Darwinian take on what was happening in the Caribbean. He divided the nations of the world into living (United States and Germany[21]) and dying nations (the Chinese and Ottoman empires, according to historian James Joll[22]):

> You may roughly divide the nations of the world as the living and the dying.... The weak states are becoming weaker and the strong states are becoming stronger.... [The] living nations will gradually encroach on the territory of the dying, and the seeds and causes of conflict among civilized nations will speedily appear.[23]

Kuyper interpreted the speech as if Salisbury were speaking of Great Britain as a living nation and was critical of the attitude of "the philosopher of the Tories" in international politics, and blamed him for still not being satisfied with the vastness of the British Empire, but continually seeking to expand it in the East and West.[24] To Kuyper the war on Cuba was waged for humanity's sake, and was thus the fruit

---

[18] Kuyper to Kuyper-Schaay, 22 Oct. 1898, in Harinck, *Kuyper in America*, 41-42.
[19] A. V. Dicey, quoted in Peter S. Heslam, *Creating a Christian Worldview: Abraham Kuyper's Lectures on Calvinism* (Grand Rapids: Eerdmans; Carlisle: Paternoster Press, 1998), 65.
[20] For example, in Holland, Michigan, "He Was Welcomed. A Distinguished Guest from Holland Here," *Grand Rapids Evening Press*, 27 Oct. 1898 (Dossier Amerika, Kuyper Archives).
[21] So Andrew Roberts, "Salisbury, The Empire Builder Who Never Was," *History Today* 49, no. 10 (1999).
[22] James Joll, "Goodbye to All That," Review of E. J. Hobsbawm, *The Age of Empire 1875-1914*, *New York Review of Books*, 14 Apr. 1988.
[23] Quoted from "The Living and Dying Nations: Lord Salisbury's Prophetic Speech at Albert Hall, London," *Daily Mail and Empire* (Toronto), 21 May 1898.
[24] A. Kuyper, "Imperialistische politiek (Het jaar 1898)," *De Standaard*, 21 Jan. 1899.

of Calvinism. The Spanish rule was replaced by the Calvinistic rule of honoring God's ordinances and human rights, first by the Dutch and now by the Americans, as he said in his lecture in the First Reformed Church in Pella, Iowa, on 1 November.[25]

Kuyper's legal view and the Spanish-American War and American expansionism

Kuyper not only gave the Americans his cultural take on international affairs, he also saw the Spanish-American War as a turning point in world history. The war cost Spain the last remnants of what was once a mighty empire on which the sun did not set. In these years it lost not only the rebelling colony of Cuba but also the Philippines. In the United States the Spanish-American War generated a debate about the nation's role in the world. The war resulted in a big expansion of the American sphere of influence both in the Caribbean and the Far East. The issue was: Should the United States withdraw now that the war had been won and hold to its Monroe Doctrine?

This doctrine stated that further efforts by European nations to colonize land or interfere with states in North or South America would be viewed as acts of aggression, requiring American intervention. At the same time, the doctrine implied that the United States would neither interfere with existing European colonies nor meddle in the internal concerns of European countries. The Spanish war made this doctrine redundant. The other option prevailed: the United States should in one way or another keep Cuba and the Philippines within its sphere of influence.

Calvinists in the United States also had to take sides. John B. Hulst of Grand Rapids published a book of 263 pages on the history of Cuba and presented the war as a war of liberation, *Het verdrukte Cuba*. It was the only book on the issue published in Dutch.[26] Dutch American theologian Henry E. Dosker (1855-1926), professor at Western Theological Seminary in Holland, Michigan, elaborated on the weight of the imperialist turn in American foreign policy. His opinion was that the United States stood before the heaviest task in all of its history.

---

[25] J. Keizer, "Toespraak van dr. A. Kuyper in het kerkgebouw van de 1ste Ger. Kerk," *Pella's Weekblad*, 4 Nov. 1898.

[26] J[ohn] B. Hulst, *Het verdrukte Cuba en zijne verlossing, of den geschiedenis van Cuba, vanaf zijne ontdekking tot aan zijne bevrijding van Spanje's juk, alsook van den Spaansch-Amerikaanschen oorlog, op eenvoudige wijze verteld aan het Nederlandsche volk* (Grand Rapids, n.d. [1898]).

Fig. 6.2. Banquet, Holland, Michigan, 1898 (*courtesy Historical Documentation Center for Dutch Protestantism*)

Until then it was a nation of hermits, locked up by itself. But now it entered the second phase of its history, a time of colonization.

Colonization: this was exactly the word Kuyper did not like to hear in relation to his view of a Calvinist American nation. Kuyper defended the Spanish-American War of 1898 as an intervention *for humanity's sake*.[27] Europe had stayed aloof when the Armenians were massacred in 1896, but the United States had stood up for the Cubans when the same fate threatened them. Kuyper claimed to be one of the few politicians in Europe who defended the military action of the United States.[28] He praised America in his newspaper *De Standaard* for its defense of law and righteousness in this case and thanked it for the liberation of Cuba.[29]

According to Kuyper, the invasion of Cuba and the Philippines had been motivated by the Christian conscience of the American people that had been alarmed by the atrocities in Armenia and wanted to prevent these in Cuba.[30] He agreed with President William McKinley (1843-1901), when he stated that the occupation of the Philippines was America's duty in order to safeguard the interests of the archipelago and the peace in the world. But expansion was something other than

[27] A. Kuyper, *Varia Americana* (Amsterdam/Pretoria: Höveker & Wormser; 's Gravenhage: Zuid Holl. Boek-en Handelsdrukkerij, 1899), 187.
[28] A. Kuyper, "Onschoon geëindigd (Het Jaar 1898)," *De Standaard*, 6 Jan. 1899.
[29] Kuyper, "Onschoon geëindigd."
[30] Kuyper, *Varia Americana*, 186.

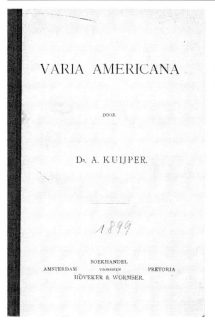

Fig. 6.3. Varia Americana, 1899 (*courtesy Historical Documentation Center for Dutch Protestantism*)

this duty. Kuyper deplored that McKinley later in 1898 gave in to the pressure of the expansionists in Congress and to public opinion, and he warned of the negative effects of an imperialist turn, not only for the United States but also for the Netherlands:

> Once the idea of expansion takes root, a country like America of course cannot be satisfied by such a small colony (less than 300.000 square miles, and a population of little more than six million), but will always press on, and become a doubtful neighbor to us. And, last but not least, annexing the Philippines will force America to take over Spain's role over against the insurgents, burden itself with heavy military expenses, and turn the character of American politics in its opposite.[31]

In lectures and interviews Kuyper gave in the United States, he shared his worries and criticized the invasion for extending American influence to the Far East. Cuba was protected, but in the case of the Philippines, it was sheer annexation, strongly promoted by the "rough rider" and Cuban war hero of Dutch descent, Theodore Roosevelt (1858-1919), who was elected governor of New York in November 1898. Kuyper enjoyed the fact that his Democrat opponent, August Van Wijck (1850-

---

[31] Ibid., 189.

1922), was also of Dutch descent,[32] but here his appreciation stopped. In an interview to a reporter of *The Democrat and Chronicle*, Kuyper stated that same month: "If you regard Cuba and the Philippines as so much gain for yourselves, you are morally sinking as a national endeavour; descending to a lower plane of national life. Just as long as America goes in for a high moral stand, it is all right." Kuyper here warned that naked annexation was morally corrupt and argued for noblesse oblige.[33]

Kuyper explained to the journalist that America's main duty in the Philippines was to protect the natives. Therefore, the nation could not be given back to Spain, for the natives would submit neither to the Spanish rule nor to another European nation, for that would cause international complications. So America was obliged to keep the Philippines. For Kuyper, the right way to proceed was to establish a government by the natives.

Kuyper was not opposed to expansion as such. In the case of Great Britain or the Netherlands, expansion was a solution to the problem that their population was too large for their home territory. But this was not the case with the United States, he explained to a Baltimore reporter in early December.[34]

Kuyper opposed the Philippine expansion and defended the rights of smaller nations against the world powers. As long as the United States defended the right of small nations and did not annex them, they did the right thing. Thus, he thrust himself into the middle of American politics on the side of those opposing annexation. Instead, the United States should use its international influence to defend the rights of nations according to the classical interpretation of international law. In November 1898, Kuyper had an audience with President McKinley in the White House. He intended to bring up the issue of the Philippines, among other issues, but his salient issue was the American policy toward the Boers. Kuyper asked McKinley to lift the embargo on the export of American horses to South Africa. He begged for support for the small Boer Republics in their pending war over against imperialistic England, which behaved immorally in Kuyper's opinion. It was perfidious Albion in *optima forma*, drunk of imperialism.[35]

---

[32] Ibid., 87.
[33] Quoted in "Dr. Kuyper on the Phillipines," newspaper clipping, no title (Rochester, n.d.) (Dossier Amerika, Kuyper Archives).
[34] "Sees danger ahead," newspaper clipping, no title (Baltimore, n.d.) (Dossier Amerika, Kuyper Archives). See also Kuyper, *Varia Americana*, 188.
[35] A. Kuyper, "Engelands wondeplek," *De Standaard*, 30 Aug. 1899; A. Kuyper, "Het Engelsche imperialisme," *De Standaard*, 25 Oct. 1899.

Fig. 6.4. Cartoon, Baltimore's Merchants Club
(*courtesy Dossier Amerika, Kuyper Archives*)

McKinley spurned Kuyper's request and gave England a free hand in South Africa. Kuyper was disappointed: this is not how a Calvinistic nation should behave. He praised McKinley as a man of prayer but at the same time dismissed him as a weak politician.[36]

In *De Standaard* of 6 January 1899, Kuyper opined on America's international interventions the previous year:

> Alas, the lustre of America's intervention would be darkened by the bright red gleam of an objectionable expansion policy! From the start we took sides with America where it aimed at liberating Cuba. And that later on, after the victory in the East, America laid its hand on the Philippines, was right, even though it had done better by restricting its wars to the West. But what it should not have done was that she in the end chose for a dangerous and disastrous conquering policy and instead of aiming at liberation, immediately annexed the Philippines and Puerto Rico.

Kuyper stated that by giving in to the expansionist groups, the United States abandoned the Monroe Doctrine, and the woes would come. The United States would get involved in the international bustle and take on a colonial and military yoke. In the end, she would act against

---

[36] Kuyper, *Varia Americana*, 185, 189.

her own tradition and principles and mark down the emancipation of the Cubans.

Kuyper's remark about military expenses turned out to be prescient. The only acquisition Theodore Roosevelt, an ardent expansionist who succeeded the assassinated McKinley as president in 1901, made in his seven years of office was the Panama Canal Zone. The nation's expansion as a colonial power thereafter came to an end.[37]

Conclusion

The cultural and the legal side were entwined in Kuyper's view on international relations. They were not based on power and threat but on a strong legal base, grounded in the diversity of nations as created by a sovereign God. It was Calvinism that honoured this insight best and since the sixteenth century had led the course of world civilization via Switzerland, the Netherlands, Scotland, and the United States. Therefore, it was especially Calvinist nations like the Netherlands and the United States that should uphold international order. This explains Kuyper's sympathy for the United States as defender of freedom and righteousness. When in 1898 the United States liberated Cuba and the Philippines from Spanish suppression, Kuyper considered the intervention to be in accord with America's tradition and principles. While in the United States, he often compared the Netherlands and United States, since both defeated Spain at vital moments in their national histories.

Because of the vital character of the moment, Kuyper became disappointed when the United States in 1898 turned liberation into expansion. Greed and power prevailed over the more noble ideals in American foreign policy he averred, to the detriment of a country he otherwise predicted would have a great future. His arguments did not win the day in 1898, but they are interesting because of their application of neo-Calvinist ideas in an international context. As in the Netherlands, his cultural take on international politics and relations was welcomed and cheered within Calvinist circles in America, such as the Presbyterians at Princeton and the Dutch Americans in the midwest. If they were not Calvinists, they appreciated Kuyper's praise of American interventions in Cuba and the Philippines.

American Calvinist historian, James D. Bratt, considered the liberation of the Spanish islands an expression of Progressivism, while

---

[37] Richard F. Hamilton, *President McKinley, War and Empire: President McKinley and America's New Empire* (New Brunswick: Transaction Publishers, 2008), 94.

Fig. 6.5. Pella train station, 1898. Volunteers waiting for the train with Company F. 3rd Iowa soldiers aboard, headed for Des Moines to be mobilized to serve in the Spanish-American war (*courtesy Pella Historical Society Archives*).

it actually preserved the old order. "In fact," he wrote, "Kuyper provides a neat cross-section of the American progressive trinity, sharing the vitalism of Roosevelt, the moralism of Woodrow Wilson, and the evangelical oratory of [William Jennings] Bryan."[38]

There was a sharp edge in Kuyper's view when the McKinley administration deviated from American traditions and adopted a foreign policy of expansionism. This had nothing to do with liberation; it was occupation, pure and simple, in Cuba and the Philippines. Kuyper's legal view of international affairs is here apparent. The United States did not have the right to violate the independence of these former Spanish colonies. As a forerunner of Wilson, Kuyper defended their right to self-determination, a defence deeply grounded in his Calvinist belief in a godly world order, including the sovereignty of nations within their own sphere. Kuyper, of course, realized that nations like Great Britain and the Netherlands had colonies, but he defended this on the rationale of a lack of territory—a problem the United States did not have. These nations were mere guardians: one day the colonies would become independent.

---

[38] James D. Bratt, *Abraham Kuyper. Modern Calvinist, Christian Democrat* (Grand Rapids: Eerdmans, 2013), 255.

Kuyper's legal view defended small nations over world powers and was a plea for a legal grounds for international intervention on their part. With regard to the Dutch nation, this was self interest, but there was more to it. Kuyper argued that the Netherlands as a Calvinist nation had an international responsibility to promote and defend the international legal order. The Dutch role in international affairs was a moral one. That is why the Dutch wanted the Peace Palace in The Hague and why Kuyper advocated in *The New York World* of 8 October 1910 the controversial conferring of the 1906 Nobel Peace Prize on Roosevelt for having negotiated peace in the Russo-Japanese war in 1904-5 and for resolving a dispute with Mexico by arbitration, as recommended by the peace movement. But opponents still saw in Roosevelt a "military mad" imperialist who fought in Cuba and completed the American conquest of the Philippines. Roosevelt, as Kuyper saw it, had been converted from expansionism and returned to the American tradition of freedom and justice.

Kuyper's neo-Calvinism was in line with the Netherlands' stance in international politics, but he added a Calvinist flavor to it. In practice this led him, unlike many European politicians, to an appreciation of America's intervention in Spanish colonies. At the same time, he stressed the limits to these interventions: it was a duty in service of the liberation of oppressed natives. He opposed power politics in international affairs and gave Calvinist nations like the Netherlands and the United States a moral responsibility in safeguarding liberty and justice in international politics. Kuyper had been in the eye of the expansionist storm when he visited the United States in the second half of 1898, but in the end, the storm blew over, just as he had argued and hoped for.

CHAPTER 7

Loyalties in Conflict: Theodore F. Koch Confronts the First World War

Robert Schoone-Jongen

When war came to Europe in the summer of 1914, Theodore F. Koch was an aging real estate agent, promoting Texas Gulf Coast farming communities from near Beaumont to beyond Corpus Christi. For three decades this sixty-year-old Dutch American entrepreneur had been buying, developing, and selling American land with capital provided by a family of Ruhr Valley screw manufacturers, the Funckes of Westphalia, Germany. So when the Great War began, Koch had solid financial reasons to monitor events beyond the Atlantic.[1] But he had motives beyond money.

---

[1] Robert P. Schoone-Jongen, "Cheap Land and Community: Theodore F. Koch, Dutch Colonizer," *Minnesota History* 53 (Summer 1993): 214-24; Robert P. Schoone-Jongen, "A Time to Gather; A Time to Scatter: Dutch American Settlement in Minnesota, 1884-1910 (PhD diss., University of Delaware, 2007); Frances Marie Schroeder, "Theodore F. Koch and the Founding of Riviera, Texas" (MA Thesis, Texas A & I University-Kingsville, 1975); Henry S. Lucas, *Netherlanders in America: Dutch Immigration to the United States and Canada, 1789-1950* (Grand Rapids: Eerdmans, 1955, 1989), 367-72, 438-41; Jacob Van Hinte, *Netherlanders in America: A Study of Emigration and Settlement in the 19th and 20th Centuries in the United States of America*, ed. Robert P. Swierenga, trans. Adriaan de Wit (Grand Rapids: Baker Book House, 1985), 626, 713-15.

While proud of their Dutch nationality, the Koch family had ties across the border in Germany as well. Great-grandfather Koch had migrated in the 1780s from the region of Westphalia to Zevenaar in the Netherlands province of Gelderland, where Koch served as the town's Protestant school teacher before being appointed to municipal offices. Theodore's mother had also been born on the German side of the border. His father, Johan Willem Coenraad Koch, managed an estate owned by German nobles. So Theodore Koch, from his earliest years, inherited both political and emotional ties to the Netherlands and both economic and familial ties to Germany.[2]

While growing up in the Netherlands during the 1860s, young Theodore had heard stories during Sunday conversations at his grandfather's table in Zevenaar and from his school lessons of Holland's humiliating Napoleonic occupation.[3] His uncles also told of fighting the Belgians in the 1830s, who then succeeded in winning independence and breaking up the United Kingdom of the Netherlands. It was another defeat for the Dutch. As a teenager Koch heard a German aunt describe the horrors she witnessed as a field hospital nurse during the Franco-Prussian War. Now, as a transplanted south Texan, Koch heard old Confederates describe the Union sacking of Brownsville in 1864. In the newspapers Koch read of Mexican marauders raiding ranches in the Rio Grande Valley, which to his expansive Texan worldview, was his very own neighborhood.

Like many contemporaries, Koch believed that human progress had rendered war obsolete in the modern era. Yet, he was no pacifist. As a young man he had thought French Catholics deserved to lose to armies of German Protestants. As an old man he nostalgically identified with the Batavians, his ancient ancestors, as they repelled the Romans in the Teutoburg Forest, led by Herman the German. Yet, to Koch, war in 1914 was serious, wasteful, and unjustified.[4]

There were deeper reasons to keep watch on the war in Europe. Koch's wife, Clara Hoeborn Koch, the daughter of a paper

---

[2] Theodore F. Koch, "Memoirs of Theodore F. Koch, 1935, Parts 1-2" (unpublished typescript in the collection of the South Texas Archive, Jerigan Library, Texas A & M University-Kingsville), 8-9; Johan Willem Coenraad Koch, "Recollections Out Of My Life" (typescript of English translation by Dirk A. Dirkse in in the collection of the South Texas Archive, Jerigan Library, Texas A & M University-Kingsville), 5, 26; (http://www.chrisvankeulen.nl/zevenaar.htm , 27 June 2013.

[3] These history lessons led many Dutch Americans to disagree with the United States' alliance with France in 1917. See Robert Schoone-Jongen, "Patriotic Pressures: The Dutch Experience in Southwest Minnesota during World War One," *Origins* 7, no. 2 (1989), 2-8.

[4] Koch, "Memoirs," 1:5, 19, 3:84.

manufacturer, had grown up during the bright early morning of the new German Empire.⁵ She remained very proudly German throughout her life. Frequent visits and constant correspondence with her mother and sisters nourished those ties. Since her father's untimely death in the wake of a business failure, the Hoeborns relied on the generosity of their prosperous son-in-law in America. Living in south Texas the Kochs dwelled among German Americans, both at home in Riviera near the coast and on holidays in New Braunfels in the Hill Country.⁶ Koch's business partner, Herbert Roedenbeck—a German cavalry veteran—boasted of visiting his brother aboard the imperial yacht *Hohenzollern* and dining with the Kaiser.⁷ The Koch's only son-in-law, Oscar Rabbethge, an officer in the Imperial German Army, marched into Belgium and on into France during August 1914.

In the United States the onset of the European war abruptly halted migration to the Gulf Coast. Surging grain prices diverted hopeful farmers to the Texas Panhandle, Oklahoma, and Kansas to profit from Europe's mayhem.⁸ With his own land business at a standstill, Koch slashed his expenses. He dismissed all his clerks (one of whom had been with him for twenty years), closed offices in St. Paul and Houston, hired his son, Theodore William, a newly minted Harvard graduate, as a general assistant, and retained a nephew, Carl Henny, as a jack of all trades—part salesman, part bookkeeper, part chauffeur, and part office manager.⁹

Obviously the war also altered the Funcke family's financial horizons. The current patriarch, Oscar Funcke, had inherited the ties to Koch in 1910, upon the death of Wilhelm Funcke III, who had

---

5   Koch, "Memoirs," 1:72. Theodore F. Koch, "History of My Engagement and Marriage to Clara D. Hoeborn and My Relations with the Hoeborn Family" (unpublished typescript in the collection of the late James T. Koch, San Antonio, TX).
6   Glen E. Lich, *The German Texans* (San Antonio: The University of Texas Institute of Texan Cultures, 1981); Idella Unterbrink Strubhart, *A Small Town in God's Country: Riviera Texas, Commemorating 90 Years of History, 1907-1997* (Norcross: Sitton Associates, 1997), 70-76, 142-57, 173, 241-316.
7   Herbert Roedenbeck, "Light and Shadow" (unpublished typescript in the collections of the Tyrell Historical Library, Beaumont, TX, and the Sam Houston Regional Library, Liberty, TX) 2, 4.
8   For a most readable account of the development of the Panhandle during this period see Timothy Egan, *The Worst Hard Time: The Untold Story of Those Who Survived the Great American Dust Bowl* (Boston: Houghton Mifflin Harcourt, 2006), 12-88.
9   Theodore W. Koch (1891-1962) Harvard class of 1912. Carl Henny (1888-1979) was the only son of Koch's only sister, Anna. Henny was born in the Netherlands and came to work for his uncle in 1905. With a three-year hiatus during which he sold Aurora trucks in Michigan, Henny remained the Koch family's factotum in Texas until his death (Koch "Memoirs," 3:121).

inherited the Koch estate upon the death of Wilhelm Funcke II in 1896.[10] The family had transformed Theodore F. Koch from a European commodity broker into an American real estate dealer and colonizer by placing deposits and letters of credit for him in New York and Chicago banks. As profits accumulated, Wilhelm Funcke III demonstrated his thanks by granting Koch the American franchise to market a German waterproofing material, Ceresit—a compound "used in all civilized countries."

When in 1910 Theodore Koch decided to branch out and develop a beach-front resort accessible by a seven-mile long railroad, a wary Oscar Funcke moved to end the relationship. This unraveling required several years. Meanwhile, nature added disasters to Koch's woes when major hurricanes struck his Texas properties in 1915 and 1916.[11] With expenses soaring and income plunging, Theodore Koch faced an ominous future. By early 1917 proceeds from farm land in Renville County, Minnesota, and his percentage from sales of Ceresit, especially in the Chicago area, provided most of his income.[12]

When the United States declared war on Germany on April 4, 1917, Koch found himself both trading with the enemy and living in enmity with his relatives and business partners. He also knew that a severe wound already had ended their son-in-law's military career by Christmas of 1914. But American involvement interdicted direct communication with Germany. It would be a year and a half before letters would flow again.[13]

Years later, like many other Americans, Theodore Koch looked back on American entry into the war with a combination of revulsion and disgust, spiced with conspiracy theories. "Most of the people of the United States went into this war as if they were going into a pleasure exposition, and they did not consider sufficiently the seriousness of participating in the World War and the consequences which would flow from it."[14] He especially resented President Woodrow Wilson's pre-war vilification of the Germans, something Koch believed stemmed from

---

[10] "Geschäftsverbinden" (unattributed typescript in the collection of the Westfälisches Wirtschaftsarchiv, Dortmund).
[11] Koch, "Memoirs," 3:6, 15-16, 115, 121; Strubhart, 225-40; Henry Stob, *Summoning Up Remembrance* (Grand Rapids: Eerdmans, 1995), 6-9; Michael Cate, ed., *Port Arthur Centennial History: The Official Pictorial History of Port Arthur, Texas*, 2 vols. (Port Arthur: Looking Glass Media, 1998), 2:446-47, 518; Margaret S. Henson and Kevin Ladd, *Chambers County: A Pictorial History* (Norfolk: Downing Company, 1988), 101-2.
[12] Koch, "Memoirs," 3: 92; 94; http://books.google.com/books.
[13] Koch, "Memoirs," 3:91.
[14] Ibid., 3:84.

secret presidential promises made to French officials. Koch believed those presidential prejudices helped warp the administration's wartime policies.

In the summer of 1917 Theodore William Koch, the heir and apprentice, caught the patriotic spirit and joined the United States Army. He was assigned to the air service and officer's candidate school. By Christmas he was commissioned a first lieutenant and, despite being a novice, ordered to train pilots. His unit, the 372nd Aero Squadron, wandered from Texas to Long Island to Dayton, Ohio, before departing for Europe early in 1918. Narrowly passed over for an assignment in Vladivostok, Teddy's unit spent the duration of the war waiting for American combat airplanes in France.[15] He did his training in a British built de Havilland, and found time to visit the real Riviera while on leave.

The war scored a direct hit on Theodore F. Koch's businesses when Congress passed and President Wilson signed the Trading with the Enemy Act on 6 October 1917. With A. Mitchell Palmer ("the fighting Quaker") serving as the Alien Properties Custodian, the federal government set about seizing every enemy-owned asset in the United States—bank accounts, real estate, patents, securities—and sending an army of lawyers and accountants fanning throughout the land in search of every hidden German-owned asset. The Funcke family's American bank deposits were confiscated, as was the Ceresit Waterproofing Company and its all-important German patents.[16]

Koch retained Edward O. Brown, his long-time Chicago attorney, to challenge the federal government's right to seize a citizen's business.[17] Appearing before the War Trade Board in Washington, Brown argued, and the board agreed, that Koch, an American citizen since 1891, retained the right to conduct his business. While the Funckes clearly were Germans and their assets subject to seizure, Theodore. F. Koch & Company was a legal, American-owned corporation and not subject to confiscation. Koch regained access to the vital funds in Chicago's

---

[15] Ibid., 3:85-7. Teddy's unit was assigned to the base at Issoudon, south of Paris, where he joined the notables Eddie Rickenbacker and the Lafayette Escadrille.
[16] Koch "Memoirs," 3:92.
[17] Edward O. Brown (1844-1923) first became Koch's lawyer in 1886 in the wake of the sudden death of Martin W. Prins Jr. By 1917 he was serving as a judge of the Cook County Circuit Court. He was a founder and leader of the local chapter of the National Association for the Advancement of Colored People, as well as the Chicago Bar Association Law Club. Edward E. Brown (1885-1959), his son, was the lawyer for the First National Bank of Chicago, which held the Funcke family deposits the federal government seized under the Alien Properties Act of 1917.

First National Bank. The board, however, demanded a monthly accounting to ensure the monies were not used nefariously. As for the Ceresit Waterproofing Company, it remained with the Alien Property Custodian's office, administered by three appointed trustees.[18]

Meanwhile, back in Riviera, the local school principal was serving as the village's self-appointed super-patriot. With German American Catholics living by themselves to the northeast of town in an enclave centered about Our Lady of Consolation church, there was much to fuel paranoia in the community.[19]

To the drawling principal it mattered little that his school had been built, in part, thanks to donations of the Germanic-accented Theodore F. Koch. Even worse, Mrs. Koch did nothing to cloak her affinities for her kinsmen. Surrounded by these threats to the nation, the principal summoned the student body to an assembly "haranguing them on pure Americanism, [saying] that he and others, full-blooded Americans, had a duty to perform, which was to clean this country of hyphen-Americans . . . and that the parents of full-blooded and true Americans should club together and wipe out these serpents and kill them off." The Kochs had no doubt as to whom the principal was referring. According to family lore, before the entire student body, the principal singled out eleven-year-old Walter Koch as one of the serpents. Theodore and Clara immediately removed Walter from the school.[20]

Thanks to the zealous principal's reports to the authorities, Theodore F. Koch soon received an unannounced visit from a federal investigator. The G-man strode into Koch's office one day and closed the door for a confidential interview. He asked Koch why he did not support the American war effort. A flabbergasted Koch retorted "that to the best of my knowledge I had not made any utterances which could be considered as unfavorable to the United States."[21]

---

[18] "Memoirs," 3:92-93; Records of the Office of Alien Property, Records of the Division of Mail and Files, Office of Alien Property Index to General Correspondence 1917-1940, box 5, files #3621-2401, #4493-6064 (National Archives, Takoma Park, MD).

[19] One sign of the parishioners' devotion was the construction of their new church. The first building (wooden) was destroyed in the 1916 hurricane. The second one was being built from bricks the church's members made themselves, using clay dredged from the bottom of Baffin Bay. This church still stands.

[20] Koch, "Memoirs," 3:85-88. Regarding Walter's departure from the school, Koch does not include this in his writings. Family lore suggests that Walter was immediately sent to St. Paul Academy (author's interview with James T. Koch, Aug. 1993). As best as can be ascertained, Walter did not formally enroll at St. Paul Academy until 1921.

[21] Ibid., 3:89.

Koch buttressed this assertion by producing a portfolio containing $20,000 in Liberty Bonds he had bought. The agent then added a second allegation; the government had reason to believe Koch had been receiving military secrets from a Lt. Koch. Again repairing to the vault, Koch produced every letter Teddy Koch had sent home since joining the service, including ones Teddy had censored himself in his capacity as an officer. The investigator noted the absence of letters sent from Georgia, the source of the incriminating letters from Lt. Koch. Theodore countered that Teddy had never been assigned to a base in Georgia. Clearly there was another Lt. Theodore W. Koch somewhere in the armed forces.

Although the agent, now satisfied, rose to leave, Theodore F. Koch was far from satisfied with the insinuations and suspicions that prompted the meeting. His honesty had been seriously questioned, something that in other times had sent him to the courts for redress. He demanded that Clara Koch, despite her verbal indiscretions, also be exonerated. Koch escorted the agent from the office to the house for a private talk with Clara to "get her version on these various questions." After spending an hour and a half hearing the Kochs refute every claim, rumor, and insinuation, the agent assured the couple that "he would give us a clean slate and from now on no accusations against us or our son would be considered."[22]

That Koch remained less than magnanimous about the local school principal should not be any great surprise. Almost twenty years later, he concluded his account of Riviera's patriotic hysteria by noting that the school board had soon removed the principal for unspecified reasons. The administrator took a position in the northern part of the state, and "within a year he made acquaintance with the inside of the County jail for having dipped personally in the funds of the school." Patriotism, indeed, had been the last refuge of a scoundrel.

For the duration of the war, the national mobilization severely restricted Theodore Koch's business activities. The government's demand for building materials severely hampered efforts to rebuild his hurricane ravaged hotel. And wartime travel restrictions kept the tourists far away from the remote peninsula in Baffin Bay. The little railroad built in 1911 stopped operating, and would be abandoned and sold for salvage after the war.

When the Armistice ended the shooting in Europe, the first letters from Germany told of hardships and shortages. Clara promptly

[22] Koch, "Memoirs," 3: 90-91.

began assembling relief packages. On slow days she sent an eleven-pound parcel; on days when others could help, she would ship even more supplies. Theodore used his New York contacts to arrange larger shipments of food, clothing, canned milk, and condiments, earmarked for relatives, friends, or general distribution in the afflicted areas.[23]

Lt. Theodore William Koch returned from France the following spring. Having seen "gay Paree" (and the Riviera and a number of other places in Europe), Teddy chose to meet his family in St. Paul, not Riviera. Old Theodore convinced young Theodore to resume working in the family enterprises, at least for a while. Theodore the Elder concentrated on rebuilding the family's fortunes in the nearby resort hotel and reviving the real estate business. Young Theodore became president of the Riviera State Bank and worked to wrest the family's assets from the clutches of the Alien Property Custodian.

Theodore Koch wrote of the Funckes, "The people in Hagen had lost millions in consequence of the war. Two large estates in Alsace and Lorraine [purchased after the Franco-Prussian War] "had been absolutely confiscated . . . without a cent of compensation."[24] The Versailles Treaty ensured that the Funckes' investments in the United States, Great Britain, and the British Empire would disappear into the black hole of reparations. Germany's new government promised to compensate citizens for documented losses in Allied countries, causing Oscar Funcke to seek an exact account of how much his bank deposits had been worth on 7 April 1917.[25] After several years, Teddy Koch finally uncovered the number in the custodian's records. To salvage a few more crumbs, Funcke hoped the Kochs might redeem the Ceresit Waterproofing Company.

Under the act of 1917, only American citizens could purchase the properties the custodian's office held. But there could be no sales without congressional authorization, and that did not arrive until 1922.[26] Then Teddy Koch moved to get cash for the Funckes and unencumbered titles to all their joint land holdings. First he worked to salvage Ceresit. The company's value had declined under

---

[23] Ibid., 3:132. The volume of parcels being sent from Riviera prompted the post office department to upgrade the local office from third to second class, meaning the town would now have a full-time paid postmaster.

[24] Ibid., 3:99.

[25] Theodore F. Koch to Alien Property Custodian, 8 Dec. 1919, in Records of the Office of Alien Property, Records of the Division of Mail and Files, File #3822 Box 66, National Archives, Washington, DC.

[26] Director of Trusts to Theodore F. Koch, 16 Dec. 1919, in Records of the Office of Alien Property, Records of the Division of Mail and Files, File #3822 Box 66, National Archives, Washington, DC.

the government's administration. Yet Teddy convinced a buyer to pay $10,000 for shares with an estimated market value of $2,000.[27] Teddy then convinced the United States Attorney for northern Illinois to plead the case for unsnarling the Texas real estate situation. Teddy and the attorney made the rounds in Washington, meeting with members of the War Trade Board, Alien Property Custodian Thomas W. Miller, and Attorney General Harry M. Daughtery.

Miller ruled that his agency would be willing to hold an auction for the Funcke's land holdings if Oscar Funcke and his relatives would state in writing their minimum price for the land Theodore F. Koch & Company controlled in Texas. During July Teddy met Oscar Funcke in Germany. Despite believing his real estate to have been worth at least $200,000 in 1915, Funcke signed a letter placing its value at only $75,000. At the public auction held that fall, Theodore W. Koch, the sole bidder, bought the properties for the agreed amount. Theodore F. Koch raised the money by mortgaging his Minnesota farms. For him the Great War finally ended in the fall of 1922, leaving him deeply in debt, but back in business.[28]

Teddy Koch left Riviera soon afterward, and headed to St. Paul where he married, minded his brother Walter during his high school years, and became the manager of the local office of Lee, Higginson & Co. When that ill-favored firm collapsed amid scandal in 1932, Teddy opened his own investment consulting business. Walter Koch followed Teddy's footsteps and went to Harvard, graduating cum laude in 1929. After a year, he enrolled in Harvard Law School, graduated, moved back to Texas, and became his father's attorney. Among the Texas lands Theodore F. Koch reclaimed in 1922 were tracts located forty miles west of Beaumont, the site of an unsuccessful Dutch farm colony near the hamlets of Winnie and Hampshire. Although he eventually disposed of the surface rights during the Depression, Koch retained the mineral rights. Beginning in the 1930s, some of those tracts proved to stand atop oil reserves worth far more than the surface would ever realize as farm land. One of the longer term consequences of the Great War was the fact that those petroleum deposits produced more returns to Theodore Koch and his descendants than the Funckes realized from all the cash they had invested in Koch's endeavors for thirty years.[29]

[27] Ceresit Waterproofing is still marketed in Europe; Henkel AG of Dusseldorf, Germany owns the brand.
[28] Koch, "Memoirs," 3:101-4; http://search.ancestry.com.
[29] Herbert Roedenbeck to Theodore W. Koch, 7 June 1958, 7 July 1958, 25 July 1958, 27 Aug. 1958; Theodore W. Koch to Herbert Roedenbeck, 2 July 1958; Theodore F. Koch to Herbert Roedenbeck, 14 Mar. 1934 (folders 9, 13, Herbert Roedenbeck Papers, Tyrell Historical Library Collection, Beaumont, TX).

When advancing age forced Theodore F. Koch into retirement, he spent time evaluating his life and recording his stories in a lengthy memoir. He continued to communicate with his living European relatives. His son-in-law and grandson paid visits to Texas in 1935 and 1936. And the letters kept flowing back and forth with the Hoeborns in Germany. Koch's Dutch connections thinned as he outlived his siblings in the Netherlands. When war again descended across Europe in 1939, Koch's caretakers worried about how Clara and he would react if Germany and the Netherlands came to blows. When that happened in May 1940, Theodore Koch's radio became "defective" and his newspapers edited to keep secret Holland's demise at the hands of the Germans. For about two months the old man remained oblivious to the occupation of his homeland. Late that summer, an old sea captain friend came to visit in Corpus Christi. During their lengthy conversation the Dutch sailor broke the news to Koch.

The country of his birth was at war with the country of his heritage, while the country of his choice officially stood aside as a spectator. Given his political bent, Koch could not be a Nazi sympathizer. But the Germans were still his relatives—grandchildren, nieces, and nephews. Here again was a contradiction Theodore Koch could not resolve. Within a matter of weeks, illness set in, as Theodore and Clara made their way toward the Hill Country to escape the late summer Gulf Coast heat. A chill turned into pneumonia when they reached New Braunfels. On 19 September 1940 Theodore F. Koch died at the age of eighty-six. A certificate listed the cause of death in medical terms, but the underlying cause was equally certain—conflicting loyalties. Part Dutch, part German, part American: proud of being each, yet not all of any one. Such was Koch's lot in life, as an immigrant, a husband, and an entrepreneur.

CHAPTER 8

Dutch Americans in World War One: In the Fog of International Law

Huug van den Dool

Introduction

Like all Dutch Americans with some interest in history, we hear stories about compatriots in times past from friends and colleagues and even from complete strangers.[1] A Dutch name and accent can invite such openness. In this way, an entirely random collection of stories emerge. I have registered some of these stories, and this publication is an occasion to relate some concerning Dutch Americans in the First World War. I first heard some of these stories from ten to twenty years ago, but only after researching the facts and context did sub-themes emerge for the chapter. A major sub-theme is the fog of international law evident in the call up of young males into military service.

There were many people of Dutch ancestry residing in the United States at the time the United States entered the Great War in April

---

[1] I wish to acknowledge the help of David Matthews, Claire and Dorothy Williams, and Paula Vander Hoven, who were essential informants for the three stories. Additionally I thank Robert P. Swierenga for allowing me to draw on *Holland, Michigan: From Dutch Colony to Dynamic City* ahead of publication, Nynke van der Hooven and Fons Baede for their help with Frisian genealogy, and David R. Rodenhuis for his critical reading of the text.

1917. The government required those who were not citizens to register for the draft, and many served on active duty. Quite a diversity of Dutch Americans did serve, although many did not or were not required to, but I will focus mostly on those who were not yet citizens. These very same Dutch citizens living in the United States were also summoned in a decree by Queen Wilhelmina in 1914, three years earlier, to serve in the army of their native country. The Netherlands did not know at this time whether they could maintain neutrality, so they built up their military in preparation for war. Although the call up was hard to enforce and just ignoring the decree would do, the Queen nevertheless netted about seventy-five men from Ottawa and Kent counties in Michigan, according to the *Grand Rapids Herald*.[2]

The experiences of Edward J. Matthews and Nicolas Williams illustrate this quirk of history. The names may not sound Dutch, because these were the names adopted some time after their immigration; originally their names respectively were Oeds van der Goot, born in 1894 in Sloten, province of Friesland, and Nicolaas Wilhelm, born in 1888 in Hoorn, province of North Holland.

Changing one's name is quite common for immigrants, and without a relative telling me about these two people, there would have been little chance to track them.[3] Oeds van der Goot made research particularly difficult by changing his name several times. Upon arrival in 1911, he changed to Edward Vander, that is, he completely dropped the "Goot" part. To the Dutch ear it is strange to drop Goot because it leaves us with Vander "nothing," but it is of course a personal decision. Edward's brother Tjeerd, who arrived in 1913, carried on as Charles Vandergoot.

By comparison, Nicolaas Wilhelm's name change is easier to understand. Changing Nicolaas to "Nicholas" may have been hard to avoid, but it is noteworthy that he ultimately insisted on Nicolas without the "h." The use of "Wilhelm" as a last name was a real liability, since it has a distinct German origin, even though this name is reasonably common in the Netherlands. Great animosity was directed during the

---

[2] Janet Sjaarda Sheeres, "The Dutch Military," *Dutch International Magazine* 44, no. 1 (June 2012): 13-16.

[3] I wish to acknowledge the assistance of David Matthews (son of Oeds van der Goot) and Claire Williams (granddaughter of Nicolaas Wilhelm). Without their initial remarks priming my interest, these stories could not be told. In spite of their Anglicized names, and living outside the well-known Dutch churches and settlements in such places as Iowa or Michigan, both Edward and Nicolas persisted in Dutch habits in their personal life (Delft blue, speculaas, Dutch tea spoons, etc). This was to the amazement and amusement of their siblings.

Fig. 8.1. Edward Matthews

Fig. 8.2. Nicolas Williams

Great War toward the Germans (e.g., "Fritz," and "Huns") and especially toward Kaiser Wilhelm II. Explaining to suspicious neighbors or the commanding officer that you are really Dutch ("not German") would not help very much. The words "Dutch" and "Deutsch" are perilously close. The Dutch were suspected to be more sympathetic toward Germany than to the United Kingdom anyway.[4] Moreover, Nicolas had married into a family of recent German immigrants, thereby increasing the suggestion he may be German himself. The modified name of "Nicolas Williams" was chosen as the right solution at that moment of history.

During the AADAS 2013 Conference in Pella, Iowa, Paula Vander Hoven, a fellow attendee, informed me of her relative, John L. Vanderhoven (originally Johan Ludwig van der Hoeven), whose life fits the theme. I also discovered the work of two individuals, Dutch journalist Jorge Groen, and Erasmus University professor Martin Kraaijestein, who were also of great help. The pair has compiled a major data collection, statistics, and personal stories on Dutch Americans in the First World War that provide context for individual biographies.

Context and sources

Given the voluminous histories of the First World War, only a brief overview is needed here. When the United States finally entered the First World War in April of 1917, its military consisted of a small

---

[4] Earl Wm. Kennedy, "Dutch Zion Besieged and Breached: Orange City, 1914-1918," Proceedings of the AADAS Conference, Northwestern College, Orange City, Iowa, 1995.

force of five hundred thousand. Both the desperate need for assistance at the front lines and President Woodrow Wilson's desire to use military power to enable him to help shape the peace led to rapid mobilization and a dramatic increase in the size of the armed forces. In May of 1917, Congress passed the Selective Draft Act, which established mandatory conscription, and by the war's end eighteen months later, the armed forces totaled more than 3.5 million service members. The rapid incorporation of new personnel forced military leaders to address issues such as the assimilation of large numbers of immigrant soldiers. They would successfully handle such concerns despite deeply divisive pre-existing ethnic antagonisms that were exacerbated by "Americanization" campaigns among the civilian population during the war.[5]

The nation had to increase its military by a factor of seven in a very short time. This was a major undertaking, and the draft board was not picky. Every young male in a certain age bracket was fair game. The government threw its net far and wide. Only draftees who were citizens of enemy countries were excused up front in the first draft, something that contributed greatly to the animosity toward the foreigners living next door. Officially, the enemy was a strange collection of far-away nations: Germany, Austria-Hungary, Turkey, and portions of the Balkan such as Bulgaria, but these enemies were invariably composited in the mind as "Germany"—facts have to be simple in time of war. In practice, the burden of proof lay with the individual to show why he did not have to serve in the army on account of not being an American citizen or a citizen born in an enemy nation.

To detail the stories of Dutch American soldiers, M. Kraaijestein's website addresses specifically the situation of non-Americans, including Dutch nationals, in the United States draft.[6] Groen studied Dutch nationals fighting in the Great War, which is puzzling considering that the Netherlands was officially neutral.[7]

The mandatory registrations (there were several) starting in June 1917 yielded twenty-five million men, of whom four million were not American citizens. Among them were 27,190 Dutch citizens. The non-

[5] Rhonda Evans, *A History of the Service of Ethnic Minorities in the U.S. Armed Forces* (Berkeley: Institute for Labor and Employment, University of California,), 2003; http://www.palmcenter.org/files/active/0/Evans_MinorityInt_200306.pdf.
[6] Martin Kraaijestein, 2002, Erasmus University, Rotterdam. See his website (in Dutch) at http://www.wereldoorlog1418.nl/oorlogsnieuws/nederlanders.htm.
[7] Jorge Groen, *Nederlanders in de Grote Oorlog* (Boom, 2004). For updates on Groen's website at http://www.greatdutchwar.nl/, click on Verenigde Staten. Groen has links on his (Dutch language) website for each of the specific countries for which Dutch nationals fought, then further links to personalized stories.

Americans were divided by the government into *declarants* (1.3 million) and *non-declarants* (2.7 million). Obviously, this was a unilateral move by the American government, not cleared with other nations. The declarants are those who had already applied for American citizenship; they had limited recourse to appeal being drafted, since they had already expressed their loyalty to the United States.

The non-declarants would keep their original nationality in many cases, and to avoid the draft, they would have to work with their own embassies. Most failed to accomplish this complicated process, either for lack of time or because they did not know the language very well. The Dutch embassy and consulates, although working overtime, did not process more than about five hundred applications. Most of the non-declarants thus ended up being drafted and inducted into military service; in some documented cases this was strongly against their will. This pool of draftees included people who had lived in the United States for only a few months or less and had no intention of staying there.

Not all draftees had to serve. Some were excused because they failed the medical examination or their number did not come up in the lottery. Jorge Groen reports that non-declarants were given distinctly worse and more dangerous assignments than declarants. Somewhere between one thousand and twenty-five hundred Dutch nationals actually served. Not much has been documented about them, but Groen gives forty-three names (see appendix), with stories (ranging in size from one sentence to a complete essay) that he collected from letters and relatives. The most famous is Louis van Iersel, a Dutch citizen who came from the Netherlands in spring of 1917.[8] He both filled out his draft registration card and applied for citizenship on the same day in June of that year. Not taking any chances, he then volunteered! It is remarkable that he received the nation's highest military honor, the Medal of Honor. Only thirty-five hundred such medals have been awarded from the Civil War to the present, a mere 191 for valor in the First World War. The Medal of Honor for a non-citizen must be very rare.

Robert Swierenga's comprehensive history of Holland, Michigan, recounts the hysteria gripping the populace. Everyone was expected to participate in the war effort in some way, and neighbors were watching each other with suspicion. Regarding the military draft, Swierenga stated that "many Dutch in Holland came in the last big wave before the war and were not yet American citizens, which made them exempt from

---

[8] See http://en.wikipedia.org/wiki/Ludovicus_M._M._Van_Iersel.

the military draft. That they prospered in the booming war economy while neighbors went off to fight aroused considerably animosity."[9] Being "exempt" seemed rational enough, but this is not how it worked for many (chapter 10). The neighbors lacked hard facts, or were not really interested in excuses anyway, so it was easier for them to make sweeping assumptions about potential draftees.

To serve or not to serve

Imagine that you lived in a foreign country, and one day you were summoned to show up to register for the draft. Thousands of Dutch Americans faced this situation in 1917. What to do? To fight a European war would have been the last thing they expected after crossing the ocean. Moreover, President Woodrow Wilson had been re-elected in 1916 on the stated achievement that he "kept us out of war." On the other hand, it was just a registration for the draft, not yet an induction. Why not go with the flow? In retrospect we know only about 10 percent of draftees actually served, the other 90 percent got off by the luck of the lottery, the medical exam, or some other ploy. Not that our boys knew these chances *a-priori*. And to refuse to register would certainly have come with some serious risks. Even the acceptance of valid excuses would have been treated differently in each community, since each draft board was composed of local people.

The young males in the general category of Dutch Americans who were facing the 1917 draft can be classified as follows:

- a. Those born in the United States to (very) recent immigrants. Examples are: Willem Zuiderveld, Abraham Desomer,[10] and Henry Wolters. Wolters was an early casualty, and the Veterans of Foreign Wars post in Holland, Michigan, is named after him. These men grew up in a largely Dutch American environment but were American citizens *de facto*.
- b. Immigrants who had already become citizens before the draft in June 1917. An example is Nicolaas Wilhelm.
- c. Declarants: immigrants who had applied to become citizens. An example is Edward Vander, who became a naturalized citizen, as did John Vanderhoven.

---

[9] Robert P. Swierenga, *Holland, Michigan: From Dutch Colony to Dynamic City*, 3 vols. (Grand Rapids: Eerdmans; Holland: Van Raalte Press, 2014), 2:1495-1540.

[10] DeSomer and Zuiderveld received the Medal of Honor for their valor in the Vera Cruz mission. See http://en.wikipedia.org/wiki/List_of_Medal of_Honor recipients %28Veracruz%29.

    d. Non-declarants: immigrants who had not yet applied, or had no intention to apply, to become citizens. An example is Rudolf Mook.

    e. Volunteers: Dutch Nationals who *volunteered* for service in the US military. An example is Louis van Iersel.

All these were Dutch Americans, actual or future, but at the moment of registering for the draft, their legal status varied greatly.

The government anticipated legal challenges from men in categories *c* and *d*, so it applied a Solomonic judgment *a-priori* by dividing the pool of non-American draftees into two groups: declarants and non-declarants. Declarants were fair game as far as the government was concerned, even if this were debatable for scholars in arm chairs. Non-declarants could appeal, but without knowing English very well, not understanding their rights, essentially without legal help, and being otherwise intimidated by their predicament, they generally could not avoid the draft.

The recruiting officers exerted pressure on non-declarants to become declarant. One of Groen's forty-three stories is of Rudolf Mook, a merchant seaman who made frequent visits to the United States. Mook was inducted under duress, caused by extreme peer pressure and even being repeatedly tied up and put in a cold shower. To end the torment, he promised to apply for citizenship, but he then managed to avoid this step with help from the Dutch consulate.[11] Concerned relatives induced the Dutch government to intervene, and in July 1918, the American government relented and excused draftees from neutral countries, in addition to those from enemy countries. It is doubtful that the soldiers already serving at the time were properly informed about this subtle change. Moreover, to discourage soldiers from opting out of service, a footnote was added: those who opted out could no longer become citizens. Clearly, the privilege of citizenship was used as a carrot and a stick.

Many draftees went to great lengths to avoid being inducted. Some married and could thus claim a dependent, their spouse. Both Edward and Nicolas married within days of the date of their draft.

Such tactics were viewed very negatively by American patriots. The Holland, Michigan, Common Council made it a misdemeanor to avoid the draft by subterfuge. "Good" neighbors turned in slackers and

---

[11] Still, Mook would become a US citizen many decades later, and he lived until the age of 91 in Oregon. Ironically he was drafted again in the Second World War in the "old man's draft."

loafers. Holland mayor Gerrit J. Diekema paused during a patriotic speech in April 1917 to look into the eyes of young women in the crowd and warn them sternly not to marry a young man to "save him from conscription." This was an act akin to treason, Diekema declared. Dentists were also warned not to pull teeth of suspected slackers.[12]

Some young men were volunteers at heart and could not wait to get into action. Louis van Iersel came to the United States to volunteer. Cornelius van Putten, an American citizen living in Holland, Michigan, traveled to Glasgow, Scotland, in 1914 to fight for the British. He announced naively that he was American, which disqualified him from serving, but the British recruiting officer told him to take a walk around the block and come back as a Canadian. And so he did—as "Patrick McCoy" from Canada. Subsequently, he became a local celebrity when the United States "finally" joined the war three years later.[13]

The three men with altered names—Edward J. Matthews, Nicolas Williams, and John L. Vanderhoven—exemplify Dutch Americans who were caught up in military service in the First World War. Oeds van der Goot (Edward J. Matthews) immigrated with brother Tjeerd (Charles) and sister Jeltje (Jean), along with van der Goot and Atte Bouma, both seventeen-year-old carpenters. The four arrived in New York on 27 March 1911 on the *Nieuw Amsterdam*. Van der Goot's stated destination was Chicago, perhaps to join Bouma's brother-in-law. Fairly soon, however, Oeds van der Goot became Edward Vander, and he moved to Cleveland, Ohio, where a small group of immigrants from Sloten had settled earlier. In a typical chain emigration, his sister Jean de Boer and brother Charles came to Cleveland in 1912 and 1913, respectively.

In June 1917 Edward Vander was drafted for military service. Ten months later, on April 1918, he was *inducted* in Cleveland into the army, and served as a machine gunner with the American Expeditionary Forces in France and Italy, until his discharge on 5 July 1918. Wounded by a shell in the battle of Piave River, Italy,[14] on 13 October 1918, he was shipped back to Ohio, where he recovered in a US Army Hospital. He lost the use of his left elbow for the rest of his life. After a long recovery, he was honorably discharged on 3 March 1921 from Walter Reed General Hospital in Washington, DC. He received the Silver Victory button and other medals. He signed his discharge papers as "Edward H. Vander."[15]

[12] Swierenga, *Holland, Michigan*, 2:1496, 1500.
[13] Ibid., 2:1502-3.
[14] http://en.wikipedia.org/wiki/Italian Campaign_%28World_War_I%29.
[15] As middle initial, he used usually *J*, but sometimes *H*, without ever spelling out these letters. Sometime late 1940, around the time of his second marriage,

Vander became a naturalized citizen on 19 July 1919 and became an FBI security guard in Washington, DC; during the Great Depression years from 1930 to 1935, he lived again in Sloten, Friesland. He died in 1955 without ever speaking to his son about the Great War. Edward Vander is buried in Arlington National Cemetery on the hillside above McCelland Gate east of Grant Road near the US Navy Cruiser Memorial in section 33, grave number 320.

Nicolaas Wilhelm (Nicolas Williams) immigrated as a seventeen-year-old around 1906; he lived first in Texas and then in Detroit, Michigan, where he held various jobs—lumbering, confectionary, farming, mail carrier, and real estate. In 1913 he enlisted in the Signal Corps as an electrician and served in the Vera Cruz occupation for six months in 1914 and then in the Philippine Islands for nine months, until his discharge in June 1916. Williams' military records state that his service was "honest & faithful," no unauthorized absences, no furloughs. He became a naturalized citizen in June 1917 under the name Nicolas Williams, and then married just ahead of the draft. Although written proof is lacking, he probably earned an "accelerated path" to citizenship for his military service from 1913 to 1916.[16]

Johan Ludwig van der Hoeven (John L. Vanderhoven) was born on 23 August 1887 in Rotterdam. He too immigrated alone, leaving four siblings behind, and arrived in February 1913 settling in Grand Rapids, Michigan. He also changed his last name, although only slightly to John Vanderhoven. He was called into military service on 22 June 1918. The order of induction read in part:

> Having submitted yourself to a local board composed of your neighbors for the purpose of determining the place and time in which you can best serve the United States in the present emergency, you are hereby notified that you have been selected for immediate military service.

Vanderhoven was inducted at Fort Custer, Michigan, in June 1918 and was assigned to the American Expeditionary Force, known as the "Polar Bears," near Archangel, Russia.[17] Despite the Armistice on 11 November 1918, this sideshow was little known at the time and

---

he changed his name to Edward J. Matthews, even if his name in the Arlington cemetery administration continues to be (to this day!) the one with which he served in the military, Edward Vander.
[16] Main advantage for enlisted men seeking US citizenship was that the five-year continuous residency requirement was reduced or waived altogether.
[17] http://en.wikipedia.org/wiki/North_Russia_Intervention.

not well understood afterward. A few thousand American troops were sent to stop the Bolshevik Revolution. The Polar Bears received a special welcome home many months later.[18]

Vanderhoven was a professional musician and played the organ and piano. He began his career as a salesman for the Friedrick Music House. He gave private lessons and concerts, and was a church organist for Christian Reformed congregations—Broadway (later Westview) in Grand Rapids, in Highland, Indiana, and in Cutlerville, a Grand Rapids suburb. In the Highland period he tried his hand at farming as well. John also was a composer. In 1933 he won a contest for composing the tune to the poem, "By the Sea of Crystal," which became the theme song for the denomination's international radio program, "The Back to God Hour." Family lore has it that Vanderhoven before immigration had been a member of the *Koninklijke Militaire Kapel*, a military band that performed for the Dutch Royal family. This means he served in the Dutch Army before doing another round in the US military. He was never wounded in war, but during the interminable Russian winter of 1918-19, he became very ill and had to be evacuated by dog sled to Archangel.

Conclusion

This chapter tells the story of Dutch Americans whose lives intersected with a horrific event in world history, the First World War. The situation of each was unique, but the most peculiar were the young men who were still Dutch citizens at the time they were registered for the United States draft. These men could possibly have avoided enlisting in the "foreign" army. In practice, however, the burden of proof for exemption was on the draftee, and it seems that some managed to avoid the draft, in spite of the fact that they may have been legally exempt.

In the fog of international law, orders to register came both from the Dutch and the US governments. The rules by which the US government drafted young men were clearly unilateral, not negotiated, and agreed upon by other nations. Neutral countries had a hard time staying neutral. The Netherlands barely made it, and having its citizens join the fight was a liability, while maintaining an official policy of neutrality.

About 10 percent of those who actively served in the US military were not citizens. In addition, a significant percentage of those who served were recent immigrants or had grown up in ethnic enclaves.

---

[18] Swierenga, *Holland, Michigan*, 2:1536-38.

English was a second language for many, so the military had a communications problem. Since all outgoing mail had to be censored, there was plenty of work for translators. From their statistics we know that Dutch was the fourth most common foreign language, after Italian, Swedish, and Danish.

The American government needed collaboration from Dutch embassies to sort out complicated cases of non-declarants in the First World War. They got some, but not nearly enough to process all cases. When, however, the shoe was on the other foot in the Second World War, the Dutch government in exile in London tried to induct its citizens living abroad into the Dutch army, and the American government gave no cooperation.[19]

Some mythology has developed over the years in terms of the military enlistments. Believing that immigrants joined the army to become citizens puts a confusingly positive spin on something far more complex. And draft avoidance took many forms, including marriage and changing one's family name. Edward Vander and Nicolas Wilhelm were both married within days of their registration, hoping it would reduce the chance they would have to serve. The trick did not work for Edward Vander. Barbara De Witt told me that her American-born Dutch uncles were able to avoid the draft by simply changing their names from Van Driel to Van Dreal, which confused the draft board.[20]

---

[19] Gerlof Homan, "Recruitment of Dutch Nationals in the United States for the Netherlands Armed Forces in the Second World War," Proceedings of AADAS Conference at Trinity Christian College, Palos Heights, Illinois, 1987.
[20] Personal communication with Barbara De Witt early 2013.

Appendix

Jorge Groen's list of Dutch Nationals who fought for the United States. One can find more details about any of them at http://www.greatdutchwar.nl.

Pieter Bil	Albert J. Decker
Hendrik Elbert	Thomas van der Feen
Theodorus de Groot	Thomas de Groot
William de Groot	Gustaaf Hermans
Albert van der Heig	Meinze Hettinga
Henry Hijlkema	Johannes Hoogeveen
Louis van Iersel	Petrus Jansen
Albertus Kamps	Dirk Kooy
Remy Leufkens	Johannes Meijer
Floris van Minden	Rudolf Mook
Johannes Nederpelt	Peter Nuiver
Johannes Overmars	Arthur Preijer
Minze Radema	Gosen Roften
Jan Romeyn	E. J. de Ronde
Abram van Rossum	John Schapendonk
Johannes Slavenburg	Pieter van Soest
Harm Timmer	Allen Tromp
Johannes Uphof	Jeremias Visser
Peter Vanderlaan	Albert Vandermeer
Peter Vanderveer	Berend Veltkamp
Edward de Vries	Catherinus van der Wal
David Witmond	

CHAPTER 9

Abraham Johannes Muste: American Pacifist Extraordinaire

Gerlof Homan

Few individuals have had a greater impact on the American peace movement in the years of the Second World War and the Cold War than Abraham Johannes Muste (1885-1967). In 1940 *Time* magazine called him the "number one US pacifist," a title he carried through the turbulent sixties.[1] His influence stemmed from his robust peace theology and active participation in the peace and civil rights movements.[2]

Unlike many peace reformers, Muste grew up in a Calvinist home. Few if any American peace activists were followers of John Calvin. Peace reform was rarely an option in Calvinist circles. Muste was born in 1885

---

[1] *Time*, 10 July 1939.
[2] The best biography of Abraham J. Muste is Jo Ann Ooiman Robinson, *Abraham Went Out: A Biography of A.J. Muste* (Philadelphia: Temple University Press, 1981). See also "A. J. Muste and Ways to Peace," *in Peace Movements in America*, ed., Charles Hatfield (New York: Schocken Books, 1974), 81-94; Nat Hentoff, *Peace Agitator:The Story of A. J. Muste* (New York: MacMillan, 1963); William G. Batz, "Revolution and Peace: The Christian Pacifism of A. J. Muste, 1885-1967" (PhD Dissertation, University of Minnesota, 1974); and Norman J. Whitney, "Number One Pacifist," *Christian Century* (10 May 1967): 622-24.

in the medieval city of Zierikzee in the province of Zeeland.[3] In 1891, when Muste was six years old, the family immigrated to Grand Rapids and joined Fourth Reformed Church. It was a very pious and religious home. Young Abraham was enrolled in a public school, where one day a potentially violent situation had an unexpected outcome. He had intentionally tripped a boy, who with the help of some of his friends, threatened to pummel him after school. Abraham, however, decided not to respond, and nothing happened. At age thirteen, young Abraham joined the Reformed Church by making a public profession of faith. As would happen again later in life, he had a mystical experience that led him to take this step of faith. After elementary school he attended Hope Preparatory School and Hope College. He was an eager and bright student with a keen and enquiring mind, who loved oratory and Shakespeare.

Upon graduation in 1905 he taught briefly at Northwestern Classical Academy in Orange City, Iowa, where he was close to his lady friend, Anna Huizinga, whom he married in 1909. Abraham and Anne had three children: Anne Dorothy, always called Nancy; Constance "Connie"; and John. Connie was the only pacifist of the three, and her death in 1965 was a serious loss for Muste. John joined the US Navy during the Second World War. Since John was only seventeen years of age, Abraham had to sign consent papers, which must have been a very difficult act for him, given his pacifist beliefs. Following the war, however, John also became a strong supporter of peace movements.

In 1906 Abraham enrolled in the Reformed New Brunswick Theological Seminary and entered the Reformed Church ministry following graduation in 1909. He served the Fort Washington Collegiate Church in Manhattan, New York, from 1909 to 1914, and was much appreciated by the parishioners. He pursued a second divinity degree at the liberal Union Theological Seminary in New York City and graduated *magna cum laude* in 1913. During his time at Union, he became increasingly disenchanted with the denomination of his birth and heritage. In 1914 he accepted a call from the Central Congregational Church in Newtonville, Massachusetts. The next year he received an honorable dismissal from the Reformed Church in America, much to the regret of his ministerial colleagues and former mentors at Hope College and New Brunswick Seminary. They rightly felt he could have had a very distinguished career as a Reformed churchman and scholar.

[3] The Martin Muste family might have been French Huguenots who escaped persecution of Calvinists by the French Catholic monarchy. Families with the surname Musté are found in France, Italy, and Spain.

Fig. 9.1. Abraham Muste lecturing at Pendle Hill, c. 1940 (*courtesy Joint Archives of Holland*)

By this time Muste espoused the Social Gospel and Progressive Movements and voted for socialist Eugene Debs for president in the 1912 national election. Muste also had joined the Fellowship of Reconciliation (FOR), a Christian pacifist group. The steps in this spiritual transformation are not clear. Besides being influenced by professors at Union Seminary, he may have read the popular Russian writer and Christian pacifist, Leo Tolstoy, and the Quaker mystic, Rufus Jones. A close reading of the New Testament, especially the Sermon on the Mount, completed the spiritual journey.

Muste's pacifist faith was severely tested when the United States in April 1917 declared war on Germany and joined the Allies in the First World War. The hyper-patriotism of the time discomfited him, and he found it very difficult to minister to Newtonville parishioners who had lost sons in France. Although his congregation tolerated his anti-war stance, he felt increasingly uncomfortable and decided to resign as pastor in December 1917. The church board reluctantly accepted his resignation in March 1918, and they wrote a sterling letter of recommendation. "We feel that we have been led these three years by a man of unusual genius and consecration. . . . His life among us has been marked by gentleness and unfailing Christian courtesy."[4]

A short while later, Muste joined the Quakers and became involved with labor union activities. In 1919 he played a leading role in the Lawrence, Massachusetts, textile workers strike and urged union

[4] Robinson, *Abraham Went Out*, 22-23.

members to remain non-violent. In 1921 he began a twelve-year stint as director of Brookwood Labor College in Katoneh, New York. He resigned in 1933 after becoming disenchanted with the college's laid back attitude. Drifting away from his Christian pacifism, he founded the left-wing American Workers Party, which formed an alliance with the Trotskyist Communist League of America. In 1936 Muste was jolted back to Christian pacifism during a visit to the St. Sulpice Church in Paris, where he had another mystical experience. When entering the church he felt "a deep and singing peace" and heard a voice saying, "this is where you belong, in the church, not outside it."[5]

Upon his return to America, Muste rejoined the Fellowship of Reconciliation and was welcomed back with open arms. FOR had been founded in England in 1914 and came to the United States in 1915. Muste helped establish the Boston chapter in 1916, and for many years he remained active in the national organization, joining the board as executive secretary in 1940 and serving until his retirement in 1953. FOR was a small organization, committed to Christian love and non-violence. In 1937 Muste also briefly directed the Presbyterian Labor Temple in New York. After retiring, Muste remained active in peace-related activities until the last day of his life. He was the spiritual leader of every major pacifist demonstration in the country and often was the actual director. In the 1950s he was active in the anti-nuclear bomb crusade, the anti-Vietnam War movement, and the civil rights struggle. Shortly before his death in 1967, he joined a peace delegation to North Vietnam.

Muste's peace theology/philosophy

Muste was a pragmatic, rather than contemplative, peace activist, but he formulated a sophisticated peace theology, which he laid out in two books, twenty-six pamphlets, and several hundred articles and oral presentations.[6] Many of his articles appeared in the journal *Liberation*, which he helped to establish in 1956. His ideas and thoughts were the reflections of a sensitive and compassionate person.

Muste was an effective peace activist because of *his* humble and gentle personality. Unlike others in peace movements, he never tried

---

[5] Hentoff, *Peace Agitator*, 97.
[6] Muste's two major books are: *Nonviolence in an Aggressive World* (New York: Harper and Row, 1940), and *Not by Might: Christianity, the Way of Human Decency* (New York: Harper, 1947). Some of his writings can be found in Nat Hentoff, ed., *The Essays of A. J. Muste*, 2nd ed. (Indianapolis: Bobs-Merrill, 1967). Muste's papers are scattered in various archives, such as the Swarthmore Peace Collection, Swarthmore College, PA, and the Joint Archives of Holland.

Fig. 9.2. Muste arrested at the Army Induction Center, New York, 15 December 1966 (*courtesy Joint Archives of Holland*)

to overwhelm or intimidate opponents or display a self-righteous attitude. He spoke with, not at, individuals and was an excellent listener. According to Sydney Lens, Muste was one of the few people who did not threaten people's egos.[7] He disavowed violence or war as ways to resolve conflicts, and deemed them evil, destructive, and self-generating.

Muste responded to violence with the most important human emotion—love. In his view, God imposed on humans an inexorable obligation to love, whatever the cost. His pacifism was rooted in his Christian faith. As David McReynolds noted, Christianity was so "central to him that his life could not be understood without realizing that he was even at the most political moments acting out of religious convictions." Christianity to Muste was the "leavening force in the world, specifically, the Sermon on the Mount, which taught the duty to love one's enemies."[8] "If I can't love Hitler, I can't love at all," Muste once declared.[9]

Individual conscience against war was the foundation for a peaceful world order. But war resistance alone would not lead to peace, according to Muste. War was the logical outcome of a capitalist economic system that was inherently unjust. War was a deeply entrenched cultural institution and could not be abolished as long as the economic order was based on a competitive quest for markets and raw materials, backed by a war machine. It was especially the war machine, he maintained, that

---

[7] Henthoff, *Essays*, xii.
[8] Robinson, *Abraham*, 82.
[9] Henthoff, *Peace Agitator*, 12.

Fig. 9.3. Peace March in New York City, 1963 (*courtesy Joint Archives of Holland*)

kept predatory imperialism alive. Without capitalism and imperialism, it would crumble.

While economic factors often led to war, Muste underestimated the importance of psychological factors. Individuals, as well as nations, can be aggressive in order to meet psychological need. Wars satisfy desires for greatness and fame. As Chris Hedges noted, "War is a force that gives us meaning."[10]

To abolish war, Muste advocated civil disobedience, tax resistance, and non-violent demonstrations. Christians are subject to a higher law and must engage in what he called Holy Disobedience.[11] They should form small cells or action-oriented, intensely committed groups, like the Catholic Workers. Eventually, if people practiced the faith they professed, Muste alleged, even Stalin might be impressed.

Muste influenced the American Peace Movement in several ways. His actions were a model for peace activists, in that he never let his ego overwhelm or humiliate opponents. His peace theology emphasized love and justice. He also served as one of the few unifying elements in a very disparate anti-Vietnam War peace movement. Muste's greatest influence was likely in the civil rights movement. Martin Luther King recognized this when he wrote Muste on his eightieth birthday: "You have climbed the mountain and have seen the great and abiding truth to which you have dedicated your life. You have been a good friend and inspiration to me and the whole non-violent movement. Without you the American Negro might never have caught the meaning of true love for humanity."[12]

[10] Chris Hedges, *War is a Force that Gives Us Meaning* (New York: Public Affairs, 2002).
[11] One of Muste's most interesting essays is *Of Holy Disobedience* (Wallingford, PA, 1952).
[12] Robinson, *Abraham Went Out*, 137. Muste was especially close to one of King's principal co-workers, Bayard Rustin. Daniel Levine, *Bayard Rustin and the Civil Rights Movement* (New Brunswick, NJ: Rutgers University Press, 2000).

PART III

Second World War

CHAPTER 10

Home Front:
Holland, Michigan, in the World Wars

Robert P. Swierenga

Fighting the world wars greatly strengthened the hand of the federal government in the lives of ordinary citizens, because both were total wars that required command economies. The home front was as critical to victory as the front lines. The national government managed people, prices, and production down to the last household. Sacrifice of human life, rationing of food and war materials, labor demands of war production, war bond drives and patriotic parades, pacifism and dissent, are all part of the story. Both conflicts changed the home front in similar ways, but the Second World War had a greater impact because it lasted twice as long, and the fighting extended from the Atlantic theater to North Africa and the Far East.

President Woodrow Wilson cast the First World War, called the "Great War," as a crusade to "make the world safe for democracy," but that war had no defining event like Pearl Harbor, except perhaps the German U-boat sinking of the passenger liner *Lusitania*. The Great War saw slackers, xenophobia, and pacifism, and the government propaganda machine had to work much harder to castigate Kaiser Wilhelm than Hitler, Mussolini, and Tojo.

When both wars started in Europe, the United States government declared strict neutrality, although public opinion backed the democracies. The United States entered the Great War almost three years in and the Second World War after more than two years. The United States declared war against Germany on Good Friday, 6 April 1917, and the war declaration against Japan came a day after Pearl Harbor, 8 December 1941. Germany and Italy then declared war on the United States, based on the Axis alliance.

Dutch Americans were torn in the Great War. Bitterness against British brutality in the Boer War (1899-1902) was still strong, their motherland had declared neutrality, and Germany had been a good neighbor to the Netherlands. It was another matter entirely when in 1940 German troops invaded the Netherlands, and German planes bombed Rotterdam, which forced the Dutch government to capitulate in four days.

For relatives and friends in West Michigan, it was unnerving to find the motherland under German occupation. Hollanders quickly donated $5,000 to the Queen Wilhelmina Fund, set up to assist displaced Dutch, for Rotterdam victims. But this effort paled in comparison to funds raised for the Boers. Strangely, 1940 engendered less of a sense of urgency than 1900, even when German rockets almost brought England to its knees.[1] But Pearl Harbor changed all that. The war became personal, and anger swelled against the fascist dictators. The fate of Western civilization was at stake, not just democracy in the abstract.

Pacifism and nationalism

Both wars roused patriots, but pacifists were largely silent until 1940. Isolationists were strong from 1914 to 1916, but not pacifists. Perhaps the "peaceniks" were lulled by Wilson's moralist rhetoric about saving the world.

The city of Holland was pulsing with patriotism in 1917. Ten days after the war declaration, civic leaders staged a patriotic rally, led by

---

[1] *Holland City News*, 2, 16, 23 May 1940; Arnold Mulder, *Americans from Holland* (Philadelphia: J. B. Lippincott, 1947), 289; Henry S. Lucas, *Netherlanders in America: Dutch Immigration to the United States and Canada, 1789-1950* (Ann Arbor: University of Michigan Press, 1955, reprinted Grand Rapids: Eerdmans, 1989), 565-70; Michael Douma, "The Reaction of Holland, MI, to the Boer War," student paper, Hope College, 2003, JAH. This chapter draws heavily on chapters 21 and 23 of my three-volume work, *Holland, Michigan: From Dutch Colony to Dynamic City* (Holland: Van Raalte Press; Grand Rapids: Eerdmans, 2014).

bands playing the National Anthem, "America," and "Battle Hymn of the Republic." Gerrit J. Diekema, the city's renowned orator-politician, whose son was a Navy pilot, waxed eloquent about the necessity of sacrificing for freedom. Looking into the eyes of the young women in the crowd, Diekema with quivering lips declared that if anyone married a young man to save him from conscription, she would be "guilty of treason and should thereafter wear dresses of yellow." When the rally ended, 125 men volunteered within ten minutes, the first of some one thousand who went to city hall to get their draft cards and lottery numbers. Local retailers sold out of American flags, and when new shipments arrived a week later, nearly every factory in Holland unfurled the flag.[2]

The most important support organization was the newly formed Red Cross chapter, with Diekema as president. By the end of 1917, the chapter had two thousand members. It helped that one hundred businesses purchased membership cards at one dollar each for all their employees.[3] city hall offered a room for the Red Cross headquarters, which became a beehive of activity, primarily women. Individuals, businesses, and churches donated clothing and hospital supplies. Women rolled bandages for the troops.[4]

The US military build up to the Second World War aroused pacifists. At Memorial Day services at Pilgrim Home Cemetery in 1940, attorney Cornelius Vander Meulen reminded the crowd of the bloody fields of Flanders, and declared: "No, my friends, wars do not end wars; war breeds wars." A Prayer for Peace service at Hope College's Memorial Chapel in September 1940 drew a capacity crowd of two thousand to hear professors John R. Mulder of Western Theological Seminary and Clarence Bouma of Calvin Theological Seminary pray and plead for "peace rather than victory."[5]

The Holland Ministerial Association drew a capacity crowd for another Prayer for Peace service in November 1941, sponsored jointly by the Reformed Church in America and the Committee of International Justice. The speakers were the outspoken pacifists Abraham J. Muste, a 1905 Hope College graduate (see chapter 9), and Frederick Olert, a Western Theological Seminary graduate and pastor of Detroit's First Presbyterian Church. Both taught that the church's role was to support

---

[2] *Holland Sentinel*, 17, 18 Apr. 1917; *De Grondwet*, 24 Apr. 1917; *Anchor*, 25 Apr.1917; Speeches (quote), Diekema Papers, box 5, HMA.
[3] *Holland City News*, 10 May, 20 Sept., 27 Dec. 1917; *Holland Sentinel*, 21 July 1917.
[4] *Holland City News*, 10 Oct. 1918; *Holland Sentinel*, 3, 8 July 1930.
[5] *Holland City News*, 6 June (quote), 12 Sept. (quote) 1940.

Fig. 10.1. Red Cross wagon in parade late 1917
(*courtesy Larry B. Massie*)

world peace through liberating individual souls. Olert warned that war could lead to the collapse of civilization. Muste also hit on Christian themes, drawing on his socialist ideology. All wars had economic causes, Muste averred, due to the competition between capitalist systems of production and their inherent inequalities. For Muste, the solution to war was to blend Calvinism and Socialism in a non-violent Christian socialism.[6]

Pearl Harbor a month later silenced all but the most ardent pacifists. Mayor Henry Geerlings, a Hope alumnus who served as defense coordinator for the Holland area, rallied the city to action with rousing speeches. "Democracy begins at home," he declared, and everyone must buy war bonds, work overtime, and make sacrifices in every aspect of life. There were shades of Winston Churchill in his language and demeanor: "If we fail, we go back to the dark ages, all of us. If we win, as I believe we will, there will be stability and plenty and happiness for every individual." For Geerlings and Muste, Hollanders had to choose patriotism or pacifism.[7]

---

[6] *Holland City News*, 19 Nov. 1941; Madalyn Northuis, "The Life and Legacy of A. J. Muste," *Joint Archives Quarterly* 22 (Winter 2013): 1-6.

[7] *Holland City News*, 17 Apr., 24 Dec. 1941, 15 Jan., 25 June 1942, 22 Apr. 1943. Geerlings' public service is unrivaled: alderman 20 years, mayor 10 years, board of education 50 years, library board 51 years, board of supervisors 10 years, Michigan House of Representatives 8 years, *Holland Sentinel* religion writer 40 years, editor of the *Leader* (religious newspaper) 25 years, church elder 17 years, Bible study teacher 25 years, etc. His public and church service exceeded 350 years (ibid., 5 Jan. 1950).

Fig. 10.2. Army howitzer attracts curious onlookers in Holland (*courtesy Myron Van Ark*)

Nativism

The First World War aroused a genuine fear of sabotage by German immigrants in America. The Wilson administration tasked its War Propaganda Committee with ferreting out "traitors" with pro-German sympathies. In the Holland area, this put under the microscope residents from Grafschaft Bentheim or Ost Friesland in the villages of Graafschap, Bentheim, and Drenthe. Anyone who failed to contribute wholeheartedly to Liberty Loan drives or Red Cross appeals became suspect.

Hollanders knew deep down that their German neighbors were decent human beings. Indeed, most belonged to Reformed churches. Diekema declared: "No better people live upon all the earth than the German people, but they must lose to win." Advertisements in local newspapers often demonized Germans. *De Grondwet* carried ads that labeled Germans as "Potsdam's Pirates" for sinking American cargo ships on the open seas. The Kaiser's minions were "Huns," rapacious barbarians bent on world domination.[8]

Even the German language became taboo. The Woman's Literary Club altered its German motto *Mehr Licht* into the English "More Light," and the national Elks Lodge board banned the German language at meetings.[9] Two watchmen were stationed on the Holland docks to

---

[8] *De Grondwet*, 18 June 1918; Diekema Papers, box 5, HMA.
[9] *Holland City News*, 11 July 1918; Marie Zingle: *The Story of the Woman's Literary Club* (Holland, MI, 1989), 29.

keep an eye out for German spies, explosive materials, and suspicious people. The Holland school superintendent investigated textbooks, censoring any that he believed were pro-German. All teaching must be "one hundred percent American," reported the *Holland City News*. The superintendent also instituted compulsory military training for high school boys.[10]

Dutch immigrants also had to toe the line, or hyper-patriots demanded their pound of flesh. The Dutch spoken in Dutch American communities sounded to Americans indistinguishable from German (*Deutsch*). When a Dutchman failed to remove his hat during a playing of the "Star Spangled Banner," a Yankee justice of the peace fined him ten dollars and would not accept his explanation that he did not immediately recognize the tune of the national anthem.[11] A Dutch farmer uttered unpatriotic comments about a Liberty Loan drive. A night or two later, vigilantes arranged a "painting bee" and gave his farmhouse and outbuildings a coat of yellow paint, a badge of disloyalty.[12] Rev. Herman Hoeksema, a Christian Reformed pastor, was castigated as a traitor by the press and by Reformed church clerics and Hope College faculty. His crime? He refused to allow the American flag in the church sanctuary during worship services, although he welcomed it during choir concerts, Sunday school programs, and other events. For Hoeksema, a strict Calvinist, unfurling the nation's banner in church was conceding too much to Caesar's realm. To honor the nation more than God smacked of civil religion, not Christianity.[13]

During the Second World War, residents of Holland joined in hatred for the enemy—"Krauts," "Dagos," and "Japs." Five hundred "enemy aliens" had to register with the postmaster. But none were charged with treason for criticizing the president or his policies, as happened during the Great War.

Conscription

In both wars the government used the draft to raise an army, a system first adopted in the Civil War. In June 1917 all men aged eighteen to forty-five had to register, and the draft board drew names by lot. In August a motley crew of farm boys, factory workers, and students gathered at city hall for their physicals. Dentists were warned

[10] *Holland Sentinel*, 11, 13 Apr. 1917; *Holland City News*, 29 Aug. 1918.
[11] *Holland City News*, 24 Oct. 1918.
[12] *Holland Sentinel*, 5 Nov. 1918.
[13] Robert P. Swierenga, "Disloyal Dutch? Herman Hoeksema and the Flag in Church Controversy during World War I," *Origins* 25, no. 2 (2007): 28-35.

Fig. 10.3. Family and friends send the "boys" off on the train at Holland depot, 19 September 1917 (*courtesy Myron Van Ark*)

not to pull teeth of "slackers" and help them avoid the draft. The next month seventy-six men left for Camp Custer, Michigan. But first they were feted with a luncheon at city hall and surrounded by hundreds of citizens as they marched to the train station. City factories closed so everyone could attend the farewell ceremony. Diekema, never short of words, again addressed the crowd. In the end, conscription culled more than 8 percent of Holland's total population (12,000).[14] Almost a full year passed before the boys left stateside army camps for Europe, while stories about the war and "our boys" filled the newspapers.

In 1940, a full year before Pearl Harbor, President Franklin D. Roosevelt called out the National Guard, and Holland's famed Company D, formed after the Great War, eighty-six men strong, was mustered in at the Holland Armory for transfer to military camps in the South. The American Legion band and color guard escorted the soldiers down Eighth Street to the train depot where, in a scene reminiscent of 1917, some five thousand people came to see them off. By 1942 Company D was fighting in the jungles of New Guinea. This company saw 654 days of combat and suffered a casualty rate of 27 percent.[15]

---

[14] *Holland Sentinel*, 5 June 1917; *Holland City News*, 12 July, 2, 9 Aug 1917, 20 Sept. 1917; 12 Sept. 1918; Ray Nies Autobiography, typescript, ch. 17, p. 9, HMA.

[15] *Holland City News*, 1, 15 Aug., 19 Sept., 3, 17, 24, 31 Oct. 1940, 30 Apr., 28 May, 27 Aug. 1942; Randall P. Vande Water, "Company D Answered Call," in *Holland: Happenings, Heroes & Hot Shots*, 1:126-28; Vande Water, "Co. D 126th Infantry Leaves

The government also reinstated the selective service system in 1940 and nearly two thousand Holland men registered, including ninety-four from Hope College and an equal number of high school seniors. Single men were drafted first, but after March 1943 married men made up most of the inductees. Only those employed in essential "war work" were exempt.[16] Young men (and their sweethearts) put their lives on hold while awaiting Uncle Sam's letter of "Greetings." A few women also volunteered for service in the Women's Auxiliary Air Corps, known colloquially as the WAACS. Carol Bremer and Hazel Ver Hey rose to the rank of major.[17]

By October 1943 a staggering 9 percent of Holland's population—nearly thirteen hundred men—were in military service, well above the national average. The 9 percent figure was only slightly higher than the 8 percent rate in the First World War. Everyone subject to the draft was affected by it, where called up or not.[18]

Home front

Both world wars were won on the home front. Through labor, conservation, and sacrifice, the country was able to supply the foodstuffs and material the troops needed. Every city was a cog in the war machine. Americans worked overtime; gave liberally to relief agencies; subscribed heavily to war bonds; and sacrificed their goods, monies, and sons and husbands in the war effort. The conflict shook social foundations. Women entered the labor force in droves; children were enlisted to collect cans, newspapers, and old tires; and soldiers went off to war and returned forever changed. Holland emerged from war a changed city.

Rationing and conservation

In 1917 the government made rationing mandatory and conservation a patriotic duty. Defense needs took priority. Victory Gardens in the back yard allowed everyone to fight. A food commissioner went door to door asking citizens to abstain from meat and bread one day each week, and to be *zuinig* (frugal) in their use of sugar and other scarce commodities listed by the government. Housewives shared

---

Holland," *Holland Historical Trust Review* 3, no. 3 (1990): 5-8; Vande Water, "Company D cheered on by excited crowd," *Holland Sentinel*, 23 Oct. 2012.

[16] *Holland City News*, 26 Sept., 17 Oct., 14, 28 Nov., 12 Dec. 1940, 2 July 1942, 14 Jan. 1943, 17 Feb., 16 Mar., 21 Dec. 1944.

[17] *Holland City News*, 24 Sept. 1942, 14 Jan. 1943, 1 June, 20 July 1944.

[18] Ibid., 7 Oct. 1943.

wheatless recipes, and some restaurants observed "meatless Tuesdays" and "wheatless Wednesdays."[19]

Herbert Hoover's US Food Administration regulated meat, sugar, and wheat, among other foods, in a program known as "Hooverizing." Staples like milk, bread, butter, and ice cream were taxed. Butter prices increased from 36¢ to 55¢ a pound, due to taxes, scarcities, and competition from manufacturers of condensed milk, which became popular. Some local creameries were driven out of business.[20]

Sugar rationing—one pound per person per week—seemed to "pinch" the most. This stingy ration caused "more dissatisfaction to the square inch" than any other issue, said the *Holland City News*. Two men went so far as to steal sacks of sugar from the Holland Sugar Beet plant, at the cost of several weeks in jail.[21]

Merchants were greatly affected. They had to follow all the price regulations and resist the temptation to sell on the black market. A Holland hardware store could buy only five kegs of nails at a time, and the cost was fifteen times higher than before the war. "I wondered, jokingly, if they were shooting nails at the Germans," the owner mused.[22]

Folks also had to deal with taxes and regulations on the newfangled automobiles. Owners had to register their vehicles with the city, and driving was restricted to "legitimate" trips, like going to church, not a Sunday jaunt to the beach. Uncle Sam taxed everything—pleasure boats, steamer berths, long distance phone calls, railroad freight, and Interurban tickets. Postage stamps went from two to three cents; postcards from one to two cents. Most important, the hated income tax, first used in the Civil War, was reinstated on incomes above $1,000 for singles and $2,000 for couples.[23]

Coal was the essential commodity during the First World War. Coal stoked home furnaces, produced steam to run electric generators at the public power plant, and yielded coal gas for heating and cooking. Coal shortages meant no electricity and no heat. Just such a situation developed in the winter of 1917-18. The Holland Gas Company reported having only a five-day supply of coal, and if a new shipment did not arrive, Holland could be without gas. The crisis was averted temporarily when

---

[19] *De Grondwet*, 30 Oct. 1917; *Holland City News*, 25 Oct. 1917.
[20] *Holland City News*, 8 Feb. 1917, 9 May 1918; *De Grondwet*, 10 Apr. 1917, 5 Nov. 1918.
[21] *Holland City News*, 27 Dec. 1917, 3 Jan. (quote), 23 May, 20 June 1918; *De Grondwet*, 18 Dec 1917, 5 Nov. 1918.
[22] Nies Autobiography, ch. 17, p. 1; *Holland City News*, 17 Oct. 1918; *De Grondwet*, 29 Oct. 1918.
[23] *Holland City News*, 1 Nov., 27 Dec. 1917, 10 Oct. 1918.

two carloads of coal arrived from Grand Rapids. During periodic coal shortages, the city fathers asked residents to turn off lights. Merchants had to limit store hours to nine per day and shut off all lighted signage and displays. The only exceptions were cigar dealers, candy stores, saloons, and poolrooms, presumably to avoid open rebellion. The city joined "lightless nights" on Thursday evenings and adopted "war time" (all year daylight savings time), to reduce electric usage.[24]

The Knickerbocker Theatre used old-fashioned kerosene lamps as an alternative light source. Churches cancelled services or gathered in unheated church basements or small heated rooms. In the middle of winter in January 1918, Holland had its first "heatless day." The National Fuel Administration had ordered cities in the Midwest to shut down industries and stores to save fuel. Several large factories in Holland had to close for longer periods due to a lack of power. Hope College kept classroom buildings at a chilly fifty-six degrees and held chapel services in a small room to conserve coal. All Holland's public and Christian schools closed for a week.[25]

Price controls

In World War Two the Office of Price Administration (OPA) rationed steel, iron, tires, and gasoline. It was the first time for tires and gasoline. Manufacturers with military contracts had no problem, but firms producing civilian goods were hurting for the duration. In May 1942 the OPA froze the price of staples, starting with sugar and coffee, and then meat, butter, cheese, and many other everyday foods except bread. The coffee limit was one pound per week per adult, and restaurant refills were on the tab. Housewives had only so many ration coupons per month and had to spend them carefully. A pound of butter or cheese required eight points; sirloin steak was six points, a jar of peaches twenty-four points, and a can of green beans fourteen points. The sugar ration book was red, the meat book blue. A "sugar for canning" program allowed an extra pound for canning and making preserves.[26]

The OPA also set prices of food and consumer goods. When local milk dealers, who felt the squeeze from rising costs, raised the price of milk from eleven to twelve cents per quart, the OPA ordered a rollback.

---

[24] *Holland City News*, 20, 27 Dec. 1917; 3 Jan. 1918; *De Grondwet*, 25 Dec. 1917; 8 Jan. 1918.
[25] *Holland City News*, 10, 17, 24, 31 Jan. 1918; *Anchor*, 30 Jan. 1918.
[26] Ibid., 23 Apr., 4, 11 June, 30 July, 6 Aug., 22 Oct., 19 Nov. 1942, 30 May 1943, 12 Apr. 1945; Hamlin, "Holland's Contribution."

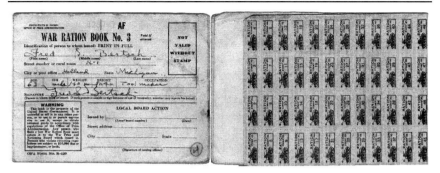

Fig. 10.4. Fred S. Bertsch's Second World War ration book with gas coupons (*Archives, Holland Historical Trust*)

The OPA also controlled restaurant menus and entrée prices. Every proprietor had to file a copy of the complete menu or price list with a local OPA board, and woe to the one caught overcharging. The board actually sent out "checkers."[27]

Most Americans had to make do with margarine, since butter was scarce and expensive. Leo Peters of Grand Rapids, a Holland native, made a fortune inventing a way to color oleo (margarine) yellow to make it look like butter. His simple invention was a bag in which housewives could squeeze and mash a butter-colored powder into gray-colored oleo sticks until the ingredients were evenly mixed.[28]

Nylon and silk hosiery were especially scarce, because the military needed nylon yarn for parachutes. Women mobbed stores on hearing rumors that nylons were in stock; nylons were the most sought-after clothing item of all.[29]

Rubber became scarce after Japan seized the plantations in the Dutch East Indies that supplied 90 percent of America's raw rubber. Gasoline was also restricted. Vehicle owners applied for mileage ration books, which allowed four gallons a week. Pleasure driving was unthinkable on that. Truckers, medical personnel, and mailmen were allowed as much gas as needed. Fortunate was the family with a member in one of these occupations, who might have unused coupons to spare. Congress set the national speed limit at thirty-five miles per hour, dubbed Victory Speed. Holland police hit on the ultimate penalty for speeding—the loss of the driver's gas ration card. They simply reported speeders to the OPA, and the federal agency did the rest.[30]

[27] Ibid., 22 Apr. 1943.
[28] *Holland City News*, 25 Mar., 30 May 1943.
[29] Ibid., 7 Aug. 1941, 19 Nov. 1942.
[30] Ibid., 1 Jan., 6, 19, 25 Nov., 3 Dec. 1942.

Fig. 10.5. Holland High School students collect scrap metal. The truck driver is unidentified (*Archives, Holland Historical Trust*).

Conservation efforts focused on collecting iron, tin, steel, aluminum, waste paper, nylons, and rubber, called Salvage for Victory. Scrap metal of any kind was golden. City trucks fanned out across town to collect the precious cargo. Tin can drives collected an estimated 90 percent of the empty cans, all washed and flattened. The Aluminum Defense Drive netted 3,095 pounds, thanks to housewives scrounging in their cupboards and closets for old aluminum kitchen utensils. Boy Scouts collected sixty thousand tons of paper, and school paper drives added many more tons. High school girls were told to raid their mother's dresser drawers for torn nylons; one drive in 1943 yielded two hundred pounds. In early 1942 tire dealers and wholesalers contributed forty tons of old tires and inner tubes, which helped Ottawa County place second in the state in a rubber drive.[31]

As the war continued, and much of the ready scrap was collected, farmers were told to scrounge for old machines lying around. A Jalopy Roundup Campaign induced owners of "junkers" to donate them for scrap. The city donated two Civil War cannons in Centennial Park, weighing 2,575 pounds each, and thirty cannon balls at eighty pounds each, which added another 2,400 pounds. City workers even dug up six thousand pounds of old Interurban tracks. Fat was valued for its glycerin, used in soap and bullets. Housewives saved cooking grease and the Camp Fire Girls collected ninety pounds in one month. Holland Rendering Works contributed fifty thousand pounds of grease.[32]

---

[31] Ibid., 24, 31 July, 14 Aug., 27 Nov. 1941, 18 June, 9, 16 July, 4 Aug., 22 Oct. 1942, 9 Dec. 1943, 7 Sept. 1944; Vande Water, "Scrap Drives, Home Front Response," in *Holland Happenings*, 3:104-7.

[32] *Holland City News*, 22 Jan., 3 Sept., 22 Oct., 25 Nov., 3 Dec. 1942, 3 May, 2 Sept., 24 Nov. 1943, 9 Apr. 1945; *Holland Sentinel*, 17 Jan. 1943; Hamlin, "Holland's Contribution."

Tulip Time was suspended in 1943 for the duration of the war. The decision was obvious. Tourists were not "festival minded," given the gravity of the war and the shortage of gasoline. The city parks department still maintained the tulip lanes, and homeowners displayed tulips in their gardens and lawns.[33] Fourth of July celebrations were also muted by a ban on fireworks, which made for a quiet day. Late in the war, even electricity was rationed to save on coal, as in the First World War, and retail merchants turned off lighted displays and signage.

War bonds

Americans were told that the best way to bring the boys back home was to purchase war bonds. In the First World War local banks issued government bonds of fifty dollars and up, with interest rates from 3.5 to 4.5 percent. The government staged four Liberty Loan campaigns. In the first campaign in April 1917, Holland fell short of its $300,000 quota, which was based on population size, by $100,000, fully one-third.[34]

In the next campaign, the Liberty Loan commission went door to door to avoid the opprobrium of missing the quota. Every major company and retail business placed full-page advertisements in the newspapers, which demonstrated their patriotic bona fides. Merchants and organizations accepted Liberty Bonds in lieu of cash at a premium. A $50 bond was worth $52.50 worth of goods, which was a better return than holding the bond to maturity. Even the city budgeted $10,000 from its board of public works earnings to buy Liberty bonds. In the second bond drive, Holland happily exceeded its quota by $150,000, more than making up the earlier shortfall.[35]

Companies competed to be the first to reach "one hundred percent," when every employee had purchased a bond. In the third Liberty Loan drive (May 1918), the local H. J. Heinz plant was the first to reach the goal. For a second time the common council took $10,000 from its treasury to purchase Liberty bonds. Once again, the drive was a success, and Holland exceeded its quota by 50 percent. Holland again met its quota in the fourth campaign in September 1918. By war's end, thrifty Hollanders had purchased over $1.5 million in Liberty bonds. They were "bloated bond holders," boasted the *Holland City News*.[36]

[33] *Holland City News*, 18 Dec. 1941, 5 Feb., 30 Apr., 11 June, 18 Mar., 22 Apr. 1943; Vande Water, "'41 Tulip Time Hosted Hollywood Stars," in *Holland Happenings*, 2:91-95.
[34] *Holland City News*, 31 May, 14, 21 June 1917.
[35] *De Grondwet*, 9, 16 Oct. 1917; *Holland City News*, 18 Oct., 1 Nov. 1917.
[36] *Holland City News*, 2, 9 May, 26 Sept., 3, 17, 31 Oct. 1918, 2 (quote), 16 Jan. 1919.

Fig. 10.6. Women march in Liberty Loan parade in 1918 (*courtesy Myron Van Ark*)

War bonds and defense stamps again helped finance the Second World War. "WHOSE BOY WILL DIE BECAUSE *YOU* FAILED?" declared newspaper advertisements during bond drives, thereby laying a heavy load of guilt on slackers. The local bond drive chair put it aptly: "The first army is our fighting front, the second army is our production front, and the third army is our bond selling front."[37]

Bond sales were of several types. Series F bonds were sold through payroll savings plans, and Treasury bonds and notes were sold via a series of seven bond campaigns. When sales lagged in the first campaign, the war bond committee devised a "buy a bomber" campaign. If the city met its quota, the air force would paint the words "City of Holland" on a B-25 or B-29 bomber. Residents rose to the challenge and exceeded the goal. In all, Hollanders bought bonds totaling $11 million in five campaigns. Holland Furnace Company employees alone bought $1 million. Children did their part by buying defense stamp books and savings bonds with small coins and dollar bills.[38]

Defense contracts

In the First World War only one quarter of civilian production was diverted to war needs, whereas in the second conflict the entire

---

[37] Ibid., 9, 16 (quote) Nov. 1944, 31 May 1945.
[38] Ibid., 24 July 1941, 8 Jan. 1942, 30 Apr., 16 July 1942, 7 Jan., 18 Feb., 29 Apr., 22, 29 July, 16, 30 Sept. 1943, 10 Feb., 9 Nov. 1944, 19 Apr., 17, 31 May, 28 June, 5 July, 1 Nov. 1945.

economy was converted to military production. In the Great War, Holland had few of the heavy industries, such as steel, rubber, and ship building that won war contracts. Dye and furnace companies thrived, but furniture factories suffered. The military needed hardware more than fine furniture.

In the Second World War local industries fared better, since fully 30 percent of the nation's industrial might was concentrated in Michigan. Holland companies inked $39 million in government contracts and earned small fortunes in profit. No factory had idle hands, including women, who took up a fair share of the jobs. "Mary gets a war job," declared a Michigan Bell Telephone Company advertisement calling on young women to apply as telephone operators. The comic strip style advertisement pictured eighteen-year-old "Mary" being interviewed and learning about her new job. The last strip read, "Mary is proud of her work, proud of the War Bonds she buys out of her pay. She has found the place she wanted—an interesting job where her abilities will count for victory." Such targeted job advertising proved effective. In the summer of 1942, the civil defense team opened a "day nursery" for mothers employed in defense plants.[39]

The Fafnir ball bearing factory employed many women; the company was one of three to earn the Army-Navy "E" pennant for production excellence. At the awards ceremony in 1944, some nine hundred employees received special "E" pins. One recipient, Fanna (Mrs. Clarence Jr.) Dokter, a serviceman's wife and the first woman to work at Fafnir, declared: "We will stay on our jobs as faithfully and as long as our soldiers must stay on theirs." Holland-Racine Shoe Co. was another employer of women. By war's end, the workers crafted 1.7 million pairs of shoes and boots, including 150,000 pairs of combat boots.[40]

Men filled the jobs at furniture factories, machine tool works, and shipbuilding wharves. Seventeen furniture companies in Holland and Zeeland joined hands to win $750,000 in military contracts. Baker Furniture made ribs for gliders, and the Charles R. Sligh Company manufactured desks for the army. Local lumber companies made pallets, and the Dutch Novelty Company produced boxes.[41]

Western Machine Tool Works won the Army-Navy "E" Award an unprecedented three times. Holland Precision Parts produced a half million motor bearings.[42] Holland Hitch made millions of pintle hooks

---

[39] Ibid., 31 Dec. 1940, 30 Jan., 6, 27 Feb. 1941, 25 June 1942, 4 Feb. 1943 (quote), 31 May 1945.
[40] Ibid., 24 Apr. 1941, 22 Jan. 1942, 27 Apr. 1944 (quote).
[41] Ibid., 1 Oct 1942, 18 Mar., 16 Dec. 1943.
[42] *Holland City News*, 24 June 1943, 3 Aug. 1944, 30 Aug., 4 Oct. 1945.

Fig. 10.7. Hart & Cooley's Holland Division of Fafnir Bearing won the coveted "E Award" for exemplary production in 1944. Holding the banner is general manager Harold S. Covell (*left*) and war veteran and employee John Flieman Jr. (*right*) (*Joint Archives of Holland*)

for military jeeps; H. L. Friedlen & Co. made more than half a million mackinaw and field jackets; Hart & Cooley manufactured mortar shells; and Donnelly-Kelly Glass crafted optical gun sights. Parke-Davis, a drug company, contributed synthetic materials and chemicals, and Holland Color and Chemical made printing inks and zinc chromate, the latter used to repair airplane fuselages.[43]

Holland Furnace shifted to military production and made parts for anti-aircraft guns, armor plating for tanks, and anchor chain for ships. Contracts over three years totaled $5 million. The company expanded its plants, doubled the workforce, and ran three shifts around the clock. In all, Holland Furnace shipped out twenty-five million tons of tank armor and thirty million tons of anchor chain.[44]

Chris-Craft boat works made minesweepers and ten thousand LSTs [landing ship tanks) for beach landings. The company also won an Army-Navy "E" Award and doubled its workforce. Jesiek Brothers constructed two submarine chasers to patrol the Atlantic and protect navy convoys. The first one took one hundred men one hundred days to complete. Armed coastguardsmen protected the plant from sabotage day and night.[45]

[43] Ibid., 24 Dec. 1942, 25 Mar. 1943, 31 May 1945; Hamlin, "Holland's Contribution."
[44] *Holland City News*, 2 Apr. 1942, 27 May 1943.
[45] Ibid., 2, 23 Apr., 14, 28 May, 11 June, 19 Nov., 3 Dec. 1942, 21 Jan., 8 Apr., 24 June 1943, 31 May 1945; *Holland Sentinel*, 29 Nov. 1941; Vande Water, "Jesiek's Builds

Fig. 10.8. Chris-Craft's 8,000th Navy Landing Craft, ready for shipment to Algonac for final water testing before shipping to the Marines in 1944 (photo Gerald Vande Vusse Sr.) *(courtesy son Robert "Bob")*

The government jawboned industrial producers to hold the line on prices, with the implied threat of price ceilings to prevent "price gouging." Charles R. Sligh Jr., president of the Grand Rapids Furniture Exposition, responded: "Of course, we want to cooperate, but it is foolish to ask the industry as a whole not to raise prices when materials costs, labor costs, and taxes all are rising." Yet most companies complied.[46]

Civil defense

Protection and defense was everyone's business, especially since officials feared German or Japanese bombing raids. Some five thousand Holland citizens volunteered for the various civil defense teams, including public school staffs, leaders of social organizations and churches, and medical and nursing personnel. There were auxiliary firefighters and air raid wardens to monitor the ubiquitous air raid drills that were a part of daily life at work and school. Emergency casualty centers were designated and supplied with medical equipment. The local Coast Guard station regulated shippers and skippers; all yacht owners, officers, crews, and longshoremen had to carry photo-IDs issued by the government.[47]

Submarine Chasers," in *Holland Happenings*, 4:123-26; Chris Hamlin, "Holland's Contribution to World War II," Hope College student paper, Apr. 1986, Joint Archives of Holland (JAH).
[46] Ibid., 2 July 1941.
[47] Ibid., 29 Jan., 9, 23 Apr. 1942, 29 Apr., 13 May 1943.

All industrial and utility plants received protection from a volunteer corps of Home Guards, which was formed to fill any security void after National Guard units were activated. The Home Guards watched for sabotage, espionage, and other threats. More than fifty men volunteered for the duty, and they were issued forest-green uniforms, black pants, and government rifles and revolvers. "America's greatest danger is not from without, but from within through the penetration of the fifth column," declared a speaker at an Americanism forum at the Holland Armory.[48]

Gold Stars

In the First World War, the first combat death in August 1918 made headlines. It was Willard G. Leenhouts, not quite twenty years old, who was killed by artillery shrapnel on the battlefield in France. Like all parents of servicemen, the Leenhouts had prayed daily for a letter from their son and hoped to hear that he was well. Ex-Congressman Diekema, a family friend and Willard's Sunday school superintendent, delivered the bad news. He took a yellow envelope from his pocket—the dreaded military telegram, and tenderly read the awful message. Later that day the mayor ordered flags flown at half-mast.[49]

In the end, twenty-six Holland doughboys (2.7 percent) made the supreme sacrifice; more were cut down by illness than battle. Hardware merchant Ray Nies recalled seeing a "pile of rough coffins" arrive at the train station "containing the bodies of fine young men, who died of the 'flu' in the training camps. . . . Why were the dead always privates, not officers," Nies mused laconically.[50] In the Second World War, forty-two Holland men (2.3 percent of all servicemen) died.[51]

Hope College at war

The Hope College community strongly supported both wars, despite the call up of male students that cut college finances. "The Orange and Blue will be found flying beneath the Stars and Stripes," declared the campus newspaper, the *Anchor*, in 1917.[52] Academic events

---

[48] *Holland City News*, 31 Dec. 1940, 3, 24 Apr., 11 Dec. 1941, 1, 15 Jan. 1942.
[49] Leenhouts, *From the Crest of the Hill*, 121; Randall P. Vande Water, "Willard Leenhouts Was First to Fall," in *Holland Happenings*, 3:128-35.
[50] Diekema Papers, HMA; Joel Lefever, "Holland residents have always stepped up to serve," *Holland Sentinel*, 26 Aug. 2007; Nies Autobiography, ch. 17, p. 3.
[51] *Holland City News*, 13 Dec. 1945. The memorial plaque in Centennial Park lists 118 World War II dead.
[52] *Anchor*, 18, 25 Apr. 1917.

Fig. 10.9. Willard G. Leenhouts, killed in action in France, 3 July 1918 (*Archives, Holland Historical Trust*)

took on a war tone. Oratory contests dealt with the evils of autocracy and Kaiserism, inauguration and commencement speakers cited German atrocities and the need to aid war victims, and news articles focused on conscription and fighting in northern France.

In the first year over ninety students signed up; most received officer's commissions. Only pre-seminary and pre-engineering majors were exempt, besides those who had failed their physicals. The college shortened the school year by holding classes six days a week and foregoing spring break, so men not called could help out on the farm. Female dorm students voted to have a weekly meatless and breadless day, and in their spare time they made bandages, pillows, and other items for the soldiers.[53]

The exodus of male students caused a sharp shift in the college's demographics. Enrollment declined by 20 percent, and for the first time in the college's history, the customary preponderance of males ended. Both wars put an end to intercollegiate athletics and social activities for the duration.[54] When the students in military training began eating at their own designated cafeteria, the women on campus saw even less of the men. "You can imagine how lonesome it has been in Voorhees Commons," one female student wrote. "There are only fourteen or

---

[53] *De Grondwet*, 6 Nov. 1917; *Holland Sentinel*, 25 Apr. 1918; Edward Dimnent Papers, JAH.

[54] Ibid., 9 May 1917; 27 Feb. 1918; Hope College Student Correspondence, JAH; Debbie Dolph, "Dr. Ame Vennema: A Biography Focusing on his Years as President," 1974, in Ame Vennema Papers, JAH; Hope Faculty Minutes, 15 May 1917, JAH.

Fig. 10.10. Army Specialized Training Program, Lubbers Hall, Hope College (*Joint Archives of Holland*)

fifteen boys who still eat with us—'little kids, cripples, and bums,' as one boy said to me."[55]

In October 1918 Hope College brought to campus the Student Army Training Corps (SATC), an early type of ROTC program, which trained and drilled men in uniform and under military discipline. The call of the bugle was heard daily for drills. The trainees went directly into the US Army. Militarizing the campus broke all precedent and tradition of the liberal arts college and aroused opposition among some supporting churches, who objected to the military presence on campus.[56]

During the Second World War, Hope College again brought servicemen to campus. First in 1942 was a federally funded, summer school for pilots, who were housed off-campus in barracks at the city airport. Several hundred pilots passed through the program. In 1943 the college joined the Army Specialized Training Program (ASTP), the modern version of the SATC, which enrolled hundreds of men for officer training. Coeds, who outnumbered men by four to one, were thrilled to see more young men on campus. "It was exciting; the uniforms, the passionate goodbyes, the promises to wait for our heroes' return," said

[55] Betty Ann (likely Hope College student Elizabeth Renskers) to Mr. and Mrs. George Kollen, Rochester, MN, 9 Oct 1918, JAH; *Anchor*, 9 Oct. 1918; *De Grondwet*, 28 May 1918, *Holland City News*, 23 May 1918.
[56] *Holland City News*, 3, 17 Oct. 1918; John W. Brink to Edward Dimnent, 10 June 1919, Edward Dimnent Papers, JAH.

a coed. "But it was also scary. We saw the newsreels. We knew that some of those we hugged goodbye would be wounded, and some would not be coming back at all."[57]

Armistice and Victory Days

Everyone flocked downtown on Monday, 11 November 1918, after they were awakened at 2:25 a.m. by Holland's official steam whistle, the "Mockingbird," at the power plant, which blew its screeching sound for over an hour to announce the signing of the armistice. The previous Thursday the town had already staged an impromptu parade for the "false armistice," so called, because the reports proved to be premature.[58]

VE-Day (Victory Europe), 8 May 1945, had also been anticipated for weeks. Everyone knew Germany had been defeated; it was only a matter of when. Berlin's fall and Hitler's suicide answered the "when." Churches quickly filled for prayer services, but the celebrations were muted, because the war against Japan continued with no end in sight. The somber 1945 Memorial Day ceremony at Pilgrim Home Cemetery brought out two thousand people to hear Hope College professor Egbert Winter speak of the high price of freedom "paid in sacrifice and blood."[59]

Americans had a week to plan for the VJ-Day (Victory Japan) celebration on 15 August 1945. Two days after the first atomic bomb, equal to twenty thousand tons of TNT, leveled Hiroshima on 6 August, Russia declared war on Japan. "Army plans for the worst, despite Atomic Bomb," read a front-page article. Three days later (9 August) the second a-bomb was dropped on Nagasaki, and President Truman demanded unconditional surrender or Japan would face "prompt and utter destruction." "Truman brings home the bacon," read the newspaper headline. Emperor Hirohito sued for peace on 10 August, but it took another five days for the Japanese warlords to accept the Allied terms of unconditional surrender. This gave Holland's VJ-Day committee time to plan the big celebration, which came on 15 August.[60]

"*Right away* there was noise just terrible. . . . We went downtown because everybody did. There was no parade but cars, cars, cars with

---

[57] *Holland City News*, 5 Sept., 31 Dec. 1940, 29 Oct. 1942, 18 Mar., 23 Sept. 1943, 9 Mar., 4, 30 Nov. 1944; Wynand Wichers, *A Century of Hope, 1866-1966* (Grand Rapids: Eerdmans, 1968), 219-25; Eileen Nordstrom and George D. Zuidema, eds., *Hope at the Crossroads: The War Years* (Holland, MI, 2008), 37, 45-54, 65-70, 106-7, 171, 195-99.

[58] Randall P. Vande Water, "Armistice Roused Celebrants in 1918," in Vande Water, *Holland Happenings*, 3: 136-40.

[59] *Holland City News*, 10, 24, 31 May 1945.

[60] *Holland Sentinel*, 6, 7, 8, 9, 10, 11, 13, 14, 15 Aug. 1945.

bells & whistles & noise. Everybody went wild. . . . Can hardly believe the war is over" (Carrie Bielfield of Holland). Business came to a virtual standstill, as stores and factories closed for the day, as did the post office and all government offices. Churches opened their doors for evening services of thanksgiving.[61]

The war did not end officially until 2 September, when representatives of the Japanese Emperor and warlords signed formal documents in the presence of General Douglas McArthur and officials from some ten allied countries on the deck of the aircraft carrier *Midway* in Tokyo Bay.

Americanization

The world wars hastened the pace of Americanization in immigrant communities across America. Serving in the military broke down the cultural isolation of ethnic cities like Holland. Christian Reformed soldiers especially were affected. They went off to war believing in the long held church motto: "In isolation is our strength," but they found themselves worshiping in military chapels with Protestants of all stripes and fighting in foxholes alongside the same Protestants and also Catholics and Jews. The old saying rang true: "How can you keep a man down once he has seen Paree?" American troops served on every continent in the Second World War, so the cultural impact was even greater. The Reformed churches in Holland introduced service flags and patriotic worship services around the Fourth of July. This blending of God and country continues to the present day and is more overt in Reformed congregations than in Christian Reformed congregations.

Many women who entered the labor force during the Second World War returned to being housewives afterward, but growing numbers did remain in the workforce. The experience of the war years made working outside the home culturally acceptable, and the economic advantages were obvious.

Although the onerous rules and regulations fell away quickly after the war, the reach of the federal government into the daily lives of citizens continued and became the new normal. To prosecute the Cold War and Korean War required continued activism and centralized direction from Washington. The Supreme Court under Chief Justice Earl Warren (1953-69) dramatically expanded federal power in the area of civil rights and civil liberties, and President Dwight Eisenhower's Interstate Highway System hastened suburbanization and permanently altered the nation's geography and culture.

[61] Carrie Bielfield, Holland, MI, to "Dear Children," Sept. 1945, Mouw Family Papers, JAH; *Holland City News*, 22 Aug. 1945.

CHAPTER 11

Packing Underwear, Cod Liver Oil, and Stockings: Holland, Michigan, Responds to War-Ravaged Netherlands, 1940s

Nella Kennedy

The May 1945 issue of *Stars and Stripes* magazine, the in-house publication of Baker Furniture for the sixty employees serving in the military, featured a cartoon of a woman in Dutch costume, carrying a basket of tulips in one hand, while the other holds a Dutch flag, titled "The Netherlands Will Rise Again." The artist, Edward M. Brolin, dedicated it to the people of the Netherlands, that "little country, the Motherland of so many people in this country."[1] As a Holland, Michigan, resident, he no doubt had many townspeople in mind who had not been able to communicate with this "Motherland" for five years. Local euphoria about the ending of the war led to initiating huge relief efforts in Dutch American communities. The question was what and how much was needed for that war-torn land? The hardships caused by the increased stranglehold of the Germans on the Netherlands was at best only known sketchily through escapees' reports, the Dutch government in exile, and illegal transmissions.

Providing assistance in alleviating needs could, at that early stage, only be imagined. With so many inhabitants with recent or distant

---

[1] *Holland Evening Sentinel*, 5 May 1945.

familial connections, it is not surprising that Holland, Michigan, ranked high in answering the call for aid, whether this was organized through church or community. This chapter will describe in brief compass the effects of German occupation in the Netherlands and how, after German capitulation in May 1945, the Dutch had to cope with crippling shortages in all spheres of life. How Holland, through its institutions and private initiatives, responded to the enormous needs is discussed in the remainder of the chapter. Was there an overarching organization in the city and county, and how well did the citizens respond to appeals for action? Were there guidelines? Who informed the organizers of the various Dutch needs? How were these gifts received in the Netherlands?

Obviously compassion and willingness to help were not lacking in Holland, Michigan, in May of 1945, but what was missing was specific knowledge about the situation in the Netherlands, especially in the spring and summer of 1945.[2] Most American citizens had very little knowledge of the five-year German occupation, and how severely all aspects of life had been impacted, especially in the last year. Apart from daily confrontations with German demands, there were increasing shortages of food, clothing, and fuel; diminished means of transportation; a damaged infrastructure; and economic stagnation due to a lack of manpower—men in hiding from the Germans or having been compelled to work in German factories.[3]

It took months to learn about the needs of this depleted nation and years to restore some kind of normalcy. Although the occupation of the Netherlands ended with Germany's capitulation on 5 May 1945, two provinces in large part had been liberated beginning in September 1944. The battles in these regions (basically south of the major rivers) caused horrendous damage. The Allied strategic bombing of the North Sea dikes in Zeeland triggered flooding in large areas, and after fierce battles on the ground, this province was liberated in December 1944. Victories came piecemeal in the eastern and northern Netherlands, beginning at the end of March and continuing through April of 1945. The big cities in the west where the food shortages were so desperate that thousands of people died of hunger had to wait until after 5 May 1945. Canadian troops entered Rotterdam only on 5 May.

---

[2] Some facts about the situation in the Netherlands during the last year of the war came from neutral Sweden. A report states that "shops are completely out of such staples as potatoes, salt, and sugar . . . electric power plants in North Holland had closed," *De Heidenwereld/Missionary Monthly* (Jan. 1945).

[3] Loe De Jong, *Het Koninkrijk der Nederlanden in de Tweede Wereldoorlog*, 14 vols. ('s Gravenhage: Staatsuitgeverij, 1982), 10b, pt.1:155.

The liberated Netherlands was in dire straits in the spring of 1945. Food, however, was not scarce during the first years of the war, although portions were smaller, and ration coupons were required.[4] During the Dutch military mobilization in 1939, the *Rijksbureau voor Voedselvoorziening* (national food supply board) was created to control and equalize the distribution of the food supply. Dutch authorities were mindful of the great shortages during World War I and sought to prevent this from occurring again. Although the Dutch were neutral in this conflict, the embargoes of Dutch harbors had created food scarcities.[5] The system worked well in the first or so war years, although the staff had to negotiate constantly with German authorities who wanted to requisition Dutch supplies. Nevertheless, the board was able successfully to manipulate statistics to deceive the enemy.[6]

Every citizen was issued a distribution card, which made them eligible for periodic ration coupons for food and other items, such as bike tires, shoes, and textiles.[7] Rising demands from Germany for food and goods, as well as shortages occasioned by Allied blockades, created greater scarcity as the war dragged on.[8] To stand in long lines in front of shops became a daily routine. Good footwear was difficult to obtain, since some shoe manufacturers were prohibited from making leather shoes, so many people went about on insoles made of wood. Frequent repairs and reconfiguring stretched the life of textile items. Tobacco, tea, and coffee were already rationed in June 1940, and by the end of the war were virtually impossible to buy, except on the black market. Coffee-loving Dutch, however, were able to make a coffee surrogate which was the best in Europe.[9]

Massive amounts of meat, fats, and dairy products, much beloved components of Dutch cuisine, were carried off to Germany early on.

---

[4] "Economisch leven," *Wegwijzer archieven wo2*, http:archievenwo2.nl/thema-overzicht/Nederland/economisch-leven, 1.

[5] Hendrik Mattheus van Randwijk, et al., *Onderdrukking en verzet: Nederland in oorlogstijd* (Arnhem: Van Loghum Slaterus; Amsterdam: J. M. Meulenhoff, c. 1949), 2:608-9.

[6] De Jong, *Tweede Wereldoorlog*, 10b, pt. 1:155. David Barnouw, *De Hongerwinter* (Hilversum: Verloren, 2005), 15. Even so, the directors and personnel were suspected, during and after the war, of having been too closely allied with the German authorities. They were exonerated from those charges.

[7] Local newspapers informed the public which coupons could be used for what products. For example, the *Utrechts Nieuwsblad* of 2 Oct. 1942 announced that coupon #405 could be used for the purchase of 125 grams of legumes or oats that month.

[8] www.hinkepint.nl/Lege%20 pagina%2012.htm, 1-27.

[9] *Onderdrukking en verzet*, 631.

Fig. 11.1. Newspaper ads demonstrate textile shortage during the war

Like coffee, these were already rationed in July 1940, and only limited amounts could be purchased. Dutch diaries and letters attest to the resulting tasteless food. Consuming less fat actually turned out to be beneficial, up to a point.[10] Ironically, the Dutch government had stocked large supplies of food and raw materials in the period from 1939 to 1940. They were forced by the German authorities to sell a substantial amount to the "Vaterland," sometimes half the total (e.g. of oil and rubber), paying less than the market value.[11]

During the last months of the war, however, no such scruples existed anymore, and widespread looting by Germans further exacerbated shortages in all areas. Food, fuel, and materials declined drastically as the winter of 1944-45 set in, especially in the urban centers of the western Netherlands. A railroad strike, called for by the Dutch government in exile in London in September of 1944, led to German retaliation. The *reichskommissar* of the Netherlands, Arthur Seyss-Inquart, stopped the transportation of food to and within the western Netherlands for six weeks. This restriction further exacerbated the scarcity of food and fuel. After the order was lifted, an extremely wet fall set in, followed by a bitterly cold winter.[12] Canals were frozen, and there were no trucks to transport food from the eastern and northern

[10] Barnouw, *Hongerwinter*, 10.
[11] De Jong, *Tweede Wereldoorlog*, 4, pt. 1:336-39. Revisionist historians, such as Gerard Trienekens, counter commonly-held notions about Germany robbing the Dutch population of their food supply by pointing to statistics that suggest Germany, with some exceptions, paid for their imported goods (although below market value). Gerard Trienekens, *Tussen ons volk en de honger: De voedselvoorziening, 1940-1944* (Soest, 1985). Barnouw, *Hongerwinter*, 7.
[12] Virtually all the winters during the war were bitterly cold.

provinces to the west. The Germans even took horses from Dutch farms.[13]

Constant strafing by Allied planes of vehicles on the roads added to the troubles.[14] As a matter of fact, transportation problems were a primary factor in the so-called Hunger Winter in the West. Most of the coal-mining province of Limburg was freed in September 1944 but was cut off from the rest of the occupied Netherlands, had there even been available locomotives.[15] By November there was no gas or electricity. Homemade small stoves,[16] fed by coal stolen from railroad storage places or from gas and electric plants, or by wood found between tram and train rails, or with small fragments from chopped down trees and shrubs, were inadequate. Authorities were obligated to allow the decimation of entire parks. People even cut down fences, docks, and household furniture for fuel. The small stoves could keep food warm but could not cook. Even to start the stoves was a daunting task that required "deep technical insight, endless patience, limitless devotion, windy weather, and a large dose of luck."[17] Energy woes hit all of the Netherlands, but the lack of food primarily affected the cities of North and South Holland and Utrecht.[18]

With store shelves bare, housewives resorted to sugar beets (with little food value), tulip bulbs (starchy), cattle fodder (inferior quality of ground peas and beans), sea gulls (not meaty or tasty), and cats as well as dogs (half of all pets disappeared).[19] The alternative was to go to local public kitchens with an empty pan and be dished up a set quantity of warm food from large containers. By February 1945 more than a million people came to these public kitchens, and by March half of all city dwellers showed up.[20] The quality was dubious, for the gruel consisted of cabbage and pea powders, meat offal, potato peels, sugar beets, and nettles.[21] This once-a-day fare did not feed the population adequately. In October 1944 people still received thirteen hundred calories a day, but by February 1945, this was reduced to only three hundred calories,

---

[13] De Jong, *Tweede Wereldoorlo*, 10b, pt.1:155.
[14] Ibid., 153.
[15] Ibid., 156, 169.
[16] De Jong, *Tweede Wereldoorlo*, 168.
[17] Ibid., 174.
[18] Ibid., 12:252.
[19] De Jong, *Tweede Wereldoorlog*, 10b:190-91. A child whose family was served virtually all parts of their pet dog remarked afterward that it was too bad that they could not feed the bones to Fido.
[20] Ibid., 166-67.
[21] Ibid., 10b, pt. 1:167; 12, pt. 1:252.

which was virtually a starvation diet. Adults need at least two thousand calories per day.[22]

In April 1945 the situation had become catastrophic in the west: no food, no fuel, no anything. It is estimated that of the three-and-a-half million residents in the provinces of North Holland, South Holland, and Utrecht, twenty-two thousand died during the Hunger Winter.[23] Beginning on 29 April, just a week before German capitulation on 5 May 1945, Allied bombers—reluctantly allowed by Seyss-Inquart—dropped food packets on various pre-determined locations near Rotterdam, The Hague, and Leiden. The tins were sorted and distributed by the National Food Supply Board.[24]

After liberation

This agency continued to function once the war was over in order to control the equal distribution of a very minimal food supply. It took several months for people to get adequate nutrition. Once the Western Scheldt opened up for Allied forces, two hundred ships containing supplies were able to dock at the Antwerp harbor in December 1944, and the freed southern Netherlands gained some relief. The first ship with provisions to dock in Rotterdam in early May 1945 contained twenty-seven thousand tons.[25] These ships (200 in all in 1945) carried supplies that the exiled Dutch government's *Voedselaankoopbureau* (goods purchasing agency) had been able to purchase from surpluses in Canada and the United States during the war years. The grain dealer Cornelis van Stolk—forced to remain in the United States after the war broke out—headed this up. The stock was regularly replenished, and by war's end was the envy of the Allies.[26]

During the month of May, Allied military trucks transported medical and food supplies, while inland waterways ships transported tons of potatoes from the eastern and northern Netherlands.[27] Red Cross bread and flour arrived, distributed without charge in various localities, but only with applicable ration coupons.[28] Posters or ads

---

[22] De Jong, *Tweede Wereldoorlog*, 12, pt. 1:252.
[23] Ibid. The number is much larger if one considers the ill-effects of long-term malnourishment revealed years after the war.
[24] Ibid. See also *Onderdrukking en Verzet*, 644-46. An article in *Trouw* informed the readers that ration coupon A450 and B456 needed to be shown to get free bread. *Trouw*, 9 May 1945.
[25] De Jong, *Tweede Wereldoorlog*, 9, pt. 2:1241-43, 1252.
[26] Ibid.
[27] De Jong, *Tweede Wereldoorlog*, 12, pt. 1:254.
[28] Ibid., 9, pt. 2:1249.

in newspapers informed the public of the kinds of food that could be picked up on a certain day. For example, between 18 and 24 May, citizens in The Hague read on a publicly-displayed notice that they could get a certain amount of potatoes in designated stores.[29]

The chaos left behind by the war affected not only food distribution. But even if one had money, there were no goods to purchase.[30] Ninety thousand houses and buildings had been destroyed; 40 percent of land was inundated, some of it with salt water. What little transport remained was in bad repair. Much of the infrastructure was gone or damaged. A mere four thousand of the pre-war twenty-eight thousand railroad cars were left; 750 kilometers of rails had been removed. Lack of transportation made it extremely difficult for Dutch people who either had been incarcerated in German concentration camps or who had worked in German factories to return to the Netherlands. Many ended up walking home. Household items and clothing were in short supply and often of bad quality.[31]

The *Holland Evening Sentinel* reported that newspapers had to serve as diapers. Even after liberation, when stores received a shipment of underwear, for example, people "lined up during the night to be the first at the [shop's] door."[32] Lack of fuel remained a problem, and parks and forests continued to be stripped.[33]

Aid from America

The government-appointed body *Nederlands Volksherstel* (Restoration of the Netherlands) attempted to create a new Netherlands out of the chaos. An executive arm of *Volksherstel* was HARK (*Hulpactie Roode Kruis*),[34] which collected and distributed the shipments of goods to the Netherlands. A number of American organizations supplied western Europe with necessities. The Queen Wilhelmina Fund, with headquarters in New York City, was one such organization. It had been

---

[29] "5000 oorlogsaffiches uit Nederland en Nederlands-Indië (1940-1945)," in Instituut voor Oorlogs-, Holocaust- en Genocidestudies, Koninklijke Bibliotheek, The Hague.
[30] Mary Pos, *Heidenwereld/Missionary Monthly* (Nov. 1946), 348 (July 1945) 210.
[31] De Jong, *Tweede Wereldoorlog*, 12, pt.1: 252-66.
[32] Letter, Alida van Eck, Amstelveen, 24 July 1946. A letter from Oostdijk (Zeeland) to a cousin in the United States bemoans the fact that cod liver oil is not available yet, Cornelia Blok-van Iwaarden to cousin Mrs. Robert Pool, 29 Jan. 1946 (Mina Pool-Bolier letters, box 97, #10, ACC).
[33] *Holland City News*, 5 July 1945.
[34] Not an arm of the Dutch Red Cross, which operated on its own authority to provide medical teams and which trained volunteers immediately after the liberation.

> **THE NETHERLANDS NEED US**
>
> - After an inspection of war havoc in Holland an official of the World Council of Churches reports property damage of almost seven million dollars to churches, parsonages and youth institutions, with sixty churches wholly destroyed and 40 seriously damaged. Fifty wooden churches could be used at once.
> - Of course the property damage does not tell the whole story. Sixty congregations have been evacuated, thirty parishes inundated. Fifty ministers have lost everything. Twelve died in captivity, nine of them leaving young children. The human suffering can be imagined.
> - Suffering as they are, the Christians of the Netherlands are said to be "greatly encouraged by promised help and planning a vigorous future." Surely we shall take note of such gallantry in action. Surely we shall aid fellow Christians, close to many of our Church by blood, as they seek to REVIVE and REBUILD
>
> **REFORMED CHURCH EMERGENCY FUND**
> 156 Fifth Ave., New York 10, N. Y.
>
> NEEDED, $300,000   ON HAND, $20,886.84

Fig. 11.2. *Church Herald* advertisement, 22 June 1945

organized already in 1940 to aid Dutch citizens, such as those who were stranded in the United States, as well as to prepare for aid to the Netherlands after the war. The fund worked with all churches of southern Ottawa County and northern Allegan County in Michigan until it was subsumed by American Relief for Holland in 1945. This became the agency through which all funds or goods collected by churches or organizations in these counties were directed and channeled. It was not the only organization, however, to provide aid. The Netherlands Office for Relief and Rehabilitation (NORR), a division of the United Nations Relief and Rehabilitation Administration (UNRRA), also sent tons of goods to the Netherlands until the end of 1947.

Reformed Christians in America provide relief

The Reformed Church in America (RCA) and the Christian Reformed Church (CRC) began in 1940 to solicit funds for Dutch relief, but they stepped up their efforts greatly at war's end. Calls for helping "our brethren,"[35] or "brethren of our faith"[36] appeared in CRC and RCA journals and synodical minutes. The *Church Herald*, the RCA organ, noted that the Emergency Fund was to help "fellow Christians close to many of our Church by blood." The Emergency Fund hoped to raise $200,000, of which $40,000 was to go to churches in the Netherlands.[37]

[35] *Banner* (5 Oct. 1945), 917.
[36] *The Link*, Graafschap Christian Reformed Church, July 1945, ACC; *Acts of Synod, Christian Reformed Church*, 1947, 380.
[37] *Church Herald* (22 June 1945), 6.

In the spring and summer months of 1945, both denominations saw aid primarily as restoring church work and religious institutions, rebuilding churches, or providing temporary barracks. The CRC perceived the necessity for spiritual aid to counter the "modernists," who were "planning extensive reconstruction projects."[38] The RCA promoted evangelism, for the church may discover "how thoroughly paganized the masses in the European countries have become ... pagan forces temporarily made harmless will reappear in other forms until they are overcome spiritually."[39]

One of the problems in the days and months after liberation was the lack of knowledge about the church situation in the Netherlands. Not having had contact with official ecclesiastical authorities in the Netherlands for five years, both denominations were at sea about whom to contact. Establishing links anew was primary. Delegates were sent to ascertain the needs of churches. With the arrival of data about the situation in the Netherlands, it became clear to the denominations that the existential needs overrode rebuilding programs of churches and religious institutions. Furthermore, a letter by two Americans from the Netherlands in the *Banner* of 20 July 1945 spelled out that the denomination's focus should be primarily on food and clothing, for "the Dutch population will die unless fed ... feed and clothe the millions destitute now."[40] Also the *Church Herald* catalogued the depleted Netherlands during the summer of 1945.[41]

The CRC Synod for a span of less than two years was involved in overseeing material aid, after which the task was turned over to classes and congregations to collect and/or purchase goods.[42] Although the RCA had set aside $40,000 of the relief fund budget in 1946 for aid to Dutch churches,[43] the denomination had cooperated—even during the war years—with secular or non-denominational relief efforts.[44] The *Church Herald* frequently published appeals from Church World Service.[45]

---

[38] Overture by Holland Classis, in *Agenda [of] Synod Christian Reformed Church*, 2 (Grand Rapids, MI, 1943), 236-37.
[39] Ibid., 13 July 1945, 3; *Acts and Proceedings of the General Synod of the RCA*, 1945, 166.
[40] *Banner* (20 July 1945), 685.
[41] *Church Herald* (19 Oct. 1945), 5.
[42] *Acts of Synod*, 1947, 223. Synod also made clear that the goods be purchased locally.
[43] *Church Herald* (8 June 1945), 15.
[44] E.g., the request from Church World Service for ninety thousand diapers (used ones were welcome, but needed to be laundered first!), *Church Herald*, 16 Dec. 1945. See also 1 June, 12 Oct. 1945.
[45] See for example ibid., 12 Oct., 16 Dec. 1945.

Fig. 11.3. Queen Wilhelmina Fund poster, 1944

Citizens of the primarily Dutch American community of Holland, Michigan,—most of them members of CRC and RCA churches—were intensely involved in the collection of funds through "drives" and collections, with purchases or donations of food and clothing to be sent to the Netherlands. As a matter of fact, even before 5 May 1945, local churches had already sent clothing to the Queen Wilhelmina Fund in New York.[46]

The guiding light of the operation of collecting and shipping goods was Willard Wichers, director of the Netherlands Information Bureau in Holland, Michigan, which was formed in 1942. By 1945 he was the official representative in Ottawa and Allegan counties for American Relief for Holland, the former Queen Wilhelmina Fund. Licensed by the government, it was the official relief fund for the Netherlands. This allowed goods to be shipped free of charge and insurance costs and on arrival in the Netherlands to be processed by HARK.

The organization was subdivided into local chapters. Wichers, representing American Relief, sent a memo to "women chairmen of churches, volunteer workers not associated with church committees, and pastors of the Ottawa/Allegan churches," listing specific Dutch needs such as diapers, breakfast foods, vitamins, and powdered milk for children; household kits (containing textiles of any sort, and kitchen items); flat irons (the old fashioned type), scissors, and toys.[47]

---

[46] A thank-you letter, preserved by the Maple Avenue Christian Reformed Church, was received on 4 Feb. 1945, from the southern Netherlands, ACC.
[47] Willard Wichers, box 8/9, n.d., Holland Historical Trust Collection (HHTC).

Fig. 11.4. Willard C. Wichers, 1909-1991

In April of 1945, in anticipation of the imminent German surrender, Wichers had block leaders appointed to launch a clothing drive. Volunteers from various RCA churches and service organizations collected nearly forty tons of used clothing and shoes which were then sorted and packed in the Holland Armory on 26 April 1945.[48] Some of this was for Allied war-torn countries, but a good amount was set aside for American Relief for Holland.[49] An enormous quantity of clothing piled high on the armory[50] floor led to the occasional packing of a volunteer's coat or to friction when a wife packed a husband's beloved jacket without his consent.[51]

The Dutch authorities and the Red Cross regularly advised Wichers' office on the third floor of Holland's city hall about various necessities.[52] Other means of obtaining information were public talks by representatives who had been sent to the Netherlands by both RCA and CRC representatives. Furthermore, individuals having just returned from visiting the "old country" and agents from various organizations spoke at churches or public gatherings about the situation.

[48] It took five days. *Church Herald*, 1 June 1945, reported that Holland's Third Reformed Church's second drive for used clothing for war victims had been met with "gratifying response," 21.
[49] *Holland City News*, 26 Apr. 1945.
[50] The armory, presently owned by the Holland Historical Museum, was built in 1923 to house the National Guard.
[51] Ibid., 3 May 1945.
[52] *Holland City News*, 4 Oct., 26 Dec. 1945.

Topping the list were shoes, especially men's shoes—extra wide requested—and work pants to allow breadwinners to go back to work,[53] warm clothing and stockings for the whole family, as well as the ubiquitous call for diapers and baby clothes. The sending of perishable foods was not possible, so canned fish, fruits, and vegetables, dehydrated soups, cocoa, tea and coffee were sent. Dutch requests for basic household objects demonstrate the all-around shortages of the most basic essentials in the home, and Holland residents sent kitchen utensils, notions such as thimbles, darning cotton, needles, woolen yarn, toiletries such as tooth brushes and soap, shoe repair kits, and toys.[54] Many church women, and even the girls at Holland Christian High, spent hours knitting sweaters.[55] Church women also made garments to be sent, and so did the Ottawa/Allegan chapter of American Relief for Holland.[56] Church basements became packing and storage places for the thousands of items collected.[57]

Not only did Wichers direct the collections, but he also instructed the donors in the regulations for shipping the goods, which ensured the safe arrival of packages in the Netherlands. His instructions also included the enclosing of maps of the United States, and a return address marking the state and town of contributors, as well as a greeting "to express . . . admiration and friendship for the brave people of the Netherlands."[58] Contents had to be listed on the outside to ensure that the packages would meet censure restrictions and that they could be sent duty free.

Ads in Dutch newspapers alerted readers that relatives or friends in the United States could send food items to them, which would be assembled by an American firm and sent to Dutch grocery chains. The great advantage was that the Dutch recipients would not have to use ration coupons.[59] Many individuals, however, sent packages on their own, often to their own relatives. The authorities actually encouraged

---

[53] *Holland Evening Sentinel*, 29 Jan. 1947. See also *Missionary Monthly* (July 1945), 210. The shoe width EEE is known as a Dutch foot.
[54] For example, *Holland City News*, 18 Sept., 4, 12 Oct., 26 Dec. 1945; Wichers, box 8/9, HHTC; *Bulletin of Maple Avenue Christian Reformed Church*, 15 July 1945, 5147, 1, ACC.
[55] Maple Avenue CRC, 27 Oct. 1946, 5147, 1, ACC. Wool was provided by the Ottawa/Allegan Chapter of American Relief for Holland (*Holland City News*, 13 Sept. 1945).
[56] Graafschap Christian Reformed Church women reported in the congregation's newspapers that they had made and sent 350 pieces of clothing, *Link*, May, 1946, 5113, 1, ACC; *Holland City News*, 4 Oct. 1945.
[57] Montello Christian Reformed Church did so in 1945, 5162, 5, ACC.
[58] Forms in Wichers, box 8/9, HHTC.
[59] See *De Gooi- en Eemlander: nieuws- en advertentieblad*, 19 June 1948, for example.

Fig. 11.5. Prospect Park CRC women pack canned goods for shipment to the Netherlands (*left to right*): Mrs. J. T. Hoogstra (pastor's wife), Mrs. Bud Westerhof, Mrs. F. Kolenbrander, and Mrs. Lawrence Veltkamp. (*Holland Evening Sentinel*, Aug. 20, 1945)

such private shipments to supplement regional or national relief.[60] The same restrictions and guidelines applied to individual shipments. Packages needed to be marked "gift" so that the Dutch recipients would not pay import duty, and a dollar value had to be included.[61] Correct labels could be picked up at Wichers' office. Proof that there was great interest to participate in sending food and goods is an entry in the *Holland City News* on 18 October 1945 that three thousand new tags had been received and could be picked up. Each tag cost one penny.[62]

The packages without a specific addressee were sent by the American Relief Agency to be forwarded to HARK. That agency sorted and distributed the goods according to the needs of the Dutch population and in consultation with social agencies. HARK compiled lists of the most needy—individuals, returned captives, orphanages, and hospitals.[63] In the first months after liberation, HARK distributed five hundred thousand items of clothing, shoes, and household articles to the especially bereft. Between 1946 and 1947, seventeen million items were distributed.[64] After 13 September 1945, HARK permitted relief goods to be consigned to a specific group.[65] Prior to that time,

---

[60] R. Neij and E.V. Hueting, *Nederlands Volksherstel 1944-1947. Een omstreden hulporganisatie in Herrijzend Nederland* (Culemborg: Lemma, 1988), 29.
[61] Wichers, box 8/9, HHTC.
[62] The actual cost was a bit less, but the remaining amount was added to the relief fund.
[63] *De Vrije stemmen van Schouwen-Duiveland: tevens mededeelingenblad militair gezag*, 16 Aug. 1946.
[64] *Nederlands Volksherstel*, 25.
[65] *Holland City News*, 13 Sept. 1945; Willard C. Wichers to Committees working for Netherlands Relief, 24 Sept. 1945 (Wichers, box 8/9, HTHC).

Christian Reformed churches had sent their packages to HARK, but after September 1945, members were instructed to address these to the *Gereformeerde Kerken in Nederland*. This denomination had a warehouse in Rotterdam.[66]

Members of the *Nederlands Volksherstel* were not very happy about having to relinquish their ideals for a less ideologically fragmented Netherlands. Although the organization was an arm of the government, it was comprised of individuals who had a clear humanistic ideology. They desired to do away with the pre-war *zuilen* (pillars) system, in which political and religious ideologies were expressed in separate institutions. *Volksherstel* had aimed at centralizing the distribution of goods and food. Wichers himself had received a plea on 30 July 1945, urging him to "to do what you can to assure those interested that relief in the Netherlands is NOT being distributed according to religious beliefs." The writer of the letter, director of Organizational Relationships of American Relief for Holland, reiterated that the distribution of food and clothing should be "religion-proof" and to make sure . . . that every person would get help, and "that no individuals or groups are favored."[67] Ultimately, *Volksherstel* functionaries capitulated and had to allow for independently operating regional and ideological groups.[68]

In spite of this recommendation, Wichers could not prevent RCA or CRC churches, or local service organizations, from sending goods to specific churches or affiliated associations, such as to Rotary Clubs. He did, however, keep records of such shipments.[69] Enormous quantities of goods were sent from Holland, Michigan. The local papers kept the public informed about the amount of goods sent. On 4 October 1945, for example, the *Holland City News* reported that American Relief for Holland had shipped seven hundred tons of canned goods, five hundred in baby food, and was preparing to ship one thousand bars of soap and five hundred children's shoes. American Relief for Holland also shipped sixty thousand cartons of oats. It has been estimated that from May 1945 to March 1946, seven hundred thousand packages were sent "by Americans and Dutch living in America, with an average weight of 5 kg."[70]

---

[66] Acts of Synod, 1946, 376. The various references in CRC publications to "Reformed churches" in the Netherlands is perhaps misleading, for it is clear from other sentences that it is a literal translation of the *Gereformeerde Kerken in Nederland*, often called "our own."

[67] Victor H. Scales to Willard Wichers, 30 July 1945. Wichers, box 8/9, HHTC.

[68] Nederlands Volksherstel (1944-47), 553-65

[69] Wichers, box 8/9, HHTC.

[70] *De Tijd: godsdienstig staatkundig dagblad*, 22 Oct. 1945; *Het Dagblad: Uitgave van de Nederlandsche Dagbladpers te Batavia*, 17 Apr. 1946.

Distribution in the Netherlands

What happened to the thousands of packages sent? Most Americans knew neither how difficult and complex the journey of a package was once it arrived at a port nor how it reached its final destination. Even after the German-placed obstacles in the Amsterdam and Rotterdam harbor were removed, administrative disorganization and lack of adequate transportation hampered the distribution of the flood of goods arriving in the Netherlands.[71] In the summer of 1946 an American observer commented on distribution problems. He saw eleven thousand packages in storage in Rotterdam awaiting personnel to deliver them. Even Rotterdam postal employees were enlisted in the fall of 1945 to unload packages from ships coming from America.[72] Part of the problem was a dockworkers' strike in the summer of 1945, when still emaciated workers[73] protested against a heavy workload and low wages. In large towns, post office back rooms resembled labyrinths with thousands of stacked packages (mostly from America) due to a lack of workers. People who had received notice that a package was awaiting them often had to stand in lines four or five wide, which sometimes stretched outside the post office.[74]

Some donors in Holland, Michigan, voiced concerns about the sure arrival of packages. Wichers dismissed these fears as unwarranted.[75] But mishaps occurred more frequently than he thought. Letters in Dutch newspapers complained that the promised package or packages, after a relative had sent a notification by mail, had not arrived. Letters were sometimes rifled by thieves, which seemed to increase after liberation.[76] Black market operations were widespread both during and after the war. Greed led some mailmen to purloin packages.[77] Others handling shipments may also have been driven by desperation to petty theft. Fully six months after liberation, it was estimated that only 9 percent of those needing relief had been helped.[78] Perhaps this statistic may need to be checked.

---

[71] *De Heidenwereld/Missionary Monthly* (July 1945), 209.
[72] *Nieuwsblad van het Noorden*, 15 Aug. 1946. *Het Vrije Volk: democratisch-socialistisch dagblad*, 17 Nov. 1945.
[73] *De Heidenwereld/Missionary Monthly* (July 1945), 209.
[74] *Amigoe di Curacao: weekblad voor de Curacaosche eilanden*, from *Algemeen Handelsblad*, 6 Sept. 1946.
[75] *Holland Evening Sentinel*, 22 Sept. 1945.
[76] *Leeuwarder Koerier*, 8, 13 Nov. 1945, for example.
[77] *Limburgsch Dagblad*, 12 Feb. 1946; *Nieuwsblad van het Noorden*, 11 July 1946.
[78] *Holland City News*, 26 Dec. 1945.

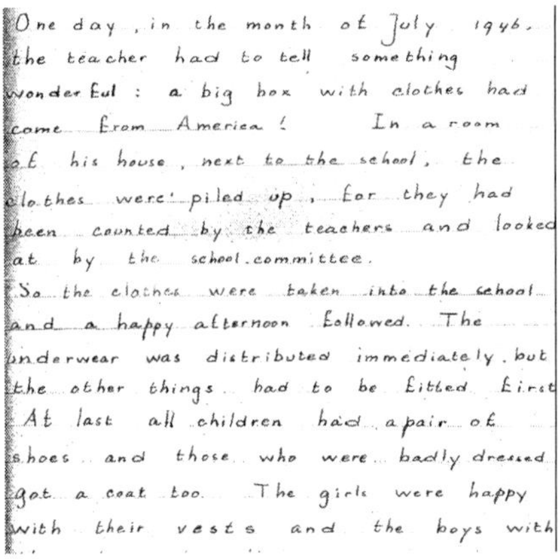

> One day, in the month of July 1946, the teacher had to tell something wonderful: a big box with clothes had come from America! In a room of his house, next to the school, the clothes were piled up, for they had been counted by the teachers and looked at by the school committee. So the clothes were taken into the school and a happy afternoon followed. The underwear was distributed immediately, but the other things had to be fitted first. At last all children had a pair of shoes and those who were badly dressed got a coat too. The girls were happy with their vests and the boys with

Fig. 11.6. Thank-you letter from a school in Werkendam (South Holland) to Montello Park Christian Reformed Church, Holland, Michigan, 1947 (*courtesy Archives Calvin College*)

Some packages simply went astray. They were improperly boxed or wrapped, damaged in transit, or undeliverable because of inaccurate names or addresses. Newspapers often included notices from the local post office with names and/or addresses that could not be traced. Some of the family contacts may have been decades old.[79]

In spite of stolen, undeliverable, or damaged packages, and an inaccurate statistic, it seems that the majority did reach their final destination. Letters of thanks were sent to many generous donors in Ottawa and Allegan Counties who had included their names and addresses on the forms Wichers had supplied. The local papers printed some of the letters.[80] Even little gifts of appreciation were sent.

Large gifts came to the United States from various governmental offices, institutions, or agencies in the Netherlands. Six hundred thousand tulip bulbs were sent to the United States. That the largesse and efforts of the Holland community were deeply valued is reflected in the many gifts to the town, now part of the artifacts collection in the Holland Museum. Gratitude was also expressed in newspapers.

Wichers had responded positively to Dutch letters for assistance after the war, and gifts small and large were sent to Holland as tokens of gratitude. One example of many must suffice. The Haarlem *Burgerweeshuis* (orphanage) sent a doll in traditional orphan dress in gratitude for having received funds to construct a playground.[81] During Holland's centennial in 1947, many "official" objects were sent, with expressions of gratitude for aid packages. The Netherlands Office of Foreign Affairs alone contributed 101 objects. The Rijksmuseum gave

---

[79] *Nieuwsblad van het Noorden*, 23 Mar. 1946.
[80] *Holland Evening Sentinel*, 7 Sept. 1945.
[81] Wichers, box 8/9, HHTC.

sixty-six valuable seventeenth-century prints. Some gifts were very large. "The Amsterdam people" sent a Frisian chaise and a barrel organ, while the province of Overijssel contributed a push sled.[82]

It was gratifying for the people of Holland, Michigan, both individually and institutionally, to receive so many indications of gratitude. Ever since Germany had invaded and occupied the Netherlands in May 1940, churches in Ottawa and Allegan Counties had raised funds for end-of-war aid. This was stepped up after German capitulation on 5 May 1945. Many gave countless hours in organizing drives for funds and goods, and in sorting, packing and shipping the relief goods. This was especially laudatory since Holland residents themselves were still living under the rationing of food and consumer goods. For the United States, V-E Day on 8 May 1945 only ended the European theater, but it was another three months before V-J Day, and concerns continued for the many from Ottawa and Allegan Counties who continued to fight in the Pacific theater. Nevertheless, the big thrust to help the people of the Netherlands had already begun months before the war with Japan had ended on 15 August 1945. Even now, more than seventy years later, the town's compassionate response is a story worth telling.

---

[82] Gifts from the Netherlands, 1938-47, box 2, T.88 0303.9, HHTC.

CHAPTER 12

By Trial and Error: The Experience of a Dutch Escape Line in the Second World War

Bruce Bolinger

During the Second World War, Dutch citizens watched the vast number of Allied bombers en route from England to their targets in Nazi Germany.[1] But those planes had to pass through a gauntlet of fire from German anti-aircraft guns and fighter planes even before they reached Germany and again on their return. On one night alone, 21 June 1943, forty-four Royal Air Force (RAF) planes were shot down over the Netherlands.[2] The US 8th Air Force from June 1942 to the end of the war experienced sixty thousand airmen shot down over western Europe, with twenty-six thousand killed, thirty thousand taken prisoner, and four thousand who evaded capture.[3]

---

[1] I am indebted to the many people in the Netherlands and the United States who, over the course of a decade or more, translated for me source documents from Dutch, French, and German and to the archivists in both countries who directed me to those records. I particularly wish to acknowledge the help of Janine Marseille-Smit, sister of Karst Smit, for sharing with me so much about her brother, including family photographs.

[2] Bob De Graaff, *Stepping Stones to Freedom: Help to Allied Airmen in the Netherlands During World War II* (Marceline, MO: Walsworth Publishing, 2003), 27.

[3] Ralph K. Patton, "La Nébuleuse de la Resistance Franco-American Colloque, Paris, Dec. 4, 2000": United States Air Forces Escape & Evasion Society *COMMUNICATIONS*, 8 Dec. 2000, 27.

As a consequence, escape lines were organized to move the evaders from the Netherlands and Belgium, through France, and over the Pyrenees to Spain, where they would be transferred by the British Embassy in Madrid to the British naval base at Gibraltar and flown back to England.[4] But the danger to those Dutch who helped Allied airmen was tremendous. In August 1940 the general commanding the *Luftwaffe* in the Netherlands announced that aiding Allied airmen was punishable by death. During the war from 150 to 165 Dutch helpers of airmen were executed.[5] Add to those figures the many helpers who were sent to concentration camps.

Escape lines in the Netherlands aided not only Allied airmen but also escaped prisoners of war, *onderduikers* (political opponents of the Nazis and men in hiding from the German labor draft, literally "under divers"), *Engelandvaarders* (young men seeking to reach England to join the RAF or the Dutch Princess Irene Brigade), and Jewish Dutch citizens. The focus of this paper is on one such line, the Smit-Van der Heijden Line, named after its principal figures, Karst Smit, a *marechaussee* (Dutch Royal Military Police), and Eugene van der Heijden, a teacher.

Karst Smit

Born 10 June 1917 in The Hague, Karst Smit was the oldest son in a multi-generational family of blacksmiths. The shop that carried stoves and other merchandise faced the street, with the living quarters above it and the grandparents on the third floor. They were a devout Dutch Reformed family, working hard six days a week and going to the Nieuwe Zuiderkerk twice on Sunday. Karst, his father, brother, and three sisters all sang in the choir.[6] Family photos suggest it was a family with a close-knit, supportive relationship.

Following secondary school, where Karst studied French, German, and English, he worked in a tax office during the day and took business school classes at night.[7] His obligatory military service began in March 1937, with Karst being promoted to sergeant in ten months. Enjoying his military service, Karst in March 1938 signed up for another six years

---

[4] Sherri Greene Ottis, *Silent Heroes, Downed Airmen and the French Underground* (Lexington: University Press of Kentucky, 2001), 174-75, and frontispiece, "Major Escape Routes through France, 1940-1945." Tom Applewhite, 2nd Lt. USAAF, discussions with the author, 2000-2006.
[5] De Graaf, *Stepping Stones*, 38, 42.
[6] Janine Marseille-Smit, letter to the author, 3 June 2005.
[7] Ibid., 2 May 2006.

Fig. 12.1. Karst Smit in Jagers uniform
(*courtesy Janine Marseille-Smit*)

and was assigned to the *Jagers* regiment, second battalion.[8] Within a week, Karst's battalion was transferred to Tilburg.[9]

Karst's assignment to Tilburg was fortunate because the city would play an important role in the escape lines. In 1939 Tilburg had a population of ninety-seven thousand and was the center of the Netherlands woolen industry. It was also the center of transportation in the province of Brabant, with the greater part of railway traffic in the southern Netherlands passing through it. Moreover, it is located on the Wilhelmina Canal, which connects Eindhoven and Tilburg to the river Maas, and sits astride the roads to 's Hertogenbosch (Den Bosch), Breda, Eindhoven, and Turnhout (in Belgium).[10] A significant proportion of Allied airmen seeking to get back to England and Dutch people fleeing the Nazis would have to go through Tilburg on their way to Belgium, France, and Spain.

During Karst's first two years in Tilburg, he made key contacts, such as Bertram Brasz, whose home later would become a stopping point for escaped French prisoners of war and Allied airmen.[11] The

---

[8] "Extract from the Service Records of the Royal Ground Forces, Royal Air Force, Royal Navy and the Royal Military Police Concerning: Smit, Karst Gerrit," Ministry of Defence, The Hague.

[9] "De Jagers Rukken Tilburg Binnen," *Nieuwe Tilburgsche Courant*, 29 Mar. 1938.

[10] Naval Intelligence, *Netherlands* (London: Naval Intelligence Division, British Admiralty, Oct. 1944), 231, 696; Tony Bosch, Penn Valley, CA, letter to the author, 9 Sept. 2006.

[11] *Vragenlijst* of Bertram Brasz, 22 Aug. 1945, Military Intelligence Service (MIS), Headquarters European Theatre of Operations United States Army (HQ ETOUSA), National Archives and Records Administration (NARA), National Archives II (NAII), College Park, MD, UD183: MIS-X Files, Holland, 1945-47.

training marches and field exercises Karst and his men conducted, fanning out from Tilburg and going as far as Baarle-Nassau on the Belgian border, familiarized him with the countryside, something that would be invaluable when it came time to move fugitives from the Nazis out of the country as quickly as possible.[12]

The German invasion

As a German invasion of the Netherlands on 10 May 1940 became imminent, Karst was assigned responsibility for three drawbridges over the Wilhelmina Canal between Oirschot and Tilburg. At any sign of the enemy, he and his men were to destroy the bridges. On the morning of Saturday, 11 May, armed only with 1890-vintage carbines and one pistol, in the face of the advancing German army, they blew up the bridges and retreated, reaching Dunkirk on 20 May. There, with fourteen hundred other Dutch troops, they boarded the French merchant ship, SS *Pavon*, intending to sail to England via Cherbourg. But the ship was bombed and strafed by German planes, with many of the Dutch soldiers killed and wounded. On fire and leaking, the ship had to be abandoned. Unable to join the evacuation of British troops at Dunkirk because of lack of space on the British ships, Karst and his men returned to the Netherlands.[13]

Nazi oppression

During the German occupation, conditions in Belgium were "relatively benign" by comparison to those in the Netherlands.[14] The former was administered by the German military, while the latter had a civilian Nazi government, headed by two Austrian Nazis, Arthur Seyss-Inquart, High Commissioner or *Reichskommissar* in charge of the civil administration, and Hanns Albin Rauter, "Higher SS and Police Leader," who received his orders directly from Heinrich Himmler.[15] Oppressive Nazi control of the civilian population included mandatory possession of identity cards with regular identity checks "on street corners and stations, on trains and in theatres."[16]

[12] Tony Bosch, interview by the author, 30 Aug. 2006.
[13] Karst Smit, "De Ramp met de Pavon," *Escape Nieuwsbulletin*, no. 90 (Oct. 1996): 16-17.
[14] Karst Smit, interview by the author, 6-7 July 2002.
[15] Werner Warmbrunn, *The Dutch under German Occupation, 1940-1945* (Stanford: Stanford University Press, 1963), 27, 30.
[16] Bob Moore, *Victims & Survivors, The Nazi Persecution of the Jews in the Netherlands 1940-1945* (London: Arnold, 1997), 159.

The systematic isolation and exclusion of Jews from the rest of Dutch society was followed by mass deportations. Dutch men were drafted to work in Germany, but when that did not produce enough workers, the Germans used mass raids to round up additional young men. University students were required to sign a declaration of loyalty to the Third Reich or face the labor draft. Radios were seized to prevent listening to broadcasts from London. Strikes, gatherings, and distribution and possession of pamphlets were made subject to the death penalty. An ever-expanding curfew was imposed. And there were reprisal executions of hostages.[17]

Marechaussee service

Determined to oppose the German occupation, in August 1940, Karst joined the *marechaussees*. This gave him the significant advantage of being able to wear a uniform, carry a weapon, be out on the streets after curfew, and because the *marechaussees* were responsible for patrolling the borders, he was free to cross the border into Belgium.[18]

Marechaussees wore distinctive uniforms (see fig. 12.5.) making them readily identifiable to non-Dutch fugitives, such as Allied airmen and escaping POWs in places such as crowded railway stations. They were predominantly from the western Netherlands, the more Protestant part of the country.[19]

Following postings in different parts of the Netherlands, in January 1942 Karst was assigned to Hilvarenbeek, a small farming town south of Tilburg and near the Belgian border. For anyone seeking to go to Brussels, Hilvarenbeek provided access to the Belgian cities of Turnhout and Antwerp. It was an ideal location for Karst to be able to help people fleeing the Nazis, not only because of his authority to patrol the border and cross into Belgium but also because of the smuggling activity common to that area. Shortages in one country and abundance in the other, plus taxes imposed on a product in one country but not in the other, created a vigorous flow of goods carried by smugglers across the border, mainly farm produce from the Netherlands to Belgium and

---

[17] Moore, *Victims* 79; Warmbrunn, *German Occupation*, 167, 72-73, 151-52, 57-58; Kees Van Kemenade, *Hilvarenbeek, 1940-1945* (Hapert: Drukkerij-Uitgeverij De Kempen, 1983), 79; Walter B. Maass, *The Netherlands at War: 1940-1945* (London: Abelard-Schuman, 1970), 143-44.
[18] Karst Smit, RTL5 Television interview, date unknown; De Graaf, *Stepping Stones*, 123.
[19] Eugene van der Heijden, "1942; De eerste 'reiziger,'" *Escape Nieuwsbulletin*, no. 85 (June 1995): 30.

manufactured products plus tobacco and chocolate from Belgium to the Netherlands.[20]

By not using the official crossing points, these enterprising individuals avoided the customs and tax officials. A large forested area on the Dutch side of the border, known as Landgoed de Utrecht (estate de Utrecht) near the town of Esbeek, provided cover for smugglers waiting for the border patrols to pass by. Not only *marechaussees* patrolled the border but also the *Deutsche Grenzschutz*, the German Border Police.[21] The *marechausees* were responsible for preventing smuggling but privately could look the other way. Professional smugglers were more likely to be arrested by them than ordinary people, who were trying to help their families survive wartime shortages and loss of income by doing a little smuggling on the side. The *Deutsche Grenzschutz* men, however, were diligent in carrying out their duties to prevent smuggling and capture fugitives, not wanting to be sent to the Russian front.[22]

Threats to the escape line

The Gestapo is probably what most people would think of as the greatest danger to an escape line or any other form of resistance during the Second World War. But there were multiple German secret police agencies. In the Netherlands there were two agencies that people feared, the SD (*Sicherheitsdienst*), the Security Service of the SS, and the Order Police (*Ordnungspolizei*), known as the Green Police for the color of their uniforms. The latter "carried out arrests, mass raids, deportations, actions against strikes, and executions."[23] By contrast, in Belgium, because of the German military administration, the escape lines' main danger was the *Geheime Feldpolizei* (GFP – Secret Field Police), part of the *Abwehr*, German military intelligence. In Antwerp the *Abwehr* set up a false escape line known as the "KLM Line," that swept up 177 unsuspecting airmen for interrogation and eventual imprisonment.[24] And always there was the risk of betrayal by collaborators. They

---

[20] Kees van Kemenade, conversation with the author, 5 May 2010; Joke Schilders, letter to the author, 28 Jan. 2013. Eugene van der Heijden, "Grensperikelen," *Escape Nieuwsbulletin*, no. 90 (Oct. 1996): 21-24; Maria van de Pol and Stan van de Pol, letter to the author, 19 Jan. 2011; Gusta and Madeleine Claes, interview by Hans Otten, *Gazet van Antwerpen*, 30 Aug. 2010; Karst Smit, "Nachtjas," *Escape Nieuwsbulletin*, no. 72 (March 1992): 27-29.

[21] Ellen Van Gilst, "In Dienst van de 'Comet Line,'" *De Telegraaf*, 9 May 1992.

[22] Karst Smit, "Tramavontuur," *Escape Nieuwsbulletin*, no. 83 (Dec. 1994): 28-30.

[23] Warmbrunn, *German Occupation*, 40-41.

[24] W. J. M. Willemsen, "Escape-avontuur eindigde in Antwerpen," *Escape Nieuwsbulletin*, no. 53 (June 1987): 30.

could be the greatest danger of all because they might be neighbors, acquaintances, people you would have no reason to suspect, and not necessarily members of the Dutch Nazi Party strutting around in their uniforms.

The first fugitives – the Frenchmen

Following the French surrender, 1.6 million French soldiers were transported east across the Rhine. They were "dispersed in work gangs: on farms, in workshops, on construction sites, in factories, in mines in Germany. More than a million were still there at the beginning of 1942."[25] Not surprisingly, many of them wanted to go home, and the work gangs presented more opportunities to escape than POW camps.[26]

In April 1942, three months after his transfer to Hilvarenbeek, Karst and another *marechaussee* were patrolling Landgoed de Utrecht near the Belgian border, when they encountered two men hiding in a ditch who at first appeared to be smugglers but, on being questioned, proved to be escaped French prisoners of war attempting to walk home. On that occasion the most the two *marechaussees* could do to help them was to take them across the border into Belgium and point them in the direction of Weelde (see fig. 6), the nearest Belgian town where they could get transportation to Brussels. Realizing there would be more such men, Karst discussed with his friend Bertram Brasz of Tilburg what could be done to provide more effective help. Brasz directed Karst to his cousin, Cornelis Brasz of Enschede, a town close to the German border, who agreed to help. It was decided that Cornelis and friends of his in the resistance would patrol the border and pick up any escaped Frenchmen they found crossing into the Netherlands. They would supply them with clothing as needed and accompany them by train to Tilburg where Karst or others in his group would take over, providing them with Belgian money and false Belgian identity cards, and guide them across the border into Belgium. From Weelde the Frenchmen could make their own way to a contact address in Brussels provided to them by Karst.[27]

[25] Peschanski, Denis, et al., *Collaboration and Resistance Images of Life in Vichy France 1940-1944* (New York: Harry N. Abrams, 2000), 94.
[26] Waldschmidt, Dominique and Odile (eds.), *Le nez au vent, Récit d'évasion*, memoirs of Charles Waldschmidt, French prisoner of war, written in 1956 and edited and reproduced in 2009 for circulation within the Waldschmidt family.
[27] Karst Smit, letter to Rijksinstituut voor Oorlogsdocumentatie (RIOD), 8 Sep. 1963. Karst Smit, testimony of 5 Aug. 1954, agency unidentified, papers of Ellen van Gilst. Karst Smit, report to the French Embassy in The Hague, 13, Aug. 1952, from file of Karst Smit, Dutch Ministry of Defence; Karst Smit, "Report of activities of Karst

Next came Jewish Dutch citizens

With mass deportations of Jewish Dutch citizens under way by July 1942,[28] more and more desperate people were seeking a way out of the Netherlands. In early May, Karst received a phone call from his friend Bertram Brasz asking him to come by. During their meeting, Brasz explained that his cousin Cornelis of Enschede had asked if they would help in the escape of Andries Hoek, the son of a Jewish dress shop proprietor in Enschede. Hoek had a contact in Brussels, Marie Krauss, who would provide temporary housing, and Hoek gave her address to Karst. On 10 May 1942, Karst guided Hoek across the border. A few days later, with one of his top aides, *marechaussee* David Jonkers, Karst paid Krauss and her brother, Jean, a visit at their home. They discussed arrangements for future refugees. Karst would see to it that the fugitives were provided with travel money and false Belgian identity cards. The more independent ones would be guided across the Dutch-Belgian border and given the Krauss address (never in writing) in Brussels, leaving it to them to get there on their own. But whenever possible, Karst would take them to Brussels himself. Jean Krauss had contacts with sympathetic Belgian police who would pass the people on to cooperative French police at the French border.[29]

The aid given to one Jewish family, the Keesing family, was particularly poignant. The father had already reached Brussels. His wife and their three children, a little boy and two girls, aged from five to nine, had been hiding in an attic in Amsterdam and were to follow him as soon as possible. The opportunity came on Christmas Eve, 1942. It had been snowing all day, and by nightfall the fields and roads were hidden under a heavy layer of snow making it difficult to walk through it and impossible to manage on bicycles. It was so cold that the German border guards remained in their huts near their fires, reasoning that no one would try to cross the border in such weather. Four members of the escape line, three *marechaussees* and one civilian, guided the little family through the forest for three hours. The children were suffering from the bitter cold, so the *marechaussees* would alternate holding them under their great coats to warm them and muffle their crying. Once across the border, one of the *marechaussees* accompanied the family to Brussels,

---

Smit," helper file of Karst Smit, National Archives and Records Administration (NARA), National Archives II (NAII), College Park, MD, UD183: MIS-X Files, Holland, 1945-47; Karst Smit, letter to National Union of War Escapees, 27 Sep. 1973, from the papers of Ed Ragas, Baarle-Nassau.

[28] Warmbrunn, *German Occupation*, 167.
[29] Karst Smit, letter to RIOD.

Fig. 12.2. Assisting the Keesing family
(*courtesy of Ewan McClure*)

while the others returned to Hilvarenbeek. It was midnight when they returned, just as the villagers were on their way to midnight mass. Some villagers were expressing disappointment about how Christmas had been spoiled—they missed the chiming of their beloved church bells, the Germans having confiscated them for metal to make armaments. But for the handful of men who had helped the Keesings, it was the most beautiful Christmas of their lives.[30]

Some people in the Netherlands exploited the desperate people fleeing the Nazis, particularly when it came to providing a false Belgian identity card with a fugitive's correct photo. But such cards were provided at no cost by Karst Smit's organization. One Jewish man writing after the war about the aid given to him in safely reaching Brussels, praised the members of the escape line for their patriotic and humanitarian work.[31]

Pillarization of Dutch society

Dutch society before the war was characterized by "four vertical *zuilen* or pillars, comprising three clearly identifiable groups, Roman Catholic, Protestant and social democratic, together with a fourth,

---

[30] Eugene van der Heijden, "De Witte Kerstnacht," *Escape Nieuwsbulletin*, no. 71 (Dec. 1991): 17-20.
[31] Lenck, John M. S. (pseudonym for C. Citroen), *Vlucht over Vier Grenzen* (Amsterdam: G. W. Breughel, n.d.), 21.

more nebulous neutral or liberal group."[32] Each pillar had its own newspapers, political parties, trade unions, and cultural organizations.[33] This pillarization undercut potential cooperation in the resistance movement among the members of the different pillars. A study of the resistance in the region of Twente found that "Protestants, Catholics, Socialists, and Communists mostly operated independently, not so much because of unwillingness to cooperate, but because they did not know each other."[34]

In 1930 Roman Catholics in the Netherlands represented 36.4 percent of the population, with the greatest concentration in the two southern provinces of North Brabant (88.6 percent) and Limburg (93.5 percent).[35] The Smit-Van der Heijden Line was centered in the province of North Brabant, particularly in the towns of Hilvarenbeek, Esbeek, Goirle, and Baarle-Nassau. Karst Smit was Protestant, as most likely were many of the *marechaussees* who assisted him.

Escape lines in the Netherlands have been described as "webs" or "networks" of resistance contacts, rather than organizations in the usual sense.[36] The Smit-Van der Heijden Line was probably unusual in that it combined a military structure (the armed, uniformed *marechaussees*) with civilian contacts scattered across several provinces. Moreover, Karst Smit, by virtue of being a *marechaussee*, was in a position of authority in Hilvarenbeek in which he came into contact with all types of people. Of these, first and foremost, were the members of the van der Heijden family, a staunchly Catholic family.

The van der Heijden family

Border crossings with fugitives from the Nazis had to be timed to avoid confrontations with the German border guards. Even though Karst and his men were prepared to shoot the German guards to protect the people they were aiding, this had to be avoided because of the consequences.[37] What they needed was a safe location near the border where the fugitives could rest, be fed, and have their false Belgian ID

---

[32] Moore, *Victims*, 10.
[33] Ivo Schöffer, "The Jews in the Netherlands: The Position of a Minority through Three Centuries," *Studia Rosenthaliana* 15, no. 1 (Mar. 1981): 86-87.
[34] Hilbrink, Coen, *De illegalen, Illegaliteit in Twente & het aangrenzende Salland 1940-1945* (The Hague: SDU Uitgeverij, 1989), 391.
[35] Naval Intelligence, *Netherlands*, 96.
[36] J. E. Van Loon-Boon, interview by Marlies van Rijn, 1 Sept. 1982, Bibliothecaris Regionaal Archief Leiden, 9; Hilbrink, *De illegalen*, 391.
[37] Lenck, *Vlucht*, 24.

Fig. 12.3. Van der Heijden family
(*courtesy van der Heijden family*)

prepared while waiting for a good opportunity to cross into Belgium. The Van der Heijden family home was ideally situated. It was a short walk from the *marechaussee* headquarters in Hilvarenbeek but at the same time located on the edge of town where there were only open fields and scattered farmhouses. Strangers could be slipped into the house through the huge garden in the rear. The family's ties to Belgium were an additional help. The mother, Elisabeth Peeters-van der Heijden, was born in Meerle, Belgium, just across the border and still had relatives there, and the father, Josephus van der Heijden, had lived in Belgium during WWI.[38] It was logical for the Van der Heijdens to cross into Begium for family visits.[39] In addition, they were as familiar with the Flemish variation of Dutch spoken in Belgium as with the standard Dutch spoken in the Netherlands.[40]

In April 1942, Karst approached Eugene van der Heijden, the second oldest son in the family, about whether the Van der Heijdens would be willing to house briefly an escaped French POW. They immediately agreed to help.[41] That man was only the first of a steady stream of refugees over the next eighteen months who stayed there.

[38] Eugene van der Heijden, "De Studenten," *Escape Nieuwsbulletin*, no. 91 (Dec. 1996): 16-22.
[39] Elly Fontaine-van der Heijden, interviews by the author, 21 Nov. 2002, 19 May 2003, 22-23 May 2004.
[40] Eugene van der Heijden, "Grensperikelen," 21-24.
[41] Eugene Van der Heijden, interview, 1994, Verzetsmuseum, Amsterdam.

C. Citroen, from Amsterdam, who was fleeing the raids aimed at Jews in July 1942, wrote of how on his arrival with a friend at the Van der Heijden home at one o'clock on a Sunday morning, they were treated to a meal of coffee, bread, butter, and cheese in the Van der Heijdens' big Brabant kitchen, then taken to a fresh, clean bedroom, where they were wished a good night. The next morning, they were treated to a "good old Dutch breakfast." During the morning Citroen played the piano while the entire family sang. Later two *marechaussees* stopped by, had a cup of coffee, and smoked a cigarette. At noon there was a bounteous warm meal, after which they were given their fake Belgian ID cards. At one o'clock that afternoon, it was time to leave for the border.[42]

But housing people fleeing the Nazis was not all the family did. The father, Josephus Cornelis, and the son, Eugene, regularly guided people to Brussels. Eugene, a teacher, had to work around his teaching schedule, using weekends and vacation periods for guiding. The mother, Elisabeth, her other sons, Marcel, Gustaf, Willy, and Jef, and daughters, Lisette and Elly, also assisted.[43]

The first escape route

With the Van der Heijdens now helping, the essential elements of the escape line were in place. After crossing the border, the guides and their charges made for the Belgian town of Weelde, a little over four miles distant (see fig. 6).[44] Their objective was the café of Maria Segers-Ooms at Groote Baan no. D56.[45] One traveler described it as a very Belgian café: "Its façade covered with all kinds of enamelled advertisements inviting one to partake of a variety of drinks or to become a member of some insurance company or another."[46] To the left of the café was the butcher shop of Maria's husband, Cornelis. Their living quarters was in the back of the building. Behind that was an inner courtyard and small stables used to raise animals or hold those that were to be slaughtered. The guides, their charges, and the general public used the stables to store their bicycles until their return. The café was very much in the center of the town, with the church and city hall directly across the street and the bus stop out front. Only beer and wine were sold in the café, with Maria

---

[42] Lenck, *Vlucht*, 19-21.
[43] Eugene van der Heijden, "De Oude Trambaan," *Escape Nieuwsbulletin*, no. 86 (Sept. 1995) 21-25; Jan Naaijkens, "Eugène van der Heijden: the salt of the earth, memories of a friend," *De Hilverbode* (1 May 2003), 9.
[44] Van der Heijden interview, Verzetsmuseum.
[45] Karst Smit, letter to RIOD.
[46] Dourlein, Pieter, *Inside North Pole* (London: William Kimber, 1953), 139.

running the bar.⁴⁷ For visitors preferring anonymity, the café could be entered from the rear via the courtyard. In her kitchen Maria fed free of charge all the people Karst's organization brought through, even providing them Belgian francs when they were short of money.

While waiting for transportation to their next stop, they might wait in a back room or prefer to relax in the café with some ersatz coffee or a beer.⁴⁸ The Segers-Ooms business was also a place where, if necessary, Karst and his men could change clothes and obtain information on German patrols on the Belgian side of the border.⁴⁹ "This data was crucial because returning to the Netherlands was considerably more dangerous since it was impossible to approach the Belgian side of the border without being seen."⁵⁰

To travel from Weelde to Turnhout, guides of the fugitives had two options, use an old-fashioned steam tram or a charcoal gas-powered bus. The former was safer because it carried farmers with baskets full of chickens for market and rarely experienced any German controls. Use of the latter may have been preferred when the departure and connection times worked better. Guides and their charges did not sit together on such trips for safety reasons.⁵¹

From Turnhout to Antwerp they used high-speed electric tram number forty-one, which could reach forty-four miles per hour and make the trip in one hour and twenty minutes.⁵² The cream-colored trams consisted of a motorcar and one or two trailer cars.⁵³ Normally the trip took place without incident but on 20 August 1943, Karst was guiding Sgt. George Duffee of the RAF on the tram to Antwerp.⁵⁴

To their dismay, at the town of Schilde, one of the intermediate stops, German police surrounded the tram and checked the ID of everyone getting off. Then, as the tram was about to get underway again, two members of the German *Feldgendarmarie*, the uniformed military police wearing their distinctive crescent-shaped gorgets, boarded and began a systematic examination of everyone's papers. It was a Friday

---

47 Laurent Woestenburg, president, Weelde historical society, and members of the society, interview by the author, Sept. 2004.
48 J. E. Van Loon-Boon, interview by Marlies van Rijn, 3; Dourlein, *Inside*, 139.
49 Karst Smit, interview by *Omroep Baarle* (Baarle-Nassau radio station), 3 July 1994.
50 De Graaf, *Stepping Stones*, 64.
51 Karst Smit, interview by *Omroep Baarle*; Eugene van der Heijden, letter to Paul Pouwels, 30 May 1995.
52 Karst Smit, interview by the author.
53 Barbara Van den Bossche and Eric Keutgens, Vlaams Tram- en Autobusmuseum, Antwerp, email to Keith Morley, 16 Nov. 2009, and timetable for Aug. 1941.
54 George W. H. Duffee, Appendix C, M.I.9/S/P.G.(-)1465, National Archives, Kew, London.

morning, and the tram was crowded with commuters. For that reason, Karst and Duffee had given up their seats and were standing on the rear platform. Even though both men had false IDs, any questioning of Duffee would mean his exposure. But Karst knew that the tram line took them on a curve around a huge abandoned fort in a forested area a little beyond the village of Wijnegem where the tram would have to slow down. Karst motioned to Duffee to join him in stalling by pretending to have difficulty finding in which pockets they had their IDs. The German MP in their car, impatient, continued on down the aisle, intending to return to them. Finally, Karst gave Duffee the signal and, ducking under the platform railing, both lept off. The *Feldgendarmarie* shouted, "Halt! Halt!" But the tram driver, realizing what was happening, delayed stopping the tram, and the two men were able to disappear into the forest. They made their way to a nearby village café, and each man had a lemonade to settle his nerves. George asked Karst, "Now what do we do?" to which Karst replied, "We catch the next tram!"[55]

Fabricating false IDs

Guiding someone across the border into Belgium and taking the person to Brussels was futile if the person was arrested at a check point for failure to have a valid Belgian ID. Fortunately, making a false Belgian ID was far easier than making a false Dutch ID. The Belgian ID had been imposed by the Germans in the First World War and remained little changed. It had the person's photo, signature, basic information, and the official stamp of the city where issued. The *marechaussees*, when they apprehended professional Belgian smugglers, would confiscate their IDs. Jef van der Heijden, who was sixteen in 1942 when his family began aiding fugitives, taught himself photography and would take a person's photo. The new photo and a confiscated smuggler's ID then went to a school teacher, Jan Naaijkens, a close friend of Eugene van der Heijden, who would remove the original photograph, substitute the new one, and painstakingly replicate on it the portion of the official city stamp that had been on the original photo. The person fleeing the Netherlands now had an ID that would stand up to routine inspection.[56]

One drawback to using a confiscated smuggler's ID was that it might be so well-thumbed and creased that it did not look at all like what a middle class individual traveling to Brussels would be carrying.[57]

---

[55] Eugene van der Heijden, "Het verzet in ons dorp," *De Hilverbode*, 10 Dec. 1948. Karst Smit, "Travamontuur," 28-30.
[56] Van der Heijden, "Het verzet," 25 Oct. 1947.
[57] Van der Heijden, "Identiteitskaarten," *Escape Nieuwsbulletin*, no. 89 (June 1996): 24-27.

For a time they were able to get good-quality false IDs by sending the fugitives' photos to their contact, Jean Krauss, in Brussels, who knew where to get blank cards. His sister, Marie, would deliver the finished product to Hilvarenbeek.[58] In 1943, however, there was a falling-out between Karst and the Krauss family over payment. The latter wanted to be paid for each airman's ID, something that was intolerable to Karst since he and his men had been paying out of their own salaries the costs of helping people. They found a solution. A paper wholesaler provided them with paper the exact same weight and shade of green as used in official Belgian IDs. Jan Naaijkens drew an image of St. George slaying the dragon that matched that used in the Brussels city seal. A stationers store in Tilburg put them in touch with a stereotype factory in Amsterdam. The factory workers, in exchange for a slab of bacon donated by a friendly farmer, made a stereotype plate that the Naaijkens' family printing press could use to generate false Belgian IDs identical to the real ones. Working overnight at the printing press in the family basement, when his family was asleep, Jan and his brother produced five hundred false IDs by morning.[59]

The student hideout: an additional way station for fugitives

Mass arrests of university students in February 1943 in retaliation for the assassination of General Hendrik A. Seyffardt were followed by a compulsory oath of loyalty to the Third Reich that students had to sign by 10 April or become subject to the labor draft.[60] Among those who went into hiding to avoid forced labor in Germany were three forestry students from the University of Wageningen—Dick Los, Jan Wolterson, and Jan de Konink. Los and de Konink were already familiar with *Landgoed de Utrecht* because of forestry training there in 1942. Using their forestry expertise, they built a hideout in the forest where they could stay for the time being. They were joined periodically by two other forestry students also from the University of Wageningen, Jan Oudemans, who was living in Esbeek, and Jan van Dongen, who was staying with a family friend in Hilvarenbeek. While patrolling the forest during the summer of 1943, Karst came across the students' hideout. Realizing that it would be a valuable additional way station in the escape route, he enlisted them into the escape line. Jan Wolterson said that becoming a part of the escape line "gave us a reason for living."

---

[58] Van der Heijden, "Mademoiselle," *Escape Nieuwsbulletin*, no. 84 (Mar. 1995): 32-36.
[59] Van der Heijden, "Identiteitskaarten," 28.
[60] Maass, *Netherlands*, 79, 140. Warmbrunn, *German Occupation*, 150-51.

Fig. 12.4. Dick Los and Jan van Dongen having breakfast in the hideout (*courtesy Jan Wolterson*)

By November 1943, when the weather became too cold to stay there, they moved into a chicken coop on the nearby De Bruijn farm which they insulated with bales of compressed hay. For several months in 1943, Allied airmen, Jews, Engelandvaarders, and others stayed at their hideout for one or more nights before being guided across the border.[61]

Practical considerations—costs, fuel, mail

The cost of running the escape line was a problem, particularly as the number of refugees increased. Karst and other members of the line had to pay for the train, bus, and tram tickets for the people they were guiding as well as for themselves. They also provided their charges with pocket money in Belgian currency and paid for the cost of feeding them in Belgium. To the extent that they could, Karst and the others paid the costs out of their own pockets. But they also took advantage of the demand in the Netherlands for tobacco. When the *marechaussees* apprehended Belgian smugglers carrying tobacco, they confiscated the tobacco. Karst's sister, Gerda, who worked in one of the government ministries in The Hague, sold it to government employees.[62] Later, one of their contacts with another escape line, Alphonse Theissing of the Dutch-Paris Line, provided financial help.[63]

Speedy transport of fugitives out of the Netherlands was a priority. The *marechaussee* headquarters in Baarle-Nassau had a pre-

[61] Karst Smit, "Zo Was Het Toen," *Escape Nieuwsbulletin*, no. 30 (Sept. 1981): 20-22; Van der Heijden, "Het verzet," 15 Nov. 1947, 10 Dec. 1948; Karst Smit, testimony of 5 Aug. 1954; Jan Wolterson, e-mails to author, 4 Jan., 6 July 2004; Joke Schilders, letter to the author, Feb. 2013.
[62] Karst Smit, letter to RIOD; Janine Marseille-Smit, letter to the author, 2 May 2006.
[63] Eugene van der Heijden, "Oliemaatschappij Petonqua," *Escape Nieuwsbulletin*, no. 88 (Mar. 1996): 21-25.

Fig. 12.5. Karst Smit and *marechaussees* on their BMW motorcycle (*courtesy Janine Marseille-Smit*)

war BMW motorcycle equipped with a sidecar that was ideal for this purpose, but there was not enough gasoline to operate it more than twice a month. But Piet van Geel, a straw merchant in Hilvarenbeek, had a contract with the German Wehrmacht to provide straw for their men and horses. In order to make his deliveries, the Germans supplied him with gasoline for his truck. He, in turn, shared the fuel with the *marechaussees*![64] Typically, Karst would pick up an evading Allied airman at the Tilburg train station. The two men would cross the street in front of the station to a hotel where Karst would have the airman don the top half of a *marechaussee's* uniform including the hat. With the airman sitting in the side car of the motorcycle, they would head for the border. One airman gave this description: "Now there followed a rather frantic and dangerous ride on a motorbike over wide main roads, through quiet avenues and narrow sandy paths until we arrived in a forest some 5 km. from the Belgian border."[65]

Karst and his contacts in Brussels needed to be able to correspond with each other regularly about deliveries of their "packages" to Brussels, but international mail was subject to inspection by the Germans, making it too risky to send across the border. Karst's solution was two

[64] Karst Smit, "Regio Noord-en Zuid-Holland," *Escape Nieuwsbulletin*, no. 79 (Dec. 1993): 13-14.
[65] Duffee, *23 Juni 1943, "Halifax" EY-S Keerde Niet Terug, Pilotenhulp tijdens de oorlog* (Rosmalen: the author, 1985), 50-51.

fold. He knew Constant Heeren, the proprietor of a café on the Dutch side of the border. Heeren's sister-in-law, Octavia Schoeters, who lived in Poppel on the Belgian side, worked in Heeren's café and needed to cross the border regularly. Equipped with a pass, she could cross back and forth without drawing attention from the German border guards. Hidden in her underwear was Karst's outgoing mail which she would pick up at the café and deposit in the mail in Poppel. For incoming mail, Karst had an arrangement with Jeanne Willems who lived in a farmhouse in Belgium a few hundred yards from the border. Her home became a mail drop for incoming correspondence. It was an easy matter for Karst to visit her farm and pick up his mail.[66]

Expanding the line

In early 1943, Karst received a phone call from the regional *marechaussee* commander, H. de Wilde, asking him to come see him in his home in Tilburg. This was unheard of! The commander never spoke to enlisted men much less invite them to his home. During their subsequent conversation, De Wilde told Karst that he knew what Karst was doing and had been asked to assist him. De Wilde was known to fraternize with German officers, but he assured Karst that it was just a "cover." After consulting with his men and warning De Wilde of the consequences of betrayal, Karst accepted the offer. What he needed, Karst told De Wilde, was the transfer of two of his *marechaussees*, David Jonkers and Huub Meeuwisse, to the town of Goirle just south of Tilburg and himself to the town of Baarle-Nassau, where Karst already had friends. That would still leave three trusted *marechaussees* in Hilvarenbeek. Within a week the transfers were complete. Karst now had three escape routes giving him more flexibility as to where and when he and his men could cross the border when guiding people to Brussels and reducing the risk of gossip about the many strangers passing through a single location.[67] An additional benefit in the case of Baarle-Nassau was its unique nature; it was actually two towns: Baarle-Nassau (Dutch) and Baarle-Hertog (Belgian), jumbled together like pieces of a jigsaw puzzle only three or four miles from the Belgian border, making it difficult for the Germans to keep track of, much less control the traffic across the border.[68]

[66] Karst Smit, letter to RIOD; Karst Smit, interview by the author.
[67] Karst Smit, letter to RIOD; Karst Smit, interview by Frans Dekkers and Wim Klinkenberg, 13 Dec. 1980, International Institute of Social History, Amsterdam.
[68] Karst Smit, "Baarle Nassau-Hertog," *Escape Nieuwsbulletin*, no. 80 (Mar. 1994): 26-28.

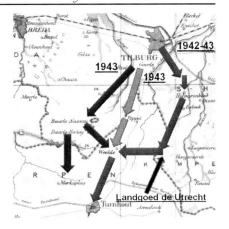

Fig. 12.6. Three escape routes

Karst's next need was for more guides to spread out the workload. During 1942-43, he noticed four young Belgian women smugglers, the Claes sisters, crossing the border three times a week, but realizing they were not professionals, he left them alone. One morning, however, after coming off night patrol duty along the border, he found three of them locked up in a cell at the Baarle-Nassau *marechaussee* barracks. The local *marechaussee* commander, Christian de Gier, was a strict, by-the-book policeman and had arrested them for smuggling. Karst promptly released them, and they hopped on their bikes and rode home. Invited over for the weekend to their home in Vorselaar, Belgium, by their grateful father, Karst became friendly with the family. They owned a small diamond-polishing factory that was shut down during the war because of a lack of raw materials. He asked if the sisters would be willing to assist by guiding fugitives from the Nazis, since they knew the smuggling routes even better than he did. His plan was to have them guide escaped French POWs. They immediately agreed, even though they were told nothing about the men they were helping. Their instructions were to meet at a large oak tree between Hilvarenbeek and Esbeek, pick up the men, who would be waiting, and guide them to Turnhout. The young women were under instructions not to talk to the men, and they guided anywhere from just one man to an entire group at a time, with everyone walking a safe distance apart to reduce the risk of their all being arrested. En route to Turnhout, they would spend the night at the Van der Pol family farm near Poppel, with the sisters delivering the Frenchmen to the tram station in Turnhout the next morning.[69]

[69] Hans Otten, e-mail message to the author, 30 Aug. 2010; Smit, "Nachtjas," 27-29; Van der Heijden, "De Oude Trambaan," 21-25; Cathy Cassiman, letter to the author, 23 Nov. 2010.

In March 1943, while patrolling the border at Baarle-Nassau, Karst noticed a young man who had been crossing it regularly. Questioning him, Karst learned that he was a student by the name of Willem Schmidt from the University of Utrecht, who was working for the underground newspaper, *Trouw*. Schmidt would deliver copies of the latest issue to Dutch nationals living in the area of Mechelen in Belgium. At first, Karst assisted Schmidt in crossing the border. Then he asked Schmidt if he would be willing to act as a guide. Schmidt immediately agreed and took on this responsibility for the next eight months, until the line was penetrated by the Germans the following November.[70]

Brussels reception center

After the falling out with the Krauss family in Brussels over their demand for payment to aid Allied airmen, Karst was in need of a new reception center for the fugitives, particularly the airmen who had begun to arrive in June 1943.[71] Briefly, Karst used the home of Pieter Neven, director of the Princess Juliana School (the Dutch school) in Brussels. From June to August, at least three airmen stayed there.[72] But with the Nevens family living above the school, it may have been too exposed a location to continue to use.[73] So Karst approached Jan Maaskant, the Protestant pastor in Brussels, whose sermons Karst had attended. Maaskant gave him a contact who, in turn, put Karst in touch with Elise Chabot and her daughter, Charlotte Ambach.[74]

Elise Chabot was from a wealthy Rotterdam family and had married a German. With the Nazi takeover in Germany, Chabot, who was fiercely anti-Nazi, separated from her husband and moved with her two daughters to Brussels. They became active in the resistance, and when approached by Karst, they were very open to his request for using their apartment as a reception center for arriving airmen.[75] Approximately thirty-one Allied airmen arrived there between July and November 1943.[76] The airmen usually were delivered to the Ambach-

---

[70] Karst Smit, testimony of 5 Aug. 1954.
[71] Eugene van der Heijden, "De Studenten," 16.
[72] *Vragenlijst* of Pieter Neven, 7 Jan. 1946, Neven helper file, NARA, NAII, College Park, MD, UD171: MIS-X Files, Belgium, 1945-47.
[73] "Document A15, Description of the Ausens [sic] route," unsigned report probably written by A. W. M. Ausems, from the file of Oreste Pinto, National Archives, The Hague.
[74] Karst Smit, interview by Dekker and Klinkenberg; Karst Smit, interview by the author.
[75] Charlotte Ambach, interview by the author, 30 Apr., 3 Aug. 2002.
[76] Service EVA Fiche d'Agent of Elise Chabot, Chabot helper file, NARA, NAII, College Park, MD, UD183: MIS-X Files, Holland, 1945-47.

Fig. 12.7. Elise Chabot and Charlotte Ambach (*courtesy Archives Générales du Royaume, Brussels and Charlotte Ambach*)

Chabot residence by Karst, Eugene van der Heijden, or Willem Schmidt. From there they would be passed on to other resistance organizations, such as Service EVA and Fiat Libertas.

Intelligence gathering and intelligence agents

Collection of intelligence was an incidental part of the work of the Smit-Van der Heijden Line. For example, maps showing installations—hangers, gas storage tanks, and more—for Havelte and Gilze-Rijen airfields were passed on to intelligence contacts.[77] The Gilze-Rijen airfield in Noord Brabant was particularly important because the Heinkel and Junkers bombers that attacked British cities were based there.[78] Every evading airman helped by the escape line who successfully returned to England was debriefed by intelligence officers. What they learned was summarized in the appendix B of the airman's escape and evasion report, and copies were distributed to all concerned parties.[79]

A special category of persons helped by the Smit-Van der Heijden Line were Dutch secret agents, most notably Pieter Dourlein and Johan Ubbink. Having parachuted into the Netherlands, they were captured by the Germans as part of the German operation "North Pole," also

---

[77] Van der Heijden, "Het verzet," 7 Feb. 1948; Jack Justice, letter to "Nico and Kees," 13 June 1945, NIOD Collection, Verzet-Noord Brabant, Doc. II-858.

[78] Gilze-Rijen, Netherlands Instituut voor Militaire Historie, Ministerie van Defensie, http://www.defensie.nl/nimh/geschiedenis/vliegvelden/vliegveldoverzicht/46190366/gilze_rijen/.

[79] Ottis, *Silent Heroes*, 19. Escape and evasion reports of American airmen from the Second World War are available online from NARA.

known as *Englandspiel*, the greatest German counterespionage triumph in which they routinely captured Dutch secret agents and "turned" them to work for Germany. Dourlein and Ubbink escaped from the prison at Haaren and were assisted in crossing into Belgium by Karst's men, thereby getting word back to London as to what had happened.[80]

Destruction of the line

On 15 November 1943, guide Willem Schmidt and an American airman were arrested at the Turnhout train station. Under duress, Schmidt provided names. The Smit-Van der Heijden Line collapsed. Karst and Eugene went into hiding after attempting to warn everyone. Four members of the Van der Heijden family were arrested, three of whom died in concentration camps—Josephus, Marcel, and Gustaf. Two of the students, Jan Oudemans and Jan de Konink, were sent to concentration camps and never returned.[81] Another, Jan van Dongen, was shot the following year by a German death squad.[82] In all, thirteen members of the line were executed or died as a result of their concentration camp experiences. Fifteen survived prison or concentration camps, some with serious physical or emotional damage. In the twenty months the line was active, it aided approximately forty-three airmen, 150 Dutch Jews, three secret agents, thirty *Engelandvaarders*, from eighty to ninety French POWs, and forty families with husbands in hiding.[83] Karst joined another escape line, was betrayed, arrested, and survived four concentration camps. After the Liberation, he was part of the investigative team of the Netherlands War Crimes Commission.[84] His decorations included the Medal of Freedom with Silver Palm (US), Most Excellent Order of the British Empire (MBE) (UK), and Knight of the Order of Oranje Nassau (NL).[85]

Why did they risk it?

In her *Memoirs*, Elsa Caspers explained simply:

[80] Ben Ubbink to David Jonkers, 11 Apr. 1979, from personal papers of David Jonkers; Hubertus Meeuwisse, "Over Leven," memoirs of Meeuwisse, Dec. 1997, 30.
[81] Vragenlijst of Johannes Oudemans, 18 Apr. 1946, Oudemans helper file, NARA, NAII, UD183: MIS-X Files, Holland, 1945-47.
[82] Eugene van der Heijden, "De studenten," 43.
[83] Report by Karst Smit, 16 July 1945, Smit helper file, NARA, NAII, UD183: MIS-X Files, Holland, 1945-47.
[84] "Extract from the Service Records . . . Concerning Smit, Karst Gerrit;" Karst Smit, interview by the author.
[85] Karst Smit, interview by the author; display in honor of Karst Smit, Marechaussee Museum, Buren, NL; Karst Smit, interview by RTL5 Television.

However hard one tries, it is never possible to reproduce in words exactly how life was lived in those days. The ever-present danger, tension, and possibility of betrayal, cannot be expressed in words. One can only try to show some of the atmosphere of life at that time. Although there were many different reasons for joining [the Resistance], there was one common denominator: not being able to endure the restriction of freedom and the infringement of the integrity of our fellow men.[86]

---

[86] Caspers, Elsa, *To Save a Life, Memoirs of a Dutch Resistance Courier* (London: A Deirdre McDonald Book, 1995), vi.

CHAPTER 13

One Soldier's Experience of War in the Pacific: Sgt. Ernest Gerritsma's Diaries and Letters in the Second World War

Donald Sinnema

This is the story of a Dutch American soldier who served in the Pacific theater in the Second World War. Ernest J. Gerritsma (1917-2001) was a second-generation Dutch American who grew up in a Dutch enclave in Sioux County in northwest Iowa.[1] The twenty-four-year old enlistee was assigned to the 147th Field Artillery Regiment of the United States Army, where he served for four-and-a-half years, from February 1941—almost ten months before Pearl Harbor—until July 1945—three weeks before the Japanese surrender. Three-quarters of that time, he spent overseas in the Pacific campaigns to safeguard Australia and defeat the Japanese in New Guinea and the Philippines.

This article recounts Gerritsma's war experience as narrated in his diaries and his many letters home. The story of the diaries themselves is a sub-theme. His experience as a soldier is treated within the larger context of the 147th Field Artillery's operations and role in the Pacific war.[2]

---

[1] Interview with Ernest Gerritsma, 7 July 1994. His father, Syne Gerritsma, had immigrated in 1908 and his mother, Gertie Feikema, in 1895, both from Friesland; after marriage they settled in Sioux Center, where Ernest was born in 1917.

[2] The most detailed history of the 147th Field Artillery is in unpublished manuscripts by Robert G. Webb, "World War II in the Pacific, 1941-1942," and "World War II

The sources

The primary source is a set of six diaries Gerritsma surreptitiously kept from the beginning to the end of his time in the service. Such personal war diaries are rather uncommon, since they were contraband; the army did not want military information to fall into the hands of the enemy, so diaries could be confiscated. Nevertheless, Ernest kept writing his diaries, and he even succeeded in getting them home without confiscation by military authorities by way of three clever strategies. The first-year diary he sent home in March 1942, soon after arriving in Australia, in a footlocker full of personal effects. Though the footlocker was shipped through military channels, it went undetected amidst the other personal items.[3]

The second diary, he sent home by a friend whom he met in Australia. While camped for several months at Rockampton on the east coast of Australia, Ernest attended services at St. Andrew's Presbyterian Church and got to know the Butters family there. The family operated a local bookshop. In June 1943, Ernest gave Butters the second diary and asked him to send it home to Iowa after the war.[4] This was not possible during the war, since even Australian civilian mail to the United States was censored.

The remaining four diaries Ernest kept with him for the rest of his time overseas. He was able to get them home in an even more daring manner. When he returned from the Philippines in March 1945, he had to pass through several inspections on Angel Island at San Francisco. At one barracks, returning soldiers were supposed to dump out their barracks bags on a cot for inspection. Instead, Ernest just walked around this barracks to the next one where they were to sleep. When his fellow soldiers warned he would never get by without a clearance slip, Ernest, now long wise to army procedures, exclaimed, "Oh, I'll see about that!" Two days later, he boarded a ferry off the island with his barracks bag (and diaries) and took a troop train home, no questions asked.[5]

Ernest was rather reflective as he wrote his diaries. They are not just a log of his daily activities. Most daily entries are a full paragraph, keenly descriptive of his experiences of the day and of his attitudes about army life.

---

in the Pacific, 1942-1945," available in the archives of Northern State University, Aberdeen, SD. Other histories of the 147th are in *South Dakota in World War II* (Pierre, 1947?), chap. 9, and Richard Cropp, *The Coyotes: A History of the South Dakota National Guard* (Mitchell, SD: Educator Supply Co., 1962).
[3] Card to his parents, 8 Mar. 1942; *Sioux Center News*, 29 Oct. 1942.
[4] Diary, 28 Mar., 8 June 1943.
[5] This story was related to me in a letter from Ernest dated Dec. 1993.

In the 1980s, Dr. Robert Webb, a history professor at Northern State University in South Dakota, was doing research on the 147th Field Artillery and learned of Gerritsma's diaries. Ernest was reluctant to hand over the diaries to Webb; instead, he typed out all the diaries during the winter of 1985 and gave this typed version to the professor. Years later, however, he did donate the diaries to the Northern State University archives in Aberdeen, South Dakota.

A second source for this topic is Ernest's many letters written to his parents and to his fiancée, Marie Ten Harmsel. He wrote to his parents about once a week, except when combat conditions made that too difficult. Over 150 of these letters (twenty-four written in Dutch) have been preserved by the Gerritsma family, along with other clippings and war memorabilia. He wrote Marie about twice a week—some four hundred letters in all—but only a dozen of these are preserved. Apparently, later in life he destroyed most of these letters; the family has only empty envelopes.

The letters offer much more detail than the diaries and express the sentiments of a perceptive observer. But their great limitation is that when Ernest went overseas, his letters were then censored by military officials. So they contain virtually no description of his military activities and only vaguely reveal his location, such as "Australia" and "somewhere in the southwest Pacific." The letters do provide vivid descriptions of non-military topics, ranging from the sights of Australia, to saw mills he visited, natives of New Guinea, and the travails of living in a tropical climate. The only uncensored letters were those written before leaving the States and after his return. In these, he could be openly critical of the United States entering the war[6]—an attitude that changed after Pearl Harbor—and he had harsh criticism of army propaganda and army training practices, such as the common hurry-and-wait routines.[7]

A third source for this article is the local weekly newspaper, the *Sioux Center News*, which regularly printed reports about local servicemen and letters from them that were shared by their families. The *News* printed a good number of Ernest's letters, including some

---

[6] Letter to parents, 9 Aug. 1941; letter to Rev. Marinus Arnoys, 5 Sept. 1941. In his skepticism about American entry into the war, Gerritsma shared a sentiment expressed by Rev. Henry J. Kuiper, editor of *The Banner*, 14 Feb. 1941, and by an article in the *Sioux Center News*, 6 Feb. 1941: "What Reason has the United States to Fight?"

[7] Letters to parents, 24 May, 15 Aug., 8 Nov. 1941. In his letter of 2 Sept. 1941, he asserted: "the army training program is an unbelievable, unprecedented waste of time and money."

not preserved by the family.⁸ In 1944 it also printed his first-year diary in thirteen installments.⁹ It is sobering to note that, during the war, the *Sioux Center News* reported on the deaths of some thirty-one Dutch American servicemen from Sioux County alone.¹⁰

A final source for this paper is personal contact with Ernest. I knew him well—he was my former father-in-law; I was married to his daughter Lois, who passed away in 2003. I read his diaries in the early nineties and talked with him about his war experiences a number of times before he died in 2001.

Gerritsma's military experience

Ernest was in the very first group of eight men from Sioux County to be drafted for military service in WWII. After President Roosevelt signed the Selective Training and Service Act in September 1940, all young men between the ages of twenty-one and thirty-five had to register for the draft on 16 October.¹¹ By lottery, Gerritsma's number (65) was selected for the first group of draftees. And so, at age twenty-four, he entered the United States Army on 24 February 1941, months before Pearl Harbor thrust the nation into war.¹² The draft was supposed to be for only one year of service, for the purpose of military training. But, by the summer of 1941, Congress had extended the term an additional eighteen months, and after Pearl Harbor, the term of service was extended to six months after the war. In Ernest's case, his term of service was drawn out to four-and-a-half long years. Keep in mind, the young servicemen who dutifully left to serve their country

---

8 *Sioux Center News*, 24 Apr., 5 June 1941; 19 Mar., 16 Apr., 16 and 23 July, 10 Sept., 19 Nov., 17, 31 Dec. 1942; 4 Feb., 25 Mar., 17 June, 9 Sept., 28 Oct. 1943; 6 Jan., 17 Feb., 1, 8 June, 13 July, 17 31 Aug., 1, 14 Dec. 1944; 15 Feb. 1945.
9 *Sioux Center News*, 24 Aug. to 30 Nov. 1944.
10 The first reported death of a local serviceman was that of Elmer Duistermars, a navy man whose ship was docked in Pearl Harbor when it was bombed on 7 Dec. 1941. A headline in the 18 Dec. 1941 issue of the *Sioux Center News* announced, "Youth Born in Sioux Center Killed in Action," after the navy reported him lost in the bombing. A week later (25 Dec.) the *News* ran an obituary about him. But the next issue of 1 Jan. 1942 blazed a large headline, "ALIVE." Duistermars was writing letters with a friend on another ship during the 7 Dec. attack. They ran on deck and helped work the largest gun, until they had to abandon ship. Elmer swam ashore through flaming oil and then manned a machine gun for two-and-a-half days before he was relieved. In the next few months he served in the battles of Coral Sea, Marshall and Gilbert Islands (cf. 23 July, 6 Aug. 1942).
11 *Sioux Center News*, 3 Oct. 1940.
12 *Sioux Center News*, 10, 31 Oct., 7 Nov. 1940; 20 Feb. 1941; Notice of Selection, 30 Jan. 1941; Diary, 24 Feb. 1941.

Fig. 13.1. Pvt. Ernest Gerritsma at Fort Ord (*courtesy Sylvan Gerritsma*)

had no notion they were leaving home for such an interminable length of time, with little reliable means of communication with their loved ones for weeks at a time.

Ernest was assigned to the Headquarters Battery of the Second Battalion of the 147th Field Artillery, a South Dakota National Guard regiment of some twelve hundred men that included draftees also from northwest Iowa and southwest Minnesota. The headquarters battery (about 120 men) was primarily a communications battery in charge of telephones, radios, signals, switchboards, setting up communications centers, and laying telephone wires.[13] Gerritsma was immediately shipped to Fort Ord in California for nine months, beginning with five weeks of boot camp, followed by field maneuvers and other military training.[14]

In letters to his folks during this period, Gerritsma was scathing in his criticism about some army procedures, especially regarding promotions in rank. As he viewed it, the headquarters battery of the 147th regiment, based in Flandreau, South Dakota, was then largely made up of lazy and drunken "good-for-nothing parasites," who could not get a decent job in civilian life and so joined the South Dakota National Guard for a living; promotions were given only to hometown guys in this old boys network and not to harder working outsiders like himself from Iowa or Minnesota:

[13] Letter to parents, 24, 30 Apr. 1941.
[14] Diary, 6 Mar. 1941.

I like to dig into the history of each man, because it reveals some interesting facts; almost without exception, all the older National Guard men were downright good-for-nothings at home who didn't amount to a straw in a whirlwind.... It seems that all these men were merely a group of drinkers who joined the National Guard because they had nothing better to do.... Most of these men never saw more money in their life; it's just the best break ever to come their way.[15]

You can well imagine how it works when the entire personnell [sic] of a battery is from the same town—like members of a large family to whom we are nothing more than intruders or outsiders.... Can you reasonably expect these ratings to go to anyone outside the hometown? In a manner of speaking, I could perhaps have a corporal's rating if it weren't for these dirty politics.[16]

I also told him [Rev. Harry A. Dykstra] about the dirty, crooked deal the selectees received here, and how we actually came here to be slaves of these men who were mainly worthless good-for-nothings at home; here we are doing all the slave details, such as K.P. duty, warehouse, guard duty, carpenter's work, etc. etc., while they get the money for it.... Rev. told me it was the same in other National Guard outfits.... Who said the army played no favorites? If only you can drink with the right men or hold your mouth nicely, which in army terms is called "sucking," your chances are a lot better, but who wants to do that—not me, army or no army, I don't want to be anyone's dog.[17]

In the army the best man surely does not win; it is knowing and associating with the right people that counts.... The army has the largest collection of politicians I ever hope to see; it operates on the principle of dog-eat-dog, and the more unscrupulous one can be, the more headway he'll make. It is a strange fact that those who were most unsuccessful in civilian life usually progress farthest and fastest in the army.[18]

After a furlough home in September 1941, Ernest and the 147th left San Francisco on 22 November on the army transport ship, SS *Willard A. Holbrook*, with about two thousand troops aboard, for the

---

[15] Letter to parents, 11 Oct. 1941.
[16] Ibid., 2 Sept. 1941.
[17] Ibid., 24 Oct. 1941.
[18] Ibid., 12 Nov. 1941.

purpose of reinforcing General Douglas MacArthur's American forces in the Philippines.[19] The ship arrived at Pearl Harbor on 27 November; Ernest described what he saw:

> This morning the ship is lying alongside a cruiser—was I surprised to see all this activity in Pearl Harbor navy yard—the work being done here is simply astounding. Cruisers, battleships, large & small craft of every type to be seen here almost without number—working day & nite [sic]. Received a pass and went to Honolulu at 2:00 p.m.—the town is a junky affair.[20]

The *Holbrook* left again on 30 November, exactly one week before Pearl Harbor was bombed.[21] The ship was now part of a larger nine-ship convoy, known as the Pensacola convoy, since it was accompanied by the cruiser SS *Pensacola*. It proceeded on an indirect course toward the Philippines, via Fiji, New Guinea, Borneo, and Singapore.[22] As the convoy sailed just south of the equator, Pearl Harbor was bombed on Sunday, 7 December 1941; the same day the Japanese bombed Manila. The United States immediately declared war. It was now too risky for the convoy to proceed to the Philippines. With the *Holbrook* now painted battleship grey, the convoy was diverted to Australia to help defend this allied country from the threat of an aggressive Japanese campaign that was rapidly moving south.

After Pearl Harbor, Gerritsma's family was very anxious to hear news from Ernest. Was he one of the victims at Pearl Harbor? On 14 December, during a brief stopover at Fiji, he was able to send a preprinted postcard, indicating only, "I am well," "Letter follows at first opportunity," and "I have received no letter from you for a long time." But his fiancée Marie did not receive this card until 18 January, a full six weeks after the bombing.[23] A cablegram to his parents arrived a week later.[24] As for Ernest, it was almost five months after leaving San

---

[19] Diary, 22 Nov. 1941.
[20] Diary, 28 Nov. 1941.
[21] For the Pearl Harbor stopover, see diary, 27-30 Nov. 1941.
[22] Webb, "World War, 1941-1942," 14.
[23] *Sioux Center News*, 22 Jan. 1942.
[24] When the cablegram, sent on 10 Jan., arrived on Sunday, 25 Jan., the Sioux Center telegraph operator personally delivered it to Ernest's father at the end of the First Christian Reformed Church afternoon service. Fearing the worst, Syne did not open the cablegram until he arrived at home and gathered his family around the kitchen table. Fortunately, the news was the same: "AM WELL LETTER FOLLOWS LONG TRIP NO WORD FROM YOU NOTIFY MARIE LOVE AND GREETINGS TO ALL." At this point the family thought Ernest was with the McArthur forces making a last ditch stand in the Philippines.

Fig. 13.2. USAT *Willard A. Holbrook* arriving at Brisbane Harbor (*courtesy State Library of Queensland, image no. 77319*)

Fransisco before he received his first mail from home on 15 April 1942.[25]

The *Holbrook* arrived in Brisbane on 23 December. After a few days, the 147th headed for Darwin on the *Holbrook* to help the Australian army defend this city in north Australia from a possible Japanese invasion. After arriving there in early January 1942, the 147th set up camp twenty-eight miles outside the city. There they were the very first American troops to raise the American flag on Australian soil. Six weeks later, on 19 February, the Japanese bombed Darwin, the first of multiple air raids that devastated the city, its harbor, and airport.[26] Ernest saw the Japanese bombers (about a hundred in the first raid), heard the explosions, and saw the extensive damage,[27] but his camp outside the city was not targeted; the 148th Field Artillery did suffer some casualties.

American victories in the great naval battle of Coral Sea (just NE of Australia) in May 1942, and in the battle of Midway in June, removed the threat of a Japanese invasion of Australia, since the Japanese lost most of their aircraft carriers in these battles.[28] So, after nearly six months at Darwin, the 147th left this area in late June and moved by truck convoy through central Australia for a three-month period of recuperation and training at Ballarat, near Melbourne in the south. From there, they moved up the eastern coast of Australia to camps near Brisbane (for

---

[25] Diary, 15 Apr. 1942.
[26] Webb, "World War, 1941-1942," 25, 34-40.
[27] Diary, 19, 25 Feb., 16, 19, 21, 28, 30 March, 2, 4, 25, 27 Apr., 13, 15, 16 June 1942.
[28] Diary, 12 May 1942.

four months) and Rockhampton (for five months), waiting to be called upon to serve in the upcoming New Guinea campaign.[29]

The American victory in the Guadalcanal campaign (August 1942 to February 1943) marked a shift from a defensive posture to an allied strategic offensive in the southwest Pacific theatre. Then operations could proceed to advance along the northern coast of New Guinea toward the Philippines.

In the New Guinea campaign, the 147th at first occupied several positions that had already been captured by other American or Australian forces, handling supplies for ongoing operations. Then it had its turn in direct combat operations to drive out the Japanese.

After nearly nineteen months in Australia, Gerritsma's 147th second battalion left Rockhampton, and then Townsville, by ship in July 1943 for Milne Bay, on the eastern tip of New Guinea. This large bay, where the Australians had repelled a Japanese invasion force in 1942, was an important staging point for further action in the New Guinea campaign.[30] The 147th spent four months camped there and then left on LSTs (landing ship tanks) for Woodlark Island briefly, and then on to Kiriwina Island, north of Milne Bay. Both these islands had been captured earlier—in late June 1943—without opposition from the Japanese; these were the first amphibious assaults in the southwest Pacific theater using LSTs.[31]

The 147th occupied Kiriwina with its important airfields for the next four months. One night Gerritsma experienced three Japanese air raids, with bombs dropping a few hundred yards away: "While still lying on my bunk, I suddenly heard a stick of bombs come whistling down, and I left for the slit-trench at the advanced pace with only helmet and shoes on. I took some kidding, too, about that burst of speed."[32]

In April 1944, the 147th moved on to the northern coast of New Guinea, to Buna for a brief stopover, and then for a month to Finschhafen, the major New Guinea supply base.[33] Buna had been captured by Allied forces in January 1943, and the Australians had taken the port of Finschhafen in October.

From there the 147th began to enter active combat engagements in the New Guinea campaign, following MacArthur's leapfrogging strategy of attacking weak Japanese positions and isolating their strong

[29] Diary, 29 June, 7 and 14 July, 8 and 10 Oct. 1942; 20, 25 Feb. 1943; Webb, "World War, 1942-1945," 1-9.
[30] Diary, 22 July, 25 Nov. 1943.
[31] Diary, 27 and 29 Nov. 1943; Webb, "World War, 1942-1945," 9-16.
[32] Letter to parents, 29 Dec. 1943; cf. diary, 20 Dec. 1943.
[33] Webb, "World War, 1942-1945, 21; diary, 4 and 6 Apr. 1944.

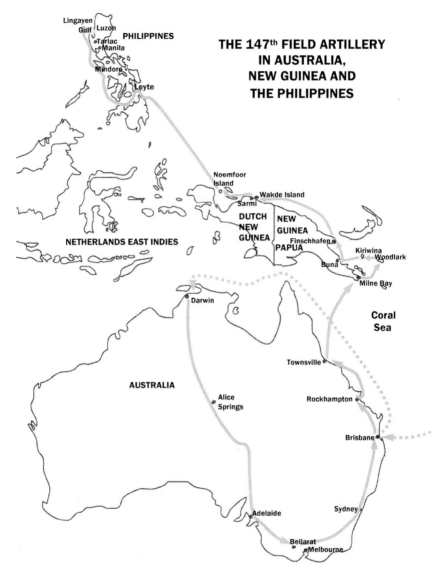

Fig. 13.3. Map of the 147th Field Artillery in Australia, New Guinea, and the Philippines

positions. The major Japanese base at Rabaul on New Britain was thus bypassed and isolated, and from Finschhafen, MacArthur's forces jumped forward along the northern coast of New Guinea to capture Aitape and Hollandia in April 1944.[34]

[34] Webb, "World War, 1942-1945," 17, 20, 29.

The 147th Field Artillery in May 1944 advanced in a convoy of Liberty ships to the Wakde Island-Sarmi area of Dutch New Guinea, and there the unit backed up the 158th Infantry in the battle of Wakde-Sarmi, to secure the capture of Wakde Island with its important airfield. Other units had already landed on 17 May after intense shelling, and they soon seized the airfield and nearby coastline. But there was a heavy concentration of Japanese troops in the dense jungle along the coast, and the 147th and 158th were called upon to secure the area. They arrived on 21 May and in a few days advanced west beyond the Tor River toward Sarmi, a nearby Japanese supply site.[35] But this advance met stiff Japanese resistance:

> Spent a sleepless night—first the noise of the artillery barrage kept me awake and later Jap snipers gave us an interesting few hours. Bullets whistled all around and over us, and so we decided the slit trench was safer. Our own guns kept firing, too. One man was killed by a Jap hand grenade, and one by a sniper's rifle; that makes two from A battery.[36]

In the fighting, the 147th and 158th forces were temporarily forced back across the river. During this retreat, Gerritsma was briefly stranded on the wrong side of the river:

> Had an exciting time this morning when a 77mm Jap mountain gun (howitzer) let loose on us with some 8 or 10 rounds—killed one man from A battery and wounded two. With Hartsfield and Osmond King, had the job of security guard quite a distance from the battery. During the day sometime the battery left to go back across the river without notifying us; when we finally became aware of this, it was an uncomfortable thought that this bit of territory reverted to the Japs. I told my companions that we should walk well separated (at first they wanted to stay tightly together) to present a less inviting target for a sniper; however, no sniper molested us, and after crossing the Tor River we got back to our outfit again.[37]

The same day Gerritsma found a large wad of Japanese occupation currency, printed in Dutch, for use in Dutch New Guinea.[38]

---

[35] Webb, "World War, 1942-1945," 30-37; diary, 21 May 1944.
[36] Diary, 29 May 1944.
[37] Ibid., 30 May 1944.
[38] Ibid., 30 May 1944.

Two nights later a Japanese suicide squad carrying land mines and dynamite was machine gunned as they tried to slip through the American perimeter and destroy the artillery guns. Gerritsma saw what was left after the explosion—chunks of flesh scattered all about.[39] A few weeks later, he spent a miserable night assigned to perimeter guard in a machine gun pit, soaked with water up to his knees.[40] When finally relieved of this difficult mission after twenty-four days of fighting, the 147th had learned the art of jungle warfare, with no front lines.

The next objective for the 147th and 158th regiments was Noemfoor Island, just off the northern coast of Dutch New Guinea; the goal was to seize the three airfields on the small island.[41] As usual, intense naval shelling and air bombardment, the heaviest yet in the southwest Pacific, first softened enemy resistance before the troops landed. Gerritsma described the landing in his diary entry of 2 July 1944:

> Before seven [a.m.] the Navy began shelling, and that indeed was an unforgettable sight—one cannot grasp the fury and destruction it causes. Soon the air was dense with powder smoke, and the shore looked like it had a smoke screen thrown over. Two or three cruisers, plus a dozen destroyers pumped shells into the island. A total of six B-24s dropped bombs. The noise of shelling and bombing was fearful. At 7:30, the "buffalos" and "ducks" left the LSTs, and perhaps an hour later, we did. Put our truck on an LCT [landing craft tank] and, with some effort, got it ashore. Began laying [telephone] wire by hand along the ridge some 500 yards back from the beach. Dead tired, soaking wet, hungry and cold. Then I was expected to go on guard [duty]—raised a rumpus about that, because laying wire is about the hardest job here.

The next day Gerritsma observed transport planes dropping a battalion of paratroopers on an airstrip on the island, but the drop was made too low, causing significant casualties among the paratroopers.[42]

Within a couple of weeks the fighting there was largely over. While at Noemfoor Gerritsma experienced the most traumatic of the more than half dozen crashes of American planes he saw or heard in his time overseas.[43] A C45 plane was taxiing when its right wheel locked

---

[39] Ibid., 1 June 1944.
[40] Ibid., 24 June 1944.
[41] Webb, "World War, 1942-1945," 37-48.
[42] Diary, 3 July 1944.
[43] He describes other American crashes in his diary entries of 31 Mar. 1942, 19 Feb., 10 and 14 Sept., 5, 16 Dec. 1944.

Fig. 13.4. LSTs landing on Noemfoor Island. Disembar- king M4 Sherman tanks and other vehicles during the Western New Guinea operation Invasion of Noemfoor Island in July 1944. (*USMC photo no. USMC-69003, from the US Coast Guard Historian's Office*)

and it hit an embankment, bursting immediately into flames, only seventy-five yards in front of his jeep. Three airmen managed to escape but were severely scorched, one without a hand. "Either one or two men were burned alive; one I saw still lying in the plane as it burned, almost opposite the door, his body still moving. I presume he was dead by then—a horrible way to die. . . . Such scenes divert your thoughts from the usual channels."[44]

After six months on Noemfoor Island, the 147th left on LSTs, on 1 January 1945, as part of a large convoy to join the Philippines campaign. MacArthur's forces had already landed on the Philippine island of Leyte the previous October and on the island of Mindoro in December; the Japanese fleet had suffered major defeat in October in the battle of Leyte Gulf. The next objective was the main island of Luzon. On 9 January the American Sixth Army landed its first units on the south shore of Lingayen Gulf, on the western coast of Luzon.[45] Two days later, Gerritsma's LST landed. For several nights his position was shelled by Japanese artillery and long-range mortars, while he tried to get some sleep in a slit trench; one shell landed sixty feet away, showering him with chunks of dirt.[46] Due to occasional "flying freight trains," shells from well-camouflaged heavy Japanese guns, he continued to sleep in trenches.[47] Another night he stayed at his forward switchboard, fifty feet back from the perimeter machine gun post that the 158th Infantry had set up:

> At 5:00 a.m. there was an explosion that seemed to lift me right off the ground. While dark, we couldn't see anyway what had caused

[44] Diary, 30 Sept. 1944.
[45] Webb, "World War, 1942-1945," 48-60.
[46] Diary, 15 Jan. 1945.
[47] Ibid., 29, 31 Jan., 3 Feb. 1945.

it, but at daylight there were chunks of flesh scattered all about. A suicide party of Japs with land-mines and powder bags strapped on had wandered close to the perimeter, and the men there opened up with the machine-gun, which set off those explosives. This morning only two bodies could at all be identified, that is, there was enough left to show they were human bodies. We had no damage whatever. These suicide squads are not interested in the infantry (they came past here by mistake), but their purpose is to sneak up on our [field artillery] gun pits, hurl themselves in, and so destroy the gun—and themselves, of course.[48]

Later one night, a man of Gerritsma's unit, Max Smith, was killed by friendly fire, while engaged in shooting flares. When a couple of Japanese were spotted outside the perimeter, a spooked young lieutenant woke up, hastily drew his 45 automatic pistol, and shot Max in the side.[49]

After a month of fighting in the Lingayen Gulf operation, and suffering heavy casualties, the 147th moved on to a rest area at Tarlac, about half way to Manila, where the first American units had pushed into the northern suburbs on 3 February. Then quite unexpectedly, on 22 February 1945, Gerritsma was selected for rotation back to the United States. The next day he left his battalion at Tarlac and traveled by plane and a Victory ship back to San Francisco.[50]

In his time oversees, he had participated in direct combat against the Japanese in three battles, at Wakde-Sarmi and Noemfoor Island in Dutch New Guinea and at Luzon in the Philippines, all in his last year overseas. But nowhere in his diaries or letters does he ever mention that he personally shot at the enemy. A couple of reasons may explain this. First, he was not part of an infantry regiment like the 158th Infantry but was part of a field artillery regiment, which supported the infantry by shelling from a distance. Second, as a member of the Headquarters Battery of his regiment, his main duty in combat situations was not to fire artillery; rather, his was a support role—to lay out telephone wire so the various units could communicate.

During his time in the service, Gerritsma rose through the ranks from private, to private first class upon going overseas, to T5 (technical 5th grade) mail corporal in late 1942 when he was in Australia, to (wire)

---

48 Ibid., 22 Jan. 1945.
49 Ibid., 6 Feb. 1945.
50 Ibid., 22 Feb.-25 Mar. 1945. The Victory class ship was a cargo and transport ship produced in large numbers during the Second World War.

corporal in November 1944 when in New Guinea, and finally to staff sergeant two months later when he was in the Philippines.[51]

In the context of the 147th Field Artillery's operations in the war, what were Gerritsma's main duties during his four-and-one-half years of service? Besides the usual soldierly responsibilities of training, guard duty, KP duty, loading and unloading equipment and rations on ships and trucks, and so forth, Gerritsma had three specific duties. First, since he had been a carpenter in civilian life before the war, he was often assigned to carpentry detail for his military regiment, starting during his training at Fort Ord and continuing throughout his time overseas. This involved making basic necessities each time his regiment would advance to a new camp—things like tables, latrines, kitchen facilities, wooden floors for tents in muddy tropical conditions, crates for the next move, and a score of other items. He constructed these mostly from scrap lumber, crating materials, or trees, and with a minimum of tools. Only on occasion did he have use of a Skilsaw, powered by a generator. At times, he was the only carpenter in his battery and the only one who could sharpen a saw, so his carpentry skills were much in demand.[52]

Second, beginning in November 1942 while in Australia, he served as a mail orderly for the regiment. He was given his own blitz buggy (jeep) to fetch mail from the nearest APO (army post office) and distribute it to the various units. Since soldiers were constantly being transferred, he had to spend a good deal of time re-addressing mail. He also handled stamps, money orders, and a mountain of Christmas packages.[53]

Third, after the 147th entered combat operations in New Guinea in May 1944, Gerritsma no longer handled the mail but became part of the wire section of his regiment.[54] This involved laying out telephone wire, at first along the ground and then in trees or on bamboo poles in Luzon, in order to establish lines of communication between units. Since Gerritsma was rather wiry in stature, he was usually one of the soldiers called upon to climb the trees, hauling up a line with the use of climbers, sometimes as high as seventy-five feet, while exposed to Japanese sniper fire. One time at Noemfoor his climbers slipped, and he sustained a gash in his armpit, requiring stitches.[55] Due to enemy

---

[51] Letters to parents, 1 Feb. 1942, 14 Nov. 1942; diary, 3 Nov. 1942, 2 Nov. 1944, 20 Jan. 1945.
[52] Letters to parents, 3 May, 19 May 1941.
[53] Diary, 3 Nov. 1942.
[54] Ibid., 27 May, 2 June 1944.
[55] Ibid., 5 July 1944.

Fig. 13.5. Gerritsma with his blitz buggy and buddies (*courtesy Sylvan Gerritsma*)

shelling and military vehicles running over the wires, he constantly had to repair lines; on one occassion they were cut by Japanese sabotage.[56] He also had to repair telephones and maintain switchboards. At Noemfoor he was made a wire corporal, and at Luzon he was promoted to wire chief, in charge of a wire crew.[57]

Gerritsma's Dutch Reformed character

It is interesting to observe how Gerritsma's Reformed background was evident during his years in the service. First, his work ethic: he was very diligent in his duties and had no stomach for laziness, incompetency, army inefficiency or meaningless busywork created just to kill time.

Second, he faithfully attended worship services whenever he could—every week except in combat conditions or when his regiment was in transit. These were usually chapel services conducted in camp by the regiment's chaplain. Here Ernest would sometimes meet one or two other Christian Reformed soldiers from nearby units and commiserate about army life and home.[58] But whenever possible, when camped near towns in Australia, he would go off base with a buddy to attend a Presbyterian church or on occasion a Methodist or Baptist church. There he was a recipient of the gracious hospitality these churches

---

[56] Ibid., 19 Jan. 1945.
[57] Ibid., 2 Nov. 1944, 20 Jan. 1945.
[58] His closest Dutch American contacts during his time in the service were Tunis Zwiep, August Piersma, Arthur Kok, Charles Dykshoorn, Lester van Muyden, and Al Broek.

showed military men. In Ballarat and Rockhampton, he even developed friendships with church families and visited their homes; in three cases, women of these families wrote to Marie on his behalf.[59]

While at Fort Ord, Gerritsma developed a special relationship with Rev. Harry A. Dykstra, a CRC military service pastor from Redlands, California, who had been one of the original Christian Reformed missionaries in China. Dykstra was not an army chaplain; as a military service pastor he pulled his small house trailer around California to regularly visit the various military bases in the state, looking up Christian Reformed soldiers, and sometimes leading the camp chapel service or a small service just for the CRC boys. Gerritsma had long talks with Rev. Dykstra about spiritual matters, army life, and world affairs, and even after he left Fort Ord to go overseas, they continued to correspond.[60] Gerritsma also kept in touch by letter with his home pastor, Rev. Marinus Arnoys, of the First CRC in Sioux Center.

During his time at Noemfoor Island, Gerritsma was impressed when he attended chapel services for six weeks in the fall of 1944, conducted by Rev. Leonard DeMoor, chaplain at the local evacuation hospital. DeMoor, a graduate of Hope College and Western Theological Seminary, had earlier been an RCA minister and recently became Presbyterian. He told Ernest about a local case of Japanese cannibalism, when chunks of flesh were cut from wounded Japanese soldiers.[61]

Though the mail was very sporadic, Gerritsma much appreciated receiving the *Banner*, the *Young Calvinist*, and the *Sioux Center News*, all of which had pages devoted to those in the military. Especially the *Young Calvinist* printed many letters of servicemen.

Another indication of his Dutch Reformed character (and perhaps his own independent mind and stubbornness) was the fact that Gerritsma would not go out on the town with the guys to carouse and drink in their free time:

> Of course I don't go along with the gang, and they can't understand why I do things the way I do, but aside from that we get along just fine, even when I tell them where they're wrong; it means going my way alone for the greater part, but even that is better than being taken in on something I'm against or don't like.[62]

[59] Diary, 18 July, 9, 16, 23 Aug., 6, 24 Sept., 4 Oct. 1942; 1, 21 Mar. 1943.
[60] Diary, 6 July 1941; letters to parents, 23 July, 9 Aug., 24 and 31 Oct. 1941; letter of Harry A. Dykstra to Syne Gerritsma, 20 Nov. 1941; letter to parents, 19 Apr. 1942. Cf. *Banner*, 19 Mar. 1943; "In Memoriam: Rev. Harry A. Dykstra," *Banner*, 16 Feb. 1987, 21.
[61] Diary, 1, 8, 10, 15, 22, 29 Oct., 5 Nov. 1944; letter to parents, 10 Oct. 1944.
[62] Letter to parents, 30 May 1941; cf. letter to parents, 4 July 1941.

> So much has been said of "the army making a man of you." Now this is true to a certain extent. But in another sense *one had better be a man* before he enters the army life, or likely he'll not be half a man when he leaves. If you are not man enough to stand on your own feet, regardless of what others do, the army will ruin you. Perhaps you can't be one of the gang, attend movies, drink, use vain language, or indulge in similar or worse evils. Now many of the boys will not understand you, but eventually when true to your Christian principles, they will think more of you.[63]

He was very critical of fellow soldiers or tent-mates who got drunk and could not fulfill their duties. He would stay back in camp to read a book or write letters or visit something interesting, especially local sawmills. In all this, he seemed to maintain the respect of his fellow soldiers.

On his return to the United States in March 1945, Gerritsma was immediately granted a three-week furlough, and he went home to Iowa to see Marie and his family for the first time in three-and-a-half years.[64] While they had been planning to marry after the war, two days after his return, Marie suggested they could decide whether or not to have their wedding during the furlough. Ernest immediately proposed, and they were married the following week, on 12 April.[65] That also happened to be the day President Roosevelt died.

After this furlough, Gerritsma spent yet another three months in Hot Springs, Arkansas, and Camp Crowder, Missouri, as he impatiently awaited his army discharge. While there, he was hospitalized twice, suffering from malaria, which he had contracted in New Guinea.[66] While hospitalized, he read *Suez to Singapore* (1942) by CBS correspondent Cecil Brown; what struck him was:

> One paragraph on the first page sums up the feelings of a soldier returned from the war fronts exceptionally well; the first sentence reads: "For the rest of my life, peace will be unnatural." The scenes, impressions and experiences of war will always be a part of the person witnessing them. How cheap is human life and how the esteem for fellow man falls.[67]

[63] Letter to Rev. Marinus Arnoys, printed in "Soldier Boys Department" of the *League Echo*, Autumn 1941.
[64] "Ernest Gerritsma Home after Forty-Two Months Overseas," *Sioux Center News*, 5 Apr. 1945.
[65] Letter to Marie, 1 Dec. 1944; diary, 3, 12 Apr. 1945; *Sioux Center News*, 19 Apr. 1945.
[66] Diary, 26 Apr., 10 May, 12-23 May, 5-10 July 1945.
[67] Diary, 16 May 1945.

Fig. 13.6. Ernest and Marie Gerritsma's wedding photo (*courtesy Sylvan Gerritsma*)

Upon his discharge, Ernest finally returned home to Sioux Center on 25 July, hitchhiking fifty miles from Sioux City to get home faster. The last entry in his diary ends with this sentiment: "I thought I was happy on April 1st [when he returned home on furlough], but I'm far happier now. And Marie was happier, and may I say, even lovelier than in April."[68]

---

[68] Diary, 25 July 1945. After his discharge Gerritsma returned to his occupation as a carpenter; then for the rest of his life, he operated his own sawmill in Sioux Center, milling mostly cottonwood and walnut trees grown in local farm groves.

CHAPTER 14

Dutch Propaganda Films in America: Documentaries from the Netherlands Information Bureau in the 1940s

Henk Aay

Introduction

The documentary films produced by the Netherlands Information Bureau (NIB) in the 1940s to advance Dutch foreign policy objectives among the American public have never been studied as to their scope, impact, and propaganda value. In this chapter, I summarize, map, and interpret the circulation records of the films borrowed from the Holland, Michigan, branch of the NIB. Foreign-policy-directed films are distinguished from culture-directed films, and the rhetoric of the former is analyzed.

The Dutch Government Information Service and the Netherlands Information Bureau

Beginning with the German occupation on 15 May 1940, and ending with the Japanese occupation of the Dutch East Indies in March 1942, the Netherlands lost all international military and economic power. The Dutch government in exile in London quickly realized that public diplomacy and information campaigns were the only forms of influence that it could still wield. It immediately established the

Regeringsvoorlichtingsdienst (RVD), the Government Information Service. For communicating Dutch information and viewpoints to the countries of the Western Hemisphere, the RVD established the NIB in March of 1941, with headquarters in New York City, the broadcast, financial, and cultural center of the nation. N. A. C. Slotemaker de Bruine, head of the Dutch East Indies news wire service, was appointed director of the NIB, signaling the importance of the colonies in relations with the United States. The rising world hegemony of the United States and its impact on the prosecution of the war and on the post-war world made this the most important arm of the RVD for pressing Dutch national objectives.[1]

Subsidiary NIB service centers were established in Washington, DC; Boston; Holland, Michigan; and San Francisco, as well as (later) in Montreal and Buenos Aires. New York; Boston; and Washington, DC, served a seventeen-state area along the east coast; Holland, a twenty-state area in the mid-section of the country; and San Francisco, an eleven-state western region (fig. 1). Holland, Michigan, became a regional NIB office because of the lobbying and qualifications of Willard (Bill) Wichers, a Holland, Michigan, native with tremendous energy and a promoter of all things Dutch. Wichers was appointed director of NIB-Holland, a position he held until the entire organization was shut down in 1974.

The NIB: culture-directed and foreign-policy-directed public diplomacy

The everyday activities of NIB regional offices were marked by the routines of a comprehensive information and promotional agency,

[1] I am following David Snyder's account, based on archival sources, of the establishment, work, and outlooks of the RVD and NIB. David J. Snyder, "The Problem of Power in Modern Diplomacy. The Netherlands Information Bureau in World War II and the Early Cold War" in *The United States and Public Diplomacy: New Directions in Cultural and International History*, eds., Kenneth A. Osgood and Brian C. Etheridge (Leiden, the Netherlands: Martinus Nijhoff Publishers, 2010), 57-80. Also helpful in this regard are David J. Snyder, "Dutch Cultural Policy in the United States," in *Four Centuries of Dutch-American Relations*, eds., Hans Krabbendam, Cornelis A. Van Minnen, and Giles Scott-Smith (Albany: State University of New York Press, 2009), 970-77; Marja Roholl, "To Put Holland on the Map: Voorlichting als Instrument van Buitenlands Beleid van Nederland, 1900-1950," paper presented to the Conference Media en Sociaal-Culturele Veranderingen, International Institute for Social History, Amsterdam, 24 May 1991, 4-12; and Bert Van der Zwan, "De Regerings Voorlichtingsdienst te London (RVD), 1940-1945 [Government Information Service (RVD) in London, 1940-45]," in *Het Londens Archief: Het Ministerie van Buitenlandse Zaken tijdens de Tweede Wereld Oorlog*, Van der Zwan, et al. (Amsterdam: Boom, 2003), 37- 45.

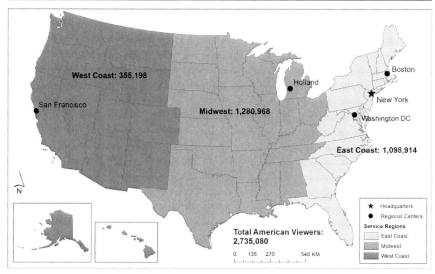

Fig. 14.1. Estimated 1940s NIB film attendance by service region

answering specific questions and furnishing information about the Netherlands to individuals, schools, libraries, and businesses, in person and by phone and letter, as well as planning and promoting cultural exhibits. Yet, such culture-directed activities, although contributing significantly to an improved American public understanding of the Netherlands, masked the bread-and-butter work of the NIB. Issues related to the war, to post-war reconstruction, and to the future of the Dutch colonies dominated a carefully planned NIB foreign-policy-directed public diplomacy.[2]

As the NIB began to ramp up this diplomacy, the United States still had not entered the war; the destructive effects (e.g., Rotterdam) of the German invasion on the largely helpless Netherlands and the hardships of German occupation were used to gain sympathy for the Dutch and importune America to join the Allied powers. When the United States did enter the Second World War after the Japanese sneak attack on Pearl Harbor on 7 December 1942, the NIB's outreach to the American public continued this theme of a suffering and innocent

[2] Foreign-policy-directed public diplomacy is related to very specific political causes and has a more activist orientation. Culture-directed public diplomacy aims to improve understanding and appreciation of a country and its way of life among the people of another country and lacks arm twisting. Information of all kinds is made available, and people are encouraged to take a look and make use of it. Both kinds of public diplomacy put their country in a positive light and both may be more or less propagandistic.

little country, as well as adding some other foci, especially that of the Netherlands as a useful ally in the war effort.

Toward the end of the war, Dutch diplomacy via the NIB turned more to the physical and human destruction of the country, to countering malnutrition and rebuilding infrastructure. But then came the Indonesian crisis and with it a renewed need for another round of propaganda and public diplomacy. No other immediate post-war issue took more attention from the NIB than restoring and maintaining Dutch sovereignty over the East Indies in the face of a growing Indonesian independence movement and American public and political sympathy for decolonization.[3]

To counter the strong anti-colonial sentiments among the American public and its political leaders, the NIB waged an information campaign that rested especially on the claim that the Dutch were different colonizers than other nations. Included in this claim were assertions of genuine improvement in the lives and conditions of Indonesian peoples, integration of Dutch and Indonesian society and institutions, as well as significant political participation by indigenous communities at all levels. Another principal claim of Communist leanings was leveled against the leadership of the Indonesian independence movement and the kind of country they would fashion. The United States would much prefer a Dutch East Indies to a Communist Indonesia.

While this propaganda campaign was not without success, its influence was not tied to hard economic, military, or international bargaining power. It could not keep American foreign policy under President Harry Truman from forcing the Netherlands' hand to grant independence to Indonesia in December of 1949.[4] This marked the end of NIB's activist propaganda and public diplomacy programs; instead, it turned to providing information to organizations and individuals who requested it. In 1951 the new national director, Jerome Heldring,

---

[3] David Snyder documents the various information strategies the NIS employed to try to win the American public over to the side of supporting continuing Dutch colonial rule in Indonesia. Films played a role in this propaganda; about half of the films distributed during the 1940s were related to the Dutch colonies. David Snyder, "Representing Indonesian Democracy in the US: Dutch Public Diplomacy and the Exception to Self Determination" in *Democracy and Culture in the Transatlantic World*, eds., Charlotte Wallin and Daniel Silander (Vaxjo, Sweden: Vaxjo University, 2004).

[4] Cees Wiebes and Bert Zeeman, "United States 'Big Stick' Diplomacy: The Netherlands between Decolonization and Alignment, 1945-1949," *International History Review* 14 (Feb. 1992): 45-70. The threat of cutting off military and other aid to the Netherlands under the Marshall Plan was part of this "Big Stick" diplomacy. One foreign policy objective undercut another.

changed the agency's name to the Netherlands Information Service (NIS). For several additional decades, the NIS supplied wide-ranging economic and cultural information to individuals, schools, social organizations, and companies. With declining budgets and shrinking political support, the Dutch government closed the agency in 1974 and transferred some of its functions to the diplomatic services.[5]

Information resource, public diplomacy, and propaganda: media, materials, and approaches

The Netherlands Information Bureau made use of all available media and other materials: newspapers, magazines and journals, photographs, material objects, films, filmstrips and slides, books, radio scripts, music recordings, lectures, telegrams, newsletters, and government reports and pamphlets.[6] Information and viewpoints about the Netherlands were disseminated through exhibits, libraries of films, books, magazines, and other print materials in each NIB office. The NIB also sent prominent Dutch authorities on lecture tours, issued press releases, and produced radio programs for broadcasts throughout the United States. The NIB widely circulated its own Dutch news magazine and enjoyed close cooperation in placing its materials with the editors of the *Knickerbocker Weekly*, a magazine for Dutch Americans.[7]

The NIB's proactive and reactive propaganda campaign included covert oversight of the Dutch wire services to manage the news; speeches to prominent audiences by Dutch diplomats; the production of films, press releases, and other quick responses to unfavorable newspaper accounts and editorials; and the use of American surrogates to make the Dutch case.[8]

In spite of its largely unsuccessful public diplomacy campaign, the NIB through its branch offices disseminated a great deal of highly

---

[5] Snyder, "Dutch Cultural Policy," 975-79.
[6] David Snyder provides a comprehensive overview of the Netherlands Information Service archive of the Holland, Michigan, NIB branch, which is held by the Holland Historical Trust and housed in the Holland Museum in Holland, Michigan (HMA). David Snyder, "The Netherlands Information Service Collection: An Introduction," *Historia Actual On Line* 8 (Fall 2005): 201-9. This is the only archive of the Netherlands Information Bureau/Service in North America; similar materials from New York and the other branches were returned to the Netherlands where, apparently, they were substantially culled.
[7] Charlotte Kok, "The Knickerbocker Weekly and the Netherlands Information Bureau: A Public Diplomacy Cooperation during the 1941-1947 Era" (MA Thesis, American Studies Program, Utrecht University, 24 June 2011).
[8] Snyder, "Problem of Power," 64-73.

diversified material about the Netherlands and its colonies to a large and broad American public during the 1940s. Millions of Americans used materials sent to schools and libraries, heard radio programs, saw films, read accounts in daily newspapers based on press releases, and attended exhibits.

After the NIS was shutdown in 1974, the Dutch government allowed NIB/NIS-Holland to keep all of its materials and records, including its film library. In time this brought about the establishment of a very extensive and complete archive of NIB/NIS materials as well as an equally extensive archive of Wichers' personal records, many of which also relate to NIB/NIS matters.

NIB-Holland 16mm documentary films and circulation records

The services of NIB film-lending libraries were much in demand, especially during the 1940s. For only the cost of postage, an organization or individual could receive a film listed in the catalog of the regional NIB office. The films could be screened multiple times and even circulated locally. While film, of course, had been around for some time (film with sound track was more recent), it remained something quite special and attractive to a very broad public, combining visual entertainment with learning, something that print media could not do. The lower cost of the 16mm format brought the film experience out of the theater into the classroom, boardroom, living room, library, and church. The films themselves, along with their circulation records, were the principal source for this study.

The film-borrowing records make it possible to analyze the cultural influence of the films, something not measurable with the films alone. The circulation records for the 1940s include fifty-five film titles, of which forty-five are found in the film collection. These records show that an estimated 1,280,968 people throughout the twenty-state Holland-NIB service area saw these films.[9]

---

[9] Although this is a reliable estimate of the number of viewers who saw films loaned out by the NIB, it significantly underestimates the total number of American viewers for two main reasons. One was the NIB practice of placing copies of films generally not available in the United States in the film lending libraries of public universities within the service region. These would be managed like any other film in their collections; if there was any viewership data, it was not shared with the NIB. Second, nineteen of the top thirty-three films that were part of a closer analysis were acquired from mainly American and some British producers and distributors. Many of these were shown as shorts in movie theaters and were available from many other public and commercial film lending agencies throughout the country.

When one applies the percentage (1.8 percent) of the total 1950 census population of this region that viewed the films to the 1950 population of the other two NIB service regions, a rough but still useful approximation of the national total comes to more than 2.7 million viewers (see fig. 1, above).[10] Such a figure assumes identical viewer participation rates and somewhat similar film libraries in each region (not likely); still, it provides something of a national ballpark figure and one measure of the films' collective cultural impact.

Data and methods

NIB-Holland prepared monthly film reports. These were alphabetically organized by film title and listed the name of the borrower (individual and/or organization), place and state, and number of viewers, and beginning in 1950, the number of showings. The film reports for the years 1966-72 have not been found. Fig. 2 shows the first page of the NIB-Holland Film Showing Report for September 1945.[11]

Each borrowing record (more than 11,000) from these monthly film reports was entered into a data base. By querying the database, several secondary data for each borrowing record were added to these primary data: type of borrower, ancestry of viewers, and geographic region of the film. Borrowers were classified into one of twelve types, such as churches, schools, libraries, and so forth. Viewers were identified as of Dutch ancestry on the basis of screenings at Reformed churches (RCA), Christian Reformed churches (CRC), Christian schools, and other Dutch American organizations, such as the Dutch Immigrant Society; all other screenings were catalogued as by non-Dutch viewers. Lastly, the films were classified into one of three geographic regions: the Netherlands, Dutch colonies, and other.

A count of total viewers for each film shown during the 1940s was generated, and the numbers were ranked to differentiate the influence of each film. Where the number of viewers at a screening was not given in the records, the average number of viewers for that type of borrower (church, school, *etc.*) was inserted. The screening locations in the database were given geographic coordinates and imported into GIS software to produce maps of film attendance throughout the Holland-NIB service region. The foreign-policy-directed films were singled out and their rhetoric examined.

[10] http://www2.census.gov/prod2/statcomp/documents/1951-02.pdf, p. 31, table 38.
[11] Film Reports, 1945-46, Netherlands Information Service, Adminstration, box 2, HMA.

FILM SHOWING REPORT FOR SEPTEMBER, 1945

An East Indian Island	
Campers, Walther League, Arcadia, Michigan	230
Junior Sunday school class, Medina, Ohio	50
Celebes and Komodo	
YMCA Camp, Terre Haute, Indiana	140
Ceremonies on Bali	
Junior Sunday school class, Medina, Ohio	50
Dutch East Indies	
Church group, Christian Ref. Church, Worthington, Minnesota	200
Dutch Guiana	
YMCA Camp, Terre Haute, Indiana	140
Glimpses of Picturesque Java	
Junior Sunday school class, Medina, Ohio	50
Sunday school teachers, Zeeland, Michigan	20
Grade school pupils, Holland, Michigan	24
American Seating Company	130
High Stakes in the East	
Convalescent patients, Station Hospital, Lake Charles, La.	21
Holland and the Dutch	
Church group, Christian Ref. church, Worthington, Minnesota	200
Landbuilders	
Grade school pupils, Holland, Michigan	24
Sunday school teachers, Zeeland, Michigan	20
Women's Club, Orange City, Iowa	275
YMCA Camp, Terre Haute, Indiana	140
Church group, Christian Ref. church, Holland, Michigan	50
Little Dutch Tulip Girl	
Church group, Christian Ref. Church, Worthington, Minnesota	200
Netherlands America	
Church group, Trinity Ref. church, Holland, Michigan	50
YMCA Camp, Terre Haute, Indiana	140
Peoples of Java	
YMCA Camp, Terre Haute, Indian	140
Junior Sunday school class, Medina, Ohio	50
Opening of DEI show, Art Gallery, Grand Rapids, Michigan	302
Quaint old Holland	
Convalescent patients, Station Hospital, Lake Charles, La.	21

Fig. 14.2. NIB-Holland: first page of film-showing report for September 1945

Film attendance

Yearly film attendance during the 1940s is shown in fig. 3. Viewership ramped up from 1943 to 1946 as the NIB's film library became more established and better known. The 1946 attendance peak is higher than that of any other year during the life of the NIB/NIS; from that peak, the general annual pattern is one of declining viewership that continues into the 1950s, punctuated by an irregular upsurge occasioned by a particularly popular film.

The total attendance of nearly 1.3 million viewers is, of course, also distributed unevenly over the fifty-five films. Fig. 4 shows the estimated

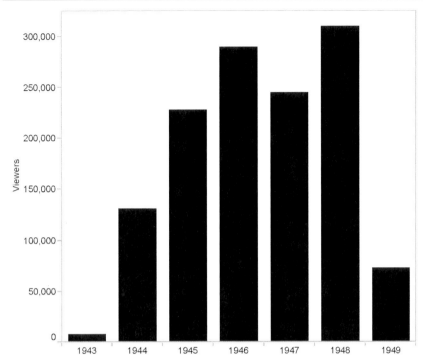

Fig. 14.3. NIB-Holland: estimated yearly attendance of films, 1940s

1940s attendance for each film arranged in descending order, from *Landbuilders*, with more than ninety-seven thousand viewers (7.6 percent of total) to *Holland-Its Cities and Industries*, with just sixty viewers (0.0 percent).[12] The decline in viewership is fairly steep for the first six films and then continues downward at a relatively constant rate. The first thirty-three films account for more than 93 percent of the total 1940s viewership. Because films with relatively small numbers of viewers have an equally small collective cultural impact, the more detailed analysis was reserved for these films (each with over ten thousand viewers).

Because these films lacked advertising, newspaper reviews, and word of mouth marketing, it is hard to know why there are such large disparities in viewership. A strong endorsement or a big yawn at a venue in one place would not readily be communicated to people in other

[12] Unless otherwise noted, the 16mm films along with their digitized versions are found in the archive of the Netherlands Information Service, HMA. In 2011 the work to digitize these more than two hundred 16mm films was begun, funded by the Meijer Chair in Dutch Language and Culture at Calvin College, the Netherland America Foundation, and the Holland Museum. The work was completed in July 2013. Several films could not be digitized because they were too damaged to run through a projector.

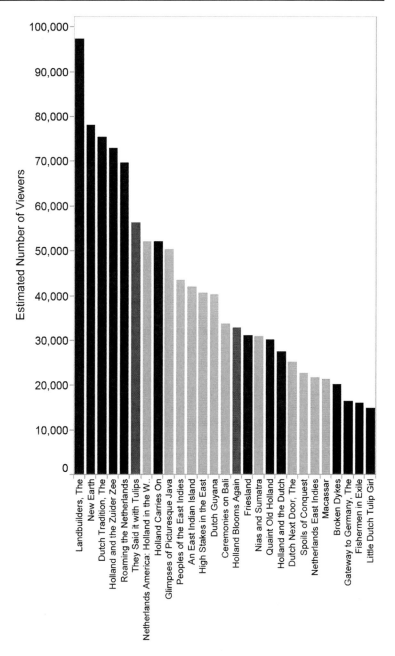

Fig. 14.4. NIB-Holland: estimated attendance by film during the 1940s

Dutch Propaganda Films in America 231

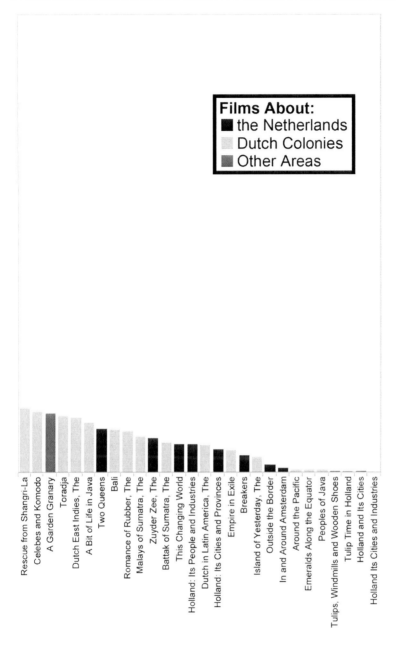

places. The NIB/NIS archive offers little help to answer this question. A plausible explanation combines marketing in the Holland-NIB office itself with local centers of film borrowers identified in fig. 5. On the one hand, the Holland office would have been asked by borrowers to recommend and send films for different occasions and interests; such preferences would help to build or dampen viewership for individual films. On the other hand, there are clusters of borrowers in some counties or centers and none in adjacent ones. In such geographic borrowing clusters, school, church, and civic networks would informally circulate information about the films that would direct further borrowing decisions and with that the viewership of particular films.

The million-plus viewers are found throughout the twenty-state NIB-Holland service region. Fig. 5 shows the geography of viewership during the 1940s. Screening locations are combined with the total number of viewers in these places. Some localities with a relatively large number of viewers/screenings have a single borrower, for example, Fort Polk, Louisiana; others have many borrowers, for example, Grand Rapids, Michigan. The first and most obvious disclosure of this map is that viewers are dispersed throughout the entire service region (and beyond); they are not overly concentrated only in the Great Lakes states relatively close to Holland, as some might expect. Cultural influence is measured not only by the number of people who are exposed to new knowledge but also by the geographic extent of that knowledge.

The distribution of screenings and viewers in general follows the distribution of the population. The films were seen by a representative geographic cross-section of the population in the NIB-Holland service area. That pattern, however, does not hold everywhere, especially along the Lake Michigan shoreline and the southern part of Lower Michigan where screenings and viewers are considerably greater than population alone would predict. Two factors play a role in this: proximity to Holland, Michigan, and the much higher concentration of Dutch Americans in this area. Knowledge about the NIB and its services would be more widespread closer to Holland, resulting in a greater use of the film lending library. Dutch American institutions, such as Reformed churches, Christian schools, and other organizations, like the Dutch Immigrant Society and Chicago's Knickerbocker Society, are much more prevalent throughout this zone. These circumstances led to higher film-borrowing rates.

Dutch American and non-Dutch viewers

The NIB's purpose was to favorably shape American public opinion in relation to particular Dutch foreign policy objectives and

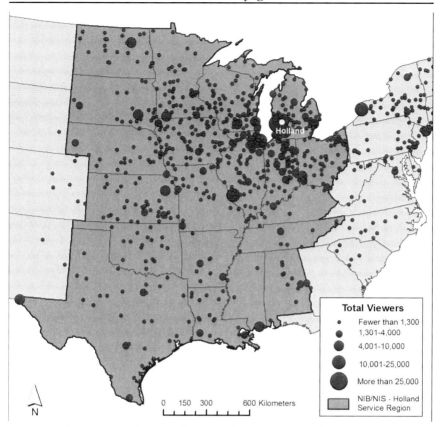

Fig. 14.5. NIB-Holland: estimated film attendance by place, 1940s

to advance knowledge about and regard for the Netherlands in general. A broad American public (not just Dutch Americans) was the primary target. Press releases were sent mainly to regional dailies and not to Dutch American institutions, newspapers, and magazines. Radio programs were not aimed at Dutch Americans but were intended for a broad audience. The film circulation records bear this out as well: of the 1.28 million estimated viewers in the Holland-NIB service region only about 12 percent (153,716) were Dutch Americans. This relatively low percentage resulted from the mission of the NIB to influence the American public opinion at large; the NIB was an agency of the Dutch government led by diplomats from the Netherlands and not by Dutch Americans.

Consul Willard Wichers was an important exception: he was a Dutch American leader whose life was very much bound up in that ethnic subculture. More than others, he saw Dutch Americans as important ambassadors in the NIB's public diplomacy and urged the New York head office to send its materials to Dutch American institutions and its print media.[13]

But there is another reason why Dutch Americans made little use of the NIB resources, including documentary films. Particularly those in and around settlements such as Holland, Michigan, and Pella, Iowa, founded in the 1840s by seceders from the Dutch state church, were of two minds and conflicted about their one-time motherland. David Zwart carefully examines these two perceptions with the help of the Netherlands Information Service as well as the Wichers archive.[14] One was a very nostalgic view of the country as a quaint pre-industrial homeland with tulips, traditional costumes, windmills, wooden shoes, and cheese markets. But the other was a rather dim view of the ancestral homeland, a country they or their forebears left because of economic hardship, religious persecution, and/or, compared to America, a country they considered to be out of date economically, technologically, and politically.

Types of borrowers

The monthly film reports list a wide variety of users along with the attendance at their screenings: Sunday schools and other church groups, camps, hospitals, grade schools, a commercial firm, civic organizations, an art gallery, and military posts (fig. 2). When all the borrowers are classified into one of nine types, the viewership of these different kinds of borrowers may be compiled (fig. 6).[15]

Among types of film borrowers, educational institutions far outnumber all other users. The type of borrower may well have a bearing on the cultural impact of these films measured by location on the continuum between entertainment and education, with schools, universities, church education, and libraries on one side, and military, care facilities, and commercial entities on the other. The preponderance of educational users clearly strengthened that impact. Educational institutions and their teachers would more likely show these films as part of a curriculum unit with possible pre-viewing commentary by the teacher, class questions with pre- as well as post-film discussion,

---

[13] David Zwart, "Constructing the Homeland: Dutch Americans and the Netherlands Information Bureau during the 1940s," *Michigan Historical Review* 33 (Fall 2007): 99.
[14] Ibid., 81-100.
[15] Most borrower types are self-explanatory. "Religious" users were all organizations administered by churches. "Care Facilities" include hospitals and institutions for the elderly.

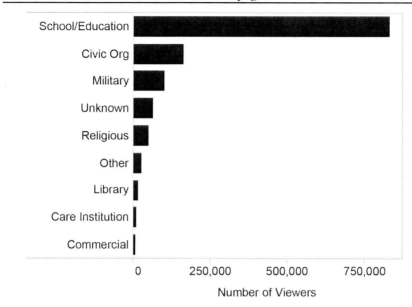

Fig. 14.6. NIB-Holland: film attendance by type of borrower

along with student written reports and possibly tests. Such teaching strategies would enhance the impact and retention of the message and meaning of the film. At the same time, students would be taught to take such materials more seriously and with more reflection than those gathered at a military base for an evening's diversion. All in all, the solid majority of educational users bolstered the cultural impact of the films, while likely lessening their more desired immediate political influence.

Up closer: the 1940 films

Fig. 4 divides the 1940 films into those mainly about the Netherlands and those about the Dutch colonies. More than half the films are about the Dutch colonies, a reflection of how important the Dutch government regarded the issue of American support of the Netherlands as a colonial power. It also references the Netherlands' enduring perception of itself as a world power. With the loss of the East Indies and prevailing anti-imperialism, the percentage of films about the colonies in the film collection understandably shrank sharply in the ensuing decades.

The top thirty-three of the fifty-five films shown during the 1940s received closer analytical scrutiny; these drew 93 percent of the attendance (1,191,310 viewers). Fig. 7 divides each of these films not only into films about the Netherlands and the Dutch colonies but also

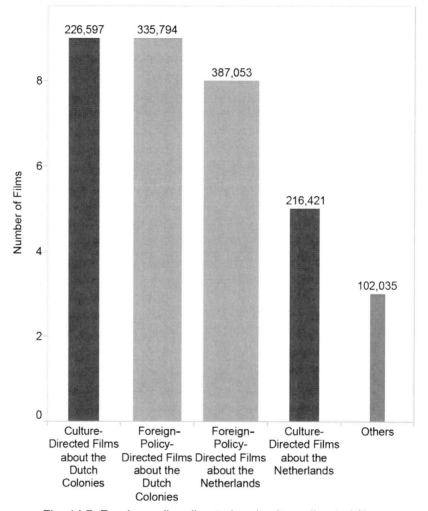

Fig. 14.7. Foreign-policy-directed and culture-directed films shown during the 1940s

into those that are foreign-policy-directed (e.g., war-related issues, postwar reconstruction, the colonies) and those that are culture-directed (e.g., to improve general understanding and appreciation).[16]

Almost all culture-directed films were not Dutch-made but rather American-made films. Many of these were shorts for movie theaters, and therefore were seen by much larger audiences. Conversely, almost all foreign-policy-directed films were produced or commissioned by Dutch government agencies, principally the NIB but also the

[16] Fig. 7 graphs 34 not 33 films; one film was placed in two categories.

Regeringsvoorlichtingsdienst (RVD), the Dutch Government Information Service, and some were acquired from the British Information Service. These circulated almost exclusively via the NIB. This study examines only the foreign-policy-directed films and not the culture directed ones.

Foreign-policy-directed films frequently were so-called compilation films. Such films were composed entirely, or almost entirely, of footage from other films, usually with new narration and music. Alternately, the same footage might be used in the production of several films. The most extreme form of borrowing footage to produce a "new" film was to use all or most of one existing film but with a new ending and possibly a new narration. The two films with the highest attendance during the 1940s (*Landbuilders* and *New Earth*) are examples of this technique. Compilation films can, of course, be produced more quickly and cheaply. In such films the narration often drives the message and meaning more than the visual portion; in some cases, the same footage with different narration takes on an entirely different message. When filming locations were inaccessible, or filming on location was prohibitively expensive and time-consuming, a documentary film could still be created. Such circumstances certainly applied to the film production unit of the NIB.

One should not assume, however, that compilation films could just be slapped together and that, as such, they were inferior creations. Suitable footage had to be located, permissions secured, a new voice-over narration written, a voice-actor hired, and a recording made. Reputable filmmakers and motion picture companies were involved in their production. For example, John Fernhout, a well-known Dutch cameraman and filmmaker who worked for the NIB film unit in New York and for the National Film Board of Canada (NFB) during the war years, made several compilation films, including *The Dutch Tradition*, an overview of the Netherlands and its colonies in relation to the war effort. The NFB was the producer of the film.[17]

Foreign-policy-directed films about the Netherlands: selected rhetorical themes

Eight of the fifty-five films (and eight of the top 33 examined more carefully as well) belong to the group of foreign-policy-directed films about the Netherlands itself (fig. 7). In terms of production methods, it is a diverse group: older existing complete films with new

---

[17] For an account (in Dutch) of Fernhout's filmmaking career go to: http://www.historici.nl/Onderzoek/Projecten/BWN/lemmata/bwn4/fernhjh.

endings and narration (*Landbuilders*, 97,483 viewers; *New Earth*, 78,098 viewers), compilation films (*The Dutch Tradition*, 75,419 viewers; *Holland Carries On*, 52,413 viewers), and completely new films shot largely on location (*Fishermen in Exile*, 16,110 viewers; *Friesland*, 31,214 viewers; *Broken Dykes*, 20,178 viewers; *Gateway to Germany*, 16,408 viewers).

Land from water, not conquest

Landbuilders and *New Earth* occupied a special place in the NIB-Holland film collection; these were the two most popular films in the 1940s and took first and third place for the lifetime of NIB/NIS Holland.[18] Unlike most others, these two had staying power. *Landbuilders* repackaged a 1932 film, *Walcheren*, about the former island at the mouth of the Scheldt estuary, part of the province of Zeeland. It retained most if not all the original footage and music track of *Walcheren*; it added English-language narration with a British accent and phrasing, and most importantly, it pasted a new minute-long piece to the end of the film.

Although *Landbuilders* was a foreign-policy-directed film in intent, it functioned equally well as a culture-directed film. This helps account for its popularity and staying power well into the 1950s. Anyone viewing the first seventeen minutes or so of the film enjoys nostalgic and folklorist scenes and commentary about Walcheren: dunes and man-made dikes as sea walls protecting the land; drainage to make fertile farmland; prosperous farming landscapes with fields, pastures, villages, roads, and canals; rural crafts and pastimes; people leaving church in traditional costumes; and the bustle on the market square in Middelburg, the capital. Together with its lyrical and moving music, the film is an ode to the way of life created and followed on the island, one that would fill most viewers with admiration. Then comes the last minute: scenes of the beautiful late-Gothic city hall situated on the market square dissolve into stills accompanied by discordant music of the ruins of the building caused by German artillery bombardment of the city. Then, against a background of the burned-out city hall and waves breaking against a dike, the narrator makes a stern summary declaration that add other layers of meaning—concern, anger, and sympathy—to the earlier feelings of admiration and respect. It is worth quoting this declaration because several other films in this category made much the same point:

---

[18] As noted, the film borrowing records from 1966 to 1972 were not recovered. The film *Holland Today* attracted nearly fifty thousand viewers in 1965 just after it had been acquired, and in 1973, it still drew more than forty thousand viewers. Any extrapolation of its viewership makes *Holland Today* the most viewed film in the NIB film collection.

A new order reigns in Holland. Zeeland was the last province to resist the German horde and had to pay the price. This man [the film shows a dike worker] has enemies a million times as powerful as any human foe and more relentless. With bare hands they have torn the soil inch by inch from the clutches of the waves and bare-handed they stood guard over the land they so rightly own. They did not come with guns and tanks and bombs like bandits to steal their fields and homes. They also needed *lebensraum* and found an answer. It was not mass murder. They built their islands and owned them with just pride. With your help they will again be masters of their hard-earned soil, reconstruct their damaged homes, and reclaim their barren fields.

The film closes with a picture of the coat of arms of Zeeland: *Luctor et Emergo* (I struggle and emerge).

If *Landbuilders* celebrated the millennium-old practice of making and protecting land from the sea and then from this land creating a rich and enduring cultural landscape, then the film *New Earth* brought this defining practice into the scale and technology of the twentieth century. The national project to drain large parts of the Zuiderzee, begun in 1927, attracted Dutch filmmakers, including Joris Ivens, pioneer and internationally renowned filmmaker of political and social documentaries.[19]

His 1933 film, *Nieuwe Gronden* (New Earth), looks at this monumental undertaking, especially the technology of dike building, land drainage, and preparation and cultivation of the new land; Ivens aims his camera particularly at the workers and skilled machine operators whose hard physical labor produced this improvement. In the last part of the film, he indicts the world economic system of the Great Depression that would rather destroy food than feed it to the poor and hungry. *Nieuwe Gronden* is the proto-film for the documentary *New Earth*, produced by the *Regeringsvoorlichtingsdienst*. Given the foreign policy objectives of the Dutch Government Information Service, it is not surprising that the third part of the film, a denunciation of the global capitalist economic system, was excised from the film.

New Earth uses short excerpts at the beginning from the film *Landbuilders/Walcheren* to set the historical context for American-Dutch friendship and American knowledge of the country. Then the footage

---

[19] For a biography of Ivens, consult Hans Schoots, *Living Dangerously: A Biography of Joris Ivens* (Amsterdam: Amsterdam University Press, 2000).

Fig. 14.8. Making new land with dike mats. Film: *New Earth*[20]

from *Nieuwe Gronden* is inserted. The close-up look at the Zuiderzee polder project in *Nieuwe Gronden* is given new meaning in *New Earth* for American moviegoers. The key to the identity of the country, according to the film, is to be found in the dikes, pumps, sluices, drainage canals, and other water works found everywhere. These have created the country and its dispositions from the beginning and continue to do so today:

> We were conquering a new portion of the Earth's surface and these [the workers on the Zuiderzee project] were our armies; this was our answer to a need for *lebensraum*. This is how a peaceful nation fights for its homeland. Holland is bounded by frontiers that Dutchmen have made.

The dominant rhetorical theme asserted by these two influential films (also asserted by others) is that the Netherlands' need for new land, for more agricultural production and greater economic welfare for an expanding population, had always been achieved by wresting more land from water rather than by military aggression against neighboring counties. While this is more or less the case for the coterminous Netherlands, it glosses over the Dutch naval military campaigns during the seventeenth century—especially against the British and Spanish—to carve out and control colonial commercial land areas around the globe. Apparently, military expansion overseas was different from military expansion over land.

[20] The Holland Museum of Holland, Michigan (HMA) has given the author the right to incorporate still images captured from films in its Netherlands Information Service Collection (T88-1182).

Moreover, this rhetorical claim creates the impression that wresting land from the sea and from other flood-prone areas was a planned national goal, when in fact, for much of Dutch history, this was prompted by local and regional community and business interests, needs, and hazards. And when this did become a national goal, as with the Haarlemmermeer Polder (nineteenth century) and the Zuiderzee project (twentieth century), protecting the inhabitants from flooding and loss of surrounding land provided the immediate impetus for these projects. Additional land was an important collateral benefit but not the driving force behind these public works.[21] There was never a political calculus: winning land from water or war against our neighbors; the Netherlands was militarily unprepared for such undertakings. These films give a moral meaning to a universal Dutch practical matter: winning land from water and protection from flooding.

We're like you

The compilation films, *The Dutch Tradition* and *Holland Carries On*, advance another rhetorical claim. These two share a lot of imagery, although the latter includes footage from the liberation and the bleak immediate post-war period as well. By pointing out parallels between the United States and the Netherlands (they're like us), the filmmakers bring the two countries closer together, give them a common identity and, as a result, attempt to evoke more understanding and sympathy from the American public. Against a background of iconic scenes from the Netherlands and from Holland, Michigan, *The Dutch Tradition* asserts:

> For centuries the people of the Netherlands have been creating the tradition that today inspires their fight for freedom. We all know the outward appearance of that tradition—tulips, windmills and wooden shoes. But what lies behind these surfaces? What is the spirit that moves every Dutchman in the world today? The spiritual [mental] legacy is the most important: a structure made up layers of individual achievements and social progress. It was one aspect of the Dutch tradition; it has become the American way as well.

---

[21] There is a very extensive literature on the history of impoldering and protection against flooding in the Netherlands. For English-language overviews consult: G. P. Van de Ven, ed., *Man-made Lowlands. History of Water Management and Land Reclamation in the* Netherlands, 2nd rev. ed. (Utrecht: Stichting Matrijs, 1994); Robert Hoeksema, *Designed for Dry Feet* (Reston, VA: ASCE Press, 2006).

Then there follows a filmic survey of noteworthy modern Dutch achievements. In *Holland Carries On* these national accomplishments are shown in scenes of Schiphol airport, modern highways, diesel-electric trains, modern housing, and most prominently, the Zuiderzee project, both the construction and the settling of the new land. Footage from Ivens' *New Earth* gets still more use.

These two films argue that the Dutch have long fought and continue to fight for their political, social, economic, and religious freedom, all precious in American life as well, and thus the United States would be inclined militarily and economically to help the Dutch recover them. Like the United States, the Dutch champion individual achievement and social progress (in housing, education, and transportation), whereas the German occupation had trampled on these achievements. As an ideological ally, the United States would want to help the Netherlands restore these freedoms and accomplishments.

For American audiences this rhetorical claim that the Netherlands was like the United States was probably not all that persuasive. It is not that Americans were indifferent to the Nazi occupation of much of Europe. While it is true that seventeenth-century Netherlands by way of its colony in America made fundamental contributions to the kind of country the United States had become, the Netherlands of the nineteenth and twentieth centuries was quite different from that of the Dutch Golden Age and its colony of New Netherland.[22]

In the collective memory of nineteenth and twentieth century European immigration-derived communities throughout the Midwest, the *differences* between America and Europe stood out. These communities remembered that, unlike the United States, Europe lacked religious and economic freedom and opportunities to get ahead; it suffered under rigid class distinctions, economic hardships and poverty, and excessive state control.

Holland carries on

In spite of the hardships of German occupation and the devastated post-war country, the NIB films strove to portray the Netherlands as a loyal and useful member of the Allied powers and a sovereign nation in exile. This theme of "Holland carries on" resonates in the films *The Dutch Tradition, Holland Carries On, Friesland,* and *Fishermen in Exile*. The establishment of the NIB itself may, of course, be seen as an expression

---

[22] See, for example, Russell Shorto, *Island at the Center of the World* (New York: Doubleday, 2004).

of this idea. It was much easier to provide filmic examples of this for the Dutch colonies—the East Indies before March 1942 and the West Indies during the entire duration of the war (see below).

But actions undertaken within the Netherlands itself also had to be shown as carrying on the fight and doing the hard work of reconstruction. Members of the Dutch resistance are shown coordinating airstrikes on military targets in their own country, distributing underground newspapers, sabotaging German trains, fighting alongside the Allied forces liberating the country, and rounding up Dutch collaborators after the liberation (*Holland Carries On*). The film *Fishermen in Exile* provides another angle on the Holland-carries-on theme.[23] Dutch fishermen escaped to British ports with their vessels when Germany invaded the country. They put their vessels at the disposal of the British navy and engaged in sweeping for mines and detonating them at sea, while they continued with their traditional fishing operations in the North Sea. Their catches helped feed their British allies.

Everyone rebuilds

The NIB got out of the business of producing and commissioning its own films soon after the war ended. That is one reason why there are so few films in the 1940s NIB collection about the physical devastation and the needed reconstruction of the country. The Dutch film industry was making a slow comeback in the release of clandestine wartime footage, especially about the Hunger Winter of 1944-45, and also in new film projects documenting the war's destruction and reconstruction in various parts of the country.[24] These films, however, did not make it into the NIB collection. US Marshall Plan films and newsreel footage about its role in the rebuilding of the country did not reach Dutch movie theaters and other venues such as the NIB film library until the early fifties.[25]

Friesland is an exception. This film takes a rather surprisingly lighthearted look at the province of Friesland coming back to life after

---

[23] This film clearly could not be classified as a foreign-policy-directed film about the Dutch colonies and therefore was classified as a foreign-policy-directed film about the Netherlands even though, strictly speaking, it is not about the Netherlands itself but about exiled Dutch fishermen operating out of England.

[24] For the Dutch film industry in the immediate war years consult Bert Hogenkamp, *De Documentaire Film 1945-1965. De Bloei van een Filmgenre in Nederland* (Rotterdam: Uitgeverij 010, 2003): 9-46.

[25] Anne-Lijke Struijk, "Negotiating the Marshall Plan: Dutch Marshall Plan Films 1948-1954" (master's thesis, American Studies, Utrecht University, 2010), 88-92.

Fig. 14.9. Ferrying cars across a canal with a destroyed bridge. Film: *Friesland*

five years of occupation, a period that became increasingly repressive as the years passed. The narration is not the customary authoritative voice over but a relaxed, even joking, conversational style. The film shows people (and cattle) coming out of hiding to pick up living somewhat normal lives once more, although against a lot of odds. The entire film underscores the Holland-carries-on and can-do themes: trucks for cattle transport become buses; cars are ferried across canals since bridges have been destroyed; bricks from destroyed buildings are cleaned and repurposed; and traffic moves very deliberately across temporary bridges built by Canadian forces during the fight for liberation. And this restart of Frisian life after the liberation is related not only to these more tangible and practical matters but also to the gamut of Frisian culture; the film shows scenes of recreational sailing and sailing races on the Frisian lakes and a parade of Frisian carriages pulled by Frisian horses with riders wearing traditional Frisian costumes.

Foreign-policy-directed films about the Dutch colonies: selected rhetorical themes

There are nine foreign-policy-directed films about the Dutch colonies produced or commissioned by the NIB among the top thirty-three films (fig. 7). They employ a trope that David Snyder calls "large Holland."[26] The geostrategic locations, the essential natural resources, and the democratic, economic, and social development found throughout the Dutch colonial empire project global power needed for success in the Second World War and ensuing Cold War. "Large Holland" is

[26] Snyder, "Problem of Power," 65.

Fig. 14.10. NIB-Holland letterhead during the 1940s

given cartographic expression (fig. 10) on the letterhead of the NIB: shown—each at a different scale!—are the Dutch colonies in the Eastern and Western Hemispheres as well as the home country itself. The Netherlands East Indies dominates the center of the map and overwhelms the mother country in area and population. The letterhead declares that the Netherlands is not a small but a large country with a presence throughout the world.

Sheer size, population, and economic investments and returns made the Dutch East Indies by far the most important colony for the Netherlands. Yet, because of their proximity to the United States, the diminutive Dutch West Indies receive more attention in these films than one would expect. All of the films about this region are foreign policy directed: *Netherlands America: Holland in the Western Hemisphere* (52,163 viewers), *Dutch Guiana* (33,763 viewers), *The Dutch Next Door* (25,225 viewers), and *The Dutch in Latin America* (6,004 viewers). Few Americans knew that these nearby parts of the Netherlands even existed, and seeing these places for the first time must have been an eye-opener. All these titles, especially *The Dutch Next Door,* brought the Netherlands geographically closer to the United States and, as a neighbor, hence more deserving of special American interest and consideration.

People of the Indies (43,519 viewers), *High Stakes in the East* (40,734 viewers), *Spoils of Conquest* (22,811 viewers) and *Netherlands East Indies* (21,731 viewers) make up the more closely examined foreign-policy-directed NIB films about the Dutch East Indies.[27] Several of these films

---

[27] The film *Rescue from Shangri-La* (13,924 viewers) is not included in the analysis. Although the film is about the war in Southeast Asia, it is not in any way related to Dutch foreign policy or to the question of the Dutch colonies. The film describes the rescue of American C-47 plane crash survivors by an American air force unit in New Guinea in 1945.

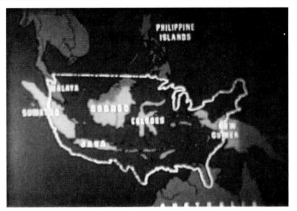

Fig. 14.11. Maps of the United States and the Dutch East Indies superimposed.
Film: *People of the Indies*

open with an overlay of an outline map of the coterminous United States on a map of the Dutch East Indies; without Alaska, the two have the same north-south and east-west extent (fig. 11); "Large Holland" strikes again.

We have the resources you need

Much is made of the fact that the first German attack in the Western Hemisphere was the 16 February 1942 shelling of the oil refineries on the Dutch island of Aruba by a submarine. Each of the films about the Dutch West Indies emphasizes that these islands provided resources critical for the war effort, especially bauxite and refined oil products but also potash. Film viewers see bauxite mining in the interior of Dutch Guiana and the shipment of the ore by river barge, under the protection of Dutch and American troops, to the coastal capital of Paramaribo for shipment to the United States. Moviegoers learn that 60 percent of the American-made aluminum necessary to make warplanes comes from Dutch Guiana; without Dutch bauxite, air warfare would be crippled. They see troops guarding the oil refineries on Curacao and Aruba, where Venezuelan crude is refined into fuels and lubricants. From *The Dutch Next Door* viewers learn that lubricating oils refined in the Dutch West Indies were "in the crankcases of the jeeps that rolled into Paris and Warsaw."

High Stakes in the East, nominated for a best documentary Oscar in 1943, makes the strategic and global importance of the Dutch East Indies economy its centerpiece, even though, ironically, tin, rubber,

Fig. 14.12. Oil storage tanks and refineries on Curacao. Film: *Netherlands America: Holland in the Western Hemisphere*

crude and refined oil, quinine, rice, sisal, and rope—each of considerable potential value to the Allies' prosecution of the war and all developed by Dutch skills and knowledge—were all flowing into Japan to maintain and expand its conquests. Indonesian settings for the excavation, cultivation, processing, and manufacture of each of these resources and commodities are shown in this film. These economic losses, the film argues, must and will be reversed, and in the post-war world, equal access for all to international trade in manufactured goods and raw materials will be essential.

Location, location, location

Another common theme in the films about the Dutch West Indies is related to their geostrategic location. With maps of the Caribbean, filmgoers see that especially the southern Dutch Antilles—Curacao, Aruba, and Bonaire—garrisoned and with a naval base, provide valuable military protection for the Panama Canal, an extremely vital asset in a two-ocean war. Moreover, these islands are shown as nodes on shipping lanes and air routes, port facilities for trans-shipment and repair, and a gateway to the Venezuelan oil fields, fifty miles away. Audiences see American war material used in joint military training exercises and the American military guarding oil refineries and building roads on the islands. Such scenes help confirm the claim of the strategic value of these places for American viewers.

We're not like other colonizers

The other foreign policy issue tackled in these films is the legitimacy and morality of Dutch colonial rule. In one way or another, this message is present in every film. It is the racial and cultural diversity of the Dutch West Indies, especially Dutch Guiana, the films assert, that points to an egalitarian, multi-ethnic global Kingdom of the Netherlands. In *The Dutch Next Door* the different groups within the population are each (visually) profiled in turn: the ethnically Dutch, Africans (freed slaves), Carib Indians, people from the Indian subcontinent, and Javanese from the Dutch East Indies. The film concludes: "These many cultures exist side by side in harmony. The entire Netherlands Kingdom may be a commonwealth of nations tomorrow [after the war], but the Dutch West Indies is a community of nations today." The film is silent, of course, about the economic power relations among these constituent groups.

The NIB liked to employ American surrogates to make its claims; these would be more credible and trustworthy for the American public than Dutch productions.[28] *Spoils of Conquest* was the August 1940 episode of *The March of Time*, the controversial and influential American newsreel series of *Time Inc.*, screened in American and foreign movie houses to millions of viewers from 1935 to 1951.[29]

Even though the episode predicts that Dutch defenders would be no match for the Imperial Japanese Army when it invaded the colony and that all its assets would become 'spoils of conquest,' the film puts Dutch colonial rule in quite a positive light. The governor general of the colonies is described as a "liberal autocrat" and the Dutch as "the most efficient colonizers" who treat "the natives not as subjects but as citizens of the empire." "Of all European colonists in the Orient, the Dutch are the most democratic" is perhaps the most congratulatory line. Little wonder the NIB kept this outdated film in its film lending library!

Notwithstanding the praises for the Dutch brand of colonialism in the narrative, when the film shows scenes of the everyday life of the colonists (home, family meal, men's club, swimming pool), viewers see a life of privilege, while the narration's focus is elsewhere. The Javanese serve meals at a colonist's home and drinks at the club, and the pool has only white swimmers.

---

[28] Snyder, "Problem of Power," 72.
[29] Raymond Fielding, *The March of Time, 1935-1951* (New York: Oxford University Press, 1978); *The March of Time as Documentary and Propaganda*: http://xroads.virginia.edu/~ma04/wood/mot/html/home_flash.htm.

Fig. 14.13. Model integrated Javanese village.
Film: *Netherlands East Indies*

Conclusion

In 1942 the Netherlands for the first time began to wage an intensive and very deliberate public diplomacy campaign in another country by showing these films and publicizing all the other kinds of information.[30] This campaign lasted until 1974. David Snyder puts the activist work of the NIB into a larger perspective in international relations and argues that the failure of the NIB to achieve some of its foreign policy objectives, such as bringing the United States into the war and keeping the East Indies, was due to a mismatch between its informational campaigns (soft power) and Dutch military and economic might (hard power).[31]

Even if the information crusade that included the films had been quite successful in shaping American public opinion in its direction, changes in foreign policy would not have followed suit. Some Dutch diplomats understood that relying on the NIB to change American policy would not be effective. At the *raison d'être* level, the enterprise of the NIB could by definition not succeed. At the level of increasing knowledge, appreciation, and understanding of the Netherlands and its point of view—some of them exaggerated, rose-colored, one-sided, and misleading—the NIB and its films had a real, largely compliant, impact on Americans' perceptions of the country. The many culture-directed films also circulated by the NIB during the 1940s need to be added to this assessment.

---

[30] In Canada and in South American countries, the work of the NIB was far more low key.
[31] Snyder, "Problem of Power," 59-61.

PART IV

Vietnam War

CHAPTER 15

Dutch American Attitudes and the Vietnam War

David Zwart

Like no other event in the twentieth century, the Vietnam War shook Americans' belief in their country. Coming off the triumph of the Second World War and consensus of the Cold War, the experience of fighting a war in a distant country created divisions within the United States that fell along new lines. Many Americans questioned the purpose, execution, and effects of the war effort in Southeast Asia. Along with the general turmoil of the era resulting from the civil rights movement, political scandals, and the counter-cultural movement, the Vietnam War contributed to a major cultural shift in the United States that altered how many Americans thought about the nation and its government.

The divisiveness of the war impacted Dutch Americans in much the same way. Dutch Americans negotiated the same shifting culture but from within their own cultural understanding. Dutch Americans saw themselves as loyal Americans supporting traditional cultural values. In stories of the migration experience and success in America, Dutch Americans highlighted the freedom that allowed them to flourish and rarely questioned why other groups might not have had the same kind of success. As patriotic Americans, they fully participated in American society (and the war) even from within their separate institutions.

The Vietnam War, however, served as one of the main catalysts for voices who questioned American traditional values and customs. Fighting a questionable war rearranged allegiances and caused new fissures among Americans of Dutch ancestry that challenged what it meant to be American. These conflicts reflected both the internal discourse of the community of Dutch Americans as well as a particular way of confronting this tumultuous time.

Scholars have examined the impact of the war on many areas of culture and society.[1] Particularly, scholars of race and class have noted the importance of the Vietnam War for changing cultural attitudes among racial minorities. War experiences of African Americans have led this research. James Westheider, for instance, showed how African American soldiers fought on two fronts, the war front and the civil rights front.[2] Civil rights leaders linked their crusade with the antiwar movement, not only because African Americans suffered a disproportionate number of casualties but also because of a deeper sense of a broken American culture at home that the military projected abroad.[3] Lorena Oropez shows how the war experience disrupted Chicano notions about the goal of assimilation for Mexican Americans.[4]

Few scholars, however, have examined the war's impact on white ethnic groups, which also experienced major changes in these years. For instance, Matthew Frye Jacobson emphasizes a revival of white ethnicity during the 1960s.[5] David Colburn and George Pozzetta perceptively connected the civil rights movement to the rise of white ethnic identity, but they did not connect these two important movements to the Vietnam War.[6] Even more comprehensive studies of white ethnic groups, such as John Bukowczyk's *A History of the Polish Americans,* did

---

[1] For just one example, see Keith Beattie, *The Scar that Binds: American Culture and the Vietnam War* (New York: New York University Press, 1998).

[2] James E. Westheider, *Fighting on Two Fronts: African Americans and the Vietnam War* (New York: New York University Press, 1997).

[3] Herbert Shapiro, "The Vietnam War and the American Civil Rights Movement," *Journal of Ethnic Studies* 16 (Winter 1989): 117-41.

[4] Lorena Oropeza, ¡Raza Si! ¡Guerra No! Chicano Protest and Patriotism during the Viet Nam War Era (Berkeley: University of California Press, 2005).

[5] Matthew Frye Jacobson, *Roots Too: White Ethnic Revival in Post-Civil Rights America* (Cambridge, MA: Harvard University Press, 2006).

[6] David R. Colburn and George E. Pozzetta, "Race, Ethnicity, and the Evolution of Political Legitimacy," in *The Sixties: From Memory to History*, ed., David Farber (Chapel Hill, NC: University of North Carolina Press, 1994), 119-48.

not consider the Vietnam War experience to be a central turning point in the ethnic identity movement of the 1970s.[7]

Scholars generally lump white ethnics together as the working class. For instance, Christian Appy notes the unequal burden the war placed on the working class, but he views that class only in binary white and black categories. He overlooks the multiple ways groups within the working class dealt with the war experience.[8]

At the same time, scholars of American religious history have been slow to recognize the impact of the Vietnam War. As Harry Stout argues, religious historians have not anchored their narratives around wars even though, by his count, the United States has participated in over three hundred conflicts since the Revolution. He places much of the cause of this almost constant state of war at the feet of American civil religion and its belief in American exceptionalism. America, in civil-religion language, was the "world savior" through its military endeavors. As Stout says, "the American consensus consists in America's faith in the institution of war as a divine instrument and sacred mandate to be exercised around the world."[9] Stout calls scholars of religion to examine more closely the relationship between American civil religion and specific religious sub-cultures.

The Dutch American experience during the Vietnam War shows how the war affected a particular white ethnic group with a particular religious outlook and also how that group came to terms with the changes brought about by the war. At that time being Dutch American meant being able to trace one's ancestry to the Netherlands, but more importantly, it also meant being part of the institutions that made up the intricate matrix of the community.[10]

The institutions of Dutch America included churches, schools and colleges, and enclaves and neighborhoods. Denominations like the Christian Reformed Church (CRC), Reformed Church in America (RCA), and Protestant Reformed Church all traced their beginnings to the Netherlands and told their histories with a strong emphasis on their Dutch roots. Individual congregations in anniversary celebrations told

---

[7] John J. Bukowczyk, *A History of the Polish Americans* (New Brunswick, NJ: Transaction Publishers, 2008), 118.

[8] Christian G. Appy, *Working-Class War: American Combat Soldiers and Vietnam* (Chapel Hill: University of North Carolina Press, 1993).

[9] Harry S. Stout, "Religion, War, and the Meaning of America," *Religion and American Culture: A Journal of Interpretation* 19 (Summer 2009): 284.

[10] For a theoretical basis for the interplay of ancestry and staying part of the institutions, see Werner Sollors, *Beyond Ethnicity: Consent and Descent in American Culture* (New York: Oxford University Press, 1986).

their histories with strong emphasis on migration from the Netherlands and subsequent success in North America. Private Christian schools as part of the National Union of Christian Schools and colleges like Hope, Calvin, Northwestern, and Dordt recounted their Dutch roots. Finally, living in enclaves and neighborhoods such as Holland or Pella brought people together to celebrate their ethnicity in community events such as Tulip Time festivals and anniversaries.

More important, being Dutch American meant participating in the network of institutions that constructed a collective memory based in the migration experience. Membership in congregations and denominations, attending and supporting private schools and denominational colleges, and living in Dutch communities, marked one as Dutch American to outsiders. While separate institutions defined the heart of the ethnic identity, members of the group did not want to be seen as "too different," and they included important aspects of being American in their collective memory. The inevitable disagreements over the "stance" toward America took place within a common discourse community.

An ethno-religious identity does not mean that everyone held the same beliefs but that they all found themselves within the same ethno-religious group. They had each other for conversation and argument partners, and they knew the definitions they were using.[11] This included defending separate institutions, making the Dutch tulip festivals "American," and emphasizing their loyalty to America. Evidence from Tulip Time festivals, church and school anniversary commemorations, and other commemorative events point to how the definition of Dutch American identity included a strong American aspect even as it continued to change in the course of the twentieth century.

Living within the matrix of Dutch America also shaped peoples' actions. Dutch Americans held certain beliefs and acted in certain ways because of their shared identity built through participating in these institutions. Dutch Americans reacted to the Vietnam War in a way that fit their cultural communal outlook and social patterns. Being faithful Americans when the war started meant support for the government in its anti-communism crusade in Southeast Asia. Dutch Americans had benefitted from the status quo, and to question the government outright or the American way went against their story of success in the United States. The institutional histories continually noted the

---

[11] For these differences, see James D. Bratt, *Dutch Calvinism in Modern America: A History of a Conservative Subculture* (Grand Rapids: Eerdmans, 1984).

Fig. 15.1. One of many soldiers in Vietnam depicted in church publications (*Banner*, 24 Nov. 1967)

freedom found in the United States and how the Dutch migrants had taken advantage of these opportunities. To question the government or America seemed an anathema.

As the war progressed, however, and the community felt its effects more and more as its sons went into combat, questions cropped up about the war's purpose and morality. Relying on religious convictions, some members began questioning the America they had so eagerly praised. At the same time, keeping the institutions strong through united efforts continued. It also meant keeping members of the community loyal and moral while serving as soldiers or objectors that reflected a religious outlook and community ethos.

By the end of the war, clear changes had occurred in the identity of Dutch America. The 1960s was one of those defining times in American history. Beside the Vietnam War, the Civil Rights and counter-cultural movements forced many Dutch Americas to re-examine their close relationship with America. They were no longer as unapologetically or unquestioningly American. Much of the rhetoric of freedom and opportunity fell to the background in the stories told about the community in commemorations. While the war was only one catalyst for change, it clearly had a major impact on how Dutch Americans thought about America and their place in it.

Questioning America was not part of the Dutch American story after the Second World War. They had thrived in America, where they found freedom and democracy protected by the government. Even if some Dutch Americans did not fully "Americanize," they still loved America. So questioning the American government went against a long tradition of not only faith in the government as a protector of freedom but also not questioning authority as outlined in Romans 13. Since the beginning of at least the Cold War, the anti-communism of the community brought them in line with government efforts to fight communism wherever it was found. For instance, Jack Stulp warned that the "threat was becoming greater," so he urged his readers to "defend the republican forms of government." Louis Benes feared communism because it had "eliminated all traces of Christianity . . . abolished churches, destroyed all Bibles," so Christians needed to "battle . . . against principalities."[12] Concern about the church under communism consistently made the headlines.[13] Articles and letters to the editors in periodicals highlighted the dangers of communism, paralleling the broader culture but with a strong "religious" bent. It wasn't just communism versus capitalism but communism versus Christianity. The dangers were clear and imminent and required constant vigilance.[14]

Writers in denominational periodicals found a receptive audience for Cold War rhetoric filled with Christian overtones. The actual case of Vietnam, however, proved a bit more complicated. The first mention in the *Banner* of the issues in Vietnam occurred in December 1961 when Richard Frens acknowledged the complexity of the situation but sided with whatever decision the leaders would make. As American commitments grew in June 1964, Frens agreed with the government message that dominoes would fall if South Vietnam became communist, but he wondered aloud what America's interest really was when the South Vietnamese did not seem interested in fighting. Ominous shadows began to grow after the Gulf of Tonkin resolution

---

[12] Jack Stulp, "Time for All-out War on Communism!," *Banner* (24 Feb. 1961), 18; Louis Benes, "What If Communism Wins?," *Church Herald* (20 Oct. 1961), 6; and Paul Schrotenboer "Understanding Communism," *Banner* (6 July 1962), 11. These are just a small sampling of the kind of coverage and rhetoric found in the periodicals of the time.

[13] See "Church Life under Communism," *Banner* (17 Aug. 1962), 6. Other articles in the 1960s showed the oppression churches faced in communist countries.

[14] *Banner* articles include: John B. Hulst, "The Threat of Communism" (4 Aug. 1961), 15-16; John Byker, "Now Behind the Iron Curtain—Over One Billion Person" (1 Sept. 1961), 6-7; Frank Einfel, "'Freedom's Holy Light'—Will it Survive?" (26 Jan. 1962), 4-5; Harold Sonnema "Challenging Our Youth" (2 Feb. 1962), 4-5; John Vander Ploeg, "Nations Disappear Behind the Iron Curtain" (8 Feb. 1963), 8-9; and Joost Sluis, "A Christian's Answer to Communism" (31 Jan. 1964), 4-5. *Church Herald* articles included: Louis H. Benes, "Communism in the Churches?" (1 Apr. 1960), 6; John W. Beardslee III, "Communism in Today's World and Tomorrow's" (19 Apr. 1963), 10; and Lester De Koster, "Marxism: Test of Faith and Conduct" (18 Sept. 1964), 16-17.

Fig. 15.2. Photo from *Church Herald* article questioning Vietnam War effort (4 March 1966)

in August 1964, yet Frens' support for the government never wavered. Other voices in both the *Banner* and the *Church Herald* raised the same banner of support.[15]

Lester De Koster voiced his support for the war in an editorial in the *Reformed Journal* in 1965, stating that it was a tricky situation, and the "President merits our wholehearted support in this delicate and dynamic situation," similarly based on the domino theory.[16] Editor John Vander Ploeg of the *Banner* defended the war as "morally defensible" in editorials.[17] The RCA General Synod sent a letter to President Lyndon Johnson in 1965 urging negotiations but also encouraging him to "continue your firm policy of resistance to Communist aggression."[18] The *Church Herald* editor, Louis Benes, came to the same conclusion, while at the same time publishing articles against the Vietnam policy.[19]

As the war progressed, and American presence in Vietnam grew to over a half-million troops by 1969, more voices expressed serious

[15] Richard J. Frens, "Shall We Write Off South Vietnam?," *Banner* (1 Dec. 1961), 10; "What Gives in South Vietnam?," ibid. (19 June 1964), 6; "Dark Shadows in South Vietnam," ibid. (30 Apr. 1965), 7; John Westra "Turmoil in Asia: Vietnam," ibid. (7 Jan. 1966), 6; Ben Hartley, "First Impressions from Vietnam," *Church Herald* (24 Sept. 1965), 4-6.
[16] Lester De Koster, "As We See It: Viet Nam," *Reformed Journal* (Oct. 1965), 3.
[17] John Vander Ploeg, "U.S. Action in Vietnam—Is It Right?," *Banner* (18 Mar. 1966), 8-9, received much praise and criticism in letters to the editor for the next few months.
[18] Reformed Church in America, *General Synod Acts and Proceedings* (1965), 220-25.
[19] Louis H. Benes, "Is Vietnam 'A Righteous Cause'?," *Church Herald* (24 Sept. 1965), 8-9; Howard Schomer, "Against Our Policy in Vietnam," ibid. (4 Mar. 1966), 12-13.

reservations about the actions taken by the government of the United States. Along with Americans in general, Dutch Americans also questioned the war's morality. Was it a worthy cause, a "just war?" Was it worth spilling blood over? The RCA General Synod's Christian Action Commission took a strong stand in 1967, when it called for the United States to stop the war.[20] While not representing a consensus, it showed how divisive the war was becoming. The same commission adopted a resolution in October 1969 calling for United States withdrawal because its war policies were not working.[21]

Other voices also pointed out ethical issues about the war. Lewis Smedes in the *Reformed Journal* regularly pointed out the difficulty of the issues surrounding the war. Smedes noted that "the Calvinist insists that there is a duty that transcends duty to country," as he defended "Vietniks."[22] The *Reformed Journal* ran a large section of diverse opinions of Calvin College faculty in the summer of 1967.[23] Some letters to the editor of the *Banner* published in "Voices" in late 1967 claimed that support for the troops meant bringing them home. Other letters questioned the morality of the war. But there were even louder voices in other publications like the *Reformed Journal* and the *Church Herald*, which had a more open editorial approach. By the late 1960s, positions in American society and in Dutch America were hardening; the polarization of the war itself put Dutch Americans in a hard place. Support for the government versus their desire not to participate in an "immoral" war pulled in opposite directions.

The theoretical discussions about the morality of the war and support for the government became concrete as the draft brought more and more young people into the armed forces.[24] Much of the war coverage also moved to the concrete during the late 1960s. The war required sacrifices by young people, and those families, nudged by advice in the periodicals, moved people to action. Like previous wars, sending young people off to war made those at home keenly aware of the dangers of the military that were not all tied to the combat itself. Efforts to keep in touch with service members focused on keeping them moral during their time in the service but also loyal to their institutional home. Supporters of the troops marshaled the institutional resources

---

[20] "A Declaration of Conscience," ibid. (22 Sept. 1967), 19.
[21] "Statement on Vietnam," ibid. (23 Jan. 1970), 11.
[22] Lewis Smedes, "The Vietniks," *Reformed Journal* (Dec. 1965), 4-5. See also "The War Nobody Wants," ibid. (Feb. 1967), 4.
[23] "Comments on Vietnam" (Reformed Journal) (July-Aug. 1967), 6-10.
[24] Appy, *Working Class War*, 11-43.

15.3   Advertisement in the *Banner*

There are some 2,500 Christian Reformed boys serving in the Armed Forces, according to the latest report. 1,800 of these boys are now receiving The Banner weekly, BUT there are yet some 700 who are not. Is your son, or a serviceman from your church, one of these 700 who are not receiving The Banner? From letters, it is evident that the church paper is appreciated more than ever when these young people are in the service far from home. Check with your consistory and ask them to order a subscription for him now, at the reduced rate of 30 cents per month. Billing will be made when the serviceman is discharged. Consistories, send names and addresses to:

THE BANNER / 2850 KALAMAZOO AVENUE. S.E / GRAND RAPIDS, MICHIGAN 49508

to support the service members. John Vander Ploeg, in the *Banner*, encouraged his readers to be "true-blue" to the servicemen and women in 1966 and to show the "solid and sincere support for all those who serve our country in these difficult times."[25] Advertisements called for local congregations to support troops by sending the *Banner* to service members.[26]

In 1967, 1968, and 1969, the *Banner* published the names of CRC members stationed in Vietnam. Home Missions of the CRC started an "Armed Forces Fund" to support servicemen homes, send publications, and support chaplains.[27] James Lont, the director of the Young

---

[25] John Vander Ploeg, "Let's be True-Blue to Those in Vietnam," *Banner* (4 Feb. 1966), 8-9.
[26] "700 Without," *Banner* (24 Mar. 1967), 35; "519 Without," *Banner* (12 Apr. 1968), 35.
[27] Herb Kredit, "Armed Forces Ministry in Action," *Banner* (27 Dec. 1968), 16-17; Melvin D. Hugen, "Hospitality House in Hawaii," ibid. (24, May 1968), 16; Herbert Kredit, "San Diego Servicemen's Center Report," ibid. (31 May 1968), 12. Servicemen homes opened during the Second World War at major military bases throughout the United States. Articles continued to remind readers to support these efforts. Dick L. Van Halsema, "Benefits of a Ministry to Servicemen," *Banner* (10 May 1968), 6; Marvin C. Baarman, "Armed Forces Ministry," ibid. (17 May 1968), 18-19; Martin Hamstra, "Is It Worth One Dollar," ibid. (7 June 1968), 6; Edwin D. Roels, "Would You Send Your Eighteen Year Old Son Three Thousand Miles Away From Home Alone? Go with Him Through the Armed Forces Fund," ibid. (16 May 1969), 16-17. The same title was used by Marvin C. Baarman, ibid. (23 May, 1969), 4; and Melvin D. Hugen, ibid. (23 May 1969), 16.

Fig. 15.4. Guides distributed by the Young Calvinist Federation helped servicemen manage their time, 1963 and 1968

Calvinist Federation, called on *Banner* readers to keep in touch with service members who could lose their morality in such an institution as the military.[28] A "Servicemen's Guide" was distributed bi-monthly to CRC service members listing churches near posts (including RCA and Presbyterian churches), service pastors and homes, and chaplains.[29]

While not duplicating the kind of denominationally-wide emphasis as the CRC, the RCA did hope to send the *Church Herald* to its members in the service, and the calls grew over time. For instance, by the middle of 1967, the editor pointed out that only one-third of the RCA men in the service received the *Church Herald*, and he encouraged his readers to rectify the situation.[30]

The work to keep in touch with service members and keep them moral also meant sending chaplains to serve in the services. Regular reports from chaplains filled both the *Banner* and the *Church Herald*.[31] These reports encouraged the readers that service members received

---

[28] James C. Long, "'In Another World'—So We Stick With Them," *Banner* (15 Mar. 1968), 15-16; Harvey A. Ouwinga, "Consistories—Support Your Servicemen!," ibid. (12 Apr. 1968), 23.

[29] Servicemen's Guides, box 1111, collection D 5.12.3, Youth Unlimited, Heritage Hall, Calvin College, Grand Rapids, MI. The name of the guides changed to "Welcome Serviceman" in the late 1960s.

[30] Louis H. Benes, "For Students and Servicemen," *Church Herald* (21 Jan. 1966), 13; Louis H. Benes, "Supporting Our Servicemen," ibid. (5 May 1967), 7.

[31] For instance, Lawrence P. Fitzgerald, "What More Can the Churches Do?" ibid. (20 Jan. 1967), 14-15, 30.

Fig. 15.5. A chaplain in Vietnam, *Church Herald*, 23 February 1968

regular Christian contact and that the denominations did their part to serve as a light in the services through their chaplains. The dangers, however, still existed. A writer in the *Church Herald* cautioned against the dangers of military service to religious faith.[32]

The dangers of "losing" soldiers to evil were all too real as one family in the *Banner* noted how they had "lost" their son to temptation.[33] Articles in the *Young Calvinist* and similar publications warned against drugs more directly.[34]

Servicemen appreciated the publications. They wrote letters to the *Young Calvinist* and other publications, thanking the editors for providing encouragement against the dangers of military life. A publication called *Alert* (from the Young Calvinist Federation) was an introduction to military life for Christian servicemen that walked inductees through the kinds of experiences they would have and how to stay faithful throughout.[35] Using the channels developed prior to

---

[32] Thomas W. Klewin, "The Christian and Military Service," ibid. (29 Apr. 1966), 4-5.
[33] "We Lost Our Son in Vietnam," *Banner* (30 Aug., 1968), 14-15; Herbert L. Bergsma, "Some Straight Talk About (and From) Servicemen," ibid. (2 Feb. 1968), 16; Helen Winters Van Dyke, "Dear Mom," ibid. (12 Mar. 1971), 2.
[34] "A Tragic Letter from Vietnam," *Young Calvinist*, Apr. 1970, 2-3. Galen Meyer, "About the Wolves," *Insight* (Jan. 1971), 22; William K. Harrison, "A Christian in the Armed Forces," *Church Herald* (5 May 1967), 8, 20.
[35] Galen Meyer, *Alert*, Young Calvinists (box 747, folder 12, records group 5.12.3, Youth Unlimited, Regional Groups, Heritage Hall, Calvin College, MI).

Fig. 15.6. "Project Thank-You Vietnam" highlighted the support for soldiers, Banner, 12 Apr. 1968

the war, the service members kept in touch with their Dutch American institutions.

Efforts to support the troops also came from the pews. Members of Dutch American churches helped start and lead Project Thank You, which was a major effort to support the soldiers by telling them they were appreciated. Started by the Christian Reformed Laymen's League, it sent gift packets to one hundred thousand front-line troops in 1967, with various items to refresh both body and soul, for example the Gospel of Mark"[36]

The organizers hoped the project would show the troops they were loved, while "putting aside the question of *why* our servicemen are there." By the beginning of 1969, the group claimed to have sent 480,000 packets.[37] The need to "stick" with the troops and support them even in the midst of some questions about the morality of the overall war dominated the discourse in the periodicals. So even as voices rose in opposition to the war itself, support continued for the troops, who were expected to stay moral even if the war itself might be immoral.

The experience of the soldiers themselves often made the distinction between the perceived lack of morality of "the war" and

---

[36] Robert J. Plekker, "Project Thank-You," *Banner* (24 Nov. 1967), 22; Robert Pekker, "Project Thank-You Vietnam," ibid. (26 Apr. 1968), 6-7. The project raised hundreds of thousands of dollars and received a Freedom Foundation Award in 1970. Martin Hamstra, "Project Thank-You Number 1 in Nation," *Banner* (6 Mar. 1970), 16-17.

[37] "Say Thanks to Our Men in Vietnam," advertisement, *Banner* (24 Jan. 1969), 27.

their personal morality hard. In oral histories conducted in the last five years in West Michigan, soldiers reported seeing multiple kinds of immorality, both in combat and on the bases. Most soldiers, however, reflected on the mundane aspects of going to war and "doing their job."[38] For instance, Larry Groothuis, from the suburbs of Grand Rapids, graduated from Hudsonville Unity Christian and was drafted at the age of twenty-three in 1966. In his training, he benefitted from the Christian Reformed Church's extensive efforts to keep him connected when he landed in Phoenix. While serving in Vietnam, he stated that being older helped him avoid the drug culture he saw in there. At the same time, he worked hard to do his job well as a radio operator but reflected very little on the morality of the war itself.[39]

The routine of being a soldier, according to chaplains, often did not fit the way the press portrayed the soldiers in Vietnam. Soldiers did their best to survive and get home.[40] Some, however, did note the difficulty of serving as a soldier in a war of dubious morality. Herbert Bergsma wrote for the *Church Herald* in 1968 about the "confusion" servicemen faced while fighting.[41] This separation of the soldier and the reasons for fighting continued to the end of 1971, when an advertisement on the back page of the *Banner* for the Young Calvinist Servicemen's Ministry noted that soldiers had to subordinate their own feelings to those of the military, but the church would not forget them.[42]

The impact of the Vietnam War experience on Dutch Americans particularly affected the community when young men sought to avoid military service. To openly defy authority and to not be willing to fight a war against communism struck at the heart of being Dutch American.[43] As the number of Gold Stars grew, more young men directly

---

[38] Chris Appy, *Working Class War*, 250-97.
[39] Larry Groothuis, interview, 17 June 2011, Grand Valley State University Veterans History Project http://cdm16015.contentdm.oclc.org/cdm/ref/collection/p4103coll2/id/1216.
[40] Marvin Konynenbelt, "What He Learned in Vietnam," *Banner* (21 Mar. 1969), 13; Jan Friend, "Vietnam Ministry," ibid. (4 July 1969), 12-13; James. W. Kelly, "Our Man in Vietnam" ibid. (part 1, 13 Feb. 1970) (part 2, 20 Feb. 1970), 12-13 (part 3, 27 Feb. 1970), 12-13. These chaplains tried to explain the mundane aspects of life in Vietnam and how they served as chaplains and express how well the soldiers carried out their tasks. Jerry Zandstra, "While Chaplains Weep," *Banner* (5 May 1972), 8; Jan Friend, "GI's Drugs, Girls, and the Chaplains," ibid. (26 May 1972), 6-7.
[41] Herbert L. Bergsma, "Vietnam: Confusion, Isolation, Opportunity," *Church Herald* (24 May 1968), 12-13.
[42] Back cover, *Banner* (12 Nov. 1971); see also ibid. (2 June 1972).
[43] Clarence Boomsma, "Conscientious Objectors and the Draft," *Banner* (15 Nov. 1965), 4-5.

Fig. 15.7. In defense of military action, *Young Calvinist*, July-Aug. 1970

challenged the legitimacy of the draft and the war. Of the nearly eleven million men under arms between 1964 and 1975, only 2.5 million were drafted. Avoiding the draft by leaving the country or claiming to be a conscientious objector was an option only for those who knew about these options.[44]

The denominational periodicals ran many articles about conscientious objectors. The contentiousness of this issue drips from every article. Those who condemned conscientious objectors noted how important it was to submit to governing authorities. Will Kirkendall II, writing in the *Young Calvinist* in the summer of 1970, cites Romans 13

[44] Appy, *Working Class War*, 11-43.

to support his position that an individual could not pick and choose when they would or would not obey the government. Raymond Van Heukelom noted in the *Church Herald* that even if a citizen did not agree, the government "must have the right to make decisions, even when they may not be acceptable to a majority of the citizens."[45] But other articles and letters pointed out the contradiction of the morality of the war and the request of young men to serve. Raymond Pontier defended conscientious objectors in the *Church Herald*: "In a world where the church has so often and so easily blessed those who make war, they are asking for a blessing on those who refuse to make war . . . [and] legality does not always equal morality."[46]

Demonstrating the growing controversy over the morality of the war and serving as soldiers in the war, denominational synods weighed in on this issue as churches and pastors requested help in dealing with young men who refused to join. The RCA took on the issue already in 1965, when its Christian Action Commission began calling for the end of the war. The conscientious objectors issue specifically came to dominate the same committee's report to the synod in 1967. The debate on the proposals of the committee in 1968 showed that not all delegates approved of the anti-war and pro-conscientious objector direction the committee had taken. In 1969, when the general synod was asked to accept draft cards from young men who refused to serve, an ad hoc committee recommended doing so, but the synod voted "no" by a vote of 123 to 109, and the motion to accept the draft cards lost. A similar motion to accept draft cards also lost in 1970, this time by a vote of 190 against and 50 for. It lost again in 1971 but continued to simmer through at least 1975.[47]

The CRC synod needed to deal with draft cards as well in 1969, when four men from the Chicago area requested selective conscientious objector status. The synod's response was to affirm the 1939 statement to obey the government, but passive resistance was permissible when the war was deemed "unjust," and a person was opposed to all wars.[48] The periodicals of the denomination provided many articles and editorials on both sides of the issue. The discord showed both the changing nature of how some Dutch Americans thought about allegiance to the United States, but also how a disagreement played out in the particular

---

[45] Raymond Van Heukelom, "What About Amnesty," *Church Herald* (19 Jan. 1973), 4-5.
[46] Raymond J. Pontier, "Conscience and the Church," ibid. (17 Apr. 1970), 11-12.
[47] Reformed Church in America, *General Synod Acts and Proceedings*, 1967, 207-8; *Acts and Proceedings*, 1969, 249-52; *Acts and Proceedings*, 1970, 213-18.
[48] Christian Reformed Church, *Acts of Synod 1969*, 96-99.

context of the ethno-religious group. As Lynn Japinga pointed out, the RCA thought of itself as a family, even with differences.[49]

The fallout of an unpopular war by the early 1970s and the "fall" of South Vietnam in 1975 meant dealing with draft dodgers and refugees. Although law and order was the default position of most Dutch Americans, amnesty for draft dodgers was problematic. At the end of the war, few defended the actions of the United States, and most were sympathetic to those who avoided the draft, even though they had broken the law.[50]

At the same time, Christian charity drove many to care deeply for the Vietnamese refugee crisis caused by the end of the war. Caring for refugees was one way to show Christian charity and deal with the fallout of the war in a positive way; congregations sponsored many families and tried to assist others.[51] In fact, the first CRC congregation to sponsor refugees was a Cuban congregation.[52] Reports on the refugees in the periodicals continued throughout the late 1970s and early 1980s. The *Church Herald* ran a series of six articles on the topic of "boat people" in 1979 to raise awareness of the crisis.[53]

The Vietnam War experience challenged Dutch Americans to deal with an ever-changing world. The Vietnam War reached into the homes of all Dutch Americans either through knowing someone serving or through the media. While there were always disagreements about what it meant to be Dutch American, there was the preeminence of a common heritage. Church institutions provided the primary avenue by which Dutch Americans encountered the war. Whether it was reading about the pros and cons of the war in church periodicals, hearing sermons from the pulpit, or having late-night conversations in the dorms, Dutch

---

[49] Lynn Japinga, *Loyalty and Loss: The Reformed Church in America, 1945-1994* (Grand Rapids: Eerdmans, 2013), xvi.

[50] Lester De Koster, "Amnesty . . . Maybe," *Banner* (11 Feb. 1972), 8-9; Herbert L. Bergsma, "I Respect the Conscientious Objector's Right to Hold His Opinion. To Regard it as Tenable is, in My Opinion, to Court Anarchy and Chaos," ibid. (2 June 1972), 10-11. Bergsma was a chaplain in the US Navy. Kenneth Konyndyk Jr., "Synod and War," ibid., 9-10.

[51] "CRC Pastor Helps Transport Vietnamese Babies to America," *Banner* (16 May 1975), 22; CRWRC Staff, "These Found a Home, But What About the Others," ibid. (17 Oct. 1975), 16-17.

[52] "Spanish CRC First to Sponsor Vietnamese Family," *Banner* (29 Aug. 1975), 25.

[53] Howard Schipper, "Escaping From Vietnam," *Church Herald* (7 Sept. 1979), 6-7; "Wretched Refuse on Malaysia's Shores" (21 Sept., 1979), 14-15; "Thailand's Untold Story" (5 Oct. 1979), 10-12; "A Floating Prison in the Philippines" (19 Oct. 1979), 12-13; "Huddled Masses in Hong Kong" (2 Nov. 1979), 16-17; "The Final Chapter: Sponsoring Boat People" (16 Nov. 1979), 12-13.

Americans engaged the war through their community. This means that the challenges brought by the war, such as serving in the military or the resulting refugee crisis, were dealt with through institutional channels. Service members received information and publications from the denomination, which worked to keep them loyal and moral during their time in the service.

The war, however, also forced many Dutch Americans to rethink their loyalties. Being loyal to America and its ideals was one of the ways Dutch Americans identified themselves. When the ideal of freedom confronted communism, it was clear where Dutch Americans would fight. As the war continued, and more and more voices rose in opposition to the conflict, it became less clear what America really stood for. So although support for America continued, there were differing visions of what "America" really was.

Being Dutch American during the Vietnam War required rethinking the American part of the Dutch American identity. And there is evidence in a number of places that that identity was changing. For instance, in Tulip Time festivals, there began a growing "authentic" movement that would emphasize the Dutchness of the festival. While clearly the Vietnam War is not the only cause of this, it is an interesting juxtaposition. A "roots" movement, and the "you ain't much if you ain't Dutch" attitude surfaced. Dutch American identity continued to be an important starting point for many to engage in America, but the particular ingredients and emphases continued to change. The Vietnam War rearranged those ingredients.

Some commentators have labeled the 1970s as the age of limits. Following the Vietnam War experience, the civil rights movement, and the counter-culture of the 1960s, the 1970s no longer held the kind of promise for the United States as was held previously. For Dutch Americans, the experience of the 1960s, but particularly the moral complexity of the Vietnam War and American involvement, caused many to question what it meant to be American with a Dutch adjective. While a roots movement and a renewed interest in ethnic identity impacted the United States and Dutch Americans, it now increasingly emphasized being Dutch rather than being American. The Vietnam War experience was a major catalyst for increasing the Dutchness of Tulip Time Festivals, genealogy and migration history, and ethnic organizations.

CHAPTER 16

The Moral Fog of War: A Christian Vietnam Veteran's Perspective

Sylvan Gerritsma

My father was a proud World War II veteran from Sioux Center, Iowa (see chapter 13). So I was born and grew up there and eventually went to Dordt College. That is not just a biographical tidbit. It is the background for the deep-seated Reformed worldview I imbibed there—a worldview developed particularly by Dutch thinkers with the heritage of Abraham Kuyper.[1] You may recognize that worldview in this essay.

My college years closely coincided with the rise and peak of national anti-establishment protest focused most sharply on the Vietnam war, although Dordt College and Sioux Center certainly were not hotbeds of counter-cultural protest. My father's generation was deeply committed to American exceptionalism (though we never heard that term) and was gravely concerned about the threat to the world of global communism, which the world depended largely on America to restrain. Those commitments pervaded the Sioux Center of my youth. But the draft indiscriminately swept up kids from Berkeley as well as from Sioux Center.

---

[1] See, for example, Albert Wolters, *Creation Regained: Biblical Basics for a Reformational Worldview* (Grand Rapids: Eerdmans, 1985).

After graduation I, too, would have been drafted, but I volunteered in order to be assured of the opportunity to become an officer. So after basic training and advanced infantry training, I completed officer candidate school in engineering, but I was commissioned as a 2nd lieutenent in military intelligence. I spent the next year in the intelligence center of the army researching POWs, interrogation techniques, brainwashing, and other related issues. I was then deployed to Vietnam in the 101st Airborne Division for a year. About half of my time there was spent as an administration officer, and for the other half, I was in charge of an electronic surveillance unit. We implanted, monitored, and maintained seismic and magnetic sensors to track enemy movement. When I was there in 1970-71, US military activity was still intense but past its peak, and the number of troops was being reduced.

For my father's generation, the need for Christian discernment about US responsibility in the world and the justification for war was not so compelling. Especially after Pearl Harbor, it did not require sophisticated insight to conclude that we Americans were on the side of the angels and that we knew who the demons were. During the next twenty years of cold war, it was still easy to cast ourselves as Christians fighting for a righteous cause against the world-wide threat of atheistic communism. But as post-war US military interventions proliferated—Korea, Egypt, Lebanon, Cuba, Thailand, Laos, Cambodia, Iran, Iraq, Grenada, Honduras, Nicaragua, the Persian Gulf, Panama, Columbia, Kuwait, Afghanistan, Bosnia, Haiti, Serbia, Pakistan, and more—the conviction of our righteous purity faltered. Central to that faltering was Vietnam. And the big question of the *purity of our cause* was upstaged by questions about the *morality of our methods*. Let me illustrate with a story.

During my first week in Vietnam, we had a training class on rules of engagement, reviewing the Geneva Conventions and combat rules. You fight soldiers; don't harm women, children, civilians, and friendlies. We all knew that from previous training. This review class was taught by an experienced sergeant who did the proper and correct job expected of him.

Then, time for questions.

Up stands a boy who looks hardly old enough to have finished high school. He was in Vietnam before, he says, serving on a long-range reconnaissance patrol team. That's a few tough, highly trained guys sent into enemy territory, lightly armed, to spy. Being lightly armed, they can't afford to be discovered. In enemy territory that means likely death. So, in a baffled, naive, almost hurt boyish voice, he asks, "Do you really mean that *now* if we are discovered in the jungle by a woman and a couple of kids, we can't kill them anymore?"

That is not merely an interesting story. The meanings and implications of it just don't quit. You could start by asking how you would feel if the woman and children killed were your mother and sisters. Or if they were not killed, how would you feel if one of the consequently dead patrol members was your brother or father. On a bigger than personal level, we were in Vietnam to "win the hearts and minds of the people." That's what counter-insurgency is mainly about. As an aside, think about what an evangelistic concept that is: "winning hearts and minds." Anyway, if you were in the community of the dead mother and children, would their deaths, to conceal the presence of a few alien soldiers, win your heart and mind?

But the story doesn't end there. The instructor has to answer the question. He is an experienced, well-trained soldier. Likely he has heard a question like that before; perhaps he has experienced it. As robotically as he would swing his rifle toward enemy fire, he presses the rewind button and carefully repeats what he mouthed earlier and what the questioner had heard repeatedly before: "The *rules* say." He did not even have to wink or continue with "but." The answer was clear, and it wasn't in his words. Nobody could say that he didn't teach the rules. Yet everybody knew he did not.

But that still isn't the end of the story. There were about fifty people there. I was there. Every one of us knew the rules. By the rules it looked like we might have right there a real live war criminal. Every one of us should have reported that. Was I, were we all, complicit in the cover up of possible war crimes? How could this happen? Is this simply a conspiracy of lawlessness? And this is not just a rare incident. You have all read in the news many variants of this story from My Lai to Abu Ghraib.

The agonizing dilemmas illustrated by that story are even further complicated by deep personal damage inflicted by previous military experience. Let me illustrate that with a story very different and at the same time containing common elements. It is a story of evil—evil deeper and more complex than we usually realize. More importantly, it also hangs on, however desperately and tenuously, to God's promise that grace overcomes evil. I relate the story leaving the moral complexity unresolved.

The scene: a hot evening forty years ago at the little sandbagged hootch where I slept in Camp Eagle about fifty miles south of the demilitarized zone between North and South Vietnam.

Fig. 16.1. Gerritsma in front of "hootsch" with motor pool in background (*author's collection*)

Knock, knock.

"Who's there?"

It is the commanding officer of my unit! This had never happened. When he wanted you, he sent a private to summon you.

"Do you know Sergeant Prince?" he asks.

Thoughts run through my mind. Sgt. Prince. Richard Prince. An appropriate name. Genuinely a prince among men. Richard, as in Richard the Lion-hearted, king of England. Richard Prince, a soft-spoken, kind, gentle, noble man. A career soldier who had already been in the army twelve years but not the stereotypical hard, macho, insensitive creature that the word sergeant brings to mind. This is his third tour in Nam. He is with us just briefly between assignments.

Then the bombshell: "He's in the bunker with a grenade threatening suicide. Can you do something?"

No longer are thoughts running sequentially through my mind. They are spasming. Auto pilot takes over, because I don't have the wherewithal to deal with this thoughtfully. Can any auto pilot be programmed for this? Auto pilot should have said, "Sir, I am just a twenty-three-year-old kid. You have been in the *army* twenty-three years. Why are you asking a kid to do a man's job?"

But that response is not programmed into my autopilot. Twenty-one years of Christian nurture and two years of Army indoctrination have programmed me to automatically take up the call of duty.

So I find myself in the bunker—Sgt. Prince, a grenade, and me. The inside of the bunker is about the size of two coffins side by side but

Fig. 16.2. Helmeted Gerritsma at "hootsch" (*author's collection*)

four feet high, sandbagged on all sides and roof, with crude benches along the walls and a few small firing ports. The entrance is a maze to prevent explosions outside from directly hitting occupants, but now also preventing quick escape or disposal of the grenade.

Other thoughts about Sgt. Prince run through my mind. Earlier he had told me that he is torn apart by the impending failure of his marriage, largely due to his absence for three of the last six years. Likely the psychological damage he suffered from combat compounded the problems. From eight thousand miles away, he is powerless to do anything about his wife's affair. He so dreaded this tour in Nam that before he left home he loosened crucial steering components of his car and drove it down a rough winding road as fast as he dared, hoping for suicide disguised as an accident.

All of these things and more had given this gentle boyish man an edge of cold, hard fury usually well concealed. He had told me of seeing a close buddy killed. A few days later the small unit he had commanded overran an enemy position. There appeared an enemy soldier, hands up, surrendering. With the thought of their almost still warm buddy in their minds, some of his men turned their guns to shoot the bastard. He stopped them. He knew the rules of war. He might have cynically articulated those rules something like this: A prisoner must be treated according to the Geneva Conventions. It's like the end of a basketball game. You shake hands. "Good game, buddy. Would you like to join us for a beer? And by the way, would you like to tell us, please, the location of the mortars from which your teammates are raining explosives on us?"

He put a furious burst of bullets through the prisoner himself.

But I digress. I am in the bunker, somehow now armed with a flashlight, obligated by duty to come out with an unexploded grenade and two live soldiers, but having no idea how that could happen. So for the next three hours Sgt. Prince and I share the crazy camaraderie of courting death. How much does he desire death? How much do I love life? Repeatedly he pulls the pin and later replaces it. If he lets it go, we have four seconds. At one point with the pin out he orders me to "turn off the damn light, sir." Throughout all this, the thought races through me, "What if he lets it go? Do I try to throw my body on it to save him? Or do I dive for the exit? Could I pick it up and throw it out of a gun port wall within four seconds? Could I even find it in the dark?"

I remember little of the conversation, perhaps because I had no strategy to deal with this. "I got the right to kill myself," he says and tells me repeatedly to get out so he can do it. The fact that I outranked him was ridiculously irrelevant in all of this. I followed *his* orders—except the order to get out.

After a few hours, he gives me the grenade. Outside the scene is surreal. There is an audience sitting on lawn chairs on the hillside as if this is live outdoor theater. The only thing missing is the popcorn.

Astonishing today, but absolutely normal then, the next day life goes on as if nothing had happened. Duty—other duty—calls. I saw Sgt. Prince only once after that, a night or two later alone, in company headquarters, handcuffed to a filing cabinet like a short-leashed dog. He looked at me plaintively. Not a word passed between us.

War. What a murky muddled moral morass! What is war anyway? To get the issues before us, I will state some of this with brutal starkness, simplification, and hyperbole. Nuance can be debated elsewhere.

First, the standard definition of war is something like this: It is an instrument of statecraft. In just war theory, that distinguishes it from private violence, even private violence on a large scale like that of drug cartels or terrorist organizations. That line gets fuzzy in cases like insurrection, terrorism, and civil war, but the pure idea is that war is between states—not between individuals or non-governmental groups. War is also subject to rules of warfare like the Geneva Conventions and just war theory.

Is that not a charmingly comforting, sterile definition of war? Fervently desired, but fanciful? One could be forgiven for likening it to professional sports. Yes, there is a bit of physical contact between players, but there are nice rules limiting that contact. Players wear pretty uniforms to distinguish the teams and to distinguish players from spectators. Rarely would spectators be involved or hurt and then only as collateral damage. There are referees, governing bodies, appeals boards, and courts to deal with violators both in the stands and on the fair level playing field.

Let's try a very different possible definition. War is a wild unrestrained melee between two or more nations (or other entities such as guerilla groups), which may require nearly the total resources (i.e., not just military) of the involved nations (meaning that civilians as part of the military-industrial complex are also mobilized), and in which almost all rules other than winning have failed or are abandoned.

But even that is a rather academic sanitized definition. So let us be blunt. What is the first thing that comes to mind when you think about war? It is killing—purposeful and large scale.

We hear about killing in the news and see it portrayed so casually in the media that we are easily desensitized to it. But did you ever think about how hard it is to kill? I mean real close-up killing in which you see the fear in the man's eyes, you see the messy blood, you bludgeon, you plunge in the knife or bayonet, and you hear him beg for his life for the sake of his children. A shudder of revulsion overwhelms most of us when we even think of it.

That's because God did not create us to kill. Genesis 9 says that when we kill, we are destroying the image of God. It is as if we are trying to destroy the closest thing we see to God—burning him in effigy. That doesn't come naturally. We are not created to do that.

But the sad reality is that in this time between the Fall and Christ's return, some evil is so powerful and threatening that most of us think it has to be opposed by deadly force. So, until Christ returns, armies have to make ordinary people into killers. That's not easy to do. Consider some of the evidence of how it can be done, beginning with relatively unsophisticated methods and proceeding to subtle, but more powerful ones.

A baffling discovery was made after battles during the American Civil War 150 years ago. The guns of the dead and wounded were collected from the battlefields to be used again. Remember that these were single shot muskets. After each shot, powder and bullet had to be pushed in from the front of the barrel. Ninety percent of these guns were found loaded, but not fired. More than half had more than one load. And that is despite the fact that it takes 95 percent of the time to load and only 5 percent to fire. How could that be?

It was discovered that soldiers had just pretended to fire and then reloaded as if they had fired. Of those who did pull the trigger, few fired to hit the enemy. All of this occurred because they could not find it within themselves to kill. They actually found it easier to risk being killed than to kill. Even as late as World War II, studies showed that only from 15 to 20 percent of individual riflemen could bring themselves to fire at an exposed enemy soldier. That is alarming for an army. If 85 percent of your soldiers really do not want to kill, it's hard to win a war. It is worse than 85 percent of librarians being illiterate. So armies had to fix that problem.[2]

By the time I was in Vietnam, the figures were inverted. Over 90 percent could kill. That is an astonishing change. You could call that behavior modification, but it is really closer to psychological DNA change. The person, the self, at a very deep level is modified into a creature God never intended that creature to be. How can that be done?

At an elementary level, armies and nations do that by demonizing the enemy. In Vietnam we were fighting the demon of godless communism. Of course, nations and armies can also manufacture demons where there are none, as Hitler did with Jews, gypsies, and others. Real or imagined, evil creatures are easier to kill than people.

Similarly, armies tend to dehumanize the enemy. It is easier to kill a gook in black pajamas than a person, even an evil person.

Demonization and dehumanization could be seen as two forms of hate. Sixty years after his war, my father still talked with bitter hatred about the Japs being a devious species, and he spoke almost with relish about seeing them asphyxiated and incinerated with flame throwers in caves to which they had retreated. When I took bayonet training, we were told to imagine we were stabbing the hated imaginary man back home in bed with our wife or girlfriend. It's easier to kill what you hate. So armies find it effective to inspire hate.

But let us go a step deeper, getting back to the definitions of war we earlier examined. Is war really a game played by nice law-abiding gentlemen under clearly defined rules? It settles us comfortably and shields us from the horrors of war to tell ourselves that. We can then dismiss atrocities simply as violations of the rules, unusual exceptions, or a few bad apples in the barrel. But is it possible that beneath this public and accepted set of rules, there is a powerfully functioning alternate set of rules more deeply indoctrinated than the official ones, and that this set of rules explains a lot of what *actually* happens in the military? Then our first story is not so much a matter of fifty men complicit in a war crime as it is of fifty men working under alternative rules so deeply indoctrinated into them that these alternative rules are mainly subconscious.

[2] Dave Grossman, "Killology," *Christianity Today* (10 Aug. 1998), 2-3. This information is widely published, including in Grossman's book, *On Killing: The Psychological Cost of Learning to Kill in War and Society* (New York: Little, Brown, 2009).

As an aside, I think quite a bit of the *non*-combat immorality often associated with soldiers (drugs, sex, language, alcohol, pillaging) is also partially explained by the unspoken definition of army as the camaraderie of those living by an intimately understood different set of rules. That would help to explain what my pastor told me before I left for basic training: a large percentage of Christian young men suspend their Christian morality and lifestyle during the two or three years they are in the army, and then revert back to their former behaviour when they return. The depth of that camaraderie also helps to explain the high rate of divorce among combat veterans: the depth of commitment and attachment to buddies is often deeper than to spouse.

I anticipate skepticism about all of this. Come on. Do not try to tell us that twenty years of Reformed nurture and education can be upended by a few months of army training. Let me present just a few examples of how the alternative values begin to supplant or at least coexist with official ones, and how all of that is unofficially indoctrinated. I will do it in bullet form, if you will allow the pun.

- When I began basic training, most of us were draftees—not volunteers. Within weeks, the army had us singing and marching to songs that glorified military camaraderie and disdained civilians. We were mainly unaware of the irony.
- Later I was in officer candidate school. Surely they would teach leaders to obey the rules. One rule was that we must be in bed from 10:00 p.m. to 5:30 a.m. But every minute during the day was regimented: when could we polish boots, get equipment and clothes ready for inspection, do the academic study, and anything personal like reading and writing letters? If we were naive enough to ask or try to use the impossibility of the rules as an excuse for not accomplishing all that, the sarcastic response was, "Ask the good fairy to do it." So we went for months getting from two to four hours of sleep per night, doing our work by flashlight, ready to hop into bed at a moment's notice if our lookout spotted an officer coming.
- Part of the time during that same officer training, we were systematically underfed. One solution was to arrange to smuggle in fast food. But that was strictly forbidden, extremely difficult to arrange, and punished severely if we were caught. But periodically we were coyly asked if we had done so yet.

Now in case your non-military minds are still reeling, wondering what the unspoken message is, it is this: if you fifty guys are too dumb to muster the collective ability to evade the rule by smuggling food when you are hungry, how could you ever lead men in battle? That is the micro message. The macro message is this: live by the real rules; watch out for the official ones. It is all about mission. Little impediments like official rules are no excuse for failing in your mission. That is the real rule, part of that alternative set of rules, the unspoken one: accomplish your mission—win. The fact that the alternative rules are so deeply ingrained explains, too, why it never even crossed my mind to report the possible war crimes of the first story. Moreover, this kind of activity cannot be merely the violation of one or two law-flouting bad apples in the barrel; it requires the complicity of everyone in the unit without exception.

So in almost any situation, you subconsciously do the calculus. Which set of rules apply? The official ones or the real ones? They exist uneasily side-by-side. And if I go by the real ones, what is the likelihood of getting caught? What are the consequences if I get caught? And how do those consequences compare with the consequences of following the official set of rules but possibly failing in the mission? I know, of course, that if I get caught, the official rules apply; the very existence of the real rules—which were only unofficially taught—will be plausibly denied. All of these considerations come to mind, whether I incinerated the village where my buddy was killed, kept a string of dead enemy ears on my belt, conducted an energetic interrogation, or just snuck in some food.

So far, in considering how to make ordinary people into killers, we have talked about demonization and de-personalization at one level. At a little deeper level there are the preparatory desensitizing effects of media and game violence before one even enters the military. There is also the effect of technology like bombs, missiles, and drones allowing easier remote killing. Then, at a still deeper and more sophisticated level, we have looked at the ambivalence of the rules. But we need to return to that still deeper question of whether military training and war itself tend to mess with our very DNA.

Let's start with psychologist and retired Lt. Col. Dave Grossman's description of basic training:

> Brutalization and desensitization is what happens at boot camp. From the moment you step off the bus you are physically and verbally abused. Countless push ups, endless hours at attention or running with heavy loads, while carefully trained professionals take turns screaming at you. Your head is shaved, you are herded together naked, and dressed alike, losing all vestiges of individuality. This brutalization is designed to break down your

existing mores and norms and to accept a new set of values which embrace destruction, violence, and death as a way of life. In the end you are desensitized to violence and accept it as a normal and essential survival skill in your brutal new world.³

Read those last two scary sentences again.

Consider also a few items from the army website a few years ago.

- "American soldiers, possessed of a fierce warrior *ethos* and spirit, fight in close combat."
- "No soldier can survive in the current battlespace without . . . continuous *immersion* in the Army's Warrior culture."
- "Inculcating the Warrior *ethos* into all soldiers of both the active and reserve components is one of their top priorities."
- "The Warrior *ethos* statement contained within the new Soldier's Creed—'I will always place the *mission* first [before the rules even??]. I will never accept defeat. I will never quit. I will never leave a fallen comrade'—is a key aspect of The Soldier focus area."
- "This is about shifting the mindset of Soldiers from identifying what they do as a Soldier— 'I'm a cook, I'm an infantryman, I'm a postal clerk' toward 'I am a Warrior,' when people ask what they do for a living."
- "This will require the deep and personal *commitment* of every member of the Army team—every leader, every Soldier, civilian, and every family member."⁴

Notice all the confessional religious language and allusions: ethos, Creed, mission, spirit, immersion (as in baptism), commitment. The change said to be required to be a soldier is eerily parallel to Christian conversion. Recall Paul's language in Ephesians 4 and Colossians 3 of taking off the old self (civilian) and putting on the new self (warrior). Or consider Paul saying in II Corinthians 5:17 that if anyone is in Christ, he is a new creation. Parallel that with the idea that if anyone is in the army, he is a new creation; the old (cook or postal clerk) is put away; the new (warrior) is put on. Some say that the army breaks you down and rebuilds you into the kind of creature they need. Do they *fully* succeed? By God's grace, no. Even the army cannot totally erase the way in which

---

3   Grossman, "Killology" 3.
4   This is from a printout from the army website in 2004, last revised Dec. 11, 2003. The quotes can be found now at: www.hsdl.org/?view&did=443218, pp. 5, 6, 10, and www.mccoy.army.mil/ReadingRoom/Triad/02132004/tf%20soldier.htm Emphasis is mine.

we reflect or image our creator God. The extent of change and damage also varies immensely from one person to the next.

Reaction to that change varies as well. One reaction was the serious problem of extensive use of mind-altering drugs. I cannot erase from my mind, for example, a child under my command.

> Yes, a child
> The child of a mother
> Perhaps her only child
> Now about nineteen years old
> Soft-spoken, and gentle
> Addicted
> Terrified
> Crying

He stood before me like a scared bunny as I told him he was being transferred to an infantry unit. His performance of duty was impaired by his addiction. He had been repeatedly warned that this transfer would happen if he did not smarten up and appreciate how good he had it.

I don't know what happened to him after that. But in my worst imagination I have to answer anguished questions from his mother:

"How did my child, trained for and holding a comparatively safe position in military intelligence, end up in an infantry unit?"

"Sending him to his death in a dangerous position was his punishment because he could not quickly drop his addiction after a few warnings?"

"The only possible treatment for his addiction was to make him canon fodder?"

I was hardly more mature than he was. One of the sad ironies of that war is that junior officers like me had to be quickly manufactured by mass production to fill the needed low-level leadership positions. So, inexperienced and ill-prepared kids were in command of other kids in life and death situations.

Now before we become too glibly critical about all of these nefarious things armies do, we need to explore our civilian complicity as well as the possible cruel irony that a lot of this may be necessary as long as we have or anticipate war.[5] The point is that we create armies

---

[5] That is an issue for another paper. Such a paper could consider theories about pacifism, just war, just policing, responsibility to protect, the sovereignty of nation states, the role and limitations of sovereign states in relationship to the United Nations and more, all considered in the context of a realistic recognition of the devastating effects of sin on international relations and conflict resolution.

to win wars. To what extent is it fair to then condemn them when they excel at manufacturing killers to do that?

But military efforts to recreate a person into a killer do immense damage at that very deep DNA level—the level of self. Training already does that; combat exacerbates it. At the same time as soldiers are trained to dehumanize the enemy, they too are partly dehumanized. That is why soldiering is arguably the most self-sacrificial of callings. Not only because of the risk of physical death or injury but also because it sacrifices the self at that very deep level. That's why soldiers so often experience post-traumatic stress disorder and the more recently recognized disorder called moral injury[6] and all of their devastating consequences. I do not know how reliable the statistics are, but already years ago, I read that about 90 percent of Vietnam combat veterans were divorced and that we lost more to suicide than to enemy action. Iraq and Afghanistan veterans experience similar statistics. There are eighteen veteran suicides a month; no, it's eighteen a week; no, really eighteen a day, one every eighty minutes.[7] With exaggeration, some have said that the dead are the fortunate casualties. They suffered for seconds, minutes, or hours before death. The walking wounded suffer for life.

And it's not just the training, the killing, and the visions and recollections of killing that torture post-war victims. It's also the moral ambiguity that eats at them for the rest of their lives:

- -ambiguity like that of our first story;
- -ambiguity they know no one will understand;
- -ambiguity that questions whether the horrific things they have seen and done were in any way justifiable;
- -and sometimes, ambiguity that they are forced to keep inside, knowing that sharing it might result in long and humiliating judgment and punishment under the official rules.

---

[6] Rita Nakashima Brock and Gabriella Lettini, *Soul Repair: Recovering from Moral Injury after War* (Boston: Beacon Press, 2012), xiv. This book explores moral injury which is now recognized by the US military and a rising number of mental health professionals. In simple terms, post-tramatic stress disorder (PTSD) results from external trauma; moral injury "comes from having transgressed one's basic moral identity and violated core moral beliefs." Analogies are always limited, but if one would compare PTSD to the results of the explosion of a nearby grenade, then moral injury could be compared to the results of exploding a grenade within one's heart.

[7] Ibid., xii. These rates of suicide continue to rise despite more research, better screening, and better treatment. I have heard that the number has now increased to 21 per day. That number does not include suicides of active duty soldiers—only veterans. In recent years, active duty suicides alone exceeded combat deaths.

War. What a murky muddled moral morass. What evil we are capable of. What opportunities for good we ignore.

Yet that is not the last word. There is grace. I want to leave you with a poem—a poem that culminates in the future, a poem that challenges us *now* to begin exchanging guns for garden tools and atomic bombs for medical isotopes. God will finish the job, but he calls us already now to begin, by his grace, to make into reality the prophecy of this poem from Micah 4:3-4.

> They will beat their swords into plowshares
>   and their spears into pruning hooks.
> Nation will not take up sword against nation,
>   nor will they train for war any more.
> Everyone will sit under their own vine
>   and under their own fig tree,
>   and no one will make them afraid,
>   for the Lord Almighty has spoken.

PART V

Dominies, Language, and the Arts

CHAPTER 17

Hendrik Pieter Scholte Roils the Christian Seceded Church in the Netherlands, 1834–1846

Eugene Heideman

Dominie Hendrik Pieter (Henry Peter) Scholte (1805-1868) was busy selling his house and church edifice in the final months of 1846 in preparation for leading a group of Dutch emigrants from the Netherlands to America. In a letter dated 29 October 1846 to his long-time friend Guillaume Groen van Prinsterer, an outstanding Dutch Christian politician and historian, Scholte explained: "Since most of the Seceders with whom I am united in the Netherlands are leaving, for me there remains no other way than to go where they are going, because for me there is in the Netherlands no field of labor outside this circle either in a temporal or religious way."[1]

In one of his last articles in the religious journal, *De Reformatie*, which he edited from its inception in 1837, he bemoaned the fact that King Willem II had not spoken a word of regret that so many Dutch citizens were departing for other countries because of conditions in the Netherlands. Even worse, many of Scholte's own acquaintances seemed to be indifferent to his impending departure. He wrote bitterly:

---

[1] Quoted in Lubbertus Oostendorp, *H. P. Scholte: Leader of the Secession of 1834 and Founder of Pella* (Franeker: Wever, 1964), 152.

Fig. 17.1. *De Reformatie*, 1845

We can do no other; we must depart. We do not leave hastily, not without spending much time in reflection, not disguising the troubles bound up with such a departure. But after careful consideration, after prayerful contemplation of our situation in the Netherlands, our decision has been made; we must depart. In spite of all that, we experience coolness and indifference from brothers; yes, there is even clandestine pleasure that we go, that they will be delivered from our annoying pushiness. This grieves us more than all the grievous silence of our king in his Royal Address to the States-General.[2]

These sentences were written by the man who in his student days at Leiden University had become the leader of the "Scholte Club." They were written in 1846 by the man, who as a young patriot had joined the military campaign of his country in the war with Belgium in 1830 and who had been decorated with a medal for his efforts. They express the isolation of the one who has been called the "driving force" behind the Secession of 1834.[3] They are almost his last words as the editor of *De Reformatie*.

What happened between 1829 and 1846 that brought forth these distressing words? This chapter will describe what happened during

---

[2] "De Troonrede," *De Reformatie* (1847), 240.
[3] Th. L. Haitjema, *De Nieuwere Geschiedenis van Neerlands Kerk der Hervorming: van Gereformeerde kerkstaat tot Christusbelijdende Volkskerk* ('s Gravenhage: Boekencentrum, 1964), 164.

those years that caused Scholte to be alienated from his erstwhile close colleagues, as well as many others in the Netherlands who were praying and working for the reform of the Netherlands Reformed Church. Although Scholte's personality was a contributing factor, the basic cause of his alienation was theological.

Nederlands Hervormde Kerk

Upon liberation from the Napoleonic regime in 1813, King Willem I ascended the throne as a constitutional monarch, and he set about to reorganize the Reformed Church. His ministers proposed a new set of "general regulations" to replace the historic Dortian church order, which the king promulgated in 1816. The *Nederlands Hervormde Kerk* was the new name given to the national church in the church order adopted by the synod of 1816.[4]

The new church order was intended to leave the theological tradition intact. Thus, every minister was required to sign his agreement with the Three Forms of Unity—the Belgic Confession, Heidelberg Catechism, and Canons of Dort. But the 1816 order powerfully centralized the administration of the entire church under a hierarchy of the synodical directorate, which had authority over provincial boards, classical boards, and local consistories. The government set up a department of religious oversight to ensure the "maintenance of doctrine, the multiplication of religious knowledge, the promotion of Christian morals, the maintenance of order and concord, and the cultivation of love for the King and Fatherland."[5]

This provision left ample room for church authorities to call upon the civil authorities to enforce the regulations, using the power of the police and courts to make arrests, hold people in jail, and impose fines on those in the church who disobeyed the regulations.

At the time the new regulations were proposed, a number of church classes, or regional assemblies, expressed their objections, but the government paid little attention. The philosophy of the Enlightenment was dominant in the ministry of religious affairs, in contrast to the theology of the Reformation. The synodical directorate did not believe it was responsible to maintain doctrinal orthodoxy. The more orthodox

---

[4] For the historical events leading up to the church order of 1816, see Karel Blei, *The Netherlands Reformed Church, 1571-2005*, Alan J. Janssen, tr. (Grand Rapids: Eerdmans, 2006), 48-49. Blei points out (56) that this was the first church order that was applicable to the church in the whole of the Netherlands. The Church Order of Dort had not been adopted everywhere in the country.

[5] Quoted in ibid., 57-58.

members insisted that the Form of Subscription of office bearers, adopted at the Synod of Dort, required signatories to accept the three forms of unity *because* they are the true interpretations of scripture, rather than *insofar as* they are true interpretations of scripture. The wider interpretation, however, prevailed. It left almost unlimited room for dissent from the confessions.

Factors leading to Scholte's estrangement from his colleagues

Church historians note that Scholte had become estranged from his colleagues in the years before his emigration to America. Some attribute this to character weaknesses. Scholte displayed an arrogant and dismissive attitude toward his teachers at Leiden University, he could be impulsive in making decisions, and he spurned advice. The same complaint, however, could be made about a number of others in the Secession movement who had not become isolated.

Some point to Scholte's experience as a factory owner. The early death of his father, Jan Hendrik Scholte, who owned a factory in Amsterdam that supplied boxes for the sugar industry, forced young Scholte at age seventeen to take over the factory. In the best interest of the company, he had to make decisions without consulting others. This contrasted starkly with church assemblies, where the consultative decision-making process was slow and deliberate. Businessmen like Scholte believed one should strike when the iron is hot.

Scholte consistently ignored decisions of Christian Seceded Church synods, as for example, in March 1836, when he wrote a compendium of the catechism for young people. Also Hendrik de Cock, the first minister to secede from the *Hervormde Kerk* in 1834, had prepared a short catechism, *Voorbeeld der goddelijke waarheden* (Compendium of divine truth"), drawn from a 1706 compendium of the Reformed pietist, Abraham Hellenbroek. When the matter of publishing a short catechism came before synod 1836, Scholte offered his short catechism. The delegates, concerned that congregations were adopting various short catechisms on their own, appointed a committee consisting of Scholte, Simon Van Velsen, and elder D. Hoksbergen to examine the short catechisms, and recommend one or more for a subsequent synod's approval.[6]

---

[6] Act 43 (1836 Minutes), *Handelingen en Verslagen van de Algemene Synoden van de Christelijk Afgescheidene Gereformeerde Kerk (1836-1869)* (Houton/Utrecht: Den Hertog, B. V. 1984), 40 (hereafter *Handelingen*). (Note: The 1984 edition has page numbers for each meeting at the top of the page; the number at the bottom of each page is that of the edition as a whole. The page number in the footnote is that of the edition as a whole.)

Scholte went ahead and published his short catechism without waiting for synodical approval. The provincial synods of Groningen and Drenthe raised objections at Synod 1837, arguing that the catechism contained statements open to a Remonstrant interpretation.[7] The Synod of Dort had strongly condemned the errors of the Remonstrants in the Canons of Dort.[8] Synod 1837 requested that the two provincial synods withdraw their complaints. Van Velsen, the chair, however, ruled that Scholte had acted contrary to Synod's 1836 action. This ruling set off a vigorous debate. Scholte admitted that he might have acted in haste but asked that the 1836 action be reconsidered. Synod 1837 instead decided that any short catechism must be approved by a "National Synod."[9] Hence, the matter was considered again at Synod 1838.[10]

Since the Christian Seceded Church synod had not yet finally adopted a church order in 1836, Scholte had not in fact violated any rule in the order. His action in moving ahead to make his catechism available in the face of the objections of two provincial synods, however, served to indicate a lack of respect for synodical decisions, even when he was the presiding officer, as he was at Synod 1836.

Scholte's treatment of synods, vis à vis a shorter catechism, in itself would not have led to a break with his colleagues. All of them displayed a similar spirit of independence with regard to matters of church polity. Scholte's actions in pursuit of his own agenda, however, fostered resentment when he moved ahead of his colleagues without adequate consultation.

Scholte, "the intentional driving force" (doelbewuste drijfkracht)[11] of the Secession movement

The fact that the Scholte family originally belonged to the Reconstituted Lutheran Church (*Hersteld Luthersche Gemeente*), which

---

[7] Antonie Gerrit Honig contended in his address at the Theological School in Kampen that it was precisely the Canons of Dort that were the central principle of the *Afscheiding*, particularly with an eye to the doctrine of predestination (Kornelis H. Miskotte, *Korte Nabetrachting over de Afscheiding van 1834* [Amsterdam: Uitgevers Mij Holland, 1934], 68-69). Miskotte was a member of the *Nederlands Hervormde Kerk* and a professor of theology at Leiden University.

[8] The Remonstrant errors included rejection of the doctrines of original sin, unconditional election, the definite number of the elect, and irresistible grace.

[9] A "National Synod" is one in which delegates of all the provincial synods are present. In the circumstances of the *Christelijke Afgescheidene Gereformeerde Kerk* during those years, some of the synod meetings did not have full participation.

[10] Actions 23-26 (1837 Minutes), *Handelingen*, 93-94.

[11] Haitjema, *Nieuwere Geschiedenis*, 7, 164.

Fig. 17.2. *Afscheiding* colleagues; *top, l-r:* Hendrik de Cock, Hendrik P. Scholte; *bottom*: Anne Maurits C. van Hall, Anthony Brummelkamp (Het Leven Van Hendrik Peter Scholte, *Nijverdal: E. J. Bosch Jbzn., 1915*)

had seceded from the Lutheran Church in Hanover, Germany, meant that his loyalty to the two-century-old Reformed Church in the Netherlands was different from that of his colleagues. He did not have the strong emotional ties with the church that had been the backbone of resistance to Spanish Roman Catholic power during the Eighty Year War. Scholte's great-grandfather, Hendrik Peter Schultzen, had migrated from Hanover and joined the close-knit German colony in Amsterdam. The Amsterdam Lutheran congregation suffered a second secession when a liberal cleric became pastor. The Scholte family became active members of the newly seceded church, the *Luthersche Gemeente in Hersteld Verband*. Hendrik's mother was a pious woman who taught her children the essentials of the faith. She was also a loyal subject of the House of Orange and taught her children to pray for the freedom of

Holland in the years when the country was under the domination of Napoleon (1795-1813).¹²

Scholte decided to join the *Nederlandse Hervormde Kerk* because he judged its confessions to be more scriptural than the Lutheran church he knew. His subsequent secession from the *Hervormde Kerk* did not carry the same emotional and theological weight that it did for other members of Scholte Club and Hendrik de Cock. He had already participated in two secessions from the Lutheran church and had also learned from one of his mentors, Willem Bilderdijk, about the secession movement in Switzerland. Secession came easily to Scholte. For the others, it was a wrenching decision. This is illustrated by comparing the secessions of Hendrik de Cock, the first minister to secede; Scholte, the second one; and Albertus C. Van Raalte, the last of the original group to join the Secession.

Scholte was the leader of the group of students known as "the club of Scholte" during his years as a theological student at Leiden University. Scholte objected to the liberal theology being taught at Leiden and seldom attended lectures, preferring instead the private lectures by Isaac da Costa and his friends in the Reveil Circle. The *Réveil* was a European Christian awakening movement centered in Switzerland. Other members of the informal Scholte club included Van Velsen, Anthony Brummelkamp, Georg C. Gezelle Meerburg, and the youngest member, Van Raalte.¹³

De Cock had studied at the University of Groningen and happily followed the liberal "Groninger" theology then in vogue. He began serving as a *Hervormde* pastor in Ulrum, Groningen, in October 1829 and preached the liberal theology of his professors. A devout parishioner, however, introduced him to experiential Reformed piety, and he read for the first time the Belgic Confession, the Heidelberg Catechism, and the Canons of Dort, and then Calvin's *Institutes,* of which he had not previously heard. De Cock's sermons gained new power, with the result that people came from great distances to hear him. In his defense of Reformed theology, he wrote a pamphlet accusing two *Hervormde* pastors, L. Meijer Brouwer and G. Benthem Reddingius, of being false teachers, "wolves in the sheepfold."¹⁴

Members of neighboring *Hervormde* parishes asked De Cock to baptize their children in Ulrum without permission from their own

---

¹² For details about the Scholte family, see Oostendorp, *Scholte,* 19-22.
¹³ Oostendorp, *Scholte,* 23; Gerrit J. tenZythoff, *Sources of Secession* (Grand Rapids: Eerdmans, 1987), 110-27.
¹⁴ *Sources of Secession,* 122-24.

pastors. This was not strictly prohibited by synodical regulations, but there were serious objections to his actions.[15]

Civil authorities, who felt responsible to uphold the authority of the church, brought charges against De Cock for violating church regulations. He was arrested, jailed, fined, suspended first from his office without loss of salary, and then suspended with loss of salary, beginning in December 1833 and continuing until January 1835, the date on which he was deposed. On 5 October 1834, De Cock received the notice of his suspension. In despair over the death of his daughter on the night of 8 October, as well as his suspension, he was encouraged by the unexpected arrival of Scholte who was on "a little side trip" to Groningen.[16]

Historians differ in assessing the extent to which Scholte's visit influenced De Cock's decision to secede. Scholte himself later wrote that he and De Cock had talked about secession, but when he left, he did not know what De Cock would do.[17] Two years later, De Cock himself wrote that Scholte was not the cause of the secession. "That the secession took place at that time was solely caused by the fact that in ecclesiastical and civil respect everything came together and all means had been exhausted, since the provincial synod had rejected all four reasons and demanded an absolute rejection of truth and Christ."[18]

Rasker, Rullmann, and Haitjema agree that Scholte played an important role in De Cock's decision to secede. Rasker points out that Scholte had already raised the matter of secession in a letter to De Cock early in 1833.[19] Rullmann says that Scholte informed De Cock about how the secessions in Switzerland had taken place.[20] Haitjema gives Scholte an even greater role. He says that Scholte helped formulate the

---

[15] Ibid., 120-22.
[16] Johan A. Wormser, *Hendrik de Cock* (Nijverdal: E. J. Bosch, 1915), 64, 20. Scholte had taken his family from Doeveren to Amsterdam. Hence, the "little side trip" from Amsterdam to Ulrum took considerable effort in 1834!
[17] Wormser, *Hendrik de Cock*, 65. Wormser notes that Scholte left on Monday morning, in contrast to Hasker, who says that Scholte left on Sunday evening (A. J. Hasker, *De Nederlandse Hervormde Kerk vanaf 1795* [Kampen: Uitgeversmaatschappij, 1974], 65). If Scholte had left on Sunday evening, more time had elapsed between the time of his departure and the meeting of the Ulrum consistory than is the case according to Wormser's timetable. Hasker's timetable supports Scholte's comment that he did not yet know when he left what De Cock would do about secession from the *Nederlandse Hervormde Kerk*.
[18] Quoted in tenZythoff, *Sources of Secession*, 127.
[19] A. J. Rasker, *De Nederlandse Hervormde Kerk vanaf 1795*, 61.
[20] J. C. Rullmann, *De Afscheiding van 1834* (Kampen: J. H. Kok, Uitgevers Mij, 1930) 5th ed., 86.

wording of the "Act of Secession and Return" that the Ulrum consistory adopted on 13 October 1834 and most confessing members signed.[21] Whatever Scholte's exact role may have been, although De Cock was the first minister to secede, it was Scholte who was the "motivating driving force" of the Secession movement.[22]

The text of the Ulrum declaration reads, in part:

> We the undersigned Overseers and members of the Reformed congregation [*Gereformeerde Gemeente*] of Jesus Christ at Ulrum, for some time having noticed the decay in the *Nederlands Hervormde Kerk*, both in the slighting of or denying of the doctrines of our fathers founded on God's Word, and in the deforming of the administration of the Holy Sacraments, which elements are all, according to our Reformed Confession, Art. 29, marks of the true church . . . hereby declare that we in accordance with the office of all believers, Art. 28, separate ourselves from such as are not of the Church, and thus will not have communion any longer with the *Nederlands Hervormde Kerk*, until this body turns back to the true service of God.[23]

Several points should be noted about the document. First, it was carefully written with full scriptural documentation. Its complexity makes it difficult to imagine that it was first drafted at a consistory meeting that was called on short notice. It is therefore easy to imagine that Scholte had a hand in putting his thoughts on paper during his time in Ulrum or even before leaving his manse in Doeveren, when he was contemplating the possibility of his own secession.

Second, the full text contains the accusation that the Nederlands Hervormde Kerk "is not the true, but the *false* church." This justified those who seceded, because according to Article 29 of the Belgic Confession, it is one's obligation to separate oneself from a false church. Third, the presence of the word *wederkeering* (returning) in the title meant that the seceders were departing from the false "Hervormde Kerk" in order to turn back to the true "Gereformeerde Kerk" and the Canons and Church Order adopted at the Synod of Dort in 1618-19. (The names *Hervormd* and *Gereformeerd* both translate in English as *Reformed*, so when the 1834 secessionists reclaimed the historic name, they were making a political statement.)

---

[21] Haitjema, *Nieuwere Geschiedenis*, 168.
[22] Ibid., 7, 164.
[23] Translation by Oostendorp, *Scholte*, 57. The full text is to be found in Wormser, *Hendrik de Cock*, 66-69.

Fourth, the full text includes the sentence, "Finally, on the authority of the Provincial Board, the preaching of the Word of God in our midst by the openly acknowledged minister of the Church, the Honorable, learned H. P. Scholte, [etc.] has been forbidden."[24] This indicates that the congregation at Ulrum regarded the action against Scholte as "an act against the prophets of the Lord."[25] Their resolution made the Hervormde Kerk's lack of regard for Scholte a matter of central concern at the outset of the Secession.

The Secession movement gained momentum after its beginning in Ulrum. On 29 October 1834, Scholte was suspended for having preached without permission in Ulrum during his visit with De Cock. He and his congregations submitted their notices of secession on 1 November 1834. Other members of the Scholte Club, Brummelkamp, Van Velsen, and Gezelle Meerburg were also suspended on various grounds over the course of the next sixteen months and seceded following their suspensions.

Albertus C. Van Raalte and the provincial synod of Zuid-Holland reached an impasse about his refusal to sign a promise to abide by *all* the regulations of the Church Order of 1816. When Van Raalte knew that he would not be accepted for ordination, he informed the synod that he was "breaking all ecclesiastical union with you." Years later, in 1862, he acknowledged that it was "the most painful sacrifice to give up the preaching so fervently desired." His father was an ordained minister in the Hervormde Kerk. Van Raalte believed that he "had done all he could to avoid an open break, for he hated 'no longer to be able to occupy the pulpits of my father, to become a shame unto my relatives and to my mother.'"[26]

Clearly, secession came more easily to Scholte than it did to De Cock, Van Raalte, and the other members of the club of Scholte. De Cock and Van Raalte had grown up in the Hervormde Kerk, which was intertwined with the history of the Dutch Republic. The Church was the defender of the Reformed faith against the power of the Roman Catholic Church, and was loyal to the House of Orange. The personal histories of the Secession leaders and their individual characters did not cause Scholte's controversies. Rather, it was deep theological differences on the doctrine of the church that led to differences of pastoral practice

---

[24] Translation by Oostendorp, *Scholte*, 58.
[25] Ibid., 58.
[26] tenZythoff, *Sources of Secession,* 135. In requiring Van Raalte to promise to obey *all* the many regulations, his examiners were asking more of him than they did of other candidates.

and interpretations of the church order. Furthermore, Scholte's involvement in the secession was irrelevant to his later estrangement from his former colleagues.

Scholte becomes estranged from De Cock

The first general synod of the Christian Seceded Church met in Amsterdam from 2-12 March 1836, with the main order of business being to prepare a petition to the King asking to be recognized as the legitimate Reformed Church. Scholte's leadership in the petition is indicated by the fact that he opened the synod with prayer and gave the meditation, after which he was chosen as chair, with De Cock chosen as clerk.[27] After preparing the letter of petition, the delegates dealt with other matters, notably differing views of infant baptism between Scholte and De Cock. Despite celebrating the Lord's Supper before adjournment, and declaring their loyalty to one another like David and Jonathon, the clerics continued the controversy until Synod 1837.[28]

The baptism of infants

At the time of the Synod of Dort the Netherlands probably counted more Anabaptists than Calvinists. Anabaptists held to believer's baptism, and refused the sacrament to infants and young children. Reformed delegates at the Synod of Dort firmly believed that God elected the church as the body of Christ to be the covenant people and that He is faithful through the generations. The delegates followed Question 74 of the Heidelberg Catechism, which states that infants are to be baptized "because they, as well as their parents, are included in the covenant and belong to the people of God." The Belgic Confession similarly declares that infants should be "baptized and sealed with the sign of the covenant, as the infants in Israel were circumcised." Although children were members of the church by baptism, Reformed churches barred them from the Lord's Supper until they were able to confess their faith publicly.

In the two centuries after the Synod of Dort, Reformed churches baptized children of confessing members. Scholte, however, was influenced by the Dutch pietists of the later Reformation (*nadere*

---

[27] *Handelingen*, 24-26. The 1984 edition has page numbers for each meeting at the top of the page; the number at the bottom of each page is that of the edition as a whole. The page number in the footnote is that of the edition as a whole.

[28] Johan A. Wormser Jr., *Het Leven Van Hendrik Peter Scholte* (Nijverdal: E. J. Bosch Jbzn., 1915), 76.

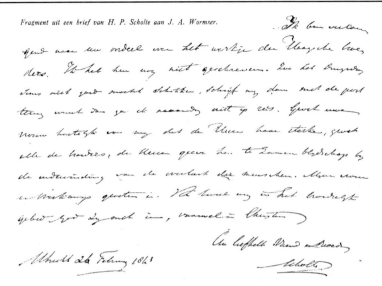

Fig. 17.3. Letter from Scholte to J. A. Wormser, 1843 (Wormser, *Het Leven Van Hendrik Peter Scholte*, pp. 136-37)

Reformatie) in the seventeenth and eighteenth centuries, who emphasized the need for personal conversion and confession of faith. He refused to baptize children of lukewarm members and even of those who, while faithful in attendance, had not made a public profession of faith. Scholte called attention to the phrase in the Belgic Confession that says it is "the children of believers" who ought to be baptized. On 8 March 1837, he wrote to the Provincial Assembly of Lower Gelderland: "Those who do not show such marks may not be recognized as members and must together with their children be denied the Sacraments until their conversion."[29]

Scholte was not the only pastor who objected to baptizing children of parents who had not yet confessed their faith. Brummelkamp in the congregation in Hattem was also uneasy about baptizing such children, although he continued to do so under certain conditions.[30]

When Synod 1836 considered the doctrine of the sacraments, it included language that favored Scholte's view that infants of non-confessing parents should be denied baptism. It taught that "no one may be considered a member of the Church of Christ, except on

---

[29] Quoted in Melis te Velde, *Anthony Brummelkamp, 1811-1888* (Barneveld: Uitgeverij de Vuurbaak, 1988), 86.
[30] Ibid., 87.

account of *confession of faith*."[31] De Cock argued against this language, but Scholte's language prevailed. At the beginning of Synod 1837, De Cock placed on the agenda his objection to an article in *De Reformatie* by the elder Smedes that incorrectly said that De Cock's practice of baptizing children of non-confessing parents had been condemned by Synod 1836. De Cock wanted the minutes to show that his practice had not been condemned. Although they favored Scholte's view, Synod 1837 agreed that De Cock's practice had not been condemned.[32]

De Cock found Scholte's practice to be too idealistic and radical. He knew that in his congregations, there were many who shared fully in the life of the congregation and its worship but did not yet feel free to make a public profession of faith. He believed that Scholte's perspective on the faith was individualistic and "labadistic."[33]

The charge of "labadism" was a serious one. Jean de Labadie (1610-1674) was a preacher in the French-speaking (Walloon) Reformed Church in Middelburg who had been suspended for declaring the Reformed Church absolutely "worldly" and no longer a genuine church. He advocated a holy community of true believers, who would separate themselves and worship in "conventicles" rather than in churches. For the Labadists, "the purity of the church took precedence over its unity."[34]

The other Seceded church leaders could not avoid making pastoral and theological decisions about whether or not to baptize children of non-confessing parents. Brummelkamp and Gezelle Meerburg sided with Scholte, who would not baptize children of non-confessing members. Van Velsen held that if the parents are unconverted, either a converted member of the church or an elder should present the child instead of the parents. At first, Van Raalte sided with Brummelkamp, but later he wavered and followed the practice of De Cock and baptized children of members who were not confessing believers.[35] Although Brummelkamp accepted Scholte's theological reasoning for refusing to

---

[31] 1836 Synod, Art. 59-61, *Handelingen*, 50-52.
[32] 1837 Synod, Art. 7, *Handelingen*, 86-87.
[33] te Velde, *Brummelkamp*, 87.
[34] Blei, *Netherlands Reformed Church*, 45-46; tenZijthoff, *Sources of Secession*, 15.
[35] Oostendorp, *Scholte*, 107. In a footnote, Oostendorp points out that Van Raalte's practice in America was that of De Cock and many early Christian Reformed leaders as well. Johan A. Wormser, *De Kinderdoop* (Holland, MI: Hope College Press, 1873), was first published in the Netherlands in 1853. Wormser had served for a year with Scholte on the editorial board of *De Reformatie* and as an elder in the *Afgescheiden* church in Amsterdam. He eventually returned to the *Hervormde Kerk*. His position was that one should not stop baptizing children of non-confessing members but that the church must help those children to understand their baptism.

baptize children of non-confessing members, in his pastoral practice he adopted a broader position that differed little from that of De Cock.[36]

The Church Order of Utrecht: disagreement between Scholte and Van Velsen

Despite their disagreements over the Dort Church Order, Synod 1836 decided that the Seceded churches should observe the document for the present. Meanwhile, the synod urged members to review developments in the two centuries since Dort and suggest possible revisions that might be needed.[37]

Dort reflected the Reformed doctrine of predestination, according to which the church is called into being by God, led by ministers and elders who are called by God to preach the Word and administer the sacraments. Governance was by assemblies of general synod, provincial synods, classes, and consistories, all arranged non-hierarchically from the broadest to the most local.[38] According to Belgic Confession Articles 27-31 and 36, the church is organized independently of the state. God ordains kings and civil authorities, but they must see that human affairs are conducted in an orderly fashion. The authorities must protect the church, encourage public worship, and ensure that the gospel is preached everywhere. God's providential rule thus permeates the spirit of Dort polity.

Following the suggestion of Synod 1836, Scholte prepared a church order for approval to the provincial synod of South Holland in March 1837. He sent his draft consisting of thirty-three articles to the churches in June. Church historian Melis te Velde considers the articles to be "a declaration of war on the Church Order of Dort."[39]

Scholte's church order said little about the authority of higher assemblies. In sending his document directly to the churches, Scholte bypassed the assemblies and allowed only fourteen days for comments and suggestions. Several regional synods reacted against his high-handed actions. It "went down the wrong throat" in Friesland, Overijssel, and Gelderland. Brummelkamp sent a letter of rebuke to the synod of South Holland.[40] The provincial synods of Utrecht, South Holland, Beneden [Lower]-Gelderland, and North Brabant, however, accepted a revised draft.

---

[36] te Velde, *Brummelkamp*, 88.
[37] 1836 Synod, Art. 23, *Handelingen*, 31.
[38] Daniel J. Meeter, *Meeting Each Other in Doctrine, Liturgy & Government* (Grand Rapids: Eerdmans, 1993), 62-80.
[39] te Velde, *Brummelkamp*, 90.
[40] Ibid.

Scholte's proposed church order was placed on the agenda Synod 1837's eighth session meeting at Utrecht. The first article stated that "All who make confession of faith and walk according to it must be recognized with their children as members of the congregation." The second article declared that this confession includes agreement with the central doctrines of the faith, forsaking the world, living according to God's commandments, and obeying the eternal King, Jesus Christ. Scholte sought to avoid the charge of "labadism" by including articles that recognized the truth that hypocrites mingle with believers, but as long as they do not give strong evidence to the contrary, those accepted by confession must be understood to be believers and they with their children remain members as long as they have not been excommunicated.[41]

Scholte's emphasis on personal confession of faith, while giving minimal attention to the office bearers and assemblies, raised suspicions that he was compromising the Reformed doctrine of election. Synod 1837 rejected accusations that Scholte had improperly translated Article 16 of the Belgic Confession on the Reformed doctrine of election and compromised the doctrine of justification of sinners.[42] Van Velsen, the chair, presented five articles of his own to follow the first six of Scholte. Van Velsen's articles recognized the rule of Christ over the church and the role of the assemblies who have guiding, but not hierarchical, power of governance. Matters not directly provided for in God's Word are the responsibility of the elders, not a matter of regulation by the broader assemblies.[43]

Synod adopted the proposals of Scholte and Van Velsen, as amended. It then followed Van Velsen's advice and considered amending the Church Order of Dort to meet the needs of the Christian Seceded Church. Forty-two of the articles of Dort were amended, eight were left out, and thirty-six were retained without change.[44] Synod in its twenty-first session adopted the amended document, which became known as the Utrecht Church Order.[45] Just before the end of the meeting, De Cock and four elders registered a protest against the many changes in the historic Dort Church Order as being inconsistent with the Belgic Confession, Article 30.[46] Scholte did not register any protest at the

---

[41] 1837 Synod, Art. 53, *Handelingen*, 103-4.
[42] 1837 Synod, Art. 14, *Handelingen*, 89; Art. 21, 23, ibid., 92-93.
[43] 1837 Synod, Art. 54, ibid., 105-6.
[44] Rullmann, *Afscheiding*, 262.
[45] 1837 Synod, Art. 120, *Handelingen*, 140-41.
[46] 1837, Art. 136, ibid., 149-50. De Cock later withdrew his protest, but the elders persisted in their protest and separated to form the *Gereformeerde Gemeenten onder het Kruis*. See Rullmann, *Afscheiding*, 287-91.

meeting, but he was displeased that the Utrecht Church Order followed Dort in its rules about the ordained offices and assemblies.

Following synod's adjournment, a storm arose in the provinces about the new church order. Some declared that it reflected too many of Scholte's ideas. Scholte himself had hoped for a more radical departure from Dort, but in the provinces of South Holland, North Holland, Utrecht, and part of Gelderland, all places where his influence was strong, the churches accepted the revisions.[47]

Van Velsen increased tensions and distanced himself further from Scholte, when in his role as chair, he wrote a "preface" to the published minutes in the synod. He stated that if anyone did not accept the decision of the synod about the Church Order, he was acting like Korah, Dathan, and Abiram (Numbers 16:23-35).[48] In this way, Van Velsen issued a direct challenge to Scholte's readiness to ignore the synod's decisions on church order. To Scholte's mind, this admonition of Van Velsen made the Church Order mandatory in detail, rather than as a guiding principal.

Scholte's persistent disregard for synodical actions

During the period 1836-40, Scholte increasingly showed disrespect for decisions made by his colleagues in the synods. It began with publishing *Kort Begrip* (short catechism) before it was approved by synod. He also ran ahead of the other members of the committee appointed to develop a denominational periodical, by issuing not only one but a number of issues of *De Reformatie* prior to the meeting of the synod in September 1837. Moreover, without synod approval, he included in the title the information that *De Reformatie* was a periodical *of* the church. Synod 1837 ordered him to say that it was a periodical *for* the church, not *of* the church.[49]

A far more serious disregard for synod occurred in 1839 when Scholte requested and received legal status from the king with the recognition of his Utrecht congregation as the *Christelijke Afgescheiden Gemeente*.

The serious nature of his action becomes clear in light of the history of the Secession. According to the Dutch Constitution, religious bodies in existence at the time of its promulgation in 1816 were free to hold public worship according to their own church orders.

[47] Oostendorp, *Scholte*, 110.
[48] "Voorwoord" 1837 Synod, *Handelingen*, vii.
[49] 1837 Synod, Art. 81, ibid., 122.

New religious bodies did not enjoy that right and were subject to the Napoleonic law of association that no more than twenty persons were allowed to assemble without permission of the civil authorities. For that reason, the civil authorities did not recognize the right of the Seceders to worship if more than twenty persons were present. Moreover, because local people often created great disturbances when Seceder ministers appeared on the scene and preached, the police accused the ministers and the congregants of disturbing the peace.[50]

In late 1835 the Seceders wrote to King Willem I, asking that he carry out his responsibility to protect Reformed worship. The king's decree on 11 December 1835 was a sharp rejection of the request. The Seceders were in violation of articles 291 through 294 of the penal code and were creating confusion and division. Therefore, he ordered civil authorities to enforce the law with power.[51]

The major reason for convening Synod 1836 was to make an official request to the king. Synod's request stated that they wished nothing else than to be *Gereformeerd*. They upheld the Church Order of Dort, the three Reformed Confessions, and worshiped using the church's liturgy from the time of 1618-19. The *Hervormde Kerk Directorate* of 1816 was in conflict with the historic *Gereformeerde Kerk*. Synod wrote that "we are not a new church association," but have the right to be recognized as in truth the *Christelijk Gereformeerde Kerk*. They added that they were not desirous of anyone else's possessions, income, or titles.[52] Scholte, as president of the synod, presented the address to the King in person on 16 March 1836.

The angry response of the King was even sharper than in 1835. On 5 July 1836, he decreed that the dissenters were claiming special privileges, and warned them of sterner measures if they did not submit to his terms. He would permit their new association to exist only on their complete renunciation of the name and title *Gereformeerd* and would permit them to meet in groups of more than twenty only if they received permission from local authorities. He was angry that they had formed a synod and claimed the name *Christelijk Gereformeerde Gemeente*, especially since there was no official doctrinal difference with the *Hervormde Kerk*.[53] From that date, the oppression of Seceders became national policy and was more severe than before.

---

[50] For a brief account of this matter, see Oostendorp, *Scholte*, 86-101.
[51] The text of the letter is found in Rullmann, *Afscheiding*, 162.
[52] For the complete text, see Rullmann, *Afscheiding*, 167-68.
[53] Oostendorp, *Scholte*, 94-95. The full text of the King's decree is found in Wormser, *Scholte*, 118-21.

The Seceded congregations increasingly felt the heavy pressure of fines, quartering of soldiers in their homes, and imprisonments. Scholte gave way under the pressure, which was especially severe in Utrecht. In December 1838, without consulting his colleagues, he led his congregation to petition the king to be organized as the *Christelijke* **Afgescheiden** (bold added) *Gemeente* under the Societies Act. The king granted the request on 14 February 1839.[54]

The other Seceders were shocked by Scholte's action, which ran contrary to the position of synod. He had not only acted in bad faith but had given up the name "Reformed" to the *Hervormde Kerk*. His friend, Johan A. Wormser Sr., lamented:

> Previously we were separated from the Directorate, not from the church. We rejected the "church association" of 1816 in order to preserve the church. That standpoint has fallen into decay by the forming of congregations, especially through the recognition in 1839 on the basis of the Utrecht Regulation. The Secession has fallen into a trap."[55]

When the legal recognition of the Utrecht congregation brought an end to persecution there, other congregations could no longer resist the pressure. Amsterdam, Groningen, Schiedam, Sleeuwijk and De Werken, and others followed suit and gained legal status. Nevertheless, there were others, including the congregations served by Brummelkamp at Hattem and Van Raalte at Genemuiden and Mastenbroek, who continued to hold out in faithfulness to the principles of the Secession. As a result, there was new tension among the Seceders until King Willem II came to the throne in 1840 and ordered the persecutions to end.

The Amsterdam quarrel and the suspension of Scholte

In the same year that the Utrecht congregation gained legal status as the *Christelijke Afgescheiden Gemeente*, a quarrel involving Scholte and Van Velsen came to a head in Amsterdam. Scholte had founded the Seceded congregation in Amsterdam, before moving to Doeveren and then to Utrecht. After his suspension from the ministry, he was never installed as pastor in any subsequent congregation. He regarded himself as a minister for all the congregations that he had supported in the provinces of South Holland, Utrecht, Noord Brabant, and Zeeland

---

[54] The text of the letter to the King is found in Wormser, *Scholte*, 131-34.
[55] Quoted in J. C. Rullmann, *De Afscheiding*, 266.

in the early years of the Secession. He had a special affinity for the congregation in Amsterdam, the city where he was born.

After Scholte, the Amsterdam congregation was served by various Seceded ministers when they had occasion to visit the city. In early 1838 the congregation felt a need for a regularly installed, resident pastor. Scholte was not willing to move to Amsterdam and Brummelkamp would not leave Arnhem, so the congregation called Van Velsen. But he did not want to leave Friesland, so he accepted on condition that he continue with the church in Friesland, while also serving as the installed pastor in Amsterdam. In 1839 Amsterdam again called Van Velsen, and he accepted without agreeing to move. Hendrik de Cock, the father of the Secession, installed him in Amsterdam on 16 June 1839. Great confusion followed, however, about the legitimacy of his acceptance of the call when he did not meet its conditions.

The confusion became greater because of the tension already existing between Scholte and Van Velsen. The tension was not just personal: the two ministers were at odds over the church order. Van Velsen favored the Church Order of Dort as amended by Synod 1837, while Scholte was becoming increasingly independent and congregational. Van Velsen also believed that it was his responsibility to emphasize the sovereign grace of God and election. Therefore, he did not always bring into full focus the call to conversion, repentance, and an experiential faith. Scholte, therefore, brought to the Amsterdam consistory charges that Van Velsen did not preach Christ. That complaint did not mean that Van Velsen ignored the great doctrines about salvation in Christ. It meant that Van Velsen, while he preached atonement by Christ, did not explore how one experienced that faith in Christ.[56] Scholte placed the complaint before the Amsterdam consistory at a meeting when Van Velsen was not present. The majority of the consistory did not agree with Scholte. Even more confusion and acrimony followed.

Finally, Seceder pastors and elders gathered at Amsterdam on 6-7 March 1838 to learn from Van Velsen, Scholte, and the consistory the facts in the case and bring about reconciliation. Brummelkamp was chosen as chair and Van Raalte and De Cock as clerks. Brummelkamp's report of the meeting concluded that Van Velsen, Scholte, and the consistory had all acted improperly at a number of points. It proposed what each must do to acknowledge their missteps and to bring about reconciliation. The strongest criticism was directed at Scholte for his interference in the Amsterdam affair and for bringing charges against

---

[56] Rullmann, *Afscheiding*, 268-69.

Van Velsen without adequate foundation. The body sent a letter to the Utrecht consistory that strongly urged them to suspend Scholte as shepherd and preacher until he publicly admitted his guilt and repented.[57]

Scholte and the Utrecht consistory refused to recognize the recommendations of the group, and Scholte continued to preach and serve as pastor. Synod 1840, which met in Amsterdam, further considered the matter. Synod heard the report that Scholte had refused to receive the communication from the March meeting. Scholte refused to attend the meeting. He advised Synod to send representatives to meet with him in Utrecht. Synod suspended him from his office and decided to send representatives to meet with him and the consistory in Utrecht.[58]

In Hendrik de Cock's report of the visit to Utrecht, he notes that only three members of the consistory appeared for a meeting on 8 December. Scholte was at home but did not appear. When the representatives sought to meet with Scholte the next day, he refused, unless Van Velsen would also be suspended. In view of his lack of cooperation, Scholte's suspension remained in place.[59] Scholte was now alienated not only from the *Christelijk Afgescheidene Gereformeerde Kerk* but also from his former Scholte Club colleagues.

Aftermath of the suspension of Scholte

Brummelkamp and Van Raalte sought to repair the breech with Scholte in the years after his suspension. But he refused to recognize the synod's authority over local church consistories, and he would not respect its decisions. He had become fully independent in spirit and in polity. He continued to carry out his pastoral ministry and preaching among those congregations that he had served prior to his suspension. Before Synod 1843 convened, Scholte had himself appointed as a delegate, but when synod convened, the question was immediately raised whether he could be seated as a delegate. Several of the delegations threatened to return home if Scholte were to be seated. After heated discussion of that and other matters, the meeting came to an end. The proceedings were not adopted as an official meeting of synod, but the discussion and other submissions by assemblies and individuals are included along with the minutes of the recognized synods of the church.[60]

[57] "Verslag," *Handelingen*, 6-7 Mar. 1840, 210.
[58] *Handelingen*, 1840 Synod, Art. 18, 246-48.
[59] Ibid., 1840 Synod, 261-62.
[60] Ibid., 267-380.

Hendrik Pieter Scholte emigrates to America

The alienation from his Scholte Club associates at Synod 1836 did not prove to be final. When Brummelkamp and Van Raalte organized their emigration society at Arnhem, and Scholte did the same at Utrecht, there was an effort to coordinate their work. Scholte published news about pending emigration to America of Brummelkamp and Van Raalte as well as his own plans. He encouraged potential emigrants to write either to himself or Van Raalte. But even with the intent to cooperate, a degree of rivalry entered in the competition to enroll persons under either man.

Hendrik Pieter Scholte was ready to leave his native land behind and move forward to America as the land of freedom and opportunity and the land where the poor could live with dignity and hope for the future under God. In his new Pella, his "city of refuge," Scholte's leadership talents, his vision for the future, and his love for personal freedom nourished by faith would result in the community that flourishes in America today.

CHAPTER 18

Significance of Hendrik Pieter Scholte's Vision of Church and State

Emo Bos

It is worth investigating where Hendrik Pieter Scholte received his outstanding political ideas about church and state, what he did with them, and whether his views were constant, consistent, and useful for the Dutch and for American churches and society.

On 11 December 1850, Hendrik P. Scholte's friend and supporter, Johan A. Wormser, wrote Guillaume Groen van Prinster: "During the *Afscheiding* I constantly had to fret between the rashness of Scholte, the narrow-mindedness of Van Velzen, and the prevarication of Brummelkamp."[1]

Perhaps Wormser painted this somewhat one-sidedly, but Scholte was someone who threw himself into a case with great enthusiasm, was

---

[1] Johan Stellingwerff, *Amsterdamse emigranten: onbekende brieven uit de prairie van Iowa, 1846-1873* (Amsterdam: Buijten & Schipperheijn, 1975), 354. An enlarged English-language edition is *Iowa Letters: Dutch Immigrants on the American Frontier*, ed. Robert P. Swierenga, trans. Walter Lagerwey (Grand Rapids: Eerdmans, 2004). Lagerwey translates the phrase: "And so in the *Afscheiding* (secession), I have always had to plod along with the rashness of Scholte, the closed-mindednes of Van Velzen, and the vacillating of Brummelkamp," 627.

Fig. 18.1. Wouter Verschuur, *Ten Days Campaign* (*Rijksmuseum*)

thick-skinned about the opinion of others, functioned obstinately, and sometimes abruptly changed his mind. He did so in the ecclesiastical as well as in the political arena. Scholte had an intense relationship with the proponents of the Church Order of Dort after 1834, while later he pursued passionately a church without denominational connections. During his time in America he joined the Whigs at first, after which he affiliated with Democrats, and in 1859, from one day to the next, he became a Republican.[2]

Was the capriciousness also manifested in his vision of the relationship between church and state? This is an important question, because Scholte had outspoken ideas on this subject. These ideas were also germaine to the issue of freedom of religion, a subject on which Scholte deviated from the prevailing opinion, also in his own circle.

Fighting for king and state

As a student at Leiden University, Scholte was predisposed to the king and state. When the Southern Netherlands (Belgium today) seceded from the Northern Netherlands in 1830 and King Willem

---

[2] Hans Krabbendam, *Vrijheid in het verschiet: Nederlandse emigratie naar Amerika, 1840-1940* (Hillversum: Verloren, 2006), 258-60.

I called for volunteers to defend national unity, Scholte immediately signed up. Characteristically, he purchased a uniform made of cloth finer than that of his fellow theology students, Anthony Brummelkamp and Simon van Velzen, who also had joined the volunteers.[3] The students were stationed in a barracks in Breda for almost eleven months, where they received training as *tirailleur* (skirmishers). Skirmishers formed the front lines to confront enemy infantrymen and slow their advance. It is not surprising that "Hein" Scholte belonged to that group; he felt at home on the front lines.

On 2 August 1831 the volunteers engaged the rebellious Southern provinces under the leadership of the Prince of Orange and won early victories. Brussels was next. But then the tide turned. The French came to the aid of the rebels, and the Prince had to withdraw against such a mighty force. The Ten Days Campaign ended a few days later. Although the army had not reached its goal, the soldiers were fêted on their return. Hein Scholte was proud his entire life for fighting in this campaign.[4]

Scholte's vision on church and state sharpened by persecution

The scene changed four years after that famous campaign, when King Willem I persecuted his faithful soldier, who had become a seceded minister. Scholte was arrested and incarcerated in the prison of Appingedam. Not long afterward, soldiers compelled him and his sick wife to leave the parsonage. But Scholte continued to preach for Reformed Seceded groups, which resulted in his being criminally persecuted and fined. That was the norm for many seceded leaders. The authorities considered them deviants, religious ignoramuses, and fanatics, who transgressed the law with their meetings and were a danger to the Reformed Church and the unity of the state. It was during the time of persecution that Scholte developed his ideas about the separation of church and state. He published articles in his journal, *De Reformatie*, pleading before courts of justice and petitioning the the king for redress. He published a number of these pleas later in book form.

Scholte developed into an outstanding fighter for the right of freedom of religion, as well as for human rights. In greater degree than can be seen in his clerical brothers, he had a well-founded vision

---

[3] G. Keizer, *De Afscheiding van 1834* (Kampen: J. H. Kok, 1934), 521.
[4] See Mees te Velde in *Anthony Brummelkamp 1811-1888* (Barneveld: De Vuurbaak, 1988), 37-39, about the Ten Days Campaign. Scholte's pride can be gleaned from an article by author/journalist J. B. Newhall in the *Burlington Hawkeye* in 1847, whom Scholte mistakenly calls professor. See H. P. Scholte, *Eene Stem uit Pella* (Amsterdam: Hoogkamer, 1848), 54.

of a citizen's right to serve God and the closely allied necessity for the independence of the church and the state. His seceded colleagues, Revs. Helenius De Cock and Simon Van Velzen, also advocated freedom of religion, but they did so by appealing to Article 36 of the Belgic Confession, which charged the authorities to protect true religion and combat false doctrine.[5] This basis would protect only adherents of the Reformed faith, who wished to return to the state of affairs as it was before the French Revolution—complete freedom for an official, public church.

Scholte saw that differently. Persecution in his view was a consequence of the centuries-old tie between church and state, in which church and state are blended. Scholte's requests on behalf of the congregations he served, such as in Amsterdam, breathed an entirely different spirit. He appealed to the king for freedom of religion and for punishment for those who disturbed public worship services, given that the authorities carry the sword to punish evildoers and protect the godly. The Amsterdam request warns the authorities emphatically not to blend the spiritual and secular police. Using history as a guide, the petitioners showed that such a mix leads to confusion.

Subsequently, Scholte asked the authorities to allow the church to rely on the Lord's governance and the ecclesiastical polity that He ordained. The state should have nothing to do with the church. After all, as the Amsterdam brothers stated, one does not have to check the Napoleonic Code to determine where Christ gathers his church. Neither does the recognition of the king present a criterium. The Amsterdam request goes far in asserting that the state must rank Jews, Christians, and atheists as equals.[6]

The request quotes Article 36 of the Belgic Confession, which declares that the Christian rulers and church members must use only the Bible, not the sword, to fight against idolatry, false religion, and the rule of the Antichrist.[7] Scholte clearly had a constricted view of the scope of Article 36.

Because of persecution, Scholte, who already rejected human rules in matters of faith, arrived increasingly at the view that the church

---

[5] E. Bos, "De Afscheiding: Afscheid van artikel 36 NGB," in *175 jaar Afscheiding van 1834*, eds. George Harinck and Mees te Velde (Barneveld: De Vuurbaak, 2012), 80-82.

[6] For the text of the Amsterdam requests, see: *De Reformatie*, 1837, I, 2-25; Cornelis Smits, *De Afscheiding van 1834*, de Classes Gorinchem, 1:36-38 (Oudkarspel: De Nijverheid, 1971), and 2: 24-25 (Dordrecht: J. P. van den Tol, 1974).

[7] *De Reformatie*, 1837, I, 21.

Fig. 18.2 Summons to pay fine for meeting illegally, December 1836

had nothing to do with the authorities.[8] He fleshed out these ideas in *De Reformatie*. It is striking that in church-state issues, he distanced himself explicitly from the "Réveil man," Alexandre Rodolphe Vinet (1797-1847).[9] Scholte noted explicitly that this Swiss scholar "published a very important work, in which the main purpose is to show the necessity of the separation of church and state." But that volume, whatever merit it may contain, is built on a philosophical foundation, not on God's Word. That foundation or principle is "the necessity of making public religious convictions."[10]

Scholte's abhorrence of philosophy is remarkable. He is of the opinion that philosophy is like a vehicle for robbery, through which

---

[8] He wrote the attorney Anne Maurits van Hall in August 1836 that he did not expect much good to come from the government "as long as it continues to interfere in the affairs of the church." Smits, *De Afscheiding van 1834*, 5:297. See also Te Velde, *Brummelkamp*, 345.

[9] Vinet, who was born in Ouchy (Vaud), is generally regarded as a brilliant theologian and historian. After serving as a docent, he became professor of French literature in Basel and in 1837 professor of practical theology in Lausanne. Already in 1826 Vinet had won a competition with his *Mémoire en faveur de la liberté de cultes*. He called for a complete separation of church and state. His motto was: "And where the Spirit of the Lord is, there is liberty" (2 Cor. 3:17). Vinet fought all his life against the interference of the state in ecclesiastical affairs. His works so impressed Scholte that Isaac Da Costa, who himself was in favor of a close relationship between church and state, warned him in a letter of 8 February 1843 against the ideas of Vinet. Smits, *De Afscheiding van 1834*, 6:90-93. The discussion focused on the interpretation of John 18:36. For Vinet's doctrine of the state, see W. P. Keijzer, *Alexandre Rodolphe Vinet 1797-1847* (Amsterdam: Uitgevers Mij. Holland, 1946), 150-62, and M. Elisabeth Kluit, *Het protestantse reveil in Nederland en daarbuiten 1815–1865* (Amsterdam: H. J. Paris N. V., 1970), 103-5.

[10] A. Vinet, *Essai sur la manifestation de Convictions religieuses et sur la separation de l'Église et de État envisagée comme consequence nécessaire et comme garantie du principe* (Paris: Paulin, 1842, Google ebook); *De Reformatie*, 1843, 2ᵉ Series, IV, 237-38.

the faithful could be seduced. It is especially philosophy that caused confusion among Christians. Appealing to Genesis 3, he stated that Satan was the first teacher of philosophy. The Word of God is the only weapon against such teaching. This gospel is a gift to childlike believers and not to the wise.[11] Scholte's views of the state are therefore based exclusively on the Bible and the history of government set forth in it. In this he showed himself a disciple of Willem Bilderdijk and Isaac da Costa.

Essence of Scholte's views on civil authorities

The nucleus of Scholte's views can be found in John 18:36, in which Christ says to Pilate: "My Kingdom is not of this world." According to Scholte, Christ indicates in this that the kingdom of God is different from an earthly kingdom. The weapons are also different; the armor of the kingdom of God is not physical (2 Cor. 10:4; Eph. 6:13-19). And when the Lord's reign over the entire world begins, "they shall beat their swords into plow shares and their spears into pruning hooks" (Is. 2:4 and Micah 4:3).[12]

These two kingdoms are not to be confused, therefore, because the state is the devil's domain, and the church is Christ's body. When he postulated that the foundation of states is from the devil, he reasoned that human activities in the establishment of states are not caused by God, but come from the Evil One. The Holy Scriptures therefore have named him the overseer of the world. Scholte referred in that respect to the story of the temptation in the desert, where the devil showed Christ all the kingdoms of the world and their glories and said that he would give everything to him "if you worship me" (Matt. 4). Apparently the devil possesses such earthly kingdoms. It is striking that Christ did not deny that.[13]

The demonic principle of kingdoms does not mean that there can be no Christian rulers. After all, God declares that kings and rulers are subject to Him. Scholte also disavowed a Christian state that submits itself to Christ in the proclamation of the gospel. Such a state is an impossibility and leads to the mixing of state and church with undesirable consequences, such as to penalize those who deny Christ openly.[14]

---

[11] *De Reformatie*, 1843, 2ᵉ Series, IV, 271.
[12] "Scheiding van kerk en staat," *De Reformatie*, series 2, vol. 4, 1843: 165-73; "Nawoord" [epilogue] in the brochure, *Het strafregt in verband beschouwd met de vrijheid van geweten en godsdienst* (Amsterdam, 1842), and Smits, 6:90.
[13] "Kerk en Staat," *De Reformatie*, series 2, vol. 4: 248-49.
[14] Ibid., 240, 305, 311; "Scheiding van kerk en staat," ibid., 167.

Fig. 18.3. King Willem II
(*courtesy Nederlands Dagblad*)

Scholte offered the following definition of the state:

A state in whatever form is a collection of native people, united under a particular government, which, with the exception of the state of Israel, takes its principles not from God but from the devil, who is, however, with the people, under the rulership of the almighty supreme authority of God, so that everything must work together for the carrying out God's counsel.[15]

It is noteworthy that Scholte exempted Israel. He ascertains that the state of Israel was founded by God as a unique theocracy. God wishes to reign as king over his people. David, called as Israel's king, points forward to Christ's kingship. All of this was extraordinary and may not be aped by us. The Israel of the Old Testament cannot be, and may not be, a model for our governments. Scholte stated with a restrained intensity that "so-called Christendom has imagined itself with high opinion and impertinence and—against the express exhortation of the apostle [in Romans 11]—taken the place of Israel on this earth, after Israel's rejection."[16]

Scholte condemned any church that transferred the concepts of Zion, Jerusalem, and Canaan to herself, and considered the state of Israel as the model for earthly government. This misconception, in his view, led to sad consequences: government salaries to clergy, mixing ecclesiastical and civilian rule, repression, persecution of those who

[15] "*Kerk en Staat*, 4:249.
[16] "Scheiding van kerk en staat," 166.

do not agree with the mainstream church, and ultimately the decay of church and state. He named Roman Catholicism as an example of this conduct, which by whoring with the rulers of the earth will be hated in the long run and will perish in fire.[17]

His negative judgment of state and authority is also seen in his assertion that the governments of the world from Babel (in Genesis 11) until the coming of Christ are components of Nebuchadnezzar's statue and the animals about which Daniel speaks (Daniel 2 and 7). Scholte believed that he and his contemporaries were living during the age of the last world power. It was, of course, true that there was a single state, such as the Roman Empire, from which all states originated. Scholte expected the victory of the Lamb over all states in the foreseeable future. He warned, however: "We expect that before that revelation of the kingdom of the Redeemer, there first shall take place a unification with, and subjection of, the states to the Antichrist."[18]

Did Scholte's views change in America?

Around 1861, after living in Pella for fourteen years, Scholte wrote a so-called *narede* (epilogue), entitled *Aan de geloovigen in Nederland* (to the faithful in the Netherlands). In this work he dealt extensively with the relationship between church and state. First, he remarked that he had always given Caesar his due and obeyed earthly governments but that he refused to give Ceasar that which belonged to God.[19]

Once again, he condemned Babylon, the great whore of Revelation 17, who claimed both spiritual and worldly powers. Christ and Belial stand in total opposition. In 1857 Scholte wrote: "The more I have come, and still come, in close contact with the powers on earth, the more I am confirmed in my earlier conviction that the governments of this world are under the influence of the Overseer of this world." Thus, it is not surprising that he resisted any forms of theocracy, such as that of the Puritans, who introduced the Mosaic model for the Massachusetts colony in the seventeenth century.[20] Theocracy is a treacherous illusion; Pella did not belong in the church but in the world.[21]

[17] Ibid., 167.
[18] "Scheiding van kerk en staat," 167; "*Kerk en staat*," 248, 312, 321.
[19] *Kompleete uitgave van de officiëele stukken betreffende de uitgang uit het Nederl. Herv. Kerkgenootschap van de leeraren, H. P. Scholte, A. Brummelkamp, S. van Velzen, G. F. Gezelle Meerburg en dr. A. C. Van Raalte* (Kampen: S. van Velzen Jr, 1863), 1:227-88, esp. 254.
[20] J. J. L. van der Brugghen, 22 Oct. 1857, in Stellingwerff, *Amsterdamse emigranten*, 285 (quote), and *Iowa Letters*, 432; A. A. van Schelven, "Het Biblicisme der Puriteinen van Massachusetts," in *Uit den Strijd der Geesten: Historische Nasporingen* (Amsterdam: W. ten Have N. V., 1944), 111ff.
[21] Lubbertus Oostendorp, *H. P. Scholte* (Franeker: T. Wever, 1964), 161-62.

On church-state issues, Scholte thought not only of Rome but also of the various Protestant churches. In Europe as well as in the United States, the spirit of Babylon predominated. In the United States, religious societies and political parties were tied together. But this is a trap, as long as governments do not recognize unconditionally that the Lord Jesus is their king, law giver, and judge. Ever since the emperor Constantine, who paired church and state, the church had lost its freedom in Christ. The church should never accept financial support from the state, because that would link it with the servants of Satan. Babylon's time is running out. The seventh world-wide empire has commenced, and the Antichrist is preparing to fight with the Lamb. "Let us go forth therefore unto him without the camp, bearing his reproach," Scholte quoted from Hebrews 13:13. Since Scholte wrote this after his emigration to Pella, it is obvious that he did not modify his antithetical vision of church and state in his American years.[22]

Active political life nevertheless

One would expect that the negative vision of the state would have led Scholte to withdraw from public life, but on the contrary, in the Netherlands as well as in America, he proudly participated in military and political affairs, such as the Ten Days Campaign. In *De Reformatie* he discussed national and international issues, although with a focus on persecutions, judicial matters, and freedom of religion. He had personal contacts with King Willem III and friendly correspondence with the minister of worship about his policy and the right of (seceded) congregations to exist.[23]

While in America, Scholte increased his activities. He wrote political articles, held political lectures, visited political party conventions, and led actions for presidential candidates of his choice. He also offered free land to volunteers during the Civil War.[24] Furthermore, he occupied positions of authority in Pella. Some accused him even of having disregarded his shepherd's staff.[25] How should we explain all of this? Did Scholte, as a politician, act against his own philosophy of government?

---

[22] Ibid., 257-58, addendum C, 286-88, 176.
[23] He received the first series of the *Archives du Maison d'Orange* from King Willem III (Stellingwerf, *Amsterdamse emigranten*, 287, and *Iowa Letters*, 433).
[24] Baron van Zuylen van Nijevelt, in Smits, *Afscheiding van 1834*, 6:251-75; Jacob Van der Zee, *The Hollanders of Iowa* (Iowa City, IA: State Historical Society of Iowa, 1912), 230.
[25] *Sheboygan Nieuwsbode*, 24 June 1856.

Fig. 18.4. Scholte's library in the Scholte House (*courtesy Pella Historical Archives*)

Scholte himself saw no contradiction, and he did not wish to argue the point. He dismissed criticism that as a pastor he should not be involved in politics with the remark that clergymen, as citizens, should be free to express their sincere feelings about politics. Scholte had two reasons for political activism in America. First, he had a very positive view of his new fatherland.[26] He even wrote that the Babylonian world powers had been destroyed at the formation of the Union.[27] Moreover, America offered him greater opportunity to be actively engaged in politics than in the Netherlands.

In a more principial vein, Scholte insisted that it was the obligation of Christians to look for good lands in which to live, even across the whole world, although true goodness could be secured by conversion to God.[28] God institutes governments to restrain evil and, according to the apostle Paul, for the wellbeing of believers. A disciple of Christ, who knows the true character and nature of governments, and those who belong to the wealthy of this world, can be employed in it for the promotion of God's Kingdom. Yes, he can do so even freer, more independently and persistently, because it basically concerns an already victorious matter. Disappointments should not confuse or paralyze him, even when the kingdoms of this world are lost, because his citizenship is in heaven.[29]

---

[26] *Pella Gazette*, 5 July 1856. In his letter of 26 June 1841 to King Willem II, he used the freedom of religion as laid down in America as a model for the Netherlands; see E. Bos, *Soevereiniteit en religie. Godsdienstvrijheid onder de eerste Oranjevorsten*, 381; Bos, *Archiefstukken*, 4:443-44.

[27] Van der Zee, *Hollanders of Iowa*, 209; *Tweede Stem*, 21, 23.

[28] *De Toekomst*, 2, 64; Philip E. Webber, "Reassessing the Visionary Thinking of H. P. Scholte," in *The Sesquicentennial of Dutch Immigration: 150 Years of Ethnic Heritage*, eds. Larry J. Wagenaar and Robert P. Swierenga (Proceedings of the Association for the Advancement of Dutch American Studies, 1997), 92.

[29] "*Kerk en Staat*," 245, 317.

Contradiction

By positioning himself this way, Scholte avoided the Anabaptist pitfall of totally rejecting authority. Yet, there is tension between his view that the principles of the state are derived from Satan, while that same state engages in the many positive and constructive activities. Scholte tried to solve this tension by concluding that everything together is an outworking of God's counsel. But the word "together" is really one word too many, because it concerns both the devil and believers. In other words, there is a clear contradiction in Scholte's view of government.

The reason for this is that Scholte judged government too negatively. His views did not come from the Bible. Although the Bible often speaks negatively about the kingdoms of this world, it does not teach that their origins are always satanic. The picture of the kingdoms of this world in the Bible is ambivalent. On one hand, the kings and rulers gather in battle array to plot together against the Lord and his anointed (Psalm 2), but on the other hand, there is a summons to kings and judges to be wise and obedient and to serve the Lord and kiss the Son. The Holy Scriptures teach us that governments are institutions of God. Paul writes that they are the ministers of God "to thee for good."[30] And this at a time when Roman authorities occupied Israel. The well being of citizens is served by maintaining the law. Kings are, therefore, occasionally called judges. The problem is that the power of the sword through devilish brainwashing is often loosened from this principle, which results in the misuse of power and arbitrariness. The Bible speaks therefore of kings who scorn law and plot against the Kingdom of God.[31]

It would be wrong, however, to consider this situation as standard for authorities and states. If they were all rooted in the devil, Psalm 2 would not call kings to be wise. The prophet Jeremiah also teaches us that we ought not disparage governments. He commanded Israelites in exile to build houses in the strange land, to live in it, to plant trees, and to eat of the fruit of the land. They also needed to marry and beget children. Very importantly, the prophet—speaking in the Lord's name—adds "and seek the peace of the city whither I have caused you to be carried away captives, and pray unto the Lord for it; for in the peace thereof shall ye have peace."[32] Also while in Babylon, the prophet

---

[30] Daniel 2:37, 38; John 19:11; Romans 13:4, but also the whole chapter.
[31] For example, in Psalm 2, the kingdoms in Daniel 7, and in Revelation 17 and 19.
[32] Jeremiah 29:4-8.

Daniel is positively disposed toward the regime. The Bible shows us that believers also have a political task in the civil realm; the cultural mandate remains despite the Fall.[33]

Scholte's abhorrence of philosophy is striking. In his day, philosophy was largely in the hands of Enlightenment and revolutionary theorists. This may explain his loathing for it. But his reaction, including that to Vinet, is nevertheless a form of Biblicism. He was, therefore, on par with his equally biblicistic teacher Da Costa. One needs to recognize that questions regarding polity and political decision making cannot be deduced from the Bible alone.

Significance of Scholte's vision

In spite of a certain inner contradiction and Biblicism, it is intriguing to consider Scholte's view of the state. He challenges believers to evaluate their views of the proper role of government in a largely secular age.

The greatest implication of Scholte's vision is his demand to break all ties between church and state. The Netherlands' government's support of churches and Christian institutions and the payment of salaries of pastors and ecclesiastical workers was anathema to him. Churches ought to exist independently from the state. I agree with him that this is indeed a *sine qua non* for genuine freedom of religion.

Additionally, Scholte's rejection of theocracy and working toward a Christian state is noteworthy. In this he preceded Groen van Prinsterer and the early Abraham Kuyper.[34] Some Christians today, unfortunately, still strive for these goals. Scholte also rightfully pointed out that the Christian church throughout the centuries too easily adopted the Old Testament distinctiveness of the people of Israel, and thereby set the state of Israel as a model for the earthly state.

In the Netherlands, Scholte's writings in *De Reformatie* about persecution by government led to changes in governmental policy. Groen van Prinsterer, while employed at the court of King Willem I, incorprated Scholte's views in his brochure "*De maatregelen tegen de Afgescheidenen aan het staatsregt getoetst.*"[35] This figuratively was like throwing a stone in the pond surrounding the Binnenhof, the seat of

---

[33] Genesis 1:28 and 2:15.
[34] E. Bos, "Balanceren tussen volkssoevereiniteit en theocratie," in *Tijdschrift voor Religie, Recht en Beleid* (2011- 13): 31-51.
[35] G. Groen van Prinsterer, *De maatregelen tegen de afgescheidenen aan het staatsregt getoetst* (Leiden, 1837).

government in The Hague. Also Scholte's zeal for seeking government recognition of the seceded congregations, who insisted on being the continuing *Gereformeerde Kerk,* emanated from his views on the separation of church from state. In his eyes the king did not have the right to decide who was *Gereformeerd.* This was the argument, as publicized by Groen van Prinsterer, that won recognition and freedom for the Utrecht congregation. Most other *Afgescheiden* congregations followed later, albeit hesitantly.

Scholte's vision drove the seceded congregations to stop seeking financial support from the government. Increasingly, voices were heard within these churches for the separation of church and state.[36] This led to the action of the general synod of the *Gereformeerde Kerk* in 1905 to eliminate the phrase, "to suppress and to eradicate all idolatry and false religion, and to utterly destroy the reign of the Antichrist" from Article 36 of the Belgic Confession.[37]

The First Amendment of the US Constitution—"Congress shall make no law respecting an establishment of religion, or prohibiting the free exercise thereof"—guaranteed the separation of church and state and freedom of religion. But this did not obviate the need for Scholte to continue the struggle against mixing church and state. With repugnance, he saw too many attempts to establish ties between church and state. We should not too readily dismiss his spirituality and pre-millinarian theology. His radicalism and independent proclivities, although leading him again and again into more isolation among his own people, give food for thought and serve as a warning for Christians today.

In summary, Scholte's writings about the relationship between church and state continue to be relevant. While he can be criticized, he nevertheless sought the full freedom of the church of Christ. His contribution to the struggle for religious freedom, for the freedom of the church from the state, is worthy of attention. The great Dutch jurist Paul Scholten said it best: "There is not one good solution for the relationship between church and state. In essence the problem is insoluble. It is not possible to have a lasting peace between church and

---

[36] Anthony Brummelkamp received the torch from Scholte. See *De Afscheiding. Afscheid van artikel 36 van de Nederlandse Geloofsbelijdenis,* 86-7.

[37] It was only in 1958 that the Christian Reformed Church revised Article 36 of the Belgic Confession. The previous English translation was judged unbiblical, because it asserted that it is the duty of the state to see to it that the gospel is preached everywhere.

state. There is not a single government that does not have, in one way or another, a world and life view. Even those states that preach neutrality do not achive it. There is a constant need to find a solution within the current legal order, even if only temporary. The foundation is crucial, and that is Christian freedom."[38] Scholte was aware of that.

---

[38] Paul Scholten, *Verzamelde geschriften*, 4 vols. (Zwolle: Uitgevers-Maatschappij W.E.J. Tjeenk Willink, 1949), 1:428.

CHAPTER 19

From Amsterdam and Antwerp to Otley and Harrison: The Rise, Fall, and Restoration of the Maverick Rev. Arie Gerrit Zigeler

Earl Wm. Kennedy

A. G. Zigeler (1833-1915) is a familiar name to a few Belgian scholars as a pioneer Reformed pastor in Antwerp who later served large independent churches in Amsterdam, while he is known, if at all, in the United States as the minister of small, rural midwestern congregations of the Reformed Church in America.[1] The story of the strange circumstances surrounding his move from Europe to the New World in 1872 was published in Dutch in 1874, but never in English.

Zigeler's early years in Amsterdam and pioneer ministry, 1856-1864, in Antwerp

Arie Gerrit (always "A. G." in print) Zigeler came from a middle-class, *Hervormd* Amsterdam broker's family, of German extraction.[2] He

---

[1] A. de Raaf, *Bewaar het pand: een eeuw Protestantse Kerk aan de Bexstraat te Antwerpen* (Antwerp: Christusgemeente, 1993), seriatim; "Ziegler [*sic*], A. G.," in Russell L. Gasero, *Historical Directory of the Reformed Church in America 1628-2000* (Grand Rapids: Eerdmans, 2001), 479. Zigeler's descendants today seem unaware of his existence. A more detailed version of the present article, too long for this publication, is forthcoming (Holland, MI: Van Raalte Press).

[2] Centraal Bureau voor Genealogie, Digitale studiezaal: familieadvertenties tot 1970, at http://www.cbg.nl; Archief van het Bevolkingsregister 1851-53 and 1874-93,

Fig. 19.1. Rev. Arie Gerrit Zigeler, c. 1900 (*drawing by Nella Kennedy*)

was probably educated for a career in business and worked as an office clerk before being drafted into the national militia at age nineteen.[3] Possibly as the result of a conversion experience, he entered the small Amsterdam theological school of the Free [Presbyterian] Church of Scotland in 1853, where he was exposed to the evangelical, ecumenical, Reformed piety of the *Réveil,* the "Christian Friends," and the Evangelical Alliance.[4]

---

and Burgerlijke Stand Amsterdam, 1832, at Stadsarchief Amsterdam (henceforth SAA); on the father's career: *Algemeen Handelsblad* (Amsterdam), 23 Jan 1850, 8 Dec. 1853, 13 Feb., 20 Mar. 1856, 6 Feb., 24, 26 Oct. 1857, 11, 20 Jan., 25 Nov. 1862, 29 Nov. 1864, 18 Sept. 1865, 16, 18 Oct. 1866, 18 Oct. 1871, in Historische Kranten: Nederlandse dagbladen uit de 17e, 18e, 19e en 20e eeuw, at http://kranten.kb.nl; www.ancestry.com; www.wiewaswie.nl.

[3] When he was inducted, Zigeler ("Arij Gerrit Ziegeler" [*sic*]) stood 5' 8 1/2" and was living with his parents, http://militieregisters.nl/zoek?l00=amsterdam&p04=arij+gerrit&p06=ziegeler.

[4] "Achtiende Bijeenkomst van Christelijke Vrienden, gehouden te Amsterdam in het Casino, Op Dingsdag en Woensdag 11 en 12 Oct. 1853," in O. G. Heldring, ed., *De Vereeniging: Christelijke Stemmen*, vol. 8 (Amsterdam: H. Höveker, 1854), 306; O. W. Dubois, "Christelijke Vrienden," in *Christelijke Encyclopedie*, George Harinck et al., eds. (Kampen: Kok, 2005), 316; Johan Stellingwerff, *Iowa Letters: Dutch Immigrants on the American Frontier*, ed. by Robert P. Swierenga, transl. by Walter Lagerwey (Grand Rapids: Eerdmans, 2004), 223-24, 226-28, 367; M. Elisabeth Kluit, *Het protestantse Réveil in Nederland en daarbuiten 1815-1865* (Amsterdam: Uitgeverij H. J. Paris N. V., 1970), 474-75. On the relationship between the Scottish evangelicals and the Dutch *Réveil,* see J. van den Berg, "De 'Evangelical Revival' in Schotland

The seminary existed from 1852 to 1861, with a curriculum modeled after that of the Free Church's New College in Edinburgh but with commitment to the Reformed Three Standards of Unity. It stressed evangelism, especially of the Jews, since its main teachers were the premillennialists Isaac da Costa and Rev. Carl A. F. Schwartz, both converts from Judaism.[5] Zigeler would remain loyal throughout his career to the spirit of the *Réveil* wing of the *Hervormde Kerk*, with its experiential, evangelistic, and mildly orthodox Reformed impulses, inclusive of other Protestants. Seceder separatism seems never to have appealed to him.

The exogenous Scottish seminary's graduates were not welcome, however, in either *Hervormd* or Seceder pulpits, so when Zigeler left the school in 1856, he went to serve with the Belgian Christian Missionary Church (BCMC) in starting a church in Antwerp, where he remained until 1864. After an initial traumatic experience facing a violent, gin-fortified, Roman Catholic mob,[6] Zigeler's difficult ministry flourished modestly for several years, so that in 1860, he was ordained by the BCMC (in a service led by Schwartz, who was visiting) and was given a larger building in which to preach (with room for at least two hundred); he

---

en het Nederlandse Réveil," in *Documentatieblad voor de Nederlandse Kerkgeschiedenis voor 1800*, vol. 13 (1990), 48-73. The mid-nineteenth century saw the convergence of chiliasm, Jewish evangelism, the Evangelical Alliance (1846), Protestant foreign missions, and anti-Roman Catholicism (all involving both the Free Church of Scotland and the Christian Friends in varying degrees), on the one hand, and resurgent Catholic Ultramontanism under Pius IX, on the other hand, along with nascent dechristianization in Europe.

[5] "Institution at Amsterdam," in *The Home and Foreign Record of the Free Church of Scotland*, vol. 3, *Aug. 1852-July 1853* (Edinburgh: James Nichol, 1853), Sept. 1852, 55; "Amsterdam," in *The Home and Foreign Record*, vol. 4, *Aug. 1853-July 1854*, Mar. 1854, 221-22; "Mission at Amsterdam," in *The Home and Foreign Record*, vol. 5, *Aug. 1854-July 1855*, June 1855, 284-87; Robert Young, *Light in Lands of Darkness* (New York: Cassell and Company, 1884), 372-76; *Proceedings of the General Assembly of the Free Church of Scotland. Held at Edinburgh, May 1854* (Edinburgh: John Greig & Son, 1854), 125-26 (copy of an English-language circular detailing the study program at the Amsterdam school). Schwartz and Da Costa were enthusiastically received (with applause and laughter recorded in the minutes!) when they spoke at length at the General Assembly of the Free Church of Scotland in 1855; *Proceedings of the General Assembly of the Free Church of Scotland. Held at Edinburgh, May 1855* (Edinburgh: John Greig & Son, [1855]), 22-29 (27-28 on the Amsterdam seminary), 80, 85-88. All book titles are at http://books.google.com/books.

[6] De Raaf, *Bewaar het pand*, 20-23; Protestantse Cultuurkring Antwerpen, "7 januari 1857. Protestantse bijeenkomst ruw verstoord," at http://www.albertschweitzer.be/1857_verstoordebijeenkomst.htm; Protestantse Cultuurkring Antwerpen, "het Réveil en het Schots seminarie." The uproar seems to have been the talk of the town, with a lot press coverage. Also graffiti was aimed at Zigeler and his ilk, e.g., *Joden* (Jews) and *keeskop* (cheese head).

had earlier expressed the unrealistic hope that he would fill a sanctuary seating a thousand people.[7] In 1859 Zigeler married Jannetje Adriana Plugge, a twenty-year-old Dutch woman, six years his junior, who had likely been one of his catechumens; she was a daughter of an immigrant harbor pilot from Vlissingen, Zeeland.[8]

Early in the 1860s, however, Zigeler became deeply discouraged with his ministry's minimal results, especially among Roman Catholics.[9] Between March 1862 and January 1863 the BCMC sent him on many forays into the Netherlands to raise money for its underfunded work; these absences from his Antwerp ministry may have contributed to its further decline.[10] On the other hand, he was developing his gift for fund raising—a talent he would employ again in Amsterdam and many years later in New York.

It was not that Zigeler did not work hard in Antwerp. He preached without notes (for lack of time) and with a loud voice (that the Catholic neighbors could hear through open windows in warm weather) three times a week (Sunday morning and evening and Wednesday evening), led daily prayer meetings, and catechized children (including those of the local *Hervormde Kerk* when it was without a pastor). He and a local *Hervormd* pastor, a friend, exchanged pulpits and, a few months before Zigeler's departure, began co-editing a weekly newspaper.[11] He was,

---

[7] De Raaf, *Bewaar het pand*, 22, 25-27, 54-55.

[8] The Plugge family arrived in Antwerp in 1855, the year before Zigeler and four years before his marriage. De Raaf, *Bewaar het pand*, 54. The 1900 census (taken in June) states that the Zigelers had been married 49 years, while the 1910 census (taken in April) says 50, thus giving only partial support for De Raaf's estimate of spring 1859; www.ancestry.com (1900 and 1910 census); *Vonnis* (decision) regarding the petition of Jannetje Adriana Plugge, 24 Apr. 1872, Arrondissementsrechtbank te Amsterdam (district court in Amsterdam), access number 198, inventory number 3482, SAA (she declared that she married in 1859, but no day or month is given); thanks to graduate student Kiki Varekamp of the University of Amsterdam for searches and scans of this and other archival materials in Amsterdam and Haarlem about the real estate of A. G. Zigeler and his wife in 1869 and 1872 (cited elsewhere as well). The Plugge family's arrival in Antwerp was registered on 25 Aug. 1855; François [sic] Plugge, in "Belgium, Antwerp, Police Immigration, 1840-1930," nr. 12409, at www.familysearch.org.

[9] De Raaf, *Bewaar het pand*, 27-28. Attendance figures fluctuated a great deal, with very few regular attendees.

[10] Ibid., 28-29; digital newspaper websites of the Royal Library in The Hague, http://kranten.kb.nl; the Leiden Regional Archive, http://leiden.courant.nu; the Dordrecht Regional Archive, http://www.regionaalarchiefdordrecht.nl/collectie/kranten.

[11] De Raaf, *Bewaar het pand*, 19, 23-24, 27-30, 58; Dick Wursten email 20 May 2013 (on catechizing *Hervormd* children). There was occasional cooperation between the Belgian *Hervormde Kerk* and the BCMC. For Zigeler's publishing work in Belgium, see ibid., 189-92. He also produced evangelistic tracts, e.g., *Waarheen?* and *Het*

however, criticized by a few of his flock for his strict doctrine, preaching too much on sin (and requiring genuine confession before forgiveness), and that he was "too young, too proud, and too insensitive."[12] After seven-and-a-half years, Zigeler left Antwerp for a church in Amsterdam, although his interest in the work of the BCMC continued, that is, he labored occasionally for it, not always successfully, as a paid fundraiser in northwestern Germany.[13]

In a significant, final "extra-curricular activity" in the Netherlands shortly before he moved back to his home town, Zigeler received wide public exposure as one of the nineteen speakers at the first Dutch, national, "evangelical," missionary festival, held on 6 August 1863 outdoors on an estate near Arnhem. Estimates of attendance range from six to ten thousand. During the day and evening, three men gave plenary addresses, while in the later afternoon, the other sixteen speakers, including Zigeler and Revs. Willem van der Kleij (Zigeler's later nemesis) and Anthony Brummelkamp, were divided into four groups and preached for twenty minutes each at four different wooded spots (so that auditors at each venue heard four consecutive messages).[14]

---

groote gebod, issued in Brussels by the Christlijke Evangelische Boekhandel, in 1864 and 1865; Fr. de Potter, compiler, *Vlaamsche Bibliographie, of Lyst der Nederduitsche Boeken, in België Sedert 1830 Uitgegeven,* vol. 3, *Tijdperk 1856-1867* (Gent: W. Rogghé, Boekhandelaar, 1868), 10, at http://books.google.com/books.

[12] De Raaf, *Bewaar het pand,* 23-24.

[13] A. G. Zigeler, Amsterdam, to L. Anet, 6 Oct. 1864, 23 Jan., 21 Feb. 1865, 25, 27 Mar., 12 Apr. 1867. Zigeler's correspondence with the Swiss-born Rev. Léonard Anet of Brussels, general secretary of the BCMC and active participant in the Evangelical Alliance (and whose wife, whom Zigeler knew also, was a Dutch-born woman whose parents were English; www.ancestry.com), gives an indication of his attachment to the BCMC. The collection of letters (1856-71) by (and about) Zigeler, almost entirely in French (showing his relative facility in the language), held in the Archives of the United Protestant Church in Belgium, Brussels (Zigeler, A., in *Anciens Ouvriers,* file box 686), was kindly photographed and sent to me by Dick Wursten, the denominational archivist.

[14] Zigeler and Van der Kleij were two of the men who replaced six of the originally chosen speakers (one was Zigeler's mentor Schwartz), who had had to drop out. Brummelkamp, unlike many Seceder leaders, was very enthusiastic about this ecumenical event, and referred to it in a report as a "camp meeting" (in English, untranslated). The festival was sponsored by at least eleven missionary societies and was a continuation of the spirit of the Christian Friends and of the *Réveil. Programma van Het Eerste Algemeen Evangelisch Zendingsfeest, te Houden te Wolfhezen, den 6den Augustus 1863* (Rotterdam: G. B. Poeschmann, 1863), 3-16; Melis te Velde, *Anthony Brummelkamp (1811-1888)* (Barneveld: Uitgeverij de Vuurbaak, 1988), 383-85. Had Schwartz suggested to the organizing committee that Zigeler, his former student whom he had ordained, replace him as a speaker? *Het Eerste Algemeen Evangelisch Zendingsfeest, den 6den Augustus 1863 te Wolfhezen gehouden, Herdacht. Verslag van wege de Commissie* (Rotterdam: G. B. Poeschmann, 1863), 28, 32-34, 62-65, 72,

Zigeler's independent ministry in Amsterdam, "Rehoboth," and disaster (1864-1872)

Although Zigeler's ministry in Antwerp ended in frustration, his eight-year ministry in his hometown of Amsterdam began hopefully but ended in disaster. He first served for less than a year as a successor of the popular evangelist Jan de Liefde, a chiliast (*inter alia*) and former Baptist who had founded his own "Free Evangelical Church" (the precursor of a Dutch denomination of that name). This independent, vaguely Reformed congregation in Amsterdam was then meeting in a rented hall called *Tecum habita* (literally, "live with yourself"). De Liefde stepped down in 1862, and his successor, A. Hardenberg, proved unsatisfactory (a good exegete but a poor preacher) and was released after about a year's service. This gave Zigeler his opportunity, but he fared no better, since the congregation found him "too churchly" and disapproved of his introduction of infant baptism.[15] This should occasion no surprise, since he was trained in the Reformed standards and had signed the Belgic Confession in Antwerp.

Next, for a couple of years, starting early 1865, Zigeler followed Schwartz (who had resigned in 1864) as pastor of the Scottish Missionary Church, which had been connected with the seminary, but Zigeler was released from this position, reportedly because something "fishy" (*niet zuiver*; literally, "impure") had been sensed about him "for some time."[16] Nevertheless, Zigeler was apparently so much in demand

---

73-76; A. Brummelkamp, "Camp-Meeting, of Algemeen Evangelisch Nationaal Zendingsfeest te Wolfhezen, 6 Aug. 1863," in O. G. Heldring, ed., *De Vereeniging: Christelijke Stemmen*, vol. 18 (Amsterdam: H. Höveker, 1864), 156-57.

[15] F. L. Bos, "Liefde, Jan de," in D. Nauta et al., eds., *Biografisch Lexicon voor de Geschiedenis van het Nederlandse Protestantisme*, vol. 2 (Kampen: Uitgeversmaatschappij J. H. Kok, 1983), 2:306-8; Kluit, *Het protestantse Réveil*, 494; G. A. Wumkes, *De opkomst en vestiging van het Baptisme in Nederland* (Sneek: A. J. Osinga, 1912), 123, at http://www.totheildesvolks.nl/jdeliefde/wumkes/hoofdstuk_4.htm; De Raaf, *Bewaar het pand*, 56.

[16] Bos, "Liefde, Jan de," in Nauta, et al., eds., *Biografisch Lexicon*, 2:307; A. G. Zigeler, Amsterdam, to L. Anet, 21 Feb. 1865 (the Free Church of Scotland has called him to its Amsterdam pulpit), 27 Mar. 1867 (he expects not to return to preaching in "Schwartz's chapel," but "the Lord will give me another field of work"); W. Van der Kleij, "Een Woord van Ernstige Waarschuwing aan de Gereformeerde Gemeente te Chicago," *De Hope*, 11 Mar. 1874 ("fishy"). Kuyper's infant Free University met 1880-83 in the Scottish Missionary Church building; once a theater, it is now again a theater, Amsterdam's oldest, *De Kleine Komedie aan de Amstel*; J. C. Rullmann, "Schotsche Zendingskerk (De)," in F. W. Grosheide et al., eds., *Christelijke Encyclopaedie voor het Nederlandsche Volk*, vol. 5 (Kampen: J. H. Kok, 1929), 120; "De Kleine Komedie," at http://en.wikipedia.org.

Fig. 19.2. *De Kleine Komedie*, formerly Scottish Missionary Church (*http://commons.wikimedia.org/wiki/ File:Klein-komedie.jpg*)

in the mid-1860s that, only a month after he had taken the Scottsh church's call, some "friends of truth" in Utrecht asked him to be their pastor; they would have paid him an annual salary of one thousand guilders (plus free parsonage), while he reportedly claimed (with an element of hubris?) that a Hamburg congregation was offering him fifteen hundred guilders; he declined both calls.[17] Zigeler's place and type of ministry between the spring of 1867 and late 1869 are unknown.

Then, on Sunday, 12 December 1869, Zigeler dedicated his very own *Evangelisatie-gebouw "Rehoboth"*[18] (evangelization building "Rehoboth"), in an evident imitation of De Liefde's *Eben-Haëzer* fifteen years earlier, which had to be abandoned because of its heavy mortgage.[19] How had the recently "fishy" but apparently magnetic Zigeler gathered a following, collected funds, and overseen the construction of Rehoboth? All that is known is that he bought three house lots in February

---

[17] *Utrechtsch Provinciaal en Stedelijk Dagblad*, 25 March 1865, at http://kranten.delpher.nl.

[18] "Rehoboth" was the name that Jacob gave a well in Genesis 26:22 because, as he said, "the Lord has made room for us, and we shall be fruitful in the land"; thus a roomy place—a "place of enlargement and flourishing."

[19] J. C. Rullmann, "Liefde (Jan de)," in F. W. Grosheide et al., eds., *Christelijke Encyclopaedie voor het Nederlandsche Volk*, vol. 3 (Kampen: J. H. Kok, n.d. [ca. 1928]), 666.

Fig. 19.3. Zigeler's evangelization building, Rehoboth (*drawing by Nella Kennedy*)

1869 for 4,250 guilders, cleared them, and had an impressive edifice erected before the end of the year.[20] With its galleries, consistory room, custodian's house, and grounds,[21] it was the capstone of Zigeler's career thus far, a kind of fulfillment of his earlier dream of filling a thousand-seat church in Antwerp. Less than a month before the dedication, he had written the BCMC, inviting it to send a delegation to attend the opening ceremony.[22]

The newspaper announcement of the sanctuary's dedication stated that it had been built for thirty-seven thousand guilders (about $500,000 USD current), all from "free-will offerings."[23] Three days after the ceremony, Zigeler began issuing shares for his "evangelization building" in the amount of thirty-five thousand guilders at four percent annual interest; there were 350 shares of one hundred guilders

[20] Land Registry, access no. 83.2 (Kadaster en hypotheekkantoren Noord-Holland), inventory no. 1969 (86) (inventory kantoor Amsterdam), Noord-Hollands Archief, Haarlem; purchase of the lots 4 Feb. 1869.
[21] These specifications for Rehoboth were given in the ad for its sale in 1872; *Het Nieuws van den Dag: Kleine Courant* (Amsterdam), 22, 23 May 1872. For a list of its furnishings at that juncture (including permanent benches, 92 chairs, organ, two hymnbooks, but no psalters or sacramentals), see 25 June 1872, in Archief van notaris G. Ruys, no. 571 in Archief van notarissen ter standplaats Amsterdam, access no. 5075, inventory no. 22012, SAA.
[22] A. G. Zigeler, Amsterdam, to L. Anet, 16 Nov. 1869.
[23] *Dagblad van Zuidholland en 's Gravenhage*, 19 Dec. 1869.

Fig. 19.4. Share issued 15 December 1869 for Rehoboth
(*courtesy author*)

each, dated 15 December 1869, individually signed by him.[24] This was evidently to provide a modest return for those who had voluntarily invested in the church's construction; in essence, they had advanced Zigeler the funds, so that he would not be hemmed in by a mortgage (contrast De Liefde); this was a not uncommon way to raise funds for such non-profit buildings.[25]

How long Zigeler preached in Rehoboth is unknown, although he was still occupying its pulpit as late as May 1871.[26] The building itself was also used by others on weekday evenings, for example, by a Spanish evangelist and a Dutch street preacher.[27] Zigeler himself is reported to

[24] Three of these one-hundred-guilder certificates are for sale on the Internet as of the present writing, from Dutch, German, and French dealers, with prices ranging from 20 to 90 euros; http://www.oudeaandelen-online.nl. The author purchased one recently from a Dutch dealer at a bargain price of 15 euros. Each of the four was signed by M. J. Pijnappel and apparently redeemed by him for 20 guilders (i.e., seventeen guilders on the principal plus three guilders interest).

[25] Information on this practice from professor James C. Kennedy, University of Amsterdam, telephone conversation, 24 Nov. 2013.

[26] A. G. Zigeler, Amsterdam, to L. Anet, 3 May 1871. His obituary claims that he preached in Rehoboth for several years (probably an exaggeration); "Ter Gedachtenis. Ds. A. G. Zigeler," *Pella's Weekblad*, 19 Mar. 1915.

[27] Rev. Antonio Carrasco, the fiery young pioneer Spanish Protestant preacher, spoke there in November 1870 (on the challenging work of evangelism in Roman Catholic Spain); Isaac Esser, the well-known, outspoken Reformed lay witness in the largely

have been a speaker elsewhere, in June 1870, once again at an annual national "camp meeting," this time in Noord-Holland.[28]

In the spring of 1871 he returned to Belgium for the wedding of his friend and successor at Antwerp, when he promised to send a thousand guilders to aid the financially needy BCMC, but he actually quickly raised twelve hundred guilders from his own flock for this cause, thus showing that his heart still beat for the BCMC.[29] Finally, in early 1872, just before he left the Netherlands, he reportedly was preaching weekly in Delft, in *Veritas* (truth), a building that since 1856 had been used for the work of evangelism and for "Bible readings."[30]

The Amsterdam press, however, was silent about Zigeler after 1869, until late April 1872, when newspaper ads appeared requesting his creditors to bring their claims "as quickly as possible" to notary Gijsbertus Ruys.[31] At the beginning of July 1872, Rehoboth was auctioned by a brokerage firm (on behalf of Ruys) for 15,901 guilders (less than half its reported cost).[32] In August 1872, it was announced

---

Islamic Dutch East Indies, street evangelist in The Hague, and millennialist, appeared at Rehoboth in Apr. 1871 (on "a prophetic, political view of missions among the Mohammedans"). *Algemeen Handelsblad*, 25, 27 Nov. 1870, 18 Apr. 1871.

[28] Zigeler participated in the seventh *Algemeene Evangelisch Nationaal Zendingsfeest* (general evangelical national missionary festival) on Wednesday, 22 June 1870, on an estate near Alkmaar, Noord-Holland; the 17 speakers (including major figures like Abraham Capadose, Nicolaas Beets, and Martinus Cohen Stuart) preached at five different locations; "Kerk- en Schoolnieuws," in *Het Nieuws van den Dag: Kleine Courant*, 17 June 1870.

[29] Zigeler pledged to send the BCMC a thousand guilders very soon. On arriving home, he fretted how he could keep this promise, but in a Saturday evening "prayer meeting" (the English words are used) the matter was taken "before the Throne of Grace," after which, at the Sunday afternoon service, he told his flock of the BCMC's need; the response was generous; Zigeler, Amsterdam, to Anet, 3 May 1871. This is the last extant Zigeler letter (to Anet).

[30] The sole source for Zigeler's brief 1872 ministry in Delft is Van der Kleij's hostile letter of March 1874; since Van der Kleij had been in the New World since 1871, this information was second hand but presumably reliable. The *Veritas* building appears to have had living quarters in addition to a meeting hall, so Zigeler could conceivably have resided as well as preached there for a time after leaving his family (see below). Van der Kleij, "Een Woord van Ernstige Waarschuwing," *De Hope*, 11 Mar. 1874; "Koornmarkt 4," in "Achter de gevels van Delft," at http://www.achterdegevelsvandelft.nl.htm, derived from Thera Wijsenbeek-Olthuis, *Achter de gevels van Delft* (University of Amsterdam doctoral dissertation; Hilversum: Verloren, 1987).

[31] *Algemeen Handelsblad*, 24, 25 Apr. 1872; *De Standaard* (Amsterdam), 24, 26 Apr. 1872; the latter daily paper had been begun by Abraham Kuyper only a little over three weeks earlier, on 1 Apr. 1872.

[32] *De Standaard*, 20 May, 4 June, 1 July 1872; *Het Nieuws van den Dag: Kleine Courant*, 22, 23 May 1872; "Afloop der Veiling van Huizen," in *De Tijd: Godsdienstig-Staatkundig Dagblad* ('s Hertogenbosch), 3 July 1872.

that the shares of the thirty-five thousand-guilder Rehoboth loan were to be paid off by Menso Johannes Pijnappel, together with Zigeler's remaining debts (if not yet settled by Ruys).[33] Ruys and Pijnappel were both reputable public figures. Ruys was an outspoken, anti-modernist, *Hervormd* elder (recently in the news), friend of Guillaume Groen van Prinsterer, and an ardent supporter of Kuyper,[34] while Pijnappel, a *Hervormd* lawyer, was a former and future Dutch parliamentarian.[35] In any case, Zigeler, by the time Ruys and Pijnappel had dealt with his creditors, was, as shall be seen, already in a far country, in the city of Chicago.

In fact, Ruys and Pijnappel were not assisting A. G. Zigeler at all but, rather, his deserted, destitute wife. On 24 April 1872, Jannetje Adriana Plugge, asked an Amsterdam court to be allowed to sell Rehoboth and their excess furniture in order to pay creditors, including those who held stock in the church (only a few hundred guilders had already been repaid). In an evident act of Christian charity, the wealthier two-thirds of the shareholders had offered to help compensate the less-well-to-do creditors for their losses and to give a cash "gift" to Mrs. Zigeler *alone* (not as common property to be shared with her husband). She based her request on the facts that the couple had, by virtue of

---

[33] *De Standaard*, 3, 6 Aug. 1872.

[34] Gijsbertus Ruys (1819-1894) was an Amsterdam notary, 1856-93. His widely publicized *cri de coeur*, shouted at the close of a 7 November 1869 church service, against the "modernist" preaching just heard (Ruys had been the elder in charge that Sunday), became a turning point in the struggle for orthodoxy within the Amsterdam consistory. W. Volger, *Om de vrijheid van de kerk. Achtergrond en ontstaan van de Doleantie* (Kampen: J. H. Kok N.V., 1954), 182-84, 186-87, 190; J. L. van Essen, ed., *Groen van Prinsterer. Schriftelijke nalatenschap*, vol. 7, *Brief wisseling 1808-1876*, vol. 6 (1869-76), GS219 ('s Gravenhage: Instituut voor Nederlandse Geschiedenis, 1992), 74, at http://www.historici.nl; "Ruys, Gijsbertus," in Archiefbank, Archiefvormers, SAA, at http://stadsarchief.amsterdam.nl/english/archives_database/archive_creators/letter18.html. At just the time that Ruys was helping Zigeler's wife extricate herself from his creditors, he was also leading in procuring a fine new residence for Kuyper, Amsterdam's rising star; its total cost was about half that of Zigeler's Rehoboth; J. Vree, *Kuyper in de kiem: De precalvinistische periode van Abraham Kuyper 1848-1874* (Hilversum: Verloren, 2006), 341-42.

[35] "Mr. M. J. Pijnappel," at Parlementaire Documentatie Centrum (Universiteit Leiden), at http://www.parlementairdocumentatiecentrum.nl. Pijnappel (1830-1906) had evidently received the money from the sale of Rehoboth; he signed each stock certificate when it was liquidated at 20 percent of its face value (the four examples of "cashed" certificates known to the present author were all settled on these terms in September 1872). Where had Zigeler planned to find the money to pay the interest (or return the principle) to the investors? If the auction of the building brought in over 40 percent of the shareholders' investment, and they received only 20 percent return, the more than 20 percent remaining from the sale presumably went to other creditors, Zigeler's wife, legal fees, etc.

their marriage, joint ownership and that her husband had permanently left the country. Initially, the court allowed her to sell their movable property (e.g., furniture) but not the building, since, although she was its manager on behalf of the shareholders, she could not legally *sell* it. Then, however, with the situation further clarified, permission was quickly granted for Rehoboth to be auctioned to the highest bidder, which presumably would give the deserted wife money for her living expenses and to pay creditors. Newspaper ads were immediately placed, inviting creditors and shareholders to settle with Ruys and Pijnappel.[36]

In spite of this public effort to square Zigeler's accounts, some suspected that he had obtained money fraudulently and that he was in fact a swindler, gone to America with ill-gotten gain. It is true that he had left the Netherlands before his shareholders and other creditors had been paid but also before Rehoboth had been auctioned (at a great loss). Zigeler would soon freely and openly confess his chief sin (see below), but he made no response in the press to the charges of financial chicanery.[37] He had, in fact, not only given the appearance of evil by his pecuniary maneuvering but had also caused loss for investors in Rehoboth, just as he himself had doubtless lost money in the collapse of his house of cards. Zigeler would not lead a life of ease in America; he would never own a home there and would labor well into his seventies, providing only a meagre living for himself and his family.[38]

[36] *Vonnis* (decision) regarding the petition of Jannetje Adriana Plugge, 24 Apr. 1872, Arrondissementsrechtbank te Amsterdam (district court in Amsterdam), access number 198, inventory number 3482, SAA; 8 and 14 May 1872, registration of copy of Jannetje Adriana Plugge petition of 29 April 1872 to Amsterdam district court, in Archief van notaris G. Ruys, no. 571 in Archief van notarissen ter standplaats Amsterdam, access no. 5075, inventory no. 22012, SAA. The court's precise reasoning in revising its decision, to allow the property to be auctioned, was hard to determine, partly due to the poor quality of the online image of the document; in any case, there is no doubt that the disposal of Rehoboth was perfectly legal. The reversal seems to have had to do with the court's realizing fully that Zigeler had left with the professed intention *never* to return.

[37] Van der Kleij, "Een Woord van Ernstige Waarschuwing," *De Hope*, 11 Mar. 1874. As shall be seen, Van der Kleij's warning with regard to Zigeler, that people in Chicago should watch their pocketbooks as well as their souls, was published only after Zigeler had provided his one and only public defense against a Chicago church member's "exposé" in *De Hope* of his chief sin and of his undermining the pastor there; the complainer had said nothing about Zigeler's supposed financial wrongdoing.

[38] His three sons became farm workers as teenagers, evidently to help support the family, and received no advanced education. A. G. Zigeler's father was probably moderately well-to-do, and his brother Gaudenz may even have been fairly prosperous, although, conceivably, some of the family lost money by investing in Rehoboth. Zigeler, "the dominie," was able to afford a maid in Amsterdam but never in America, except for a low-cost granddaughter later.

Fig. 19.5. Interior of the *Plantagekerk* (formerly "Rehoboth") (*www.reliwiki.nl from Stadsarchief Amsterdam*)

In hindsight, Zigeler's big mistake may have been to succumb to "blind ambition" or a "cult of personality" featuring himself, since it was he alone who owned Rehoboth (although the church may have had a consistory), and since he had evidently provided for no continuation of its ministry. Thus, when he and Rehoboth parted, either due to trouble with the church or marital problems, or both, the ministry simply collapsed, leaving the shareholders and flock (not to mention his wife and children) in the lurch. Nevertheless, Zigeler's Rehoboth emerged from the shadow cast by his downfall to serve as a place of worship for over a half century.

The *Christelijke Gereformeerde Gemeente*, the Seceder congregation of Amsterdam, bought Rehoboth through a broker that fateful summer of 1872 for a bargain price (only 43 percent of its original cost of thirty-seven thousand guilders) and renamed it the *Plantagekerk* (for its location). In June 1892, the last synod of the *Christelijke Gereformeerde Kerk* took place in it, just before the majority of the congregations merged with the churches of Kuyper's *Doleantie* to form the *Gereformeerde Kerken in Nederland*. Church services ceased in the *Plantagekerk* in 1927; the building was sold to a printing business the next year and eventually (1998) taken over by squatters; it was totally renovated (not "razed," as one source claimed) and is now the "Plantage Doklaan," owned and occupied by a collective. Rehoboth's late eighteenth-century German organ lives on today in a church in Alphen aan den Rijn.[39] Zigeler evidently built to last.

How widely the details of Zigeler's departure from Amsterdam were known in that city is unclear. Although an online word search of the leading Amsterdam newspapers around 1872 yields no report of the sad end of his ministry, there are indications that it was common knowledge, especially "on the street."[40] A good example of this comes from the pen of a contemporary, Cornelis ("Kees") Meijer, the popular Amsterdam versifier and street-corner singer known as "Meijer the Rhymer." He had once lampooned Carl Schwartz (among many others) but now pilloried Zigeler as a swindler in the ditty, *"Ziegler* [sic] *en de gefopte vromen"* (Ziegler and the duped pious ones):

Wie heeft hier niet gehoord van de dominé,
Den dominé hier in ons wijkje
Hij maakt er een reisje over de zee

---

[39] "Rehoboth," *De Bazuin*, 19 July 1872, p. 3; real estate sale, 2 Aug. 1872, in Archief van notaris G. Ruys, no. 571 in Archief van notarissen ter standplaats Amsterdam, access no. 5075, inventory no. 22013, SAA; Hermann Moritz Rex, "Die lewe en werk van Sytze Wopkes Wierda in Nederland" (PhD thesis, Universiteit van Pretoria, 1974), 215, at http://upetd.up.ac.za/thesis/submitted/etd-08202008-111647/unrestricted/00front.pdf; "Amsterdam, Plantage Doklaan 8-12—Plantagekerk," at http://www.reliwiki.nl/index.php?title=Amsterdam,_Plantage_Doklaan_8-12_-_Plantagekerk; H. C. Endedijk, *De Gereformeerde Kerken in Nederland*, part 1, *1892-1936* (Kampen: Uitgeversmaatschappij J. H. Kok, 1990), 81; "De Plantagekerk te Amsterdam," in *De Gooi- en Eemlander: nieuws en advertentie blad*, 27 Dec. 1928; "Plantagedok," at http://plantagedok.nl.greenhost.nl; Rogér van Dijk and Cees van der Poel, "Three organ restorations by the firm Gebr. Van Vulpen," at http://www.hetorgel.nl/e2006-06a.htm. Incidentally, Rev. Hendericus Beuker, later Calvin Theological Seminary professor, occupied "Zigeler's pulpit" from 1873 to 1881.

[40] Van der Kleij's 1874 letter suggests that it may have been well known, since his Amsterdam informant knew of it, writing 4 May 1872; Kuyper's Amsterdam daily, *De Standaard* (Amsterdam), briefly summarizes, without comment, Van der Kleij's accusations, as though they needed no explanation. Similarly, although the Seceder weekly *De Bazuin* (Kampen) made no mention of Zigeler (in a search from February to October 1872), it rejoiced about the purchase of Rehoboth in July 1872, as though it needed no introduction to its readers. Finally, Zigeler was already out of the country by 24 Apr. 1872, according to his wife's petition of that date, and a few days later, she explained to the court that she had failed to give the specific grounds for her request for the immediate sale of Rehoboth, because she had *assumed* that his departure was *common knowledge*. Van der Kleij, "Een Woord van Ernstige Waarschuwing," *De Hope*, 11 Mar. 1874; "Binnenland," in *De Standaard*, 28 Mar. 1874; *De Bazuin*, 19 July 1872; 8 and 14 May 1872, registration of copy of Jannetje Adriana Plugge petition of 29 April 1872 to Amsterdam district court, in Archief van notaris G. Ruys, no. 571 in Archief van notarissen ter standplaats Amsterdam, access no. 5075, inventory no. 22012, SAA.

In Amerika neemt hij een kijkje.
Dominé
Dominé
Op reis de centen mee
Broer Kees die houdt de preek
Hij heeft verlaten zijn bef en steek[41]

The piecemeal, painful extrication of Zigeler and his family from Amsterdam lasted from the spring of 1872 to the following winter. He was the first to leave, followed by his parents and two of his young children (apparently to live with their paternal and maternal grandparents), leaving only his wife (and his live-in cousin, a widow) to care, in straitened circumstances, for the remaining two children during the latter part of 1872.[42]

---

[41] This rhyme, dated ca. 1872, shortly after Zigeler's exodus, is apparently a bastardization of a popular folksong about the Dutch sea hero Piet Hein, may be translated as follows: "Who here has not heard of the dominie, the dominie here in our little neighborhood. He takes a little trip across the ocean. He takes a little look around in America. Dominie. Dominie. Taking a trip with the cents [money, with him]. Brother Kees [i.e., Meijer] – he preaches the sermon. [Because] He [Zigeler] has left behind his robe and [three-cornered] hat [i.e., old-fashioned minister's pulpit apparel]." H. F. Wijnman, "De Amsterdamse Liedjeszanger Kees Meijer (1818-1885)," in *Een en zestigste jaarboek van het Genootschap Amstelodamum* (Amsterdam: J. H. de Bussy N.V., 1969), 165-66, at www.amstelodamum.nl.

[42] The family's breakup may be traced in Amsterdam's *Bevolkingsregister* (population register), the ads mentioned above, Van der Kleij's letter, and Mrs. Zigeler's petition to sell Rehoboth. The couple had four children from 1861 to 1867 but none thereafter, although Zigeler's wife was only twenty-eight when she bore her last child; "A. G. Zigeler, Vrij Evangelische Kerk," in Stamboom Forum, at http://www.stamboomforum.nl/genealogie/2/12955/1. The family lived at four Amsterdam addresses from 1864 to 1872; a cousin, an older widow, joined the household in May 1871. Successive maids (including a Remonstrant and a Lutheran) lived with the Zigelers at their first three places (i.e., until the end of April 1872). The dominie must have left the family early in 1872, since he was out of the country by mid-April and had been preaching (and living?) in Delft that spring (Van der Kleij data; see above). In early May the Zigelers' daughter, aged 8, followed her paternal grandparents to Oldenzaal, Overijssel, the birthplace of the grandfather, who had just moved back there from Amsterdam (19 Apr. 1872), conceivably because of the dominie's troubles; Jacob Zigeler would die two years later, at sixty-five. On 18 June 1872 the middle son, aged six, moved to Antwerp, presumably to be with his maternal grandparents. On this same day A. G. Zigeler was signed out of the civil registry of Amsterdam to go "temporarily" (it said) to America, although his wife's petition of 24 April to sell Rehoboth shows that he had already emigrated, *not* to return. These departures left only the oldest and the youngest sons (ages 10 and 4) still at home with their mother and the cousin, who remained with the decimated family until January 1873, about the time Zigeler's wife and four children left for the US (the official date for their removal from the city was "May/June 1874," which is obviously an *ex post facto* entry by a scribe). Archief van het Bevolkingsregister 1864-1874/75, at SAA; *Algemeen Handelsblad*, 10 July 1874.

Zigeler's exile and eclipse: American wilderness wanderings, 1872-1885

Thus, by the spring of 1872, the family of Rehoboth's Rev. A. G. Zigeler was in total disarray. The dominie had left his wife, offspring, flock, and calling and gone off to America with an unmarried twenty-year-old woman. He had obviously suffered a personal meltdown, either because of "the temptations of the flesh," marital difficulties, the financial burden of Rehoboth,[43] a general "mid-life crisis," or a combination of factors. His decision to emigrate[44] was likely occasioned by a general desire to escape all prior commitments and to start afresh with his new-found love, "Marie." All that is known of her is that she was from Amsterdam, an only child, and just slightly more than half his age of thirty-nine. She may have been one of his flock, as his wife had been, or just possibly a household servant.[45] The fugitive couple arrived in Chicago via England by early summer.[46]

A first-hand account about Zigeler soon after he came to Chicago appeared in a letter from Rev. Bernardus de Beij, immigrant pastor of the First Reformed Church of Chicago, to a fellow Seceder dominie in the Netherlands. In the course of the missive, after De Beij referred to Ulrum's former Seceder pastor who had recently run off to America with a younger woman not his wife, he continued:

> You have surely learned about the Rev. Zigeler of Amsterdam. I heard and read about him here, too. Fourteen days ago he came

---

[43] Zigeler's collection of 1200 guilders from his congregation for the BCMC in the spring of 1871, as well as his having paid several hundred guilders to his shareholders by April 1872, suggest that financial problems were not the chief cause of his unseemly departure. *Vonnis* [decision] regarding the petition of Jannetje Adriana Plugge, 24 Apr. 1872, Arrondissementsrechtbank te Amsterdam [district court in Amsterdam], access number 198, inventory number 3482, SAA.

[44] Zigeler's family had international interests, and he had already lived "abroad" (albeit only as far as Belgium).

[45] Bernardus de Beij, Chicago, to Pieter Ariens Lanting, 30 July 1872, at Heritage Hall, Calvin College, translation by Henry Ten Hoor, revised by the writer; photocopy in De Beij folder at Van Raalte Institute, Hope College. The Maria (not "Marie") ter Horst who was a maid in the Zigeler home in Amsterdam was not an only child. De Beij's letter, which is very hard to read, is the only source for her Christian name. Her surname may never be known. Zigeler's wife had also been twenty years old when he married her about thirteen years earlier.

[46] The pair cannot be found in the presently available US passenger lists; perhaps they traveled incognito. It may safely be assumed that they did not visit Mrs. Zigeler's younger brother, living in Yorkshire, on their way to America. His wife claimed that Zigeler, trying to cover his tracks, had intentionally left no forwarding address; 8, 14 May 1872, registration of copy of Jannetje Adriana Plugge petition of 29 April 1872 to Amsterdam district court, in Archief van notaris G. Ruys, no. 571 in Archief van notarissen ter standplaats Amsterdam, access no. 5075, inventory no. 22012, SAA.

to me (although he had been to my church now and then) and began to tell me his black and pathetic history in the presence of the young girl with whom he had fled. I listened to him, witnessed his confession of sin, recognized visible signs of regret and sorrow, and saw his condition as well as human eye can see. He desired me to release him from the object of his adulterous love. I did that by arranging to place her in a decent boarding house for $3.00 per week, where she feels at home. Meanwhile, he is a clerk in a store and earns from $12 to $15 per week. His wife is inclined to come over and live with him. He has written her that Marie (that is her name) is no longer with him, and I have assured her of the truth of that statement. Whether or not I have helped with this help, and done a good work thereby, the results will show. I understand that I must forgive where God forgives and help where he helps as far as our light reaches to show on the outside what we may surmise to be on the inside.[47]

A member of Chicago's church reported, further, that Zigeler, after being apart from "the girl" for three or four weeks (during which time De Beij must have written the above letter), "managed to abduct her craftily" and, after living with her again for a while, repented once more, even more deeply and with much emotion, and then returned her to her parents, after which his wife and children voyaged to join him (De Beij had written to arrange this).[48]

On 17 December 1872, Mrs. Zigeler petitioned the Amsterdam court to appoint her older brother, living in Brussels, as the agent in her affairs, since she was about to leave the country for America.[49] She and her children arrived in New York in the middle of January 1873 after a voyage of about fifteen days on the SS *Rotterdam*, the first ship of the future Holland America Line,[50] for which Zigeler may have already been working as an agent in Chicago.[51] The reasons for the betrayed

[47] De Beij to Lanting, 30 July 1872. Where had De Beij already *read* about Zigeler's Amsterdam misdeeds, since neither the Amsterdam newspapers nor *De Bezuin* appear to mention the matter?
[48] Een lid der Holl. Ger. Kerk, "Een waarschuwing," *De Hope*, 4 Feb. 1874.
[49] *Volmagt* (power of attorney), 17 Dec. 1872, in Archief van notaris G. Ruys, no. 571 in Archief van notarissen ter standplaats Amsterdam, access no. 5075, inventory no. 22013, SAA.
[50] *Dutch Immigrants in U.S. Ship Passenger Manifests, 1820-1880*, Robert P. Swierenga, comp. (Wilmington, DE: Scholarly Resources Inc., 1983), 1189.
[51] An anonymous, liberal, Dutch correspondent living in Chicago complains in an Amsterdam paper in August 1873 about the preferential treatment given in Chicago to orthodox immigrants, e.g., Zigeler, "the former Seceder [sic] pastor from Amsterdam who, after heartily repenting of his sin with this unmarried woman"

Fig. 19.6. SS *Rotterdam I*, 1872-1883 (*www.wrecksite.eu*)

and abandoned wife's return to her husband may only be surmised, but chief among them would probably be financial support for herself and her children, as well as the expectations of church and society, the demands of Christian forgiveness, the children's need of a father, and of course the vows of marriage, if not the remnants of love.

Early in the next year (1874) two letters appeared in *De Hope* "exposing" Zigeler as a "hypocrite." One was written by an anonymous member of De Beij's congregation,[52] and the second by Rev. Willem van der Kleij, the newly installed pastor of Graafschap, Michigan, who knew (of) Zigeler in the Netherlands. Among other things, they recounted the old story of Zigeler's long-confessed sin of adultery as well as the news of his more recent alleged treacherous ingratitude to De Beij by attacking his sermons (in two letters to him) and in further undermining his ministry by preaching in private homes, under the guise of "Bible readings."[53] Zigeler, still in Chicago, published in *De Hope* what he stated would be his one and only reply to the unsigned letter, again admitting the adultery but denying that he had betrayed De Beij's kindness in any way, and certainly not in two *private* letters he

---

(implying the case was well known to his readers), quickly found office work and was currently Chicago agent for the *Rott. Stoomboot-Maatschappij* (Rotterdam steamboat company); "Gemengd Nieuws," in *Het Nieuws van den Dag. Kleine Courant*, 27 Aug. 1873; "The Holland-American Line: A History," at http://www.halpostcards.com/unofficial/line.html.

[52] Een lid der Holl. Ger. Kerk, "Een waarschuwing," *De Hope*, 4 Feb. 1874.
[53] Zigeler's ministry in Antwerp had begun in a similar way, which seems to have been common in *Réveil* circles.

had written to the dominie (whose contents could not, in the nature of the case, have been known to the critic). Moreover, he claimed that his house ministry was never undertaken on his own initiative but only at the request of others.[54]

Zigeler's letter could not have answered the additional accusations, put forth by Van der Kleij, of financial impropriety and of not being Reformed, because Van der Kleij's missive was published a week after Zigeler's "final word," whose publication had been delayed because the editor had misplaced it. In any case, Van der Kleij relied heavily upon a May 1872 letter to him in Pella from a well-known, prominent, respected but anonymous, Christian brother in Amsterdam.[55] Although the publication of unsigned letters and articles was not unusual then, it is unfortunate that two of the three witnesses against Zigeler in *De Hope* were nameless. Van der Kleij's accusation about Zigeler's dishonesty with regard to money is likely an exaggeration, if not a misrepresentation, in light of the previously described, legally correct way his accounts were settled; this is not to say, however, that Zigeler was not morally culpable in the economic loss caused to the Rehoboth investors.

Van der Kleij's second charge of Zigeler's not being "Reformed" is only partly true, based on his knowledge of the man before he (Van der Kleij) emigrated in 1871; for example, the two of them had been among the sixteen "stump" speakers at the national Dutch "camp meeting" in 1863, as noted above. Furthermore, Van der Kleij certainly knew of Zigeler's ministerial career outside both the *Hervormd* and Seceder churches. Thus Zigeler, unlike the Seceder Van der Kleij, had not subscribed to the Three Standards of Unity, simply because the BCMC that ordained him required subscription only to the Belgic Confession, not to the Heidelberg Catechism or Canons of Dort.[56] And certainly none of the three independent congregations he served in Amsterdam were either *Hervormd* or Seceder, although he seems to have brought a generically Reformed presence to them.[57]

---

[54] A. G. Zigeler, "Een verklaring" (letter written 9 Feb. 1874 but publication delayed by editor's error), *De Hope*, 4 Mar. 1874.

[55] Van der Kleij, "Een Woord van Ernstige Waarschuwing," *De Hope*, 11 Mar. 1874.

[56] De Raaf, *Bewaar het pand*, 10; in 1849 the BCMC took as its doctrinal standard the Belgic Confession of Faith, except for Article 36 (about separate in Belgium). Unlike the Seceder Van der Kleij, Zigeler only implicitly repudiated the *Hervormde Kerk* by his church affiliations in Belgium and the Netherlands and was even recorded as *Hervormd* in the Amsterdam *Bevolkingsregister* about 1870.

[57] Zigeler of course began as a student at the seminary of the Free Church of Scotland, which denomination was separate from the state, like the BCMC and the churches of the Secession in the Netherlands. Nevertheless, the school was openly committed, confessionally, to the Reformed faith.

Zigeler was never sectarian, being first and foremost an "evangelical" and ready, willing, and able to preach the gospel anywhere and at any time, for example, in Methodist, Baptist, and other evangelical pulpits; a Methodist minister took part in his funeral.[58]

The 1874 warning letters may well have helped end Zigeler's informal ministry in Chicago and precipitate his departure for parts west,[59] since he surfaced that same year as an "evangelist" supplying the struggling little RCA congregation in the hamlet of Otley, near Pella.[60]

Zigeler had reached the exact halfway point—a critical juncture in his long life: the first forty-one years had been spent in three major urban centers, while the last forty-one years would be spent in several relatively obscure rural communities.

The Otley church was founded by the Classis of Illinois in 1871 with seventeen members as an English-language congregation, with a minority of Dutch speakers, which situation caused discord, so that its first pastor, an Anglophone, had left already in 1872, and the pulpit remained vacant throughout much of the 1870s, during which period the general synod reported that Otley had ten families and twenty-eight communicant members. Thus "Evangelist A. G. Ziegler" [sic] filled a need in Otley from 1874 to 1875 as unofficial pulpit supply,[61] and it allowed him to exercise his preaching gifts well out of the limelight.[62]

---

[58] Zigeler's involvement in the *Réveil*, the Christian Friends, and the "camp meetings" indicates his "ecumenical" attitude. As minister in the Le Mars, Iowa, RCA congregation, he preached at evening services of both the local Baptist and Methodist churches; *De Volksvriend*, 2 Nov. 1893, 6 Feb. 1894. No record was found of his preaching for the CRC, perhaps because that denomination's pulpits would have been closed to *any* RCA man. His three surviving children (sons) seem to have left the RCA; www.ancestry.com; www.familysearch.org.

[59] Zigeler appears once in an annual Chicago city directory, published summer 1874, as "George Ziggler," clerk, living at 620 West Fourteenth Street (this street was renamed after his February 1874 *De Hope* letter giving his address as 620 Mitchell Street); *The Lakeside Directory of the City of Chicago, 1874-5* (Chicago: Williams, Donnelley & Company, 1874), 1186, 99, 92, at www.ancestry.com (US city directories, 1821-1989).

[60] In any event, Zigeler probably felt happier preaching in a church than conducting "Bible readings" in private homes, even though he may have had a relatively secure source of income as a clerk in Chicago.

[61] *1871—Through the Years—1971* (Otley Reformed Church, 1996), 2-3, at http://www.otleychurch.org/assets/pdf/orcHistory.pdf.

[62] Zigeler was bilingual, at least by then, but it might not have been necessary, since the congregation, with the influx of Dutch immigrants in the late 1870s, may have lost most if not all of its native Americans; *1871—Through the Years—1971*, 1-3. Zigeler could well have honed his English homiletical skills in non-Dutch, non-RCA churches in the Otley/Pella area between 1875 and 1885, before officially entering the RCA ministerial fold.

But Zigeler's nemesis, Van der Kleij, now a member of the Classis of Holland, which body had evidently learned of Zigeler's preaching in Otley, was part of a three-man classical committee appointed in April 1875 to inform—and warn—the Classis of Illinois about "a certain Ziegler" [sic]. This quickly brought Zigeler's work in Otley to a close, although twelve years later he would be back there as its regularly-installed RCA pastor. This suggests that it was the Classis of Illinois, not Otley, who ended his service there in 1875.[63]

Very little is known of Zigeler's doings over the next decade. He appears in the 1880 census as "Ira Sigler," "a preacher," in Otley with his wife and four children; his oldest son, aged eighteen, was working then as a "day laborer." The Zigelers may have been living in the little local hotel, along with the young, recently married Otley Methodist preacher.[64]

In the fall of 1882, Zigeler made a two-week visit to preach to the pastorless Dutch Reformed settlers of the new colony of Harrison, [South] Dakota, who later were said to have had a "pleasant memory" of his ministry. He subsequently returned to Harrison (as to Otley) as an installed RCA pastor.[65] At the end of 1882, his daughter married a Marion County farmer and died young, leaving an infant daughter who was probably raised by the Zigelers after her father remarried. By the

[63] Classis of Holland Minutes, 8 Apr., 9 Sept. 1875. The classical committee, composed of Van der Kleij and two other ministers, was appointed in April and, having done its work, discharged in September; the minutes for both actions said nothing as to Zigeler's supposed offense(s). Had Zigeler committed fresh offenses? or did Van der Kleij, a respected but ailing member of classis, spearhead an anti-Zigeler campaign, in the spirit of an Inspector Javert? The Classis of Holland could inform the Classis of Illinois of a danger in the latter's midst because the three committeemen all had recent close ties with Pella, which lay very near to Otley. Zigeler's entrance into the RCA ministry may have been delayed for about a decade by these actions of 1875. The Otley church's centennial history calls Zigeler "Evangelist" in 1874 (as its supply preacher) but "Reverend" in 1887 (as its installed pastor). *1871—Through the Years—1971*, 2-3. Unfortunately, the minutes of the Classis of Illinois and the Otley consistory are lost.

[64] www.ancestry.com (1880 census). At the very end of the enumeration for the town of Otley were the Zigelers, the Methodist couple (Levi Meade Hartley and wife), and the hotel owner and his family; this leads to the likelihood that both ministerial families were living in the small hotel. *Yearbook of the Southern California Annual Conference of the Methodist Episcopal Church* (n.p.: The Conference, 1906), 80, at http://books.google.com/books. The Otley Reformed Church was listed as "vacant" in the RCA records in 1880, when the census recorded Zigeler as "a preacher." Was he even then preaching surreptitiously in Otley? The congregation's centennial history does not say.

[65] "Frank LeCocq's Douglas County, South Dakota," in Henry S. Lucas, ed., *Dutch Immigrant Memoirs and Related Writings*, rev. ed., vol. 2 (Grand Rapids: Eerdmans, 1997), 316, 323.

1885 Iowa state census, the Zigelers had moved from Otley to nearby Polk Township, where A. G. was still listed as a "preacher," living with his wife and three sons; the oldest just married and farming may have been providing a home for his parents and brothers.[66]

Zigeler's rehabilitation: pastor and churchman within the Reformed Church, 1885-1915

With two children wed and the other two old enough to fend for themselves, A. G. Zigeler finally came out of eclipse, so to speak, when in October 1885, he began to supply the small, English-language, RCA congregation in Havana, Mason County, Illinois. Its former pastor, Rev. William Gilmore, A. C. Van Raalte's son-in-law, had died the previous year. The church's annual report in the spring of 1886 stated that Zigeler's services "are highly appreciated by the community at large and quite a number of conversions have occurred." The congregation had grown; so that the total number of communicants was thirty-three (twenty-one families), with fifty in the Sunday school. Even so, Zigeler remained in Havana only around a year.[67]

At this point he "transferred" his clerical credentials to the Classis of Illinois from "the Christian Mission Church of Belgium" that he had left over two decades earlier. But the May 1886 Particular Synod of Chicago, to which the Classis of Illinois belonged, "reminded" the classis of the need to comply with the "requirements of the RCA Constitution regarding the reception of ministers" in having "received into the ministry Mr. A. G. Zigeler."[68] This mild reproof presumably had to do with the status of "*Mr.*" Zigeler's credentials (outdated or non-existent), or with the lack of any ecclesiastical discipline for this "fallen" minister, or both.

After affiliating with the RCA and his brief stint at Havana, Zigeler served mostly small Dutch-speaking flocks for the next seventeen years, until ill health forced him to retire. The churches included Spring Lake and Manito, Illinois (jointly served; English-language; 1887), Otley

---

[66] www.ancestry.com (1885 Iowa census); www.familysearch.org (marriages). The Zigeler children and their descendants mostly remained in or near Marion County, initially close to the soil.

[67] There were four adult baptisms, while seven people joined on confession of faith and five by letter. *Minutes of the Particular Synod of Chicago, Convened in Chicago, Illinois, May 5th, 1886* (Grand Rapids: W. W. Hart, Printer, 1886), 15-16; *The Acts and Proceedings of the . . . General Synod of the Reformed Church in America, June 1886* (New York: Board of Publication of the Reformed Church in America, 1886), 170.

[68] *Minutes of the Particular Synod of Chicago, 1886*, 16, 35.

(again) and Bethel [Pella], Iowa (jointly served; 1887-93), Le Mars, Iowa (1893-94), Harrison, South Dakota (1894-1900), and, finally, the Fourth Church of Pella (1901-4).[69]

In spite of his previous history as a sometimes independent operator, Zigeler seems to have become a "team player" in the RCA, active in classis and diligently ministering to his rural midwestern churches. But occasionally he was able to vary this routine with visits to the more urban world of his earlier life. For instance, in the summer of 1890, he took his wife and young grandchild across the Atlantic. The trio returned via Hull, England, in August as the only (cabin) passengers on a freighter.[70] Zigeler was twice a classical delegate to the Particular Synod of Chicago (1887 in Chicago and 1891 in Pella) and was sent three times (1889, 1896, and 1898) to the general synod in the East, which lasted over a week.[71]

Zigeler's most significant activity outside the Midwest in these later years was the seeming culmination of his second career. He was sent by the destitute farmers of Douglas County, South Dakota, to New York City for some seven weeks in early 1895 to seek desperately needed aid for them during the severe winter. He was then the recently installed pastor of the Harrison RCA congregation, the biggest in the Classis of Dakota (with almost two hundred communicant members).[72]

---

[69] "Ziegler," in Gasero, *Historical Directory*, 479 (a few of these dates have been revised, based on contemporary newspaper reports, e.g., in *De Volksvriend*). Van der Kleij had been pastor of a forerunner of this Fourth Reformed Church of Pella just before he went to Michigan in 1873; ibid., 613.

[70] Their cargo ship, "The Hindoo," sailing from Hull, Yorkshire, would have cost less than a Holland America Line passenger vessel from Rotterdam. There was regular service from England to the Continent. Did any relatives subsidize their journey? The New York customs form called the grandchild "Tom," but the Zigelers almost certainly had no grandchild named Tom, so "he" may well have been their motherless (since 1888) five-year-old granddaughter, probably already living with them since her father's remarriage in February 1890. De Raaf, *Bewaar het pand*, 56; www.familysearch.org; www.ancestry.com (New York, Passenger Lists, 1820-1957; 1900 census).

[71] The manuscript minutes of the Classes of Iowa (Le Mars) and of Dakota (Harrison) show that Zigeler attended classis sessions regularly (except when ill), fulfilled committee and pulpit assignments, and examined candidates for the ministry (in church history or in church government). He served on no "key" committees at the particular synod or at the general synod, where the West was underrepresented anyway. Thanks to Tim Schlak, director and archivist, De Witt Library, Northwestern College, Orange City, Iowa, for photocopies of these minutes.

[72] *First Reformed Church, Harrison, South Dakota, 1883-1983: "One Hundred Years of His Faithfulness"* (n.p.: 1983), 16. Although Harrison was both the largest church in the classis and the largest Zigeler would serve in the United States, his acceptance of this suffering flock's call of desperation (after nine successive turndowns in the previous two years) seems to illustrate either Zigeler's self- (or God) confidence or

Fig. 19.7. First Reformed Church, Harrison, South Dakota
(*courtesy Northwestern College Archives*)

Since 1890 the Douglas County farmers had experienced three poor harvests and one total loss, so the RCA churches in the East had been sending clothing, bedding, and shoes to the sufferers. Zigeler, through newspaper publicity (in the RCA's *Christian Intelligencer* and even in the *New York Times*) and personal appearances, sought to raise $10,000 to buy coal to heat homes, seed, and especially grain to feed the horses for spring plowing. He succeeded in collecting a bit over $5,000 (about $141,000 current). Fortunately the drought eased.[73]

---

his compassion, or both. Many left South Dakota during the hard times of the mid-1890s, so that the Harrison church went from a high of 198 communicant members (100 families) in the spring 1895 report to the general synod (shortly after Zigeler came), to a low of 113 members (76 families) in the 1897 report. The 1894 statistics, when the pulpit was vacant, were 165 members (94 families), while in 1900, just before Zigeler left, there were 141 members (89 families); *Acts and Proceedings*, various years. In a rare appearance in print, Zigeler, Harrison's new pastor, wrote an article urging South Dakota settlers not to leave because of hard times; A. G. Zigeler, "Wederwoord," *De Volksvriend*, 6 Dec. 1894, p. 6.

[73] *New York Times*, 21 Feb. 1895, p. 16, at http://www.newspapers.com/newspage/20526010; *Newtown Register*, 14 Mar. 1895, p. 2 (quoting the Jamaica, Long Island, *Standard*, 9 Mar. 1895), at http://fultonhistory.com/Newspaper4.pdf. Judging from these articles and those in the *Christian Intelligencer*, the New York City-based RCA weekly, which promoted and reported on Zigeler's New York efforts (in addition to the Classis of Dakota minutes), he was on site collecting funds in the New York City area from about 12 February to the beginning of April 1895. Did he stay with Rev. Giles Mandeville, the corresponding secretary of the RCA

Upon his return to Douglas County, the grateful people gave his family gifts, having collected twenty-five cents (sometimes borrowed) per person: "a beautiful armchair and a platform rocking chair [for Zigeler and his wife] . . . and a large and well-dressed doll" for their young granddaughter.[74] Thus once again Zigeler's talent for raising money was put to use, this time for the physical needs of others, not for a Rehoboth as a platform for his preaching— and not only for his own flock but also for the Christian Reformed and other people in the area.[75] The later *Réveil*, of which Zigeler was a representative, was concerned with social amelioration in addition to evangelism.[76]

Zigeler, by his time in New York, appears to have had a fine command of English, judging from the occasional pieces bearing his name, as well as the fact that the Classis of Dakota, whose business was conducted in English (with translations, when needed, for Dutch and German speakers), declined to let him and his Dutch-language Harrison church transfer to the adjacent Classis of Iowa, since his/their English was so good.[77] Also, Zigeler participated in, if not led, a

---

board of education, who oversaw the "honest and careful distribution" of the funds donated? Who paid for Zigeler's trip east? *Christian Intelligencer* regularly published the amounts given by each church, group, and person during Zigeler's eastern campaign. On the results of his efforts and the drought-ending rains, see *Christian Intelligencer*, 17 Apr., 8 May 1895. There was criticism, however, by an anonymous Dakotan in a Michigan paper, of this "begging" and "stealing," by Zigeler et al., from the eastern RCA for people in South Dakota (lured there by greed, they should have cared for themselves); A.B.C., "Wat denken onze Stam- en Geloofsgenooten van Charles Mix en Douglas Counties, in South Dakota?" *De Grondwet*, 26 Feb. 1895. Also a pastor, a South Dakota booster in *Christian Intelligencer* later admitted that he had overlooked Douglas County's problems; F. N. Nickerson, "Dakota Jottings," *Christian Intelligencer*, 20 Feb., 20 Mar. 1895; with response by Zigeler, 6 Mar. 1895.

[74] A. G. Zigeler, "Letter from Dakota," *Christian Intelligencer*, 8 May 1895, p. 8.
[75] *Diamond Jubilee, 1883-1958. Historical Sketch and Seventy-fifth Anniversary of First Reformed Church, Harrison, South Dakota* (n.p., [1958]), 8. *First Reformed Church, Harrison, 1883-1983*, 16-17.
[76] O. W. Dubois, "Réveil," in *Christelijke Encyclopedie*, Harinck et al., eds., 1536-37; Kluit, *Het protestantse Réveil*, 378-472.
[77] Zigeler and his consistory claimed that their church's members' English was inadequate to function in the classis, which responded that their proposal was written in excellent English, better than that of most classis members, and that, in any case, the official business of the Classis of Iowa was also conducted in English; Classis of Dakota Minutes, April 1896. In addition to Zigeler's mastery of English, he was sufficiently fluent in German to preach occasionally that language at the Ebenezer Church near Scotland, South Dakota; Classis of Dakota Minutes, Sept. 1895 and 28 Oct. 1896. Three decades earlier, he had done fundraising preaching for the BCMC in northwestern Germany; see above.

modest Americanizing and modernizing of the Harrison congregation during his pastorate. When he resigned in 1900, due to ill health, "all the consistory went home heavy-hearted."[78]

Zigeler's last congregation, Fourth Reformed Church of Pella, being much smaller than Harrison, enabled him to transition into an easy semi-retirement, except that Fourth Church was in sharp decline, having just been rent by a controversy over millennial teaching. That charge may have served, in a sense, to bring the aged Zigeler full circle to his premillennial beginnings and continued leanings. The congregation met in the former church of the premillennial Scholte and included remnants of his flock.[79]

After fully retiring from Fourth Church in 1904, Zigeler continued to preach in area churches and schoolhouses as opportunity and health permitted. His granddaughter cared for him and his wife in Pella until 1911, when she died unmarried, to be followed by Mrs. Jannetje Zigeler in 1912, after which A. G. lived at his oldest son's farm in Kellogg, Iowa, for a couple of years, spending his final four months at his namesake grandson's farm in Newton, Iowa. He was buried in March 1915 beside his wife in nearby Pella. Her well-attended funeral at First Reformed Church was led by the ministers of First, Second, and Third Churches (Fourth Church had disbanded), while her husband's service in the same sanctuary was conducted by the First and Second Reformed Churches' pastors (Third Church was vacant), together with the ministers of Otley Reformed and of the Pella Methodist churches (but not of the two local CRCs).

Unlike the perfunctory English-language obituary for "Ziegler" [sic], the longer one in the Pella Dutch newspaper recapitulates his service, including his Belgian and Scottish Missionry Church work,

---

[78] Zigeler's pastorate began with organizing a Ladies Aid and Missionary Society (of which his wife was a charter member), while in his final year (1899) a Christian Endeavor Society was started, English was introduced in the morning communion services for the church's non-Dutch members, "36 Evangelical hymn books in the English language" were bought, insurance was purchased for the sanctuary and parsonage, and the local cemetery was set up, owned jointly by the Reformed and Christian Reformed. *First Reformed Church, Harrison, 1883-1983*, 10, 17; *Diamond Jubilee, 1883-1958*; *Historical Sketch of First Reformed Church, Harrison*, 13.

[79] Zigeler's predecessor at Fourth Church, Rev. Jan Willem Poot, had been in a Free Evangelical church (like De Liefde) in the Netherlands and was a premillennialist admirer of Dwight L. Moody; William D. Allison, "From Poot to Poat: A Dutch American Family History," ch. 14, "Published in Pella," 1-6, at http://www.jrpoot.eu/pdffiles/14-pella-smaller.pdf. One of Zigeler's very few known published sermons, from 1865, echoed the (premillennial) evangelistic concerns of his teachers Schwartz and Da Costa: *Bidt gij voor Israël?* (Amsterdam: H. de Hoogh, 1865); http://boekwinkeltjes.nl/singleorder.php?id=120626837.

pointing out that "he preached for several years in a church built especially for him in the Plantage" in Amsterdam.[80]

The RCA General Synod obituary aptly describes "A. G. Zieglar" [sic] as an "intensely evangelical rather than doctrinal [preacher] and successful in leading many to the Savior. He was emotional and a magnetic speaker, not always free from peculiarities in address."[81] Not surprisingly, there is no word in any of the obituaries about his midlife troubles, but neither is anything said of his fundraising for the destitute farmers of South Dakota.

In 1865, near the apex of his career in Amsterdam, Zigeler delivered an address at Scottish Missionary Church for the fiftieth anniversary commemoration of the Battle of Waterloo, in which he urged the Dutch to repent in view of their double deliverance: by God from Napoleon's tyranny and especially by Christ from the wrath to come. Among the many evils catalogued by Zigeler was rapidly increasing immorality: "In former times fingers were pointed at an adulterer, but presently one is almost no longer ashamed to transgress this commandment of God."[82] Forty-five years later, when Zigeler was nearing the end of his life, the Pella census enumerator put down the detail that the old minister had been *married twice*, which testifies to the lingering pain—and shame—of the adulterous episode of long before, when he had met his personal Waterloo.[83]

The "moral" to this story could easily be that pride goes before a fall, but also that humbled, chastened, and repentant sinners can still be fruitful ministers. Zigeler's case also illustrates the fact that the midwestern RCA could and needed to be "flexible" in using imperfect vessels to serve its immigrant churches.

---

[80] "Mrs. A. G. Zigeler," *Pella's Weekblad*, 8 Mar. 1912; "Ziegler" [sic], *Pella Chronicle*, 7 Mar. 1912; "Ter Gedachtenis. Ds. A. G. Zigeler," *Pella's Weekblad*, 19 Mar. 1915; "Ziegler" [sic], *Pella Chronicle*, 18 Mar. 1915; thanks to Elizabeth McMahon of the Geisler Library, Central College, for photocopies of these obituaries. Pella Historical Society, *History of Pella, Iowa, 1847-1987*, vol. 1 (Dallas: Curtis Media Corporation, 1988), 622 (granddaughter's death). Oddly, perhaps, Zigeler's wife spoke only Dutch and not English after many years in the New World; was this covert protest against her forced emigration? www.ancestry.com (1900 and 1910 census).

[81] *Acts and Proceedings*, 1915, 606-7.

[82] A. G. Zigeler, *Neerlands verlossing herdacht: toespraak bij gelegenheid van het halve eeuwfeest van de overwinning te Waterloo, 18 Junij 1865* (Amsterdam: H. de Hoogh, 1865), 9; this was a strong, well-crafted address of thirty-one pages. One of Zigeler's two known published sermons, also from 1865, is about the (sexually?) sinful woman who anointed Jesus' head and washed his feet with her tears; Jesus forgave her sins because of her faith (Luke 7:48-50); A. G. Zigeler, *De Zondares aan de voeten van Jezus. Leerrede over Luk. 7:48-50* (Amsterdam: H. de Hoogh, 1865); 23 pages long. De Hoogh was a major publisher of literature for a *Réveil* public.

[83] www.ancestry.com (1910 census). It is highly unlikely that Zigeler had become a "bigamist" in 1872 by actually marrying Marie (e.g., in England); rather, the census datum is simply one final confession of his sin of adultery 38 years earlier.

CHAPTER 20

On the Shift to Standard Dutch: Pella, Iowa Compared to Holland, Michigan

Jaap van Marle

Students of Dutch American history and culture seem to take a much greater interest in the vicissitudes of the Dutch and their descendants in Michigan than in Iowa. In Jacob Van Hinte's *Netherlanders in America*, for instance, the chapter "The Rooting of the Young Dutch Branch in Michigan" has a length of fifty pages, whereas the size of its counterpart on Iowa is fewer than thirty pages.[1] The same holds for Lucas where sixty pages are devoted to Michigan, whereas the parallel discussion of the immigration to Iowa is assigned only forty-five pages.[2] A similar focus on Michigan can also be found in Hans Krabbendam's *Freedom on the Horizon*.[3] In his monograph there are only nineteen

---

[1] Jacob Van Hinte, *Netherlanders in America: A Study of Emigration and Settlement in the 19th and 20th Centuries in the United States of America*, ed. Robert P. Swierenga, trans. Adriaan de Wit (Grand Rapids, MI: Baker Book House, 1985). I am indebted to Caroline Smits for comments and discussion.

[2] Henry S. Lucas, *Netherlanders in America: Dutch Immigration to the United States and Canada, 1789-1950* (Ann Arbor, MI: University of Michigan Press, 1955).

[3] Hans Krabbendam, *Freedom on the Horizon: Dutch Immigration to America, 1840-1940* (Grand Rapids, MI: Eerdmans, 2009).

references to Pella, whereas Holland has forty-six references, Zeeland thirty, while Grand Rapids has even fifty-two references.[4]

Clearly, from an historian's point of view, there may be good reasons for this uneven treatment of Iowa and Michigan, for instance, the fact that the Dutch in Michigan not only founded Holland and the other "Dutch colonies" in the Holland area but that they also settled in "American" cities such as Grand Rapids. For a linguist, however, this greater interest in Michigan is far from obvious. As far as the vicissitudes of the Dutch language are concerned, Pella, Iowa, should by no means be considered second rate, since the development of Dutch in Pella is no doubt highly remarkable. Of course, this is also directly reflected by the fact that there is a monograph on the position of Dutch in Pella, Iowa— Phil Webber's well-known *Pella Dutch* from 1988 which was recently reprinted (and expanded) in 2011—whereas there is no such book on the Dutch in Holland (or any other "Dutch town") in Michigan.[5]

From a socio-cultural point of view, the Pella, Iowa, settlements are culturally unique, especially when considering the use of the Dutch language.[6] This is evident in their maintenance of the Dutch language in everyday life.

There can be no doubt that in Pella the position of Dutch has been much stronger than in Holland, Michigan. When Phil Webber researched spoken Dutch in the 1980s for his book, *Pella Dutch*, the language was still very much present in the Pella community, even if, at that time, Dutch was no longer generally used as the language of informal, in-group communication among Dutch Americans. As late as the 1950s Dutch was still used in public life. As was stressed by our informants, till that time Dutch could still be heard in Pella shops.[7]

In Holland the situation was completely different. By the 1950s, Dutch had virtually disappeared from public life. During the time that Caroline Smits and I were involved in our fieldwork project on American Dutch, we always asked our Michigan informants the following question: "Do you remember if you heard Dutch spoken in

---

[4] This seems to be parallelled by the fact that more attention is paid to Van Raalte than to Scholte. Consider, for instance, Krabbendam's concise treatment of the Dutch immigration to the United States (*Freedom on the Horizon*), in which 35 references to Van Raalte can be found versus 28 to Scholte.

[5] Philip E. Webber, *Pella Dutch: Portrait of a Language in an Iowa Community* (Ames: Iowa State University Press, 1988); Philip E. Webber, *Pella Dutch: Portrait of a Language in an Iowa Community, an Expanded Edition* (Iowa City: University of Iowa Press, 2011).

[6] Webber, *Pella Dutch*; Webber, *Pella Dutch . . . an Expanded Edition*.

[7] When Van Hinte visited Pella in 1921, he visited the "park" and heard nothing but Dutch; Ester, Kennedy, and Kennedy, eds., *The American Diary of Jacob van Hinte* (Holland, MI: Van Raalte Press, 2010), 166.

Fig. 20.1. Central Park Café, Pella, Iowa, c. 1940s
(*Pella Historical Society*)

Holland while you were shopping?" Interestingly, nobody could! Since most of these interviews were held between 1989 and 1997, and since most of our informants were in their seventies or older, this seems to imply that in Holland the Dutch language had disappeared from public life before the Second World War. It is my impression that the position of Dutch in Holland was already seriously affected in the 1920s. This generalization relates exclusively to Holland, Michigan, itself and not to the smaller Dutch towns and villages in the region where the language held on longer.

In Pella the situation was very different. When we made our fieldwork trips to Iowa (between 1989 and 1995), the Dutch language had not yet completely disappeared from public life. In the Central Park Cafe, isolated Dutch phrases and expressions could still be heard, and in some of the shops, older folks switched to Dutch when they found out that we came from the Netherlands. Thus, in the 1980s and early 1990s, the last vestiges of the use of Dutch in Pella were still present. This is also the conclusion of Webber's *Pella Dutch*.

During our fieldwork in Pella, we found that the number of people who could still speak (their variety of) Dutch well was relatively large. In Holland, Michigan, by contrast, Dutch Americans who could still speak Dutch were hard to find. Dutch Americans who could still speak Dutch mostly lived in the outlying settlements. [8]

---

[8] And, more often than not, they spoke a different type of Dutch: American Dialectal Dutch (see below).

These observations have important consequences. Since most of our informants were in their 70s or older, this implies that in the 1920s and 1930s, Dutch was still very much alive in many Pella households and families.[9] Clearly, the shift to English was different from that in Holland.

There were certainly many Dutch Americans in both cities who shifted to English relatively soon in the early twentieth century. This is referred to as the rapid shift scenario.[10] But the number of "early shifters" was much higher in Holland than in Pella. This helps to explain why most of the early complaints about "bad Dutch" heard as early as the 1880s, primarily related to Michigan and not to Iowa. In contrast, until far into the twentieth century, the inhabitants of Pella were praised for the quality of their language.[11]

Is is no doubt true that the turning point for many Dutch Americans to embrace English and hence American culture was at the very end of the nineteenth century.[12] But there were many exceptions, particularly in Pella.[13] This is why, even in 1989, American Dutch had not completely disappeared, as was evidenced by the large number of Dutch Americans who could speak Dutch well and by the number of people who had clear recollections of the time in the 1950s when Dutch was commonly heard in public life.[14]

---

[9] As a matter of fact, quite a few of our informants were brought up monolingually in Dutch.

[10] Jaap van Marle and Caroline Smits, "American Dutch: general trends in its development," in *Language Contact across the North Atlantic*, eds. P. Sture Ureland and Iain Clarkson (Tübingen: Niemeyer, 1996), 427-42; Jaap van Marle and Caroline Smits, "De ontwikkeling van het Amerikaans-Nederlands: een schets," in *Overzees Nederlands*, eds. J. B. Berns and J. van Marle (Amsterdam: Meertens Instituut, 2000), 63-83.

[11] Van Hinte, *Netherlanders in America*, 992.

[12] Herman J. De Vries Jr., "Henry Van Andel's Dutch Grammar Books and the Language Problem," in *Dutch American Arts and Letters in Historical Perspective*, eds. Robert P. Swierenga, Jacob E. Nyenhuis, Nella Kennedy (Holland, MI: Van Raalte Press, 2008), 92 (with reference to Krabbendam, *Freedom on the Horizon*).

[13] This claim is also doubtful for some of the smaller settlements in the Holland area where the position of American Dialectal Dutch (see below) was remarkably strong. See also Jaap van Marle, "The Acculturation of Dutch Immigrants in the USA: a Linguist's View," in *The Dutch Adapting to North America: Papers Presented at the Thirteenth Biennial Conference for the Advancement of Dutch American Studies*, ed. Richard H. Harms (Grand Rapids: Calvin College, 2001), and Jaap van Marle, "Over de rol van godsdienst bij taalbehoud, in *Streven* 70, 512-22.

[14] For Pella, the Second World War seems to have been crucial, not only for reasons of nationalism but also because these were the years the grandparents of our informants died. In many families it was the generation of the grandparents of our informants that vehemently stuck to Dutch.

The shift to Standard Dutch

The central claim of this chapter relates not to the maintenance of Dutch but to its unique *development*. To appreciate this completely different dimension of Dutch in Iowa, one must study dialects that were generally used as the vehicle for oral communication. At the time of immigration in the nineteenth century, there was *no* spoken standard language in the Netherlands; people simply spoke their local dialect. As in many other European countries, there was only a standard for writing and not for speaking. It was only after 1850 that a spoken standard language gradually came into being in the Netherlands. Further, it was only in the course of the twentieth century that a large part of the population started to use the spoken standard language on a regular basis. The implication of the above is that a majority of the immigrants who came to Pella must have been dialect speakers. Hence, the variety of Dutch that was spoken in Pella was *not* "dialectal" at all. The first linguists who seriously studied American Dutch, that is, the dialectologists, Jo Daan and Henk Heikens, observed this "non-dialectal" character of Pella Dutch immediately. In an interview in the *Pella Chronicle* in 1966, Daan observed the following:

> We expected to find here in isolation, an older form of the dialects than could be found in the Netherlands. . . . But this has not been true, because most people have learned Dutch through association with other dialects. The result has been very near the standard Dutch language, but more mixed up than in the Netherlands.[15]

That is, Daan came to the United States hoping to find "older dialects," but in Pella she found a kind of standard Dutch instead.

This observation is all the more remarkable because in the United States "dialectal Dutch" is by no means uncommon. In the smaller Dutch settlements in the Holland, Michigan, area, in the Alto/Waupun area in southeastern Wisconsin, and in the "Brabantic" Little Chute area in northeastern Wisconsin, for instance, "American Dialectal Dutch" was spoken for a long time.[16] Indeed, it was by far the prevalent type of

---

[15] *Pella Chronicle*, 18 Oct. 1966. When speaking of the "mixed up" character of Dutch spoken in Pella, Daan alluded to the influence of English.

[16] For Michigan, see Jaap van Marle, "On the Divergence and Maintenance of Immigrant Languages: Dutch in Michigan," in *Language Diversity in Michigan and Ohio*, eds. Brian D. Joseph, Carol G. Preston, and Dennis R. Preston (Ann Arbor, MI: Caravan Books, 2005), 169-87; for Wisconsin in general, see Jaap van Marle, "Dutch Immigrants in Wisconsin: Their Linguistic Heritage," in *Diverse Destinies: Dutch Kolonies in Wisconsin and the East*, eds. Nella Kennedy, Mary Risseeuw, and Robert

Dutch. In Pella, however, we did not find clear instances of "dialectal Dutch;" it was always standard Dutch that was spoken.

How did this standard-like variety of Dutch come into being? There are two possibilities: First, it came into existence as a result of some sort of levelling process, by means of which "salient" dialect features were levelled out. That is, the original dialects became "standard like" because of the loss of their most distinguishing characteristics.[17]

A second possibility is that the spoken standard language that gradually developed in the Netherlands was, as it were, copied in Pella. The first possibility is the most: "natural," predominantly linguistic development (dialect levelling) whereas the second may be considered the purely "socio-cultural" possibility, which exclusively involves the imitation and adoption of the prestigious new standard for speaking that developed in the Netherlands.

As is clear from the above quote, Daan opted for the more "natural" process of dialect levelling. In her view, the clash of different dialects is essential to the rise of the standard-like variety of Dutch used in Pella. I believe that the socio-cultural view is correct.

A crucial point is that this standard-like variety of Dutch is not restricted to Pella but can be found in Michigan (particularly Holland and Zeeland) and Alto, Wisconsin, as well. Interestingly, in these cases it was usually the more educated, cultural elite who spoke like that. In my view, this observation is very important. It implies that in these circles, Dutch Americans were not only aware of the new norm that was gradually developing in the Netherlands but that they were also still oriented toward the Netherlands to such an extent that they adopted this new norm. As a result, the rise of a spoken standard in the Netherlands was, as it were, paralleled by a similar development in the United States.

This thesis fits with the following anecdote. During one of my fieldwork trips I had an interview with two Dutch American women in Alto, Wisconsin. Both still spoke Dutch well, but there was a marked

---

P. Swierenga (Holland, MI: Van Raalte Press, 2012), 221-33, and for the Brabantic dialect of the Roman Catholic immigrants in the Little Chute area in Wisconsin, see William Z. Shetter, "Brabants dialekt in Wisconsin," *Taal en Tongval* 9 (1957):183-89. To a certain extent, the survival of Frisian in Wisconsin is comparable to this continued use of the dialects in the United States. See Jaap van Marle, "On the Survival of the Frisian Language in Wisconsin," *Diverse Destinies*, 235-46.

[17] Note that these dialects differed from each other so much that the Dutch immigrants had great difficulty in understanding each other (e.g., Van Hinte, *Netherlanders in America*, 991; Krabbendam, *Freedom on the Horizon*, 225).

difference between the two. One spoke a prototypical variety of American Dialectal Dutch.[18] The other spoke standard-like American Dutch. Interestingly, both were perfectly aware of this difference, and the latter had extremely interesting comments on the standard-like variety that she spoke. She told me that in her family, they had originally used the dialectal variety, but her father went to Calvin College in Grand Rapids to study for the ministry and there discovered that he *had to learn* the standard-like variety of Dutch. This was the language taught at Calvin College around 1900 that all students who wanted to become a minister had to master. Although my informant's father never became a minister, he held to this standard-like variety learned in Grand Rapids and this variety remained in use in the woman's family.

This story is important in that it shows that the educated and cultural Dutch American elite was very well aware of the fact that in the Netherlands a standard for spoken Dutch had become the norm. Moreover, this elite had still such strong ties with the Netherlands that they adopted this new norm as well. In the United States, as in the Netherlands, the gradually developing spoken standard became the prestigious norm used by the educated elite. This is why in the United States this standard-like variety can be found in Iowa, Michigan, and Wisconsin alike, as long as one focuses on ministers, journalists, and other informants who had had more education and a prominent position in the church.[19]

In language development in Pella, therefore, it is important to note that not only the more educated elite adopted this standard-like variety but also the community as a whole, particularly shopkeepers and farmers, opted to use this prestigious variety of Dutch in the course of everyday conversations. This development resulted in the more or less complete disappearance in Pella of the original dialects, as well as the Frisian language. In sum, I have never found American Dialectal Dutch in Pella as I have in Michigan and Wisconsin.[20] It is these developments

---

[18] In the case of Wisconsin, American Dialectal Dutch comes in different types. The language of the lady at issue, for instance, was clearly based on the dialects spoken in the Dutch province of Gelderland (Gelders) whereas in the Little Chute area, American Dialectal Dutch is Brabantic in nature.

[19] The many contacts with the Netherlands via the churches have no doubt played a prominent part in the adoption of Standard Dutch by the elite. Krabbendam, *Freedom on the Horizon*, 223-28, gives examples of such contacts.

[20] With respect to Pella, I completely agree with Daan's observation in the *Pella Chronicle* that no dialectal Dutch can be found. As was indicated above, in Pella, Frisian was ousted by standard-like American Dutch at an early stage as well (Van Marle, *On the Survival of the Frisian Language*).

Fig. 20.2. Conversing on Franklin Street, Pella, Iowa, after 1922
(*courtesy Pella Historical Society Archives*)

that explain why the Dutch Americans in Pella have been praised for the quality of their language.[21]

Thus, Dutch Americans in Pella copied the gradual rise of a spoken standard language that occurred in the Netherlands. Consequently, an American variety of Standard Dutch came into being, a variety that particularly in the early years must have been remarkably similar to its counterpart in the Netherlands.[22]

Let us take a closer look at this copying of the developing spoken standard language. In all probability, there was interplay of several factors which in combination resulted in the developing spoken standard language as the new norm. First is the differing socio-cultural context. The Pella Dutch in the early years were economically better off than their kinfolk in Michigan. In addition, the number of "educated residents" was high in Pella.[23] From this one can assume that the majority of Pella's inhabitants had a relatively strong cultural orientation toward the culturally and politically dominant parts of the Netherlands. This made them more inclined to follow trends in the Netherlands, including the new norm for speaking. This paralleled what

---

[21] Van Hinte, *Netherlanders in America*, 992.
[22] In later American Dutch, the similarity with the standard language spoken in the Netherlands was seriously affected by factors such as: (1) the influence of English, and (2) language attrition (due to the decreasing use of Dutch). See Caroline Smits, *Disintegration of Inflection: The Case of Iowa Dutch* (The Hague: Holland Academic Graphics, 1996). Also, see the literature mentioned in footnote 10.
[23] Van Hinte, *Netherlanders in America*, 992.

happened in the Netherlands, where the use of the spoken standard was also restricted to the socio-cultural elite.

Second, "linguistic distance" was a factor in the use of spoken standard Dutch. The majority of the inhabitants of Pella came from the western parts of the Netherlands where, not surprisingly, the spoken standard developed. This variety is much more closely related to the western dialects than to the eastern or southern dialects. As a result, the linguistic distance between the western dialects and spoken standard Dutch is relatively small. Thus, the spoken standard was easier to acquire for the Dutch Americans in Pella than for their Michigan kin.

One, however, should not exaggerate this factor. Pella had quite a few immigrants with a Frisian, Gelderland, or Groningen background, and they, too, adopted the standard-like variety. In these cases, the linguistic distance between the dialects and the spoken standard was much bigger, but apparently, it did not hinder the spread of the new standard among these speakers.[24]

The spread of standard-like American Dutch also was dependent on the existence of a cultural "infrastructure," such as Christian schools, which played a crucial part in the maintenance of Dutch and churches, particularly the "Dutchy" Christian Reformed congregations. As in the Netherlands and other European countries, schools and other cultural institutions constitute important vehicles for the spread of standard languages.[25]

Conclusion

The fact that in Pella, Iowa, a specific kind of Dutch developed is no coincidence. It was the conscious choice of the residents to imitate and adopt the prestigious new norm that developed in the Netherlands. Due to their orientation toward the western parts of the Netherlands, they were aware of this trend. The fact that the linguistic distance between the majority of the dialects spoken in Pella and the new spoken standard was close certainly helped in the spread of the standard-like variety. The fact that the Dutch Americans in Pella imitated the new norm indicates the extent to which they were still oriented toward the Netherlands.

It is clear that Dutch Americans in Pella consciously chose to adopt Standard Dutch. At the time we did fieldwork, the language of

---

[24] Recall, also, that this standard-like variety could be found outside of Pella, Iowa, as well. It was simply the variety of Dutch used by the Dutch American elite, irrespective of their geographic background in the Netherlands.
[25] Krabbendam, *Freedom on the Horizon*, 231.

most of our informants was "disintegrating," because of the fact that it had been affected by forces such as the influence of English and language erosion. Of course, there were still speakers of American Dutch whose language was affected hardly at all, and these speakers strongly disapproved of the disintegrating language of their fellow Dutch Americans. These speakers clearly considered themselves speakers of "High Dutch" (as they called it themselves), the language of the Netherlands. Importantly, to them High Dutch was also the language of their faith and their church.

These speakers in Pella really cherished their language, and they were proud that they spoke "the real Dutch." This is evident from the fact that they knew facts about their language that were unfamiliar to most other American Dutch speakers. One Pella informant, for instance, was proud that he still knew that there was a gender distinction in Dutch (i.e., the difference between nouns associated with the article *de* and nouns associated with *het*). He was perfectly aware that this distinction had been lost in the language of nearly all other speakers of American Dutch. Some speakers of American Dutch displayed a clear "anti-dialect" attitude. One of our informants, a retired farmer, told us: "In my house it is only High Dutch that is spoken." In conformity with this rule, he forbade his wife to speak the Groningen dialect with her sisters. To him, speaking a dialect was some sort of an insult. Nearly all speakers of American Dutch strongly disapprove of the use of English words while speaking Dutch.[26]

Speakers of American Dutch clearly favor "pure Dutch." They start from a norm that is typical of standard languages; dialect speakers are usually far less sensitive to language norms that are based on purity. Even at the time we made our recordings, there were speakers of American Dutch who could also read and write Dutch. To them, American Dutch still functioned as a standard language.

In the literature it has often been stressed that there are regional differences in the maintenance of Dutch. In this chapter, however, we focus on the differences in the development of Dutch. In many places the original dialects were maintained, resulting in American Dialectal Dutch. But among the educated elite there was a trend to imitate and adopt the gradually emerging spoken standard. Crucially, in Pella this new spoken standard became the norm of the population as a whole. This shift to Standard Dutch illustrates how different the diverse

---

[26] Van Marle and Smits, "On the Decrease of Language Norms in a Disintegrating Language."

Dutch settlements actually were in socio-cultural terms. This implies that one should be careful in making strong generalizations about Dutch American culture in general, since both the regional and the socio-cultural differences were tremendous.

CHAPTER 21

Gerhard Hendrik Nollen: Portrait of the Artist

Susan Price Miller

In 2008 the Scholte House Museum, part of the Pella Historical Society, sent a dark and damaged landscape, titled *Pastoral Scene*, by Dutch-born artist Gerhard Nollen, to Barry Bauman Conservation in Chicago. After careers at the Art Institute of Chicago and in private practice, Bauman offers conservation services at no charge for non-profit institutions. While repairing the canvas and uncovering the original colors, he discovered the work of someone he now considers "one of the most unknown great artists in America, let alone Iowa."[1]

Gerhard Nollen was a nineteenth-century painter, photographer, and teacher in southeast Iowa, but since his death in 1901, few people have been made aware of his work. Thirty years ago, Carl and Paul Nollen published family stories and documents in *The Nollen Family in America*, and Kathleen Goldzung (Vanden Oever), a Central College

---

[1] Barry Bauman, email to author, 7 July 2012. To see *Pastoral Scene* in color, go to Bauman's website at http://www.baumanconservation.com, click on: enter, 2008, 51, #244. All paintings owned by the Pella Historical Society will be designated PHS followed by PHV (Pella Historical Village) or SHM (Scholte House Museum) for the present location.

Fig. 21.1. *Pastoral Scene*, c. 1874
(*Pella Historical Society, Scholte House Museum*)

student, interviewed owners of Nollen paintings for an honors paper.[2] Recently, I have found more information in on-line digital sources of a larger data base of paintings attributed to Nollen. I have also made close observations of his style, materials, and techniques. The results reveal much about his life and accomplishments.

Researchers may have trouble finding artist Gerhard Nollen in record sources and identification of his oeuvre. Gerhard, Gerard, Gerrit, Geo, and George appear in some sources, and Nollen turns up spelled in a variety of ways. He most often signed paintings and documents "G. H. Nollen," although a few paintings have a monogram with a large "G" crossed at the top with "H" and at the bottom with "N." As an independent photographer in Keokuk, Iowa, he simply imprinted "Gerhard" on his cabinet cards. Unfortunately, he left many paintings unsigned. The lack of anything significant in his own words only adds to the challenge of capturing this artist.

Gerhard Hendrik Nollen, the second son of Hendrikus and Zwaantje Nollen, was born on 9 March 1830, in Didam, the Netherlands. Family stories tell of the child's impetuous indulgences. For example, once when carrying a basket of *poffertjes* (silver-dollar-size pancakes)

[2] Carl Nollen and Paul Nollen, *The Nollen Family in America* (Macomb, IL: self-published, 1981); Kathleen Goldzung (Vanden Oever), *Schilder Nollen*. Central College Archives, Pella, IA; reprinted in *Artisans and Musicians Dutch and American*, ed. James E. McMillan (Pella, IA: Pella Printing Co., 1997), 34-52.

to a man across town, he ate all but one on the way then finished the last one when invited to do so by the intended recipient. Another time, Gerhard emptied his brother's bank of coins and spent them on merry-go-round rides at the fair.[3]

Father Hendrikus was the local school teacher, which included the extra duties of sexton (*koster*) and song leader (*voorzinger*) at the Didam Reformed Church (*Hervormde Kerk*). He also served as the *burgemeester's* secretary. Nevertheless, in a society very conscious of status, Hendrikus Nollen felt "low in the hierarchy of the village," in spite of his talents and hard work. He and Zwaantje took extra steps to educate their children, have books in the house, and prepare the children for good positions in society.[4]

But son Gerhard, who had little interest in academic subjects, filled his copybooks with drawings and sketched on his slate. Seeing this, Hendrikus arranged for the ten year old to learn a trade with a house painter in Arnhem, thirteen miles away, where art lessons were also available. He wanted his son to have "a chance to become somebody and at the same time . . . learn a trade that he [could] fall back upon in case of necessity."[5]

From an early age, the boy had to cope with being on his own for fifty-one weeks of the year. Under the guidance of the house painter at Arnhem, Gerhard was able to attend the Arnhem Academy of Design. No later than 1845, when Nollen was fifteen, he made a confident realistic portrait in pastels (colored chalk) of Joannes ter Laak, which is now in the collection of the Openluchtmuseum (Open Air Museum) in Arnhem.[6]

While still a student in 1849, Gerhard signed his first known oil painting, a double portrait of his brother John and himself. Nollen intentionally made the heads and eyes in conventionalized oval shapes, a style that he would use again from time to time. The painting was not only a "faithful representation of the boys' features" but also a "work of art [that] had decided merits, and it excited the admiration of all."[7]

---

[3] John Scholte Nollen, "My Father and Others," *Pella Chronicle* (13 May 1943). John Scholte Nollen, the son of Gerhard's older brother, John, was born in 1869 and knew the artist for thirty years.
[4] Nollen and Nollen, *Nollen Family*, 10.
[5] John Nollen, "The Tower of Babel," in Nollen and Nollen, *Nollen Family*, 181.
[6] Ibid., 183; Hans Piena, email to author, 27 May 2013. Piena wrote that Joannes ter Laak died in 1845, although the website gives "ca. 1850-1855" as the date of the portrait. See the portrait at: http://www.geheugenvannederland.nl.
[7] John Nollen, "Tower of Babel," 185. This painting, signed G. H. Nollen and dated 1849, came to the United States with the family and now belongs to a family descendant (Carl Nollen, letter to author, 30 July 2010).

In 1851 the Academy of Design awarded him the gold medal for being the top artist at the school. His public remarks of thanks made the father doubly proud. Hendrikus wrote to his brother, "If the dear God will further spare him with life and good health, we can have much joy together in this well-beloved boy."[8]

Gerhard had learned the painting techniques passed down since the seventeenth-century Golden Age of Dutch painting. Barend Cornelis Koekkoek, one of the best known Dutch landscape painters during Nollen's formative years, followed the tradition of layering glazes of paint. Koekkoek first established the "sky in thin, transparent layers, an operation that took him a few days. After this, he would build up the rest of the landscape layer by layer, from pale tints to full tones and from sketchy to detailed, taking care that each layer was perfectly dry before applying the next one. Only when the painting was almost finished did he add the figures."[9] There is no record that Nollen studied with Koekkoek, but he or his teachers no doubt knew of the famous painter who lived in Cleves, Germany, about twenty-five miles from Arnhem.

Gerhard used the same method of layering tinted glazes to create textures and luminous skin tones in approximately two dozen portraits, which are the majority of his surviving work painted before 1875. By 1854 Nollen had produced exceptional realistic portrayals of his mother and father and of Wilhelmina Nass, the wife of Joannes ter Laak.[10] Barry Bauman, who treated the two paintings of the parents, says they are "highly accomplished," the work a "mature artist."[11]

As Gerhard began to prosper in the early 1850s, his father experienced some personal conflicts with the church minister. He also lost his position as secretary for the *burgemeester* after new laws broadening the electorate resulted in the domination of municipal government by the majority Catholic population.[12] Hendrikus Nollen "reluctantly . . . severed his connection with his native country, and sought a pleasanter home in the Land of Promise beyond the sea."[13]

---

[8] Hendrikus Nollen to Hendrik Nollen, 14 Oct. 1851, in Nollen and Nollen, *Nollen Family*, 143-44.

[9] Marjan van Heteren, Guido Jansen, and Ronald de Leeuw, *The Poetry of Reality: Dutch Painters of the Nineteenth Century* (Amsterdam: Waanders Publishers, 2000), 74-75.

[10] The parents' portraits at Bauman, 2011, p. 83, #403, PHS, PHV. Wilhelmina Nass, Openluchtmuseum at: http://www.geheugenvannederland.nl.

[11] Barry Bauman, email to author, 12 Nov. 2012.

[12] Nollen and Nollen, in *Nollen Family*, 11-12.

[13] John Nollen, "Tower of Babel," 194.

In 1854 son Gerhard gave up his promising career as an artist and left the Netherlands with his parents and siblings. The family entered the United States through New Orleans and came up the Mississippi River by steamboat to St. Louis and Keokuk, Iowa. The family settled in Pella, a small Dutch colony on the Iowa prairie, founded in 1847 under the leadership of Dominie Hendrik P. Scholte. Hendrikus Nollen expected to be the master of an estate worked by servants, but he found himself struggling to survive on a frontier farm that was physically and culturally isolated.[14]

Gerhard tried to restart his career as an artist in town. On 1 February 1855, he advertised in the first edition of Scholte's *Pella Gazette*. Anyone wanting a portrait or painting lessons could contact him at the "Book Store." Dr. Benjamin Keables, the husband of Scholte's daughter, Sara, had only recently added books and school supplies to his drug store on the northwest corner of the central square.[15] Dr. Keables, a member of the first class at Medical College in Keokuk, Iowa, graduated and started his practice in Pella in 1852. The 4 October 1855 issue of the *Gazette* announced Nollen's intention to open a studio for architectural, landscape, and portrait drawing. He built a large room with an attached bedroom near the corner of Washington and Main Street, where he and brother John were living the following spring.[16]

Gerhard continued to experiment in Pella with oval eyes and heads, as is evident in portraits of Henry Scholte Jr. and a group of three girls—his two sisters and their neighbor, Jenneke Welle.[17] At the same time, however, he produced a sensitive, realistic portrayal of Mrs. Hendrik Eysink, a family friend who had emigrated with the Nollens and died in 1857.[18]

Gerhard's known landscapes from this time are three drawings of early Pella. His 1856 sketch of the north side of the central square, including the Scholte house and the *Pella Gazette* office, is now kept at a

[14] John Nollen, "The Rise of Omega," in Nollen and Nollen, *Nollen Family*, 198, 218-19.
[15] "Keables' Column," *Pella Gazette* (27 Dec. 1855).
[16] 1856 State Census of Iowa, Marion County, Lake Prairie Township, 514, at http://iagenweb.org. John married Johanna Scholte in 1864, at which time Gerhard sold him the building for $400. Carl Nollen, *The Nollen Family in America: Twenty Year Update* (Runnels, IA: self-published, 2002), 103.
[17] As Barry Bauman was working on the picture of the three girls, he discovered the initials "J. W." on the bow of the one in the middle, which indicates she was Jenneke Welle and not Nollen's third sister, Gezina Hendrika, who died 8 March 1855. See image at Bauman, 2010, p. 78, #378; PHS, PHV; Henry Scholte Jr., portrait, PHS, SHM.
[18] Interview with the owner by author, 19 Nov. 2009.

Fig. 21.2. Portrait of Mrs. Hendrik Eysink, c. 1855 (*courtesy Verle Boot*)

bank. Two other drawings of local landmarks from the same year went to a publisher in the Netherlands to be used as illustrations in a book by his brother John. Since the artist was not in Iowa at the founding of Pella, he had to imagine the view, titled *Pella in 1848*, where the only recognizable building is a side view of the Scholte House. The print of *Pella 1856*, however, should be a fairly accurate representation of Central College, Scholte's church, and the central square in the distance.[19]

During 1856 Nollen decided to leave Pella for a region that might have more opportunities for an artist. He moved to Keokuk, Iowa's, "Gate City" on the Mississippi River, where increasing riverboat traffic and real estate speculation were fueling rapid growth. Dr. Keables, who had graduated from medical school in Keokuk only four years earlier, knew the territory and may have made arrangements when he passed through the city in the spring of the year on a trip to Cincinnati.[20]

During his first years in Keokuk, Nollen worked solely as a painter at Emerson's Photographic Palace, which specialized in daguerreotypes and ambrotypes, two kinds of early photographs that used metal and glass mounted in a case. The proprietor advertised in the form of bank notes with the line, "Life size portraits painted at this

---

[19] Jan [John] Nollen, *De Hollanders in Iowa, brieven uit Pella van een Geldersman* (Arnhem: D. A. Thieme, 1858).

[20] Mary Scholte to her father, 9 Mar. 1856, Central College Archives, Pella, IA. Mary wrote from her school in Monticello, IL, that she was not in good health and mentioned a possible visit from "Dr. K.," who was going to Cincinnati.

Fig. 21.3. Self-portrait with Marble Pillar, c. 1857 (*author's collection*)

establishment," printed across the bottom.[21] Hendrikus wrote in 1859 that his son "does nothing but painting, and earns more than he needs. ... He lives economically and well, just as the circumstances were in the Netherlands."[22]

For three years Nollen worked with the energy and boldness of youth, showing off his skills and experimenting with portrait styles, materials, subject matter, and scale. A three-quarter length, almost life-size painting of a confident, well-dressed young man with oval eyes and head is probably a self-portrait displayed in his studio. With a limited palette of colors, the artist recreated the textures of a marble pillar, brocade drapery, and metal-edged buttons.

In 1856 and 1857, Nollen produced seven paintings of the family members of two brothers, Charles and Garret Van Weerden, both natives of the Netherlands.[23] Charles ran a tobacco shop, and Garret,

---

[21] Private collection of Allan Janus at Luminous Lint for Connoisseurs of Fine Photography, http://www.luminous-lint.com.
[22] H[endrikus] Nollen to brother, June 1859, in Nollen and Nollen, *Nollen Family*, 17.
[23] Vanden Oever, "Schilder Nollen," 42-43. The author identified one couple as Mr. and Mrs. Samuel Van Grieken. Samuel Van Grieken, however, was only about eighteen years old at the time and unmarried. The adults were probably Mr. and Mrs. Garret Van Weerden, the parents of the children in another painting, one of whom married Van Grieken in 1863. After the death of the owner interviewed by Vanden Oever, the seven paintings were dispersed, and their present locations are unknown.

who rented a room to the painter, was a confectioner.[24] A Van Weerden family story that Nollen paid his room and board with the portraits may be true, since it is unlikely that the shopkeepers could have afforded them otherwise.[25] Nollen was probably learning to copy photographs, especially with the groups of children, and also practicing both realistic and stylized forms.

Nollen also copied a variety of subjects from small commercial images or prints available at the time. In 1857 he signed and dated a portrait of Native American Chief Keokuk, wearing a blue robe, now at the Samuel F. Miller House Museum. A larger signed portrait of the chief in an orange robe hangs in the Keokuk city council chambers, and another almost identical canvas from the Miller House is being investigated as a possible third Chief Keokuk by Nollen.[26]

In an entirely different vein, he painted a beautiful copy of Raphael's *Sistine Madonna* on a sheet of metal in 1857.[27] At the same time, the busy young man worked on a very large painting based on a small black and white engraving of Thomas Cole's landscape *Dream of Arcadia*.[28] John C. Hughes, the head of the Keokuk Medical College, commissioned or bought the sixty-eight-by-eighty-four-inch painting, which his son donated to the State Historical Society of Iowa in Des Moines.[29]

In 1859 Gerhard and nineteen-year-old Samuel Van Grieken, the Dutch-born "operator" for Emerson's "Gallery," took over this business and advertised that they would pursue "their respective arts and will be at all times ready to supply any kind of pictures, from the smallest miniature to the size of life."[30] About this time they acquired the equipment to make *carte de visites*, or CDVs, on standard two-and-a-half-by-four-inch cards. The new technology, which swept the country about 1860, greatly reduced costs, and many Civil War soldiers who passed through Keokuk had their pictures taken for family members back home.

[24] Nollen lived at the same address as Gerret [sic] Van Weerden on 4th Street between Main and Blondeau (*Keokuk City Directory*, 1859), http://iagenweb.org.
[25] Vanden Oever, "Schilder Nollen," 43.
[26] Barry Bauman, 2013, p. 115, #565. The Lee County Historical Society owns two paintings of Chief Keokuk in the Samuel F. Miller House Museum.
[27] Hazel Veith, a descendant of the photographer Emerson, donated the painting to the United Presbyterian Church in Keokuk.
[28] Thomas Cole, a leader of the Hudson River School, painted *Dream of Arcadia* in 1838. James Smilie made an engraving that was printed by W. E. Smith in 1850 and by Appleton & Co. in 1854.
[29] Bauman, 2012, p. 103, #501.
[30] Keokuk, *Daily Gate City*, 6 Dec. 1859, in Carl Nollen, *Nollen Family*, 66.

In the middle of the Civil War, Gerhard took up the challenge of painting a major historical work based on an engraving of the painting [Stephen] *Decatur Boarding the Tripolitan Gunboat* by Dennis M. Carter. (Admiral Stephen Decatur had boarded an enemy boat soon after learning of the death of his brother James during the first Barbary War in 1804. His heroic action and subsequent victory made him an American hero.) Edward S. Carter, a local store owner, bought Nollen's *Decatur at Tripoli* from Emerson in 1889. When Carter's son gave it to the Elks Lodge in Keokuk, a Des Moines newspaper called it "one of the most famous paintings by an Iowa artist" which "[had] won fame not only in the country, but abroad." The paper also reported that "Mr. Nollen had a vision that he would paint a great historical picture, and this was felt to be realized when he painted *Decatur at Tripoli*."[31] Unfortunately, the one Nollen painting with the most published information disappeared from the Elks Lodge, and all attempts to locate it have been unsuccessful.[32]

Gerhard's partnership with Van Grieken probably ended some months before the two men paid separate license fees in 1865. Nollen's income that year was $463.[33] With the departure of the soldiers after the war, however, his earnings dropped to only $191 the following year.[34] Between 1866 and 1871, the city of Keokuk directories listed his profession most often as a portrait painter, although the 1868 edition identified him as both photographer and portrait painter. Nollen owned a solar camera that made "pictures of any size desired, either plain or colored," and he retouched images in India ink or colored them with oils or water colors for other photographers.[35] His four-and-a-quarter-by-six-and-a-half-inch photos, called cabinet cards, were imprinted simply with the name "Gerhard" and his address. All are in the author's collection.

After the war, the railroad from the Mississippi River reached Pella, and the small town grew larger and more prosperous. In 1871, a year after the United States census for Keokuk listed his personal worth

---

[31] Des Moines *Register and Leader* (21 Dec. 1915), quoted in Zenobia Ness and Louise Orwig, *Iowa Artists of the First Hundred Years* (Ames, IA: Wallace Homestead Co., 1939) 154-55.
[32] Carl Nollen, *Nollen Family*, 66.
[33] IRS Tax Assessment Lists, 1862-1918, IA, District 1, Annual Lists, 1865, at Ancestry.com. Nollen paid $25 for a business license, $23.15 in income tax, and $1 for his watch.
[34] Tax Assessment Lists, 1866.
[35] Keokuk, *Daily Gate City*, undated clipping in Bickel Collection, "Iowa Towns," 47, Keokuk Public Library.

Fig. 21.4. Self-portrait, c. 1874 (*courtesy Pella Historical Society, Scholte House Museum*)

at $4,000, Nollen moved back to Pella and set up a studio on the west side of the central square in a building owned by Dr. Keables.[36] In the early 1870s, Gerhard painted a series of portraits on canvas mounted on oval wooden frames, which was a new format for his work. Photographs of most of the subjects exist, indicating he probably used them as the basis of the poses. Among the portraits are his brother John; his sister-in-law, Johanna; himself; and his wife, Gertrude Kramer Nollen, whom he married in April 1874. Gertrude, who at age thirty-five, was ten years younger than her husband, had worked for Dr. Keables' family since she was in her teens.[37]

While Nollen painted a few more portraits from time to time until four years before he died, his interest turned to the landscape genre in the 1870s. Possibly his best work, what is now called *Pastoral Scene*, seems to be his own version of ideal rural life reminiscent of his copy of Thomas Cole's *Dream of Arcadia* (image 1). A family story says the man leaning against a tree is Gerhard. The image does resemble his self portrait from

[36] "William Fisher, et al., vs. M. H. E. Beard," *In the Supreme Court of Iowa* (December Term, 1874), 30 (known as the Garden Square Controversy), Central College Archives. G. H. Nallen [*sic*] was listed as a business on the square next to B. F. Keables' drug store. Keables had originally built the building for his brother's furniture business.

[37] Johanna's portrait, dated 1874, is in a family collection (Nollen and Nollen, *Nollen Family*, 70-71). John's portrait was donated to the Pella Historical Society in 2012. Gertrude's portrait, now lost, is listed on the appraiser's bill of Nollen's estate, along with his self portrait. Gerhard's estate information from Carl Nollen, email to author, 10 Dec. 2009.

the period, and the woman—a milk maid—is probably Gertrude. Both are wearing clothes in earlier European styles, a characteristic of most figures in his landscapes. The setting, however, is for the most part an Iowa scene with animals and a pond in the country with a house, a mill wheel, a church tower, and curiously, a distant Dutch windmill, all signs of human habitation. Two focal points skillfully draw the viewer into the woods on the left and to the windmill centered on the distant horizon.

Sadly, Gerhard's hope for personal happiness ended the year after his marriage. Gertrude gave birth to a son on 10 June 1875, but she died eight days later. The baby died on 1 September 1875. One can only imagine the devastation experienced by Gerhard and the Nollen and Keables families. The loss deeply affected Gerhard, who was left "solitary and a mildly eccentric spirit." By 1880 he was living with his mother and younger brother Henry in an apartment over the Pella National Bank.[38]

After 1875 Nollen's landscapes changed in both materials and subject matter. In 1877 he created two melancholy scenes in shades of gray on light-weight cotton fabric tacked to thin, narrow strips of wood, mitered and glued at the corners. One has a coach, much like a nineteenth hearse, accompanied by a lone rider on a horse, while in the other, a group of people gather at the edge of a large body of water.[39] Another painting with the same flimsy materials is thought to be the family farm west of Pella. Here a large dark gray sky contrasts with sunlight shining on bright green fields.[40] A road bordered by a fence runs across the bottom of the picture plane where a single figure stands looking at the farm, and a little dog far to the right turns toward town. Nollen wrote on a stretcher, "this scene—1867," which is the year his father died. It is possible that the artist returned to Pella at that time and made sketches, which he finished in oils a decade later. The fact that he made this notation reveals the importance of the subject for him.

The poor quality of Nollen's materials may indicate a low point financially, or a period of exploration, or both. Another example with small, rough-cut, wood bars and glued mitered corners is *Tending Sheep*.[41]

[38] John Scholte Nollen, "So Many Yesterdays: Reminiscences of an Octogenarian," *Grinnell College* (Iowa City: State Historical Society of Iowa, 1953), 239.
[39] Bauman, 2012, p. 96, #470; PHS, SHM. Nollen wrote the date 1877 on the stretchers of *Landscape with Coach* when he gave it as a wedding present to a nephew in 1896.
[40] Bauman, 2011, p. 90, #440; PHS, SHM.
[41] Bauman, 2013, p. 112, #548; PHS, SHM.

Fig. 21.5. *The Farm*, c. 1877 *(courtesy Pella Historical Society, Scholte House Museum)*

The monochromatic color scheme in shades of brown creates a rustic barnyard setting for a young girl in vintage peasant clothing with her back to a group of sheep in the foreground, one of whom looks directly at the viewer. Gerhard's version of a published print demonstrated how to create a variety of textures within a range of light to dark values of one color.[42]

Understanding the use of light and dark is an important step in learning how to paint. It is possible that Nollen used these one-color studies when he was teaching Maria Scholte Beard, the widow of Dominie Scholte.[43] Her simple, moderately-size compositions have the same type of stretchers as *Girl with Sheep*. Nollen probably supplied materials and prepared her canvasses. Over time, they sagged, and the paint flaked and cracked. Her later, larger, and more ambitious work held up better due to stronger supports and better technique. She skillfully copied or adapted elements from published prints. In Maria Scholte Beard, Gerhard had not just a student but almost an equal.[44]

In the late 1870s, Nollen had another protégé of note. Augusta Arnold Macy from Oskaloosa, Iowa, studied with him before her move to Des Moines in 1880, where the newly established Drake University

[42] The exact print for Nollen's painting has not been located, but a similar oil painting for sale on eBay in September 2013 indicates there was a common source for both.
[43] "Maria" is the original spelling of her name. If she had signed her paintings, she would have used Maria Beard. Paintings signed "Scholte" are by Nora Scholte, who changed the spelling of her mother-in-law's name to Mareah in the book, *Stranger in a Strange Land*.
[44] See examples of Maria's paintings at Bauman, 2011, p. 83, #403; 2011, p. 90, #440; 2013, p. 107, #525.

hired her to teach drawing and painting. Macy had two daughters who also became artists. Harriet Macy exhibited widely and taught art for years at East High School in Des Moines.[45]

Gerhard, the teacher, also instructed Central College students during the 1885-86 school year. At the end of March, just after the winter term ended, he left Pella for New York State. His return date is not known, but he intended to be gone long enough for the consistory at the Second Reformed Church to name a new deacon in his place. A year later, in April 1887, he departed again, this time to paint the "scenery" in California.[46] The only recorded work from his eleven months in the Sacramento and San Francisco areas, however, is a "crayon" portrait of Lily Langtry, which he entered in the Mechanics Institute Exhibition in San Francisco.[47] He may have also produced at this time the unsigned pastel scene of a waterfront with palm trees that appears in a photograph of Henry Scholte Jr.'s, apartment in the Scholte House and still hangs in the dining room of the museum.

Nollen reappeared in Pella in March 1888 but soon left for the Netherlands in the company of a Dutch minister and his family. After a year visiting friends in Europe, he landed in New York, having traveled from Amsterdam in a first-class cabin. He reached Pella on 6 April 1889.[48]

It was probably after the trip to Europe that Gerhard Nollen began teaching Nora Keables Scholte, the wife of Henry P. Scholte Jr. As with Maria, he again supplied materials for his student. Nora's early oil paintings have stretchers held together at the corners with metal fasteners with an 1885 patent date, the same fasteners found on several of his landscapes. Nora taught art at Central College for a few years in the late 1890s, painted for the rest of her life, and covered the walls in the Scholte House with her oils and watercolors.

In the early 1890s, Gerhard Nollen moved forty miles southeast of Pella to Ottumwa, where his student Clarence Timbrel lived. When Zwaantje Nollen died in January 1892, her son was too ill to attend the funeral.[49] That was the year he completed one of his best portraits,

---

[45] Ness and Orwig, *Iowa Artists*, 134-35.
[46] *Pella Blade*, 30 Mar., 6 Apr. 1886, 12 Apr. 1887, 28 June 1887, in Nollen, *Family Update*, 33, Newspaperarchive.com.
[47] *Report of the Industrial Exhibition of the Mechanics*, Mechanics Institute (San Francisco, 1887) 63, 177, Google Books. G. H. Nollen received a diploma for his entry in the category of "crayon," probably meaning "pastel," drawings. Lily Langtry was in San Francisco at the time, having just divorced her husband.
[48] *Pella Blade*, 27 Mar., 15 May 1888, 9 Apr. 1889, in Nollen, *Family Update*, 33-34; Robert P. Swierenga, comp., *Dutch Immigrants in New York Passenger Lists*, 1881-94, Ancestry.com.
[49] Ness and Orwig, *Iowa Artists*, 206; *Pella Blade*, 22 Jan. 1892.

a remarkably realistic image of the Baptist pastor Lewis A. Dunn, president of Iowa Central University from 1871 to 1881, and of the renamed Central College from 1886 to 1888.[50] Three years later, in 1895, the court decided that he was unable to take care of his own affairs and named his brother John as guardian.[51] Gerhard went to live on his sister's farm west of Pella and painted portraits and landscapes on art boards that eliminated the need for stretchers and canvas. Although he made rather mechanical copies of family pictures of Dominie Scholte and his daughter, Mary Scholte Bousquet (two copies), his portrait of Nora Scholte, based on an existing photograph and observations of the live model, has the old translucent skin tones, clothing details, and solidity.[52] He produced his last painting in 1897, when he secretly sketched Dr. Ira Stoddard for a surprise fiftieth-anniversary gift.[53] The surface has a rougher paint texture, which shows some decline in technique, although the face is warm and alive.

Nollen's landscapes after his extensive travels in the 1880s show a progression toward more imaginative and emotional scenes. Although the settings are probably not of any particular place, they do show the influence of the time spent in California in the ground formations and types of trees. Two landscapes from late in the decade are painted mostly in browns. They have a western look with mountains rising up in the distance. One setting is a rocky land with scrubby vegetation. Here a man with a dog leads a horse ridden by a woman into a river, while another man pushes a boat loaded with belongings away from shore. Two children stand in the water, and two horsemen approach. The travelers move from left to right across the bottom of the frame toward an unseen destination. Patches of color with undefined edges give the painting an impressionistic quality.[54]

Three final landscapes from the 1890s depict only one or two figures and a dog, alone in nature, devoid of any other sign of human activity.[55] Large, smooth horizontal areas of paint represent sky and ground and create a quiet, peaceful effect. Plants and people are not clearly formed. Composed from the artist's imagination, the three

---

[50] Bauman, 2007, p. 39, #183.
[51] "Henry Nollen vs. Gerhard H. Nollen," 10 Oct. 1895, Probate Records, Marion County, IA, District Court, courtesy of Carl Nollen, 19 Oct. 2012.
[52] *Dominie Scholte*, PHS, PHV. *Mary Scholte Bousquet*, PHS, PHV, and SHM; *Nora Keables Scholte*, Bauman, 2010, p. 75, #364; PHS, SHM.
[53] Bauman, 2007, p. 39, #183; Central College; Anna Howell Clarkson, *A Beautiful Life and its Associations* (New York: Historical Department of Iowa, 1899), 41-42.
[54] Bauman 2010, p. 75, #364, PHS, SHM.
[55] Two of the paintings can be seen at Bauman, 2013, p. 112, #548. PHS, SHM.

Fig. 21.6. *Landscape with Pine Trees*, 1896 (*courtesy Pella Historical Society, Scholte House Museum*)

paintings all have a hazy, dream-like quality suggesting memory, loneliness, and uncertain journeys. In the one dated 1896, a man, a woman on a horse, and a dog, appear against the low, distant horizon. Nollen had come a long way from his idyllic vision in *Pastoral Scene*.

When Gerhard Nollen died on 1 April 1901, he left investments worth over $7,000, and a dozen paintings, some of which have been located. His books about art, poetry, and religion, and numerous photographs and drawings have disappeared. The local paper published an obituary that mentioned nothing about his life after his return to Pella, except that "he has been living quietly with his relatives here in the country and lately in the city."[56] Apparently, his family and others did not know what to say, nor had they known how to deal with him in his final years. The stigma of mental illness or dementia carried the perception of moral failure. In addition, some members of the family felt he had not lived up to his potential as an artist. Writing many years later, his nephew, John Scholte Nollen, one of five very successful children of John Nollen, summed up the attitude:

> Father's artist brother Gerard... never won the success to which his talent might have entitled him. His experiment as a photographer in Keokuk proved only his lack of practical business sense, and

[56] *Pella Advertiser*, 4 Apr. 1901.

even though he was a minor Ruysdael as a landscapist, and better than most of his contemporaries at portraiture, there was naturally little market for his work or for his skill as a teacher of painting in rural Pella. He was quite lacking in the enterprise that could have gained him fame in a city in competition with other artists. Like my father, whose light also was hidden under the Pella bushel, Uncle Gerard preferred to "let well-enough alone."[57]

Clearly the nephew did not appreciate the challenges Gerhard had faced in leaving his career in the Netherlands, coping with the situation in Iowa, and enduring the disappointments in his personal life. He showed plenty of enterprise in taking on challenging painting projects and learning a variety of photographic techniques in Keokuk, where during at least one year, he earned more than twice as much as his brother John, the bank cashier. He had acquired a fair amount of personal worth by the time he returned to Pella and had earned a few favorable words in the press. Somehow, he could support himself on long sojourns in distant places while teaching himself and others, and he had over $7,000 in investments when he died. During his lifetime, art began to change from a way to record people, events, and nature to a means of self-expression, and Nollen moved in that direction either accidentally or by choice. He drew and painted as he wished from a very early age until almost his last days.

A generation after Gerhard died, the *Souvenir History of Pella*, published in 1922, offered a better evaluation of his life and contributions: "G. H. Nollen was a talented artist who did much to develop the artistic character of the community. . . . He was an artist of unusual ability, and in addition to doing artwork, he taught a number of pupils. He was a man of earnest religious convictions and a blameless life."[58]

---

[57] John S. Nollen, "So Many Yesterdays," 240-41. The writer was a German language and literature scholar and president of two colleges. His two brothers had each become president of a major insurance company in Des Moines, and his two sisters were well known educators in Des Moines.

[58] *Souvenir History of Pella, Iowa: 1847-1922* (Pella: Booster Press, 1922), 90, 170.

Index

101st Airborne Division, 272
Abernethy, Alonzo, 57
Afscheiding of 1834. *See* Christian Seceded Church
Alexander College, 63
Alien Properties Act, 111n
Allegan, MI, 78
Allegan County, MI, 166, 168, 170, 174-75
Alto, WI, 355-56
Ambach, Charlotte, 196, image 197
American Anti-Slavery Society, 72n
American Dialectal Dutch, 354n, 355-57, 360
American Expeditionary Force, 124-25
American Legion, 36, 143
American peace movement, 129, 134
Americanization: and war, xxi, 120, 158
Amsterdam, NL: and Arie Gerrit Zigeler, xxiv, 323-36, 338-39, 341, 349; and Christian Seceded Church, 304-6, 312; German Lutherans in, 292; and Gerhard Nollen, 375; and Henry P. Scholte, 290, 304-6, 312; and the Holocaust, 184, 188; and Jan Pijnappel, 74n; and Klaas Zuidema, 45, 50; and Second World War, 173, 175, 191; Amsterdam Stock Exchange, 81
Anabaptists, 297, 319
Anchor, The (newspaper), 154
Anet, Léonard (Brussels), 327n
Angel Island, CA, 202
Anti-Revolutionary Party, 91, 93; politics of, 90; principles of, 90-91
anti-slavery, 72-73; and Abraham Lincoln, 83, 86n; and Albertus C. Van Raalte, 68; and Civil War, xv; and Henry P. Scholte, 5, 11, 14, 68; and John Brown, 82; and Lucretia Mott, 72; and Maria Margaretha Storm-van der Chijs, 68, 77, 82, 86; and Newton A.

Patterson, 79; and Pieter Zonne, 68; and Roane County, TN, 83; and territorial expansion, 64; and William Vandever, 54-55, 64, 66
Antwerp, Belgium: and Arie Gerrit Zigeler, 323, 325-30, 332, 337n; and Dutch Escape Line, 181-82, 189; harbor of, 164
Apache Indians, 61
Appomattox, VA, 26
Archangel, Russia, 125-26
Arkansas Post, AK, 48, 52, 59
Arlington National Cemetery, 125
Armistice Day (11 Nov. 1918), 113, 125, 157
Army Specialized Training Program, image 156
Army-Navy "E" Award, 151-52
Arnhem Academy of Design, NL, 365
Arnhem Emigration Society, 307
Arnoys, Marinus, 217
Atkinson Griffin House, KY, image 36
Atlanta, GA, xvii, xviii, 37, 58-59
Auburn, NY, 9
Australia: and Ernest Gerritsma, 201-3, 207-10, 215-16; and Maria Margaretha Storm-van der Chijs, 85

Baarle-Nassau, NL, 180, 186, 192, 194, 195-96
Babylon: as Biblical symbol of evil, 316-17, 319
Baede, Fons, 117n
Baffin Bay, CA, 112n, 113
Baflo, NL, 51
Bagelaar, Anna Suzanna (Mrs. Jacobus van der Chijs), 69
Baker, Nathaniel B., 21, 23
Baltimore, MD, 54
Baltimore's Merchants Club, image 102
Banks, Nathaniel P. (gen.), 59
Banner, The, image 261; and Ernest Gerritsma, 217; and Vietnam War voices, 258-65
baptism: infant, 297-98, 328; adult, 344n
Barry Bauman Conservation, Chicago, 363

Battle of Green River (KY), 35, 37
Bauman, Barry, 366, 367n
Beard, Maria Scholte, 9, 18, 374-75
Beets, Henry, 31
Beets, Nicolaas, 332n
Belgian War for Independence, 20, image 310
Belgic Confession: and Arie Gerrit Zigeler, 328, 341; and doctrine of election, 301; and church and state, 295, 300-301, 312, 321; and infant baptism, 297-98
Belgium: and Arie Gerrit Zigeler, 332, 344; and Dutch Escape Line, 178-83, 187, 190, 192, 194-98; and Secession of 1830, 288, 310; and First World War, 109; and War for Independence, 20, image 310
Benes, Louis, 258-59
Benthem Reddingius, G., 293
Bentonville (NC), Battle of, 56
Bergsma, Herbert, 265, 268n
Bertsch, Fred, image 147
Bielfield, Carrie, 158
Bil, Pieter, 128
Bilderdijk, Willem, 293, 314
Black Hills, SD, 60
blitz buggy, 215, image 216
Boer Republics (South Africa), 92; war for independence, xvi, and Abraham Kuyper, 101, and Dutch Americans, 138
Boer War, xvi, 138
Bolshevik Revolution, 126
bombing: Dutch New Guinea, 212; Japanese raids, 153; North Sea dikes, 160; Pearl Harbor, 207
Bos, Geertje, 50
Bos, Simon, 50
Bouma, Atte, 124
Bouma, Clarence, 139
bounty (enlistment): Civil War, 39
Bousquet, Mary Scholte, 376
Bowling Green, KY, 34, 47
Bragg, Braxton (gen.), 47
Brasz, Bertram, 179, 183-84
Brasz, Cornelis, 183
Bratt, James D., 103
Bremer, Carol, 144

Brolin, Edward M., 159
Brookwood Labor College, NY, 132
Brown, Cecil (war correspondent), 218
Brown, Edward O., 111
Brown, John (abolitionist), 82
Brownsville, TX, xviii, 59, 108
Brummelkamp, Anthony, image 292; and congregation in Hattem, 298; and Henry P. Scholte, 298-300, 304-7; and Scholte Club, 293, 296
Brussels, Belgium: and Arie Gerrit Zigeler, 327n, 339; and Dutch Escape Line, 181, 183-85, 188, 190-91, 193-94, 196; and Secession of 1830, 311
Bryan, William Jennings, 104
Buchanan, James (US president), 73
Buckner, Simon Bolivar (gen.), 47-48
Bukowczyk, John, 254
Buna, New Guinea, 209
Burke, Edmund, 90

Calvin College, 256, 260, 357
Calvin, John, 95, 129
Calvin Theological Seminary, 139, 336n
Calvinism: and Abraham Kuyper, 95-98, 103, 105; Dutch variant of, 93; English variant of, 66; Neo-, 89, 105; and Socialism, 140; as worldview, 93
Cameron, Simon, 19n, 21
Camp Butler (Springfield, IL), xvii, 39, 40
Camp Crowder (MO), 218
Camp Fire Girls, 148
Camp meetings (NL), 327n, 332, 341, 342n
Camp Morton (Indianapolis, IN), 45, 48, 52, image 46
Camp Tuttle (IA), 22
Campbellsville, KY, 35
Canada, xxii, 73, 124, 164, 237, 249n
Canadians, 124; and Second World War, xxi, 160, 244
Canons of Dort, 289, 291, 293, 341
Capadose, Abraham, 332n

Cape of Good Hope: and Dutch settlers, 71
capitalism, 134, 258
Caribbean, 94, 97, 98, 247
Carrasco, Antonio, 331n
casualties: in war, xix, xxii, 28n, 34, 208, 212, 214, 254, 283
Catholics: and Arie Gerrit Zigeler, 325-26; in Caribbean, 94; and the Catholic Workers, 134; and Dutch Escape Line, 185-86; and French, 108, 130n; and German American, 112; and Henry P. Scholte, 316; and House of Orange, 296; in Iowa, 55; and Jews, 158; in the NL, 296, 366; and Spain, 292, 331n; and William Vandever, 64-65; in Wisconsin, 356n
Centennial Park: cannons in, 148; fountain in, image 41; memorial plaque, 154n
Central College: and Gerhard Hendrik Nollen, 368, 375-76; and Nollen family, 363-64
Central Park Café (Pella), image 353
Ceresit Waterproofing Co., 111-12, 114, 115n
Chabot, Elise, 196, image 197
Charles R. Sligh Co., 151
Charleston, SC: harbor, 18-19
Chase, Salmon P., 24
Chicago: and Arie Gerrit Zigeler, xxiv, 334n, 338-40, 342, 345; Dutch Americans in, 81; and Oeds van der Goot, 124; and Particular Synod of 1886, 344-45; and Republican National Convention (1860), xvi, 5-8, 10; and Theodore F. Koch, 110-11; and Wigwam, 5
Chicago's *Press and Tribune* (newspaper), 11
Chris-Craft Co., 152, image 153
Christian Reformed Church (CRC): and Americanization, 158, 167, 359; and Arie Gerrit Zigeler, 342n, 347-48; and Harry Dykstra, 217; institutions, 255; and missionaries, 216; and Ne-

therlands films, 227; and NL relief, 166, 168-72; and Herman Hoeksema, 142; and John L. Vanderhoven, 126; and soldiers, 216-17, 264; synods,167, 267; and Vietnam War views, xxii, 261-62, 267-68
Christian Reformed Laymen's League, 264
Christian Seceded Church: and government summons, image 313; and Henry P. Scholte, 287-307, 309-22
Christian socialism, 140
Church Herald (periodical), 167, 260, 262-63, 265, 267-68, images 166, 259
Church World Service, 167
Churchill, Winston (English prime minister), 140
Cincinnati, OH, 8, 9, 368
Citroen, C., 185n, 188
civil disobedience, xix, 134
civil rights movement, 129, 134, 253, 254
Civil War: and Henry P. Scholte, 3-29, 317; and Holland Colony, 33; and income tax, 145; and John Douma, xvii, 39-41; and Klaas Zuidema, xviii, 43-52; and military draft, 142; and Roane County, TN, xix, 67-68, 82-84; and John Van Lente, 33-38, 41; and West Michigan veterans, 31; and William Vandever, xviii, 53-66
Claes sisters, 195
Clarke, William Penn, 7
Classis of Dakota, 345, 347
Classis of Holland (RCA), 343
Classis of Illinois (RCA), 342-44
Cleveland, OH, 124
Clinch River, TN, 79-80
Clum, John P., 61-62
coal, 346; and First World War, 145-46, 149; and province of Limburg, NL, 163
Cohen Staurt, Martinus, 332n
Colburn, David, 254

Cold War, xix, 129, 158, 244, 272
Cole, Thomas (artist), 370, 372
colonization of NL by US, 224, 248; Kuyper's critique of, 98-99
Communists: Indonesian, 224; Netherlands, 186; South Vietnam, 258-59; Soviet, 132
concentration camps, 165, 178, 198
Condict, J. Elliot, 65
Confederate States of America, 83
conscription, xix, 23, 120, 124, 139, 142-43, 155
conservation: and First World War, 144, 146, 148; in Second World War, xxi, 144, image 162
Copperhead Movement: and Democratic Party, 23
Coral Sea: battle of, 204n, 208
Corinth, MS, 22
Corpus Christi, TX, 107, 116
counter culture, 269
counter insurgency, 273
Cox, J. Murray, 12
Coyl, William H. (col.), image 58
Crook, George (gen.), 60
Cuba: and Abraham Kuyper, 90, 94, 97-105; and Dutch, 78, 94-95; and US military intervention, 272
Custer, George Armstrong, 60
Cutlerville, MI, 126

Daan, Jo, 355-56
Da Costa, Isaac, 293, 313n, 314, 320, 325
Darwin, Australia, 208
Daughtery, Harry M. (gen.), 115
Davenport, IA, 56
De Beij, Bernardus, 338-39, 340
De Boe, Martinus, 35-36
de Boer, Jeltje (Jean) nee Van der Goot, 124
De Bruijn farm, 192
Debs, Eugene, 131
Decatur, Stephen (admiral), 371
Decker, Albert J., 128
De Cock, Helenius, 312
De Cock, Hendrik, image 292; career, 293-94; and Henry

P. Scholte, 294-300; and
Nederlandse Hervormde Kerk,
293; as father of secession of
1834, xxiii, 290, 293-97; 301; 305
defense, 144; and Aluminum
Defense Drive, 148; civil, 151,
153; contracts, 150; plants, xxi,
151; stamps, 150
de Gier, Christian, 195
de Groot, Theodorus, 128
de Groot, Thomas, 128
de Groot, William, 128
de Konink, Jan, 191, 198
De Koster, Lester, 259
Delaware: Swedish colony in, 54
Delft, NL, xix, 68-70, 76, 86, 332, 337n
Democratic Party: and Abraham Kuyper, 100-101; and Benjamin Franklin Keables, 25-26; and Copperheads, 23; divisions in, 9; and Dubuque, IA, 55; and Henry Hospers, 27; and Henry P. Scholte, 6, 11-15, 19-21, 26, 28, 310; and Holland (MI) Dutch, xv; and Lake Prairie Township, IA, 12-13; and Marion County, IA, 5; and Pella Dutch, xv, 5, 11-12; and Peace Democrats, xv, 25; and Stephen Douglas, xv, 6, 12-13, 17-18, 55; and William Stone, 25; and William Vandever, xviii, 64
demonization: and war enemies, 278, 280
Den Andel, NL, 51
de Ronde, E. J., 128
Des Moines, IA: and state political conventions, 5
Desomer, Abraham, 122
de Vries, Edward, 128
De Wilde, H., 194
De Witt, Barbara, 127
Diekema, Gerrit J., 124, 139, 141, 143, 154
disease: and the Civil War, 34, 39, 44, 46
Dodge, Grenville M. (gen.), 57, 59
Doesburg, Jacob O., 34-35
Dokter, Fanna (Mrs. Clarence), 151

Dordt College, 271
Dort, Synod of, 289, 291, 295, 297; and Canons of Dort, 289, 291, 293, 295, 341; and Church Order, 289, 291, 295-97, 300-303, 305, 310; and Nederlandse Hervormde Kerk, 289-90
Dosker, Henry E., 98
Douma, Jan (John), xvii, 31-32, 39-41, images 33, 40
[Douma], Romke, 32
Dourlein, Pieter, 197-98
draft (military): avoidance of, 127; and Civil War, 22-23, 142; dodgers, 268; and Dutch nationals, xix, 120-23, 127, 324; and First World War, xix, 118, 120-24, 126-27, 142, declarants, xix, 121-23, 127, non-declarants, xix, 121, 123, 127; and German draft (forced labor), 178, 181, 191; and Second World War, 139, 142-44, 204-5; and Selective Draft Act, 120; and Vietnam War, 260, 265-68, 271-72, 279, 295, 300
Drake University (Des Moines, IA), 374
Dubuque, IA, 55, 63
Dubuque *Times* (newspaper), 11
Duffee, George, 189-90
Dunn, Lewis A., 376
Dutch: confused with Deutsch, 119, 142
Dutch East Indies, 147, 221-22, 224, 245, 248, image 246
Dutch Guiana, 246, 248
Dutch Nazi Party, 183
Dutch New Guinea. *See* New Guinea
Dutch Reformed Church, xix, 69, 71, 74. *See also* Netherlandse Hervormde Kerk (Netherlands Reformed Church)
Dutch Reformed Church, US. *See* Reformed Church in America
Dutch West Indies, 245-48
Dykstra, Harry A., 206, 217

Earp, Wyatt, 12
Ebben, Gerard, 81

Eisenhower, Dwight (US president), 158
Elbert, Hendrik, 128
election: doctrine of, 291n, 301, 305
elections, Abraham Lincoln, xiv, 7, 9-15, 22, 25, 38; William Vandever, 55, 57n; and Abraham Muste, 131
Emancipation Proclamation, 86
Emanuel II (king of Spain), 70
Enlightenment, 90, 289, 320
Eppink, Berend H., 39, image 33
Erasmus University, 119
Erie County, NY, 73
escape lines: Dutch in Second World War, 178-79, 182, 184-86, 188, 191-92, 197-98, map, 195
ethnicity: and Dutch American enclaves, 126, 158, 233, 256, 269; in NL, 248; and 1970s movement of, 254; and white ethnics, 254-55; and William Vandever, 54, 57, 63, 66
Evangelical Alliance, 324
Eysink, Mrs. Hendrik, 367, image 368

Fafnir Co., 151, image 152
Fellowship of National Reconciliation, 131-32
Fernhout, John, 237
Fillmore, Millard (US president), 72
Fillmore Township, MI, 39
First Christian Reformed Church, Sioux Center, IA, 207n, 217
First Presbyterian Church, Dubuque, IA, 63
First Reformed Church, Harrison, SD, 345n, image 346
First Reformed Church, Pella, 98
First World War: and Abraham Muste, 131; and Boer War, xvi; and combat deaths, 154; and conservation, 145, 149; and defense contracts, 150; and draft, 144; and Dutch Americans, 117, 119, 121, 124, 126-27; and false IDs, 190; and fear of German sabotage, 141; ends Great Migration, xix; and NL foreign policy, 93; and Theodore F. Koch, 107-16
Flandreau, SD, 205
Flemish language, 187
Fort Custer, MI, 125
Fort Donelson, TN, 45, 48
Fort Laramie, Treaty of, 60
Fort Ord, CA, 205, 215, 217
Fort Sumter, SC, 43
Fort Washington Collegiate Church, Manhattan, NY, 130
Fourth Reformed Church, Grand Rapids, 130
Fourth Reformed Church, Pella, 345n, 348
France: and American Expeditionary Forces, 124; and escape lines, 178-79; and First World War, 131; and Willard G. Leenhouts, 154-55
Franco-Prussian War, 108, 114
Free Church of Scotland, 325n, 328n, 341n
freedom: American, 72, 103, 105, 307; civic, 74, 90, 253, 257-58; and Henry P. Scholte, 310-12, 320-22; in NL, 241-42, 292, 320-21; political, 14, 103, 139, 157, 199, 269, 321; religious, 11, 74, 90, 310-12, 317-18, 320, 321-22; theory of, 90
Free University of Amsterdam, xix, 328n
French Revolution, 90-91, 96, 312
Frens, Richard, 258-59
Friesland, NL, 32, 73, 118, 125, 141, 201n, 243, 300, 305
Frisian(s), 73, 76-77, 244, 359; horses, 80; language, 356n, 357
Fulton, IL, xviii, 43-44, 50
Funcke, Oscar, 109-10, 114-15
Funcke, Wilhelm II, 110
Funcke, Wilhelm III, 109-10
Funcke family, 107, 109, 111, 114-15

Gazetteer (Roane County, TN, newspaper), 79
Geerlings, Henry, 140
Geneva Conventions, 272, 275-76

Georgetown Cemetery, Ottawa Co., MI, 50
Georgia: and Civil War, xviii, 37, 59, 67, 113
Gereformeerde Kerken in Nederland, 172, 335. *See also* Nederlandse Hervormde Kerk
German Americans, 109, 112
German Theological School, 63
Germans: American nativism toward, 141-42; as American soldiers, 49, 52; confused with Dutch, 119, 142; and escape lines, 177-219; and First World War, xvi, xx, xxi, 110-14, 116, 119; immigrants, 6, 10, 51, 55, 119, 141; and pastors, 63; as Presbyterians, 63; as Protestants, 108; as Roman Catholics, 112; and Second World War, 153, 155; in South Carolina, 81; and Theodore F. Koch, 107-12, 115-16
Germany: culture of, 378n; empire of, 108-9; and escape lines, 177-219; and First World War, 110-14, 116, 120, 131, 137-38, 141-42; Imperial Army of, 109; and Lutheran Church, 292; nation of, 70n, 97, 107-8; and occupation of NL, 159-65, 173, 175, 223, 238, 242-43; and Second World War, 138, 155, 157, 169, 177, 246, and U-boats, 137; and Zigeler family, 323, 347
Gerritsma, Ernest, images 205, 216, 219; biography, 201, 219; character of, 216-18; diary of, xxii, 202-3; marriage, 218-19; military promotions, 214-15; military experiences, 204-16
Gerritsma, Gertie (Mrs. Syne) nee Feikema, 201n
Gerritsma, Lois (Mrs. Donald Sinnema), 204
Gerritsma, Sylvan, images 274-75; biography, 271-72; military experiences, xxiii, 272-75; and morality of war, 275-84
Gerritsma, Syne, 201n, 207n

Gettysburg, battle of, 35
Gezelle Meerburg, Georg C., 293, 296, 299
Gilmore, William, 344
Gilze-Rijen airfield, 197
Gold Stars, 154, 265
Goldzung, Kathleen, nee Vanden Oever, 363
Grafschaft, Bentheim, 141
Grand Rapids, MI: and Abraham Muste, 130; and Johannes Van Lente, 38; and John B. Hulst, 98; and John L. Vanderhoven, 125-26; and Larry Groothuis, 265; and Leo Peters, 147; as market center, 146; and Netherlands Information Bureau films, 232; and Standard Dutch usage, 352, 357
Grand Rapids Furniture Exposition, 153
Grand Rapids Herald (newspaper), 118
Grant, Gen. Ulysses S., xix, 25-27, 54, 60, 62
Great Britain, 92, 97, 101, 104
Great War. *See* First World War
Greeley, Horace, 17
Greeneville, TN, 47
Grimes, James (US senator), 6, 18
Groen, Jorge, 119, 120-21, 123, 128
Groen van Prinsterer, Guillaume, 90, 287, 320-21, 333
Grondwet, De (newspaper), 141
Groningen, NL: dialect of, 360; immigrants from, xviii, 49, 51, 359; and Klaas Zuidema, 43, 49-51; provincial synod of, 29; secession of 1834, 293-94, 304; University of, 293, and theology, 293
Groningers, xvii, 49, 51, 77
Groothuis, Larry, 265
Grossman, Dave (lt. col.), 280
Guadalcanal, 209
Guizot, Francois, 90

Haitjema, Theodorus L., 294
Hamlin, Hannibal, xvi, xvii, 8, 11
Handelsblad (Amsterdam newspaper), 81

Harlan, James, 18
Harpers Ferry, WV, 82
Haaren, NL, 198
Harris, Isham G. (TN governor), 80
Harrison, SD, 345
Harrison, William H. (US president), 11
Hart & Cooley Co., image 152
Hayes, Rutherford (US president), 62
Hedges, Chris, 134
Heeren, Constant, 194
Heidelberg Catechism, 289, 293, 297, 341
Heikens, Henk, 355
Heldring, Jerome, 224
Heldring, Otto G., 70
Hellenbroek, Abraham, 290
Helvetia (ship), 51
Henny, Carl, 109
Hermans, Gustaaf, 128
Herron, Francis J. (col.), 56, image 58
Hettinga, Meinze, 128
Hicks, Thomas (portrait painter), 9
Highland, IN, 126
Hijlkema, Henry, 128
Hilvarenbeek, NL, 181, 183, 185-87, 191, 193-95
Himmler, Heinrich, 180
Hitler, Adolph, 133, 137, 157, 278
Hoeborn family, 108, 116
Hoek, Andries, 184
Hoeksema, Herman, 142
Hogeweg-de Haart, Huiberta P., 82
Holland City News (newspaper), 142, 145, 149, 171-72
Holland Colony, xvii, 31-32, 37, 75
Holland Color & Chemical Co., 152
Holland Fire of 1871, 33, 41
Holland Furnace Co., 150, 152
Holland High School, image 148
Holland Hitch Co., 151
Holland, MI: Americanization, xxi; and Albertus C. Van Raalte, xvi; and Civil War, xvii, xix, xx, 31-41, 84n; colony of, 31-41, 352-53; and Dutch language usage, xxiv; Fire of 1871, 41; and First World War, 121-24, 138-40, images 141, 143, Americanization, 158, armistice, 157-58, civil defense, 153-54, and conservation, 142-46, and Hope College, 154-56, and nativism, 141-46, and price controls, 146-49, and relief effort, xxi, war bonds, 149-50, defense contracts, 150-51; and Maria Margaretha Storm-van der Chijs, 74-75; and Netherlands Information Service, xxii, 226; and patriotism, 138; politics of, xv, xvi; and Second World War, 137-39, 142, 150-51, 154, 156, Americanization, 158, defense contracts, 150-53, and Hope College, 156-57, and NL relief, 159-75, victory days, 157-58; Tulip Festival, 256
Holland, MI, Common Council of, 123, 149
Holland Precision Parts, 151
Holland-Racine Shoe Co., 151
Holland Sentinel (newspaper), 39
Hollander, De (newspaper), xvii, 74, 78
Holy Disobedience, 134
Hoogeveen, Johannes, 128
Hoover, Herbert (US president), 145
Hope College: and Abraham Muste, xx, 139; and Civil War, xvii; and First World War, 142, 144, 146, 154-56; and Memorial Chapel, 139; and Second World War, 156-58, 217
Hope, De (newspaper), 340-41
Hope Preparatory School, 130
Hospers, Henry, 26-27
Houston, TX, 109
Howard, Oliver O. (gen.), 58
Huizinga, Anna (Mrs. Abraham Muste), 130
Hulst, John B., 98
Hunger Winter, xxi, 163-64, 243

Imperial German Army, 109
Inauguration Day (Washington), 17
Indian reforms, 60-66
Indiana: and Civil War, xviii, 44, 47, 49; and John Vanderhoven, 126; and Klaas Zuidema, 43-44

Indiana Infantry, 60th, 44-45, 47-49, 52
Indiana Infantry, 67th, 49
Indiana Soldiers and Sailors Monument, 44
Indianapolis, IN, xviii, 34, 44-45, image 46, 48-49
Indians: and government policies, xviii, 53-54, 60-62, 64-66
indoctrination: army, 274
Institutes of the Christian Religion (John Calvin), 293
International Calvinist League, 89
Iowa: and Abraham Kuyper, 98; and Abraham Lincoln, 20, 26, inauguration of, 16-18, assassination of, 28; and Abraham Muste, 130; and Arie Gerrit Zigeler, 344-45, 347-48; and Civil War, 21-24, 40, 53; and Copperheads, 23, 25; and Democratic Party, 6, 15, 25; and Dutch immigrants, xv, 6, 71, 351-52; and Dutch language usage, 351-61; and Ernest Gerritsma, 201-2, 205, 218; and Gerhard Hendrik Nollen, 363-78; and German immigrants, 6; and Henry P. Scholte, xxiii, 3-29, 68; and Native Americans, 23; and Pella, xvi, 119, 234; and Peoria, xvi; and presidential election of 1864, 26; and Republican National Convention (1860), 7-8; and Republican Party, xvi, 6-7, 10, 16-18; and Republican State Convention, 5-6, 8-9; and Spanish-American War, image 104; 33rd Iowa Volunteer Infantry, 25; and William Vandever, xviii, 53-66
Iowa Central University. *See* Central College
Iowa City, 7-8
Iowa infantry, 9th, xviii, 56; 38th, 58
Iowa Volunteer Infantry, 33rd, Company G, 24
Irish, 55

Jackson, MS, 49

Jacobson, Matthew Frye, 254
Jansen, Petrus, 128
Japanese campaign, 207
Jews, 312; and Americanization, 158; evangelism of, 325; and Holocaust, 278; sheltering of, in NL, xxi, 181, 188, 192, 198
Johnson, Lyndon (US president), 259
Joll, James, 97
Jones, Rufus, 131
Jonkers, David, 184, 194

Kaiserism, 155
Kalamazoo, MI, xviii, 33-34, 39
Kamps, Albertus, 128
Kautz, August (gen.), 62
Keables, Benjamin Franklin, 22, 25-26, 367-68, 372
Keables, Sarah Scholte, 22, 367
Kellogg, John, 78
Keokuk, IA: and Nollen, xxiv, 364, 367-68, 370-71, 377-78
Keokuk Medical College, 370
Keesing family, 184, image 185
King, Martin Luther, 134
Kingston, TN, xix, 74, 78-81, 84
Kirkendall II, Will, 266
Kirkwood, Samuel (IA gov.), image 21, 22-23, 56
Knickerbocker Society (Chicago), 232
Knickerbocker Weekly, 225
Know-Nothings, 17
Knoxville, IA, 7, 11, 14
Knoxville, TN, 74, 75n, 84n
Koch, Clara Hoeborn, 108, 112-13, 116
Koch, Johan Willem Coenraad, 108
Koch, Theodore F.: and Alien Property Custodian, 112, 114-15; ancestry, 108; beliefs, 108; and Ceresit Waterproofing Co., 110, 112-14; and First World War, 110-11; loyalty questioned, 111-13; real estate business of, xix, 107, 109-15; retirement, 115; views of war, 108
Koch, Theodore "Teddy" William, xix, 111-15

Koch, Walter, 112, 115
Koekkoek, Barend Cornelis, 366
Kooy, Dirk, 128
Korean War, 158
Kraaijestein, Martin, 119, 120
Krabbendam, Hans, 351
Krauss, Jean, 184, 191, 196
Krauss, Marie, 184, 191, 196
Kuiper, Henry J., 203n
Kuyper, Abraham, image 96; and American colonization, 98-103; and Arie Gerrit Zigeler, 333; and banquet in Holland (MI), image 99; and Free University of Amsterdam, xix; and Henry P. Scholte, 320; and international affairs, 91-95, 98, 104-5; and international law, 90-94, 103-5; and national defense, 91; and neo-Calvinism, 89, 105; and Princeton Stone Lectures, xviii, 95-96; "world and life" perspective of, 271; and Spanish-American War, 94-103; Varia Americana, image 100

labadism, 299, 301
Lafayette Park (Washington, DC), 9
Lake Prairie Township, IA, 12, 23
Lakota Indians, xix, 60, 65, image 61
Lancaster, NY, 73, 76, 78
landing craft tank (LCT), 212
landing ship tank (LST), 152, 209, 212, image 213
Langtry, Lily, 375
Le Mars, IA, 345
Lee, Robert E. (gen.), 24, 26-27, 38
Leenhouts, Willard G., 154, image 155
Leeuwarder Courant (newspaper), 72, 74, 76
Leiden University, 288, 290, 291n, 293, 310
Lens, Sydney, 133
Leufkens, Remy, 128
Liberation (periodical), 132
Liberty Bonds, 113, 149
Liberty Loan drives, 141, image 150. See also war bonds.
Liberty ships, 211

Limburg (province of), 81, 163, 186
Lincoln, Abraham (US president): image 7; assassination, 27-29, 39; funeral train, 39-40; as Great Emancipator, xv; and Henry P. Scholte, 3-29; and Johannes Van Lente, 38; and John Douma, 39-40; and Klaas Zuidema, 52; presidential election (1860), xv, xvi, 3-16, 83, (1864), 26-27; presidential inauguration, 16-18, image 18; vault, image 40; and William Seward, 7-16
Little Bighorn, Battle of, 60
Little Chute, WI, 355, 357n
Little Rock, AR, 25
Livingstone, David (African explorer), 83n, 85
Lokker, Cornelius J., image 33, 39
Lord Salisbury, 97
Los, Dick, 191, image 192
Louisville, KY, 34-35, 46, 59
Louisiana, 48-49, 67n, 77, 232
Lucania (steamship), 95
Lusitania (ship), 137
Lutheran Church: and Scholte, 291-93
Luzon, Philippines, 213-16

Macy, Augusta Arnold, 374-75
Macy, Harriet, 375
Mahaska County, IA, 11
Manypenny, George, 62
Marion County, IA: and Civil War volunteers, 25; elections in, 11-12, 26; and Henry P. Scholte, 11-12, 29
Marseille-Smit, Janine, 177n
Marx, Karl, 54
Mason-Dixon Line, 34
Matthews, David, 117n, 118n
Matthews, Edward J., 118, image 119, 124, 125n
McArthur, Douglas (gen.), 158, 207n
McCoy, Patrick, 124
McKinley, William (US president), xix, 99, 100-104
McReynolds, David, 133
Medal of Freedom, 198

Medal of Honor, 56, 121, 122n
Meeuwisse, Huub, 194
Meijer Brouwer, L., 293
Meijer, Cornelis ("Kees"), 336, 337n
Meijer, Johannes, 128
Methodist Church, Pella, 348
Methodists, 64
Mexican-American War, 3
Michigan Bell Telephone Co., 151
Michigan Infantry: 24th, xvii, 39; 25th, xvii, 33, 35, 84n
Midway (ship), 158
Miller, Thomas W., 115
Missouri Compromise (1820), 64
Mokma, Germ W., image 33, 39
Mokma, Wiebe, 32
Monroe Doctrine, 98, 102
Montello Park Christian Reformed Church, image 174
Mook, Rudolf, 123, 128
Moore, John (Civil war surgeon), 58
Moore, John C. (col.), 35
Morgan, John Hunt (Conf. gen.), xvii, 34-37, 47
Morgan, Joseph S. (col.), 59
Mott, Lucretia, 71-72
Mulder, John R., 139
Munfordville, KY, 35, 47-48, 52
Murray, Andrew Jr., 71n
Murray, Andrew Sr., 71n
Murray, John, 71n
Muskegon, MI, xviii, 50, 51
Muste, Abraham Johannes, xix, images 131, 133-34; biography, 129-30, 139-40; Christian theology of, 132-34, 140; pacifist views, 131-32, 140; as Quaker, 131-32; and Social Gospel, 131
Muste, Anne Dorothy (Nancy), 130
Muste, Constance (Connie), 130
Muste, John, 130

Naaijkens, Jan, 190-91
Nadere Reformatie, 297-98
Napoleon Bonaparte, 92, 108, 289, 293, 303, 312, 349
Nass, Wilhelmina (Mrs. Joannes ter Laak), 366
National Guard, Company D, 143

"National Synod" (NL), 291
National Union of Christian Schools, 256
Native Americans, 23, 370
nativism: and Dutch Americans, 141-42
Nazi: oppression by, xxi, 178-83, 185-86, 188, 195-96, 242
Nederlands Hervormde Kerk (Netherlands Reformed Church), 289, 292, 293-97, 299n, 303-4, 311, 325-26, 365
Nederpelt, Johannes, 128
Neo-Calvinism, xix, 89-91, 94, 103, 105
Netherlands: and Abraham Kuyper, 93-96, 100-104; and Anti-Revolutionary Party, 90-91, 93; and Dutch escape lines, 177-99; and economic conditions in the 1840s, 71; and emigration, 43, 50-51; and First World War, 118, 120-21, 126, 138; and Henry P. Scholte as prospective foreign minister, 17; and Koch family, 107-8, 116; and Maria Margaretha Storm-van der Chijs, 68-69, 73-75, 78, 80-81, 84-86; and pillarization, 185-86; and Nollen family, 364, 367-69, 375, 378; religious history of the, 287-307, 309-22; and Second World War, 159-75, image 162, food shortages, xxi, 160-63, liberation, xxi, 160-61, relief aid, 160, 164-72, 173-75; and Standard Dutch language, 353, 355-60. *See also* Zigeler, Arie Gerrit; Christian Seceded Church; neo-Calvinism; Netherlands Information Bureau films
Netherlands Antilles, 94, 247
Netherlands East Indies, 94, 245
Netherlands Information Bureau: circulation records, 226-27; culture-directed, 222-25; films of, xxii, 221-49, film attendance, 227-32, film lending libraries, 226-27; and Government

Information Service, 221-22; and public diplomacy, 225-26, 249; rhetorical themes, 237-48; viewership, 232-37
New Brunswick Theological Seminary, 130
New College (Edinburgh), 325
New Guinea, xxii, 143, 201, 203, 207, 209-12, image 213, 214-15, 218, 245n
New Orleans, LA, 59, 367
New York City, 130, 165, 222, 345, 346n
New York Infantry, 90th, 59
New York Times (newspaper), 67, 346
New York Tribune (newspaper), 17
New York World (newspaper), 105
Nies, Ray, 154
Nieuw Amsterdam (ship), 124
Nieuwe Zuiderkerk, NL, 178
Niles, MI, 34
Nobel Peace Prize (1906), 105
Noemfoor Island, 212-14, 217
Nollen, Carl, 363
Nollen, Gerhard Hendrik, xxiv; biography, 363-65; early paintings of, 365-73, images 364, 369, 372; post 1875 paintings of, 373-75, images 374, 377; painting techniques of, 365-70
Nollen, Gertrude nee Kramer (Mrs. Gerhard), 372-73
Nollen, Gezina Hendrika, 367n
Nollen, Hendrikus, 364-69
Nollen, John, 365, 367-68, 372, 376, 377-78
Nollen, Paul, 363
Nollen, Zwaantje (Mrs. Hendrik), 364-65, 375
Noord Brabant, 197, 304
Northern State University, SD, 203
Northwestern Classical Academy (college), 130
Notier, Matthew, xvii, 39, images 33, 40
Nuiver, Peter, 128
Nyland, Gerrit J., 39, image 33

Office of Price Administration, 146

Ohio: and Civil War, 36, 47; and First World War, 111, 124
Olert, Frederick, 139-40
onderduikers, xxi, 178
Open Air Museum, NL, 365
Orange City, IA, 130
Oskaloosa, IA, 11, 22, 374
Ost Friesland, 141
Otley, IA, 342-44
Oudemans, Jan, 191, 198
Overmars, Johannes, 128
Owen, Richard (col.), 45-46, 48

pacifism: Christian, 132-33, 282n; and First World War, 137-40
Palmer, A. Mitchell, 111
Parke-Davis Co., 152
patriotism, 34, 57, 92, 113, 131, 138, 140, 254
Patterson, Newton A., 78-81, 84, image 79
Pea Ridge (AR), Battle of, xviii, 56-57
Peace Democrats. See Democratic Party
Peace Palace (The Hague), 94, 105
Pearl Harbor, 137-38, 140, 201, 203-4, 207, 223, 272
Peeters-van der Heijden, Elisabeth, image 187
Pella, IA: and Arie Gerrit Zigeler, 343n, 345, 348-49; Central Park, 21, 353; and Civil War casualties, 28n; colony, xxiii, 234; ethnicity, 256; Franklin Street, images 4, 358; Garden Square, 12, 21, 26, 372n; and Gerhard Hendrik Nollen, 363-78; and Hendrik P. Scholte, 316-17; Main Street, 367; and Methodist Church, 348; *Pella Chronicle*, 355, 357n; *Pella Gazette*, xvi, xxiv, 5, 367; politics in, 3-29; Reformed churches, 345, 348; Scholte Church in, 27, 348, image 28; and Standard Dutch Language, 351-61; train station, image 104; Washington Street, 11
Pella Home Guard, 22
Pensacola (ship), 207
Peters, Leo, 147

Petersburg, VA, 38
Philadelphia, PA, 16, 54
Philippine Islands: annexation of, Kuyper's critique of, 90, 98-105; and First World War, xix, 125; and Second World War, 201-2, 207, 209, 213-14
Pijnappel, Menso Johannes, 331n, 333-34
Pike, James Shepherd, 17
Pilgrim Home Cemetery (Holland, MI), 41, 139, 157
Pillar Church, 32
pillarization, NL, 185-86
Plugge, Jannetje Adriana (Mrs. Arie Zigeler), 326, 333, 337n, 338n, 339, 348
"Polar Bears," 125-26
Pontier, Raymond, 267
Pope Pius I, 70
popular sovereignty doctrine, 55
Port Hudson, LA, 37
potato famine (1840s, NL), 31, 71, 160n; and Second World War, 163-64
POW camps, French, 183, 187, 195, 198
Pozzetta, George, 254
predestination, doctrine of, 300
Preijer, Arthur, 128
Presbyterian church, 65, 216-17, 262; and William Vandever, xviii, 54, 61, 63-64, 66
Presbyterian Labor Temple (NY), 132
Presbyterians at Princeton, 95, 103
Prince of Orange. *See* Willem I, King (NL)
Prince, Richard (sgt.), 274-76
Princess Juliana School (Brussels), 196
Princeton University: and Kuyper, xix, 96
Prospect Park Christian Reformed Church, image 171
Puerto Rico, 102

Quakers, 71, 111, 131
Queen Sophia (NL), 69
Queen Wilhelmina Fund, 138, 165, image 168
Quintus, Jacob, 11, 74n

Rabbethge, Oscar, 109
Radema, Minze, 128
Rasker, A. J., 294
Rauter, Hanns Albin, 180
Red Cloud Agency (NE), 60
Red Cross, 139, image 140, 141
Red Cross, NL, 164, 165n, 169
Reformatie, De, xxiii, 287, image 288, 297-99, 302, 311, 313, 317, 320
Reformation, Protestant, 90, 289, 297
Reformed Church in America: and Abraham Kuyper, 98; and Abraham Muste, 130, 139; and Apache Indian missions, 61; and Arie Gerrit Zigeler, xxiv, 323, 338, 343-48; and Christian Action Commission, 260, 267; and Herman Hoeksema, 142; and Maria Margaretha Storm-van der Chijs, 74-76; Netherlandic roots of, 255; and NL relief (1940s), 166-72
Reformed Protestant Dutch Church in North America, 75.
Rehoboth (Amsterdam church of Zigeler), 328-37, images 330-31, 335
Religion, freedom of, 11
Remonstrants, 291
Renville, MN, 110
Republican Party, xvi, 5, 8, 9, 11, 13-15, 26, 55, 57
Réveil, 71, 293, 313, 324, 325, 347
Richmond, VA, 38
Rio Grande Valley, 108
Riviera State Bank, 114
Riviera, TX, 109, 111-15
Roane County Agricultural Society, 78
Roane County, TN, xix, 67, 73, 78-81, 83-84
Rock Island, IL, 54
Rodenhuis, David R., 117n
Roedenbeck, Herbert, 109
Roften, Gosen, 128
Roman Catholics. *See* Catholics

Romeyn, Jan, 128
Roosevelt, Franklin Delano (US president), 143, 204, 218
Roosevelt, Theodore (US president), 100, 103-5
Rot, Arie, 34
Rotterdam (ship), 339, image 340
Rotterdam, NL, 69n, 125, 172, 345n; and Second World War, 138, 173, 196, 223
Round Valley Reservation, CA, 64
Rullman, J. C., 294
Ruys, Gijsbertus, 332-34

sabotage: and Second World War, xxi, 141, 152, 154, 216
San Carlos Agency (AZ Terr.), 61
San Francisco, CA, 96, 202, 206, 214, 222, 375
San Jago, Cuba, 94-95
Schapendonk, John, 128
Schmidt, Willem, 196-98
Scholte Church, 27, image 28, 348, 368
Scholte Club, 288, 293, 296, 306-7
Scholte, Henry Jr., 367, 375
Scholte, Henry (Hendrik) Peter (Pieter), images 4, 292, 298; and Abraham Lincoln, xvi, 3-29; anti-slavery views, 5, 11, 14, 68; career, 290-93, 307, 310-11; and Christian Seceded Church, xxiii, 287-307, 309-22; church of, 27-28, 348, 368, image 28; desk of, image 14; and Dort Church Order, 300-305, 310; emigration of, 307; family, 290-93, 376; as father of Secession of 1834, xxiii, 288-305; and Hendrik de Cock, 294-300; house of, xxiv, images 6, 318; and Johan A. Wormser, 309; and Nederlandse Hervormde Kerk, 293; as newspaper editor, 367; founds Pella Colony, xv, 3, 367; political career of, xvi, 3, 5-29; and Scholte Club, 288, 293, 296, 306-7; and Simon Van Velsen, 291-93, 300-302, 304-6, 311; suspended by Christian Seceded church, 302-6; theology of, 348; vision of church and state, xxiii, 309-22; and William Seward, 5-17
Scholte, Jan Hendrik, 290
Scholte, Maria (Mrs. Henry P.), 9, 18, 374-75
Scholte, Nora Keables, 375
Scholte, Sarah, 22, 376
Scholten, Paul (NL jurist), 321
Schultzen, Hendrik Peter, 292
Schurz, Carl, 62
Schwartz, Carl A. F., 325, 327n, 328, 336
Scottish Missionary Church, 328, image 329, 348-49
Second Presbyterian Church (Dubuque, IA), 63
Second Reformed Church (Pella), 348, 375
Second World War, image 147, 253, 257, 353; and Abraham Muste, 127, 129-30; and Americanization, 158; and Dutch escape lines, 177, 182-99; and Ernest Gerritsma, 201-19; and Holland, MI, 137-39, 142, 150-51; and Hope College, 156-57; and NL, 127; as total war, xix
Segers-Ooms, Maria, 188
Sermon on the Mount, 131, 133
Seward, William H., xiv, xvi, 5-10, image 8, 13-19, 24, 38
Seyffardt, Hendrik A. (German gen.), 191
Seyss-Inquart, Arthur, 162, 164, 180
Sheboygan County, WI, 68
Sheboygan Nieuwsbode (newspaper), 11, 74
Sherman tanks, image 213
Sherman, William T. (gen.), xvii, xviii, 37-38, 57-59
's Hertogenbosch (NL), 179
Shiloh, TN, 83
Sioux Center, IA, 217, 219, 271
Sioux Center News (newspaper), 203-4, 207n, 217
Sioux County, IA, xxii, 201, 204
Sioux Indians: war of, 62

Slavenburg, Johannes, 128
slavery. *See* anti-slavery
Sligh, Charles R. Jr., 153
Slotemaker de Bruine, N. A. C., 222
Sloten, Friesland, 118, 124-25
Smedes, Lewis, 260, 299
Smit, Karst, xxi, 177n, 178-81, 183-98, images 179, 193
Smit-Van der Heijden Line, xxi, 178, 186, 197-98
Smith, Donald (historian), 39
Smith, Max, 214
smuggling: of people, xxi, 181-82, 195; of food, 280
social Darwinism, 93
Social Gospel, 131
South Africa, 69-71, 85-86, 92-93, 101-2. *See also* Boer War; First World War
South Dakota National Guard, 205
Spanish-American War, xix, 94, 98-99, image 104
Springfield, IL, xvi, xvii, 8-10, 39
St. Andrew's Presbyterian Church (Australia), 202
St. Louis, MO, 18, 367
St. Paul, MN, 109, 114-15
Stahl, Friedrich Julius, 90
Standaard, De (newspaper), 99, 102
Standard Dutch: usage of, Pella compared to Holland, 352-61
Stanton, Edwin M., 24
Stars and Stripes (magazine), 159
State Historical Society of Iowa, 370
Stoddard, Ira, 376
Stone Lectures: at Princeton University, xix, 95-96
Stone, William M. (IA governor), 7, 25, 28
Storm, Willem, 69
Storm-van der Chijs, Anna Maria Margaretha (Mienette), images 68, 76, 86; advertisements, Netherlands newspapers, 76-78; and Albertus C. Van Raalte, 74; family history, 68-70; interest in America, 71-74; and Newton A. Patterson, 78-80; philanthropy, 85-86; and Reformed Church in America, 74-76; Tennessee colony of, xix, 68, 73-74, 80-85; as world traveler, 70-71
Stout, Harry S., 255
Stulp, Jack, 258
Suez Canal, 85
Suikerbakker, Grietje, 50
Suikerbakker, Hendrik, 50
Surinam, 94
Sweeny, Thomas W. (gen.), 59
Swierenga, Robert P., xx, xxi, 117n, 121
Snyder, David J., 224n, 244, 249

te Velde, Melis, 300
Tebb's Bend (KY): Battle of, 35-36
Ten Eyck family, 54
Ten Harmsel, Marie, 203
Tennessee: and Dutch colony, 73-74, 80-85
ter Laak, Joannes, 365-66
Texas: and Civil War, 49, 59; Panhandle, 109; and Theodore F. Koch, 107, 109-11, 115-16, 125
Theodore F. Koch & Co., 111, 115
Third Reich, 181, 191
Thompson, J., 58
Tilburg, NL, 179-80, 183, 191, 194
Timmer, Harm, 128
Tippecanoe County, IN, 49-50
Tolstoy, Leo, 131
Tremont House (Chicago), 7-8
Tromp, Allen, 128
Truman, Harry S. (US president), 157, 224
Tulip Time, 256; and war, 149, 269
Turnhout, Belgium, 179, 181, 189, 195, 198
Tyler, John (US president), 11

Ubbink, Johan, 197-98
Union Theological Seminary, 130
Unity Christian High School (Hudsonville, MI), 265
University of Amsterdam, 326n
University of Groningen, 293
Uphof, Johannes, 128
US Army, 147th Field Artillery, 201, 203, 205-6, 208-15, image 210

US Army, 158th Infantry, 211-14
US Coast Guard station (Holland, MI), 153
US Commissioner of Indian Affairs, xviii, 60
US Marshall Plan, 224n, 243
Utrecht, NL, xxiii, 69, 163-64, 329; synod of, 300, 301-2, 304, 306-7, 321

van Dam, Cornelis, 37
van den Bosch, Maria, 71
van der Heijden, Jef, image 187, 188, 190
Vander, Edward H. 118, 122, 124-25
Van der Chijs, Jacobus (brother), 69, 70
Van der Chijs, Jacobus (father), 68-69
van der Feen, Thomas, 128
Vandergoot, Charles, 118, 124
van der Goot, Nicolaas (Nicholas) Wilhelm, 118, 125
van der Goot, Oeds, 118, 124
van der Goot, Tjeerd, 118, 124
van der Heig, Albert, 128
van der Heijden, Elly, 188
van der Heijden, Eugene, xxi, 178, image 187, 188, 190, 197-98
van der Heijden, Gustaf, image 187, 188, 198
van der Heijden, Josephus, image 187, 188, 198
van der Heijden, Lisette, 188
van der Heijden, Marcel, image 187, 188, 198
van der Heijden, Willy, 188
Van der Hoeven, Johan Ludwig. See Vanderhoven, John L.
van der Hooven, Nynke, 117n
Vanderhoven, John L., 119, 122, 124-26
Vander Hoven, Paula, 117n, 119
van der Kleij, Willem, 327, 332n, 334n, 336n, 340-41, 343, 345n
Vanderlaan, Peter, 128
Vandermeer, Albert, 128
Vander Ploeg, John, 259, 261
Van der Pol family, 195

Vanderveer, Peter, 128
van der Wal, Catherinus, 128
Van Der Weer, Myron, 54
Vandever, Florence, 63
Vandever, Jane (Mrs. William), 63
Vandever, William, images 55, 58; career, 53-55; and Civil War, xviii, 56-59; as US Indian Inspector, xviii, 59-62; religious views, 54, 63-66
Vandever, William (father), 54
van Dongen, Jan, 191, 198, image 192
Van Driel family, 127
van Geel, Piet, 193
Van Grieken, Samuel, 369n, 370-71
van Hall, Anne Maurits, 313n, image 292
Van Heukelom, Raymond, 267
van Iersel, Louis, 121, 123-24, 128
Van Lente, Frederick, 3-32, 37-38
Van Lente, Hein, 32, 37
Van Lente, Janice, 33, 36
Van Lente, Johannes, xvii, images 32, 41; and Civil War, 33-37; family, 31-32, 37; as gardener, 41
van Minden, Floris, 128
Van Peyma, Worp, 73-74, 76-77
van Putten, Cornelius, 124
Van Raalte, Albertus C., 68, 78; and Civil War, 32, 35, 37, 84n; as immigrant leader, xvi; and Maria Margaretha Storm-van der Chijs, 70, 74-75; and Secession of 1834, 293, 296, 299, 304-5, 307
Van Raalte colony, xvii, 31-32, 37, 75
van Rossum, Abram, 128
van Soest, Pieter, 128
van Stolk, Cornelis, 164
Van Velsen, Simon: career, 305; and church polity, 299, 301; and Henry P. Scholte, 291-93, 300-302, 304-6, 311
Van Vliet, Adrian, 63
Van Weerden, Charles, 369
Van Weerden, Gerret, 369-70
Varekamp, Kiki, 326n
VE-Day: celebrated in Holland, MI, 157

Veltkamp, Berend, 128
Ver Hey, Hazel, 144
Versailles Treaty, 114
Veterans of Foreign Wars (VFW), 122
Vicksburg, MS, xviii, 25, 37, 48-49, 59
Vicomte De Bonald, Louis, 90, 91n
Victory Gardens, xxi, 144
Vietnam War, 253-59, image 257; and CRC, images 261-64, 266; and Dutch American attitudes, xxii, 132-69; and Muste, xx, 132, 134; and RCA, image 259
Vinet, Alexandre Rodolphe, 313
Visser, Jeremias, 128
VJ-Day, celebrated in Holland, MI, 157
Vliedorp, NL, 51
Vriesland, MI, 50
VU University, 89

Wakde Island (Dutch New Guinea), 211
Walter Reed General Hospital, 124
war bonds, xxi, 137, 140, 144, 149-51
Warren, Earl (chief justice), 158
Washington, DC, 55, 62, 222
Webb, Robert (professor), 203
Webber, Philip E., 352-53
Weekblad (Pella newspaper), 26-28
Weelde, Belgium, 183, 188-89
Welle, Jenneke, 367
Welles, Gideon, 19
Western Machine Tool Works, 151
Western Theological Seminary, 98, 139, 217
Westphalia, Germany, 107-8
Whiteside County, IL, 43, 50-51
Wichers, Willard C., xxi, xxii, 168-72, image 169, 173-74, 222, 226, 233
Wide-Awake Clubs, 11
Wiersema, Klaas, 50
Wiersema, Trientje, 50-51
Wigwam Convention, Chicago, 5-8. See also Republican Party
Wilhelm II, Kaiser of Germany, 119
Wilhelmina, Queen (NL), 118
Willard A. Holbrook (ship), 206, image 208
Willard Hotel (Washington, DC), 9, 17

Willem I, King (NL), 289, 303, 310-11, 320
Willem II, King (NL), xxiii, 69, 287, 304, image 315, 318n
Willem III, King (NL), 69, 73, 317
Williams, Claire, 117n, 118n
Williams, Dorothy, 117n
Williams, Nicolas, 118, image 119, 124-25.
Wilson, Woodrow (US president), xvi, 104, 110-11, 120, 122, 137, 138, 141
Wisconsin, 17, 40, 68, 71, 77, 84, 355-57; and *Sheboygan Nieuwsbode*, 11, 74
Witmond, David, 128
Wolters, Henry, 122
Wolterson, Jan, 191
Woman's Literary Club, 141
Women's Auxiliary Air Corps (WAACS), 144
Wormser, Johan A., image 298, 299n, 304, 309

Young Calvinist (periodical), 217, 263, 266
Young's Point, AR, 48, 52

Zeeland, MI, 36, 151, 352, 356
Zevenaar, NL, 108
Zierikzee (province of Zeeland), 130
Zigeler, Arie Gerrit, xxiv, image 324; American wanderings, 338-44; biography, 323-27, 336-39; as evangelical, 325-27; as independent minister, 328-36; as Reformed pastor, 344-49
Zigeler, Jacob, 337n
Zijpe, NL, 50
Zonne, Pieter, 68
Zuidema, Anna nee Bos, 50
Zuidema, Dutmer, 50
Zuidema, Nicholas, xviii, images 44, 51; and Civil War, 44-49; postwar career, 50-54; death, 44
Zuidema, Simon, 50
Zuiderveld, Willem, 122
Zwart, David, xxii, 234

Notes on Contributors

Henk Aay, PhD, Clark University; professor of geography and environmental studies and Meijer Chair in Dutch Language and Culture Emeritus, Calvin College; and Senior Research Fellow, Van Raalte Institute. Henk taught geography and environmental studies at Calvin College for thirty years before retiring in 2012.

Douglas Firth Anderson, PhD, professor of history emeritus and reference librarian/archivist, Northwestern College, Orange City, Iowa, and co-author of *Orange City* (2014).

Bruce Bolinger, MA, UCLA, has spent several decades researching Resistance rescues of downed Allied airmen in the Netherlands, Belgium, and France during WWII. He served as Nevada County (CA) clerk-recorder and president of the county historical and genealogical societies.

Emo Bos, JD, VU Amsterdam; PhD, Erasmus University, had a distinguished career as prosecutor, judge, and deputy justice. His chapter is based on his thesis published under the title: *Soevereiniteit en religie. Godsdienstvrijheid onder de eerste Oranjevorsten* (Sovereignty and religion: freedom of religion under the first Orange kings).

Sylvan Gerritsma, retired businessman residing in St. Catharines, Ontario, is a native of Sioux Center, Iowa, where he graduated from Dordt College. He served as a military intelligence officer in the 101st Airborne Division in Viet Nam in 1970-71.

George Harinck, PhD, professor at VU Amsterdam and Theological University Kampen. He is widely published on Protestant Dutch American relations in the 19th and 20th centuries and is writing a biography of theologian Geerhardus Vos.

Eugene Heideman, PhD, University of Utrecht; author of *The Practice of Piety: The Theology of the Midwestern Reformed Church in America, 1866-1966*. His current research is focused on Hendrik P. Scholte as editor of *De Reformatie*.

Gerlof D. Homan, professor of history emeritus, Illinois State University, Normal, has written extensively in peace studies and Mennonite history.

Notes on Contributors

Earl Wm. (Bill) Kennedy, ThD, Princeton Theological Seminary; Senior Research Fellow, Van Raalte Institute; and professor of religion emeritus, Northwestern College, Iowa. Forthcoming publication, annotations on the minutes of the Classis of Holland, Reformed Church in America, 1848-76.

Nella Kennedy, MA in art history, University of Iowa, and Senior Research Fellow, Van Raalte Institute, in which capacity she has translated numerous documents, written articles, and has been a co-editor of three AADAS conference volumes. She has also been a guest curator at the Holland Museum.

Susan Price Miller is an independent quilt and local history researcher who has published in *Uncoverings*, the American Quilt Study Group journal. While a volunteer at the Scholte House Museum, she curated an exhibit of drawings and paintings by individuals connected to the Scholte family, including those of Gerhard Nollen.

Ronald D. Rietveld, PhD, University of Illinois, Champaign-Urbana; professor of history emeritus, California State University, Fullerton; and author of many articles on 19th century Dutch American subjects, most notably Abraham Lincoln and the Civil War.

Marten Rustenburg, BA, Calvin College, has served as an AADAS board member, newsletter editor, and representative on the West Michigan Dutch Heritage Committee. This chapter is his first formal foray into historical research for AADAS.

Robert Schoone-Jongen, PhD, Delaware, associate professor of history at Calvin College, is currently researching Dutch immigrant communities in Minnesota and New Jersey. His biography of Theodore F. Koch is under consideration for publication.

Janet Sjaarda Sheeres is an independent scholar and the author of articles on Dutch immigrant and family history in various historical and genealogical journals. She edited and annotated *The Classical Assembly, General Assembly and Synodical Assembly Minutes of the Christian Reformed Church 1857-1880* and is an associate editor of *Origins*.

Donald Sinnema, PhD, St Michael's College, University of Toronto; professor of theology emeritus, Trinity Christian College, IL; author of *The First Dutch Settlement in Alberta*; and currently preparing a definitive edition in English of the proceedings of the Synod of Dort, 1618-19.

Robert P. Swierenga, PhD, University of Iowa; research professor, Van Raalte Institute; professor of history emeritus, Kent State University; and author and editor of numerous books, most recently *Holland, Michigan: From Dutch Colony to Dynamic City*.

Michael Swanson, a native of Fulton, Illinois, is the assistant archivist in the Elwyn B. Robinson Department of Special Collections at the University of North Dakota. His varied research interests include documenting the Dutch of Whiteside County, Illinois.

Huug van den Dool, PhD, University of Utrecht principal scientist at the Climate Prediction Center, has published on topics such as the history of Waddinxveen, family history, Noordeloos (Zuid Holland) emigration to North America, secondary migration of Dutch Americans in the United States, and biographies of other noteable Dutch Americans.

Jaap van Marle, PhD, linguistics, University of Utrecht; vice dean and professor of the Department of Humanities at the Open Universiteit Nederland in Heerlen and author of dozens of articles on morphology, language contact, and language change among overseas Dutch.

David Zwart, PhD, Western Michigan University; assistant professor of history and social studies education at Grand Valley State University; and author of several chapters and articles, including "For the Next Generation: Commemorating the Immigration Experience in the United States and Canada," *Tijdschrift voor Sociale en Economische Geschiedenis*.